CLOSED

VOLUME 36

Gosho Aoyama

Case Briefing:

Subject:
Occupation:
Special Skills:
Equipment:

Jimmy Kudo, a.k.a. Conan Edogawa
High School Student/Detective
Analytical thinking and deductive reasoning, Soccer
Bow Tie Voice Transmitter, Super Sneakers,
Homing Glasses, Stretchy Suspenders

The subject is hot on the trail of a pair of suspicious men in black when he is attacked from behind and administered a strange substance which physically transforms him into a first grader. When the subject confides in the eccentric inventor Dr. Agasa, they decide to keep the subject's true identity a secret for the safety of everyone around him. Assuming the new identity of first-grader Conan Edogawa, the subject continues to assist the police force on their most baffling cases. The only problem is that most crime-solving professionals won't take a little kid's advice!

Table of Contents

CASE CLOSED

CONFIDEN

C A S E   C L O S E D

Volume 36
Shonen Sunday Edition

Story and Art by GOSHO AOYAMA

© 1994 Gosho AOYAMA/Shogakukan
All rights reserved.
Original Japanese edition "MEITANTEI CONAN" published by SHOGAKUKAN Inc.

Translation
Tetsuichiro Miyaki

Touch-up & Lettering
Freeman Wong

Cover & Graphic Design
Andrea Rice

Editor
Shaenon K. Garrity

VP, Production **Alvin Lu**
VP, Sales & Product Marketing **Gonzalo Ferreyra**
VP, Creative **Linda Espinosa**
Publisher **Hyoe Narita**

Printed in Canada

Published by VIZ Media, LLC
P.O. Box 77010
San Francisco, CA 94107

10 9 8 7 6 5 4 3 2 1
First printing, October 2010

W.SHONENSUNDAY.COM

www.viz.com

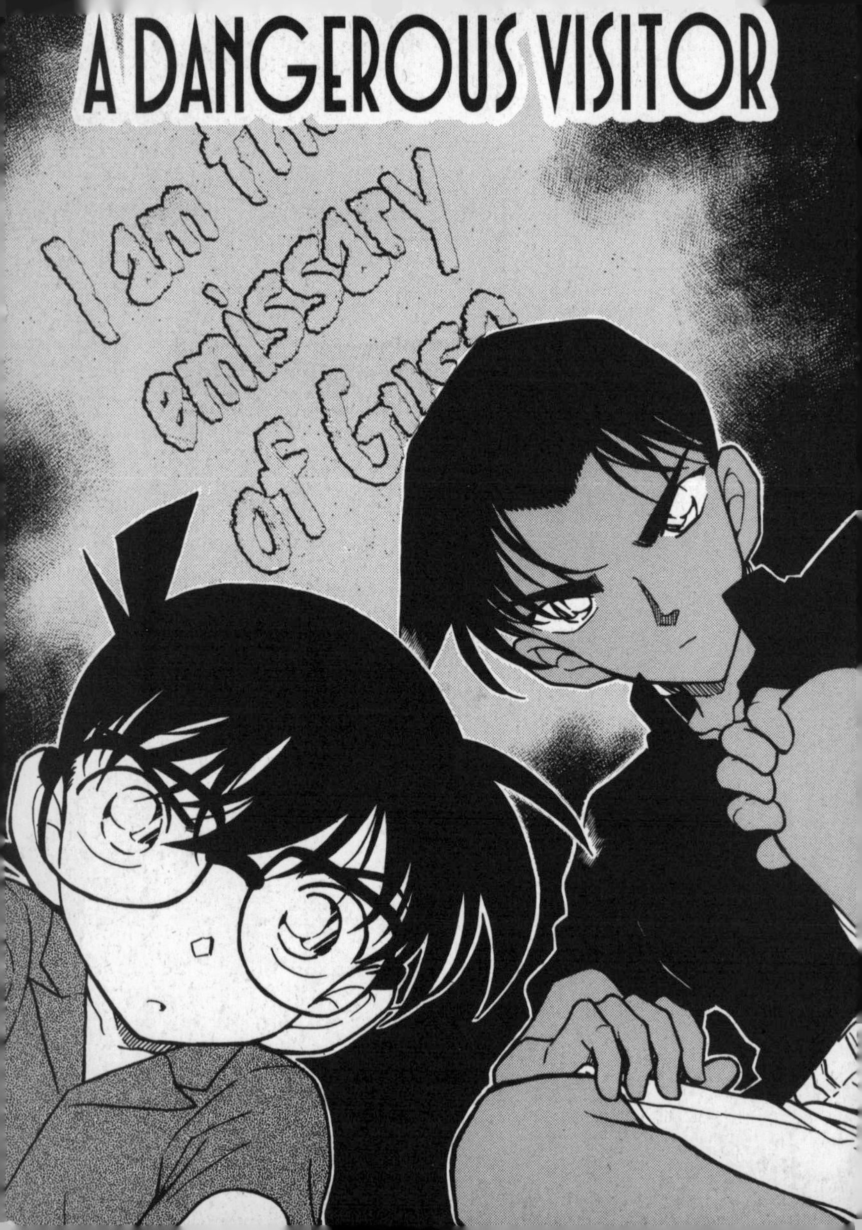
A DANGEROUS VISITOR
I am
emissary
of Gus

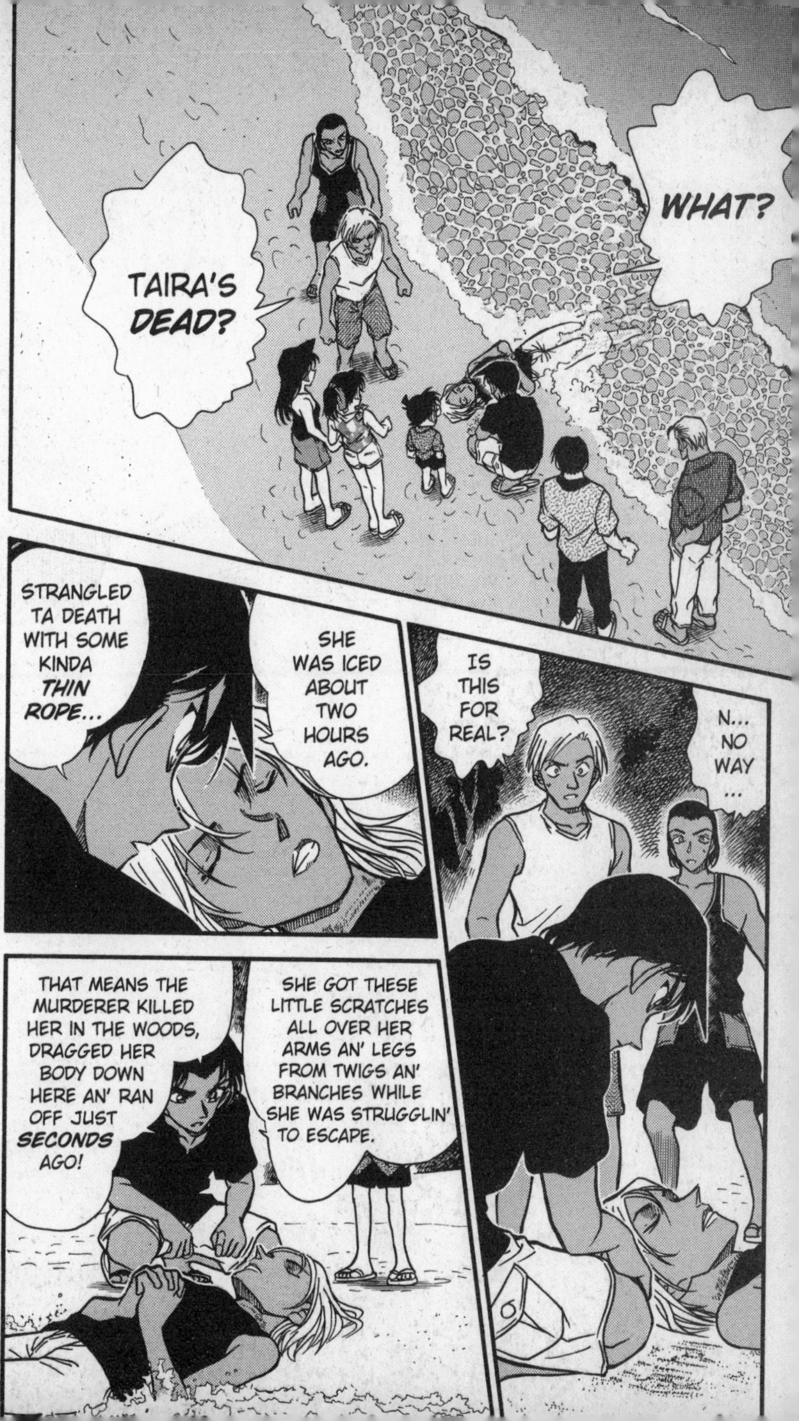
WHAT?
TAIRA'S DEAD?
N... NO WAY...
IS THIS FOR REAL?
SHE WAS ICED ABOUT TWO HOURS AGO.
STRANGLED TA DEATH WITH SOME KINDA THIN ROPE...
SHE GOT THESE LITTLE SCRATCHES ALL OVER HER ARMS AN' LEGS FROM TWIGS AN' BRANCHES WHILE SHE WAS STRUGGLIN' TO ESCAPE.
THAT MEANS THE MURDERER KILLED HER IN THE WOODS, DRAGGED HER BODY DOWN HERE AN' RAN OFF JUST SECONDS AGO!

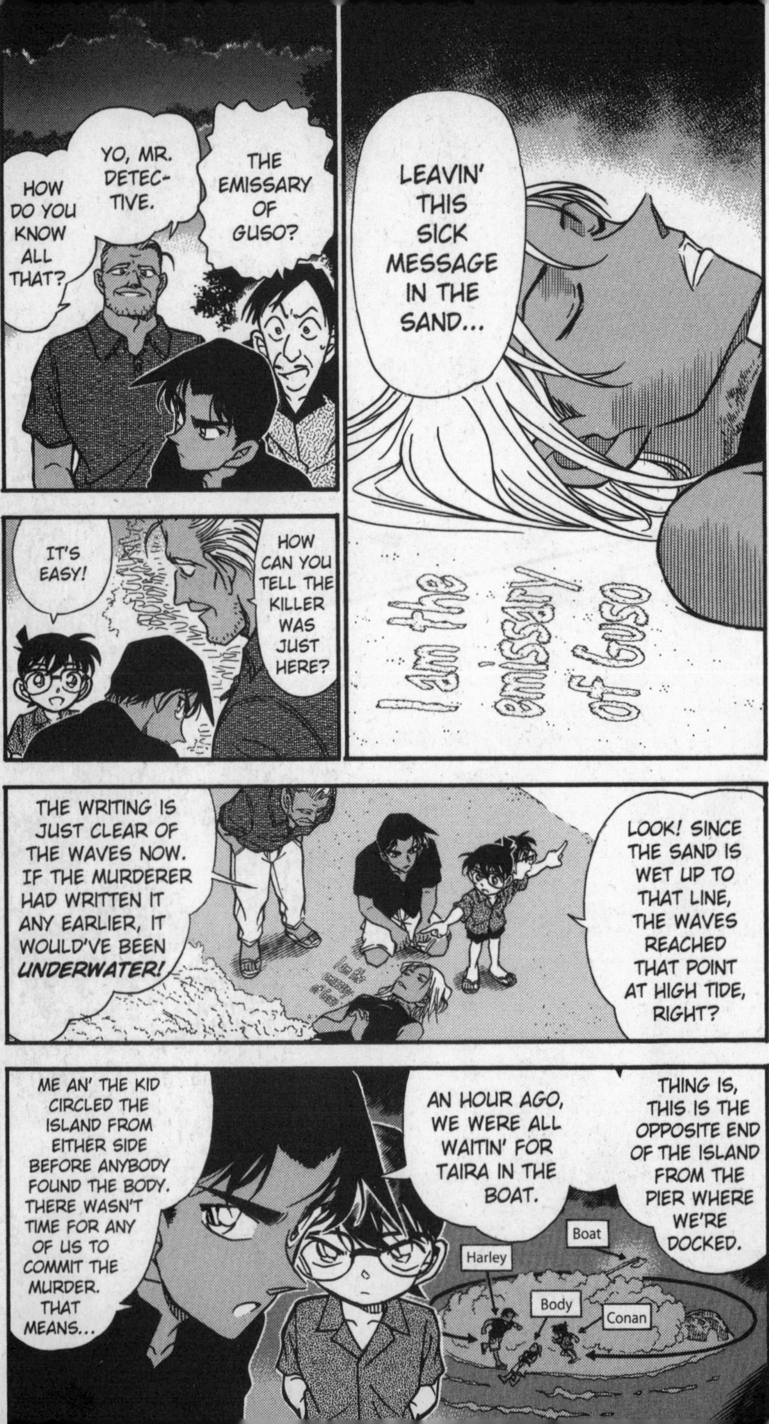
LEAVIN' THIS SICK MESSAGE IN THE SAND...
I am the emissary of Guso
THE EMISSARY OF GUSO?
YO, MR. DETECTIVE.
HOW DO YOU KNOW ALL THAT?
HOW CAN YOU TELL THE KILLER WAS JUST HERE?
IT'S EASY!
LOOK! SINCE THE SAND IS WET UP TO THAT LINE, THE WAVES REACHED THAT POINT AT HIGH TIDE, RIGHT?
THE WRITING IS JUST CLEAR OF THE WAVES NOW. IF THE MURDERER HAD WRITTEN IT ANY EARLIER, IT WOULD'VE BEEN UNDERWATER!
THING IS, THIS IS THE OPPOSITE END OF THE ISLAND FROM THE PIER WHERE WE'RE DOCKED.
AN HOUR AGO, WE WERE ALL WAITIN' FOR TAIRA IN THE BOAT.
Boat
Harley
Body
Conan
ME AN' THE KID CIRCLED THE ISLAND FROM EITHER SIDE BEFORE ANYBODY FOUND THE BODY. THERE WASN'T TIME FOR ANY OF US TO COMMIT THE MURDER. THAT MEANS...

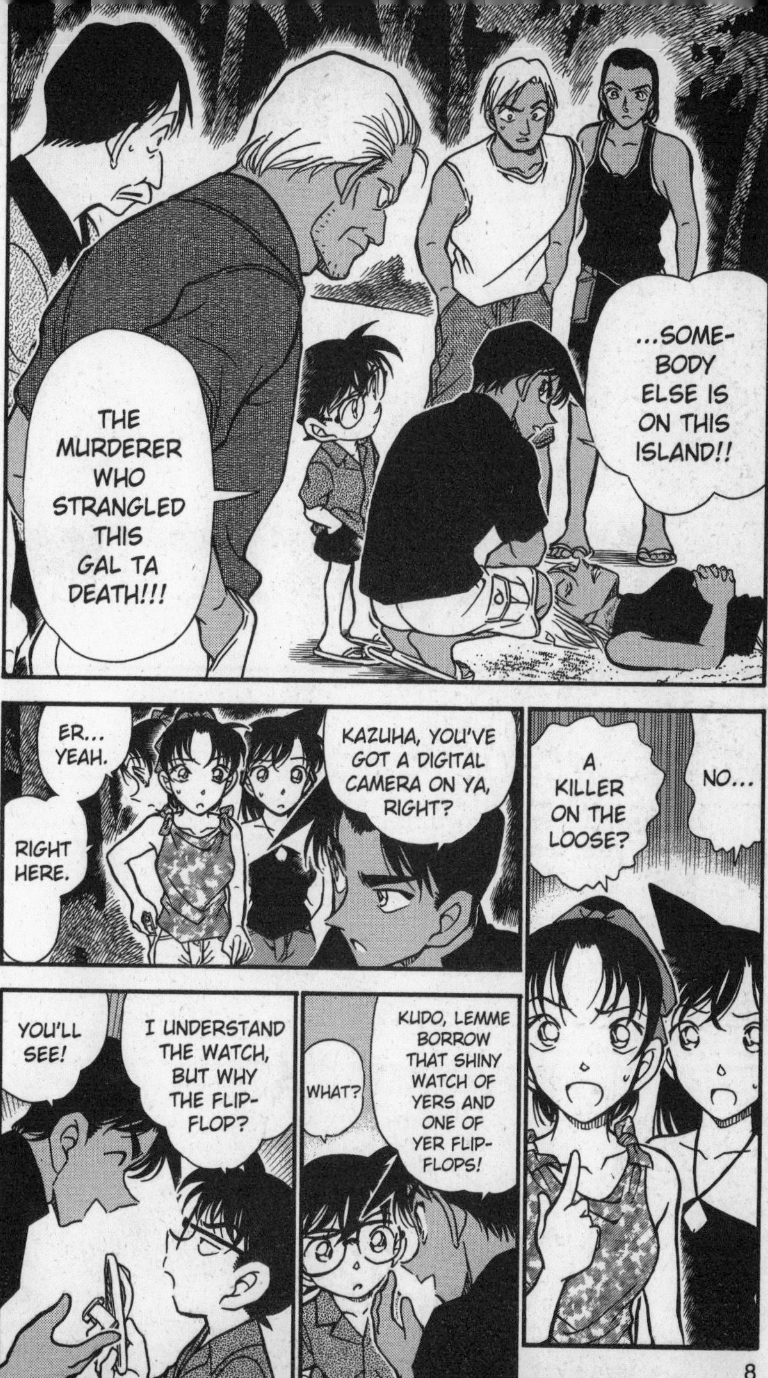
...SOME-BODY ELSE IS ON THIS ISLAND!!
THE MURDERER WHO STRANGLED THIS GAL TA DEATH!!!
NO...
A KILLER ON THE LOOSE?
KAZUHA, YOU'VE GOT A DIGITAL CAMERA ON YA, RIGHT?
ER... YEAH.
RIGHT HERE.
KUDO, LEMME BORROW THAT SHINY WATCH OF YERS AND ONE OF YER FLIP-FLOPS!
WHAT?
I UNDERSTAND THE WATCH, BUT WHY THE FLIP-FLOP?
YOU'LL SEE!

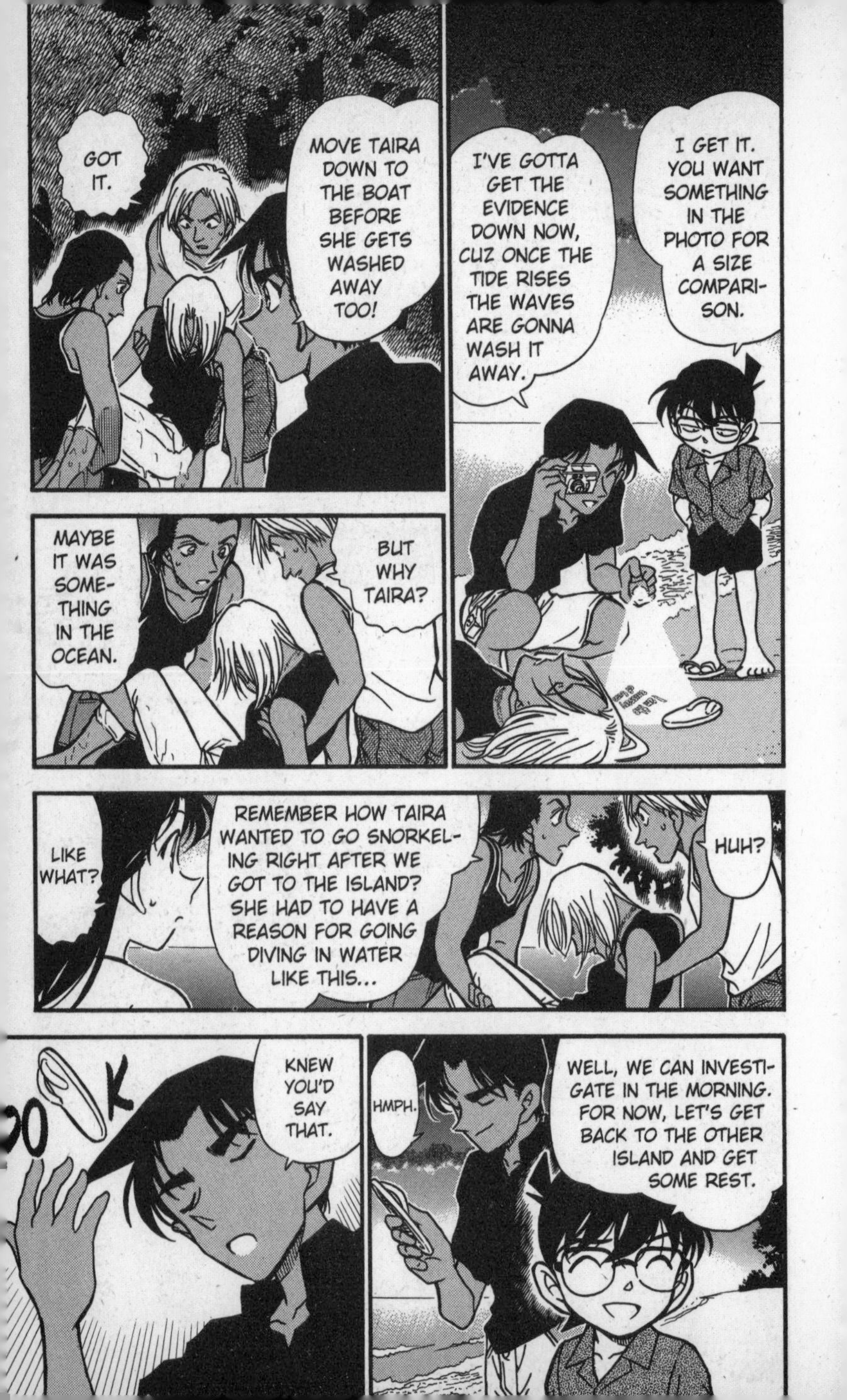
I GET IT. YOU WANT SOMETHING IN THE PHOTO FOR A SIZE COMPARI-SON.
I'VE GOTTA GET THE EVIDENCE DOWN NOW, CUZ ONCE THE TIDE RISES THE WAVES ARE GONNA WASH IT AWAY.
MOVE TAIRA DOWN TO THE BOAT BEFORE SHE GETS WASHED AWAY TOO!
GOT IT.
BUT WHY TAIRA?
MAYBE IT WAS SOME-THING IN THE OCEAN.
HUH?
REMEMBER HOW TAIRA WANTED TO GO SNORKEL-ING RIGHT AFTER WE GOT TO THE ISLAND? SHE HAD TO HAVE A REASON FOR GOING DIVING IN WATER LIKE THIS...
LIKE WHAT?
WELL, WE CAN INVESTI-GATE IN THE MORNING. FOR NOW, LET'S GET BACK TO THE OTHER ISLAND AND GET SOME REST.
HMPH.
KNEW YOU'D SAY THAT.

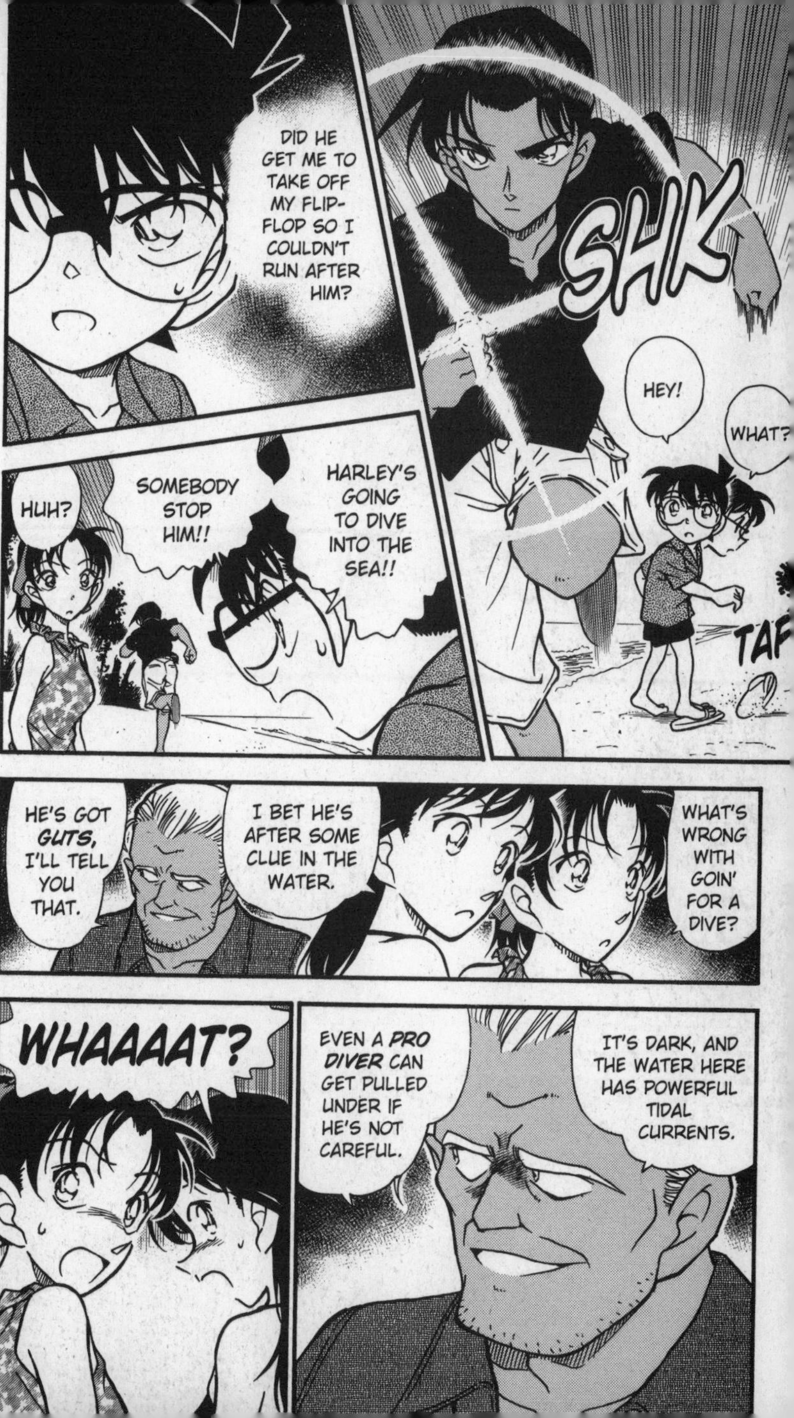
SHK
HEY!
WHAT?
TAP
DID HE GET ME TO TAKE OFF MY FLIP-FLOP SO I COULDN'T RUN AFTER HIM?
HARLEY'S GOING TO DIVE INTO THE SEA!!
SOMEBODY STOP HIM!!
HUH?
WHAT'S WRONG WITH GOIN' FOR A DIVE?
I BET HE'S AFTER SOME CLUE IN THE WATER.
HE'S GOT *GUTS*, I'LL TELL YOU THAT.
IT'S DARK, AND THE WATER HERE HAS POWERFUL TIDAL CURRENTS.
EVEN A *PRO DIVER* CAN GET PULLED UNDER IF HE'S NOT CAREFUL.
WHAAAAT?

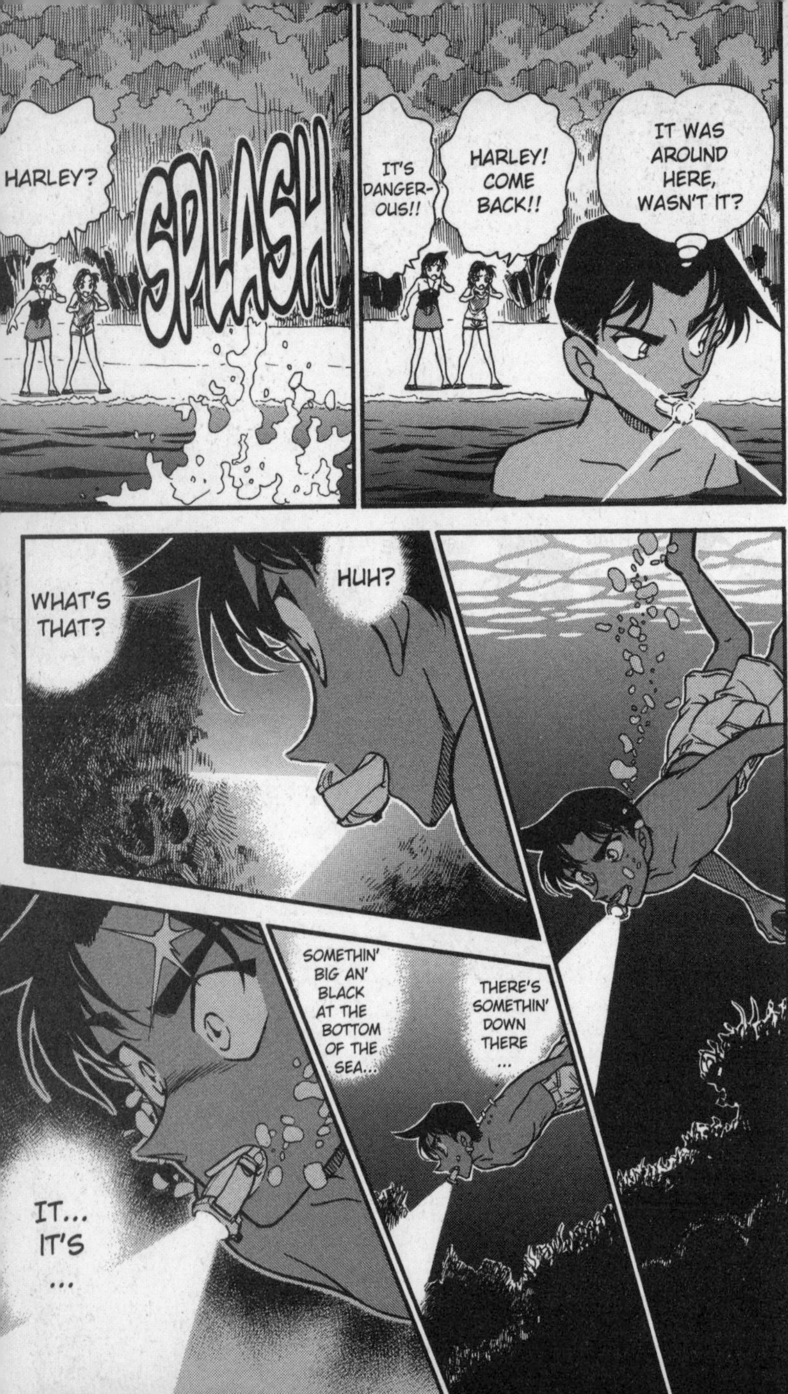
IT WAS AROUND HERE, WASN'T IT?
HARLEY! COME BACK!!
IT'S DANGER-OUS!!
SPLASH
HARLEY?
HUH?
WHAT'S THAT?
THERE'S SOMETHIN' DOWN THERE ...
SOMETHIN' BIG AN' BLACK AT THE BOTTOM OF THE SEA...
IT... IT'S ...

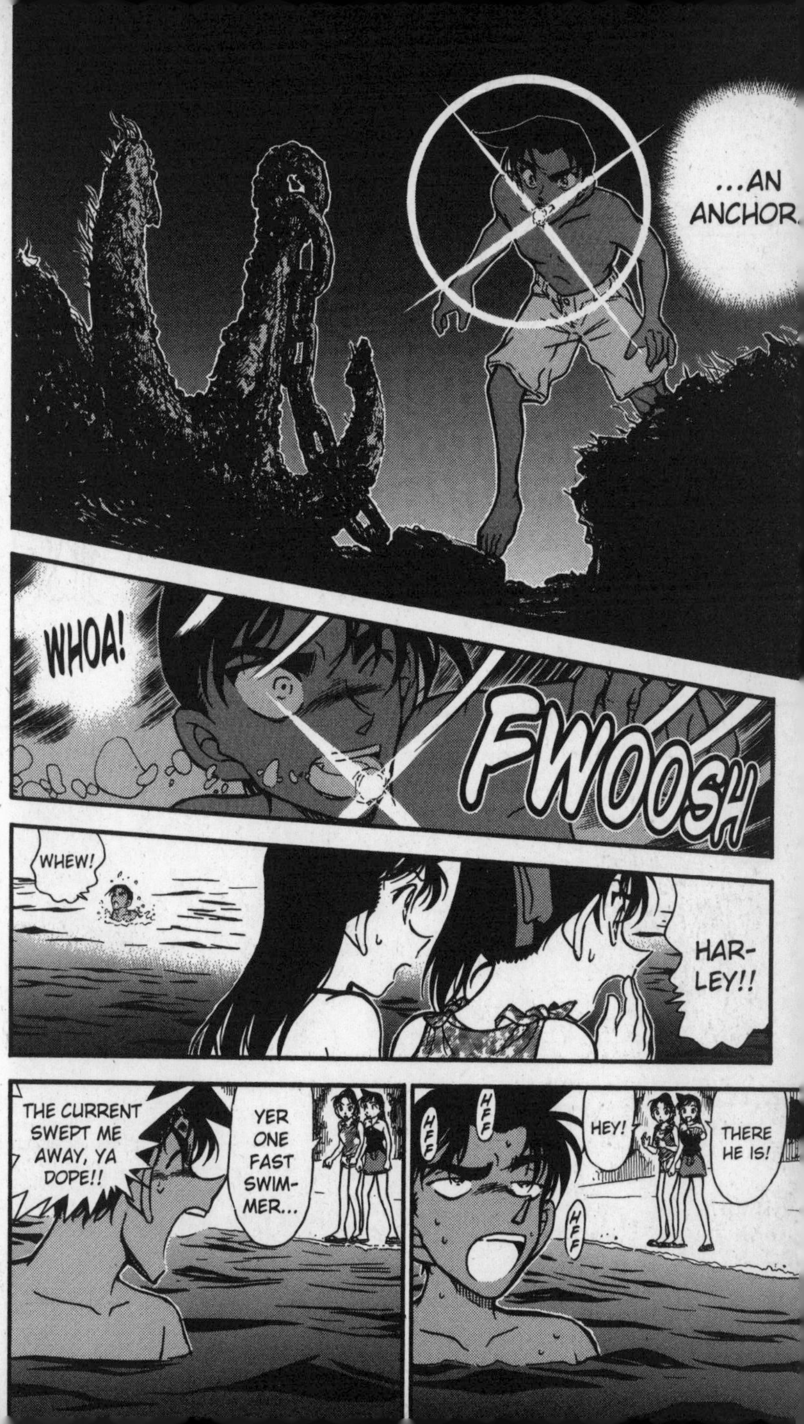
...AN ANCHOR.
FWOOSH
WHOA!
HAR-LEY!!
WHEW!
THERE HE IS!
HEY!
HFF
HFF
HFF
YER ONE FAST SWIM-MER...
THE CURRENT SWEPT ME AWAY, YA DOPE!!

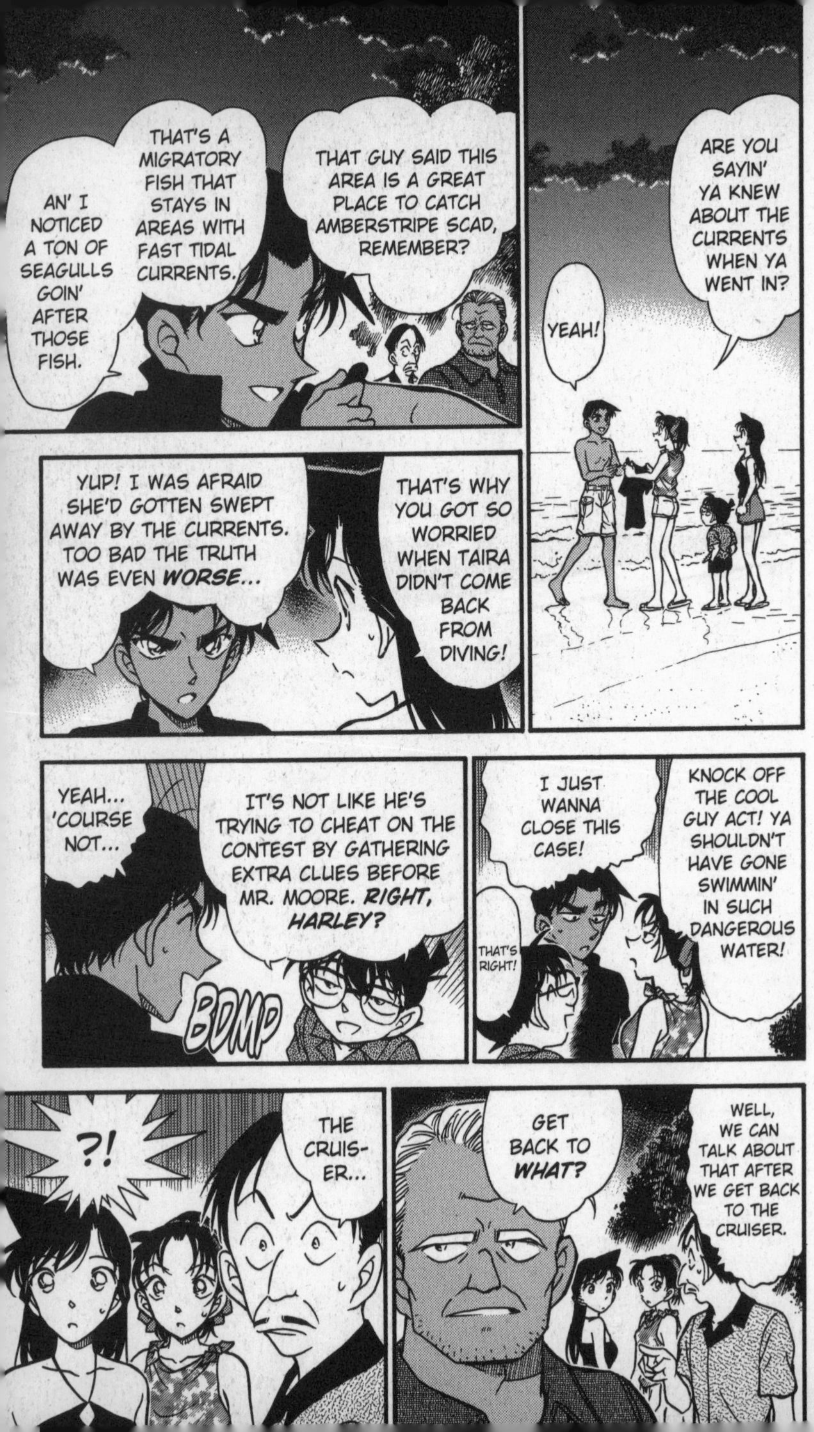
ARE YOU SAYIN' YA KNEW ABOUT THE CURRENTS WHEN YA WENT IN?
YEAH!
THAT GUY SAID THIS AREA IS A GREAT PLACE TO CATCH AMBERSTRIPE SCAD, REMEMBER?
THAT'S A MIGRATORY FISH THAT STAYS IN AREAS WITH FAST TIDAL CURRENTS.
AN' I NOTICED A TON OF SEAGULLS GOIN' AFTER THOSE FISH.
THAT'S WHY YOU GOT SO WORRIED WHEN TAIRA DIDN'T COME BACK FROM DIVING!
YUP! I WAS AFRAID SHE'D GOTTEN SWEPT AWAY BY THE CURRENTS. TOO BAD THE TRUTH WAS EVEN **WORSE**...
KNOCK OFF THE COOL GUY ACT! YA SHOULDN'T HAVE GONE SWIMMIN' IN SUCH DANGEROUS WATER!
I JUST WANNA CLOSE THIS CASE!
THAT'S RIGHT!
IT'S NOT LIKE HE'S TRYING TO CHEAT ON THE CONTEST BY GATHERING EXTRA CLUES BEFORE MR. MOORE. ***RIGHT, HARLEY?***
YEAH... 'COURSE NOT...
BDMP
WELL, WE CAN TALK ABOUT THAT AFTER WE GET BACK TO THE CRUISER.
GET BACK TO ***WHAT?***
THE CRUISER...
?!

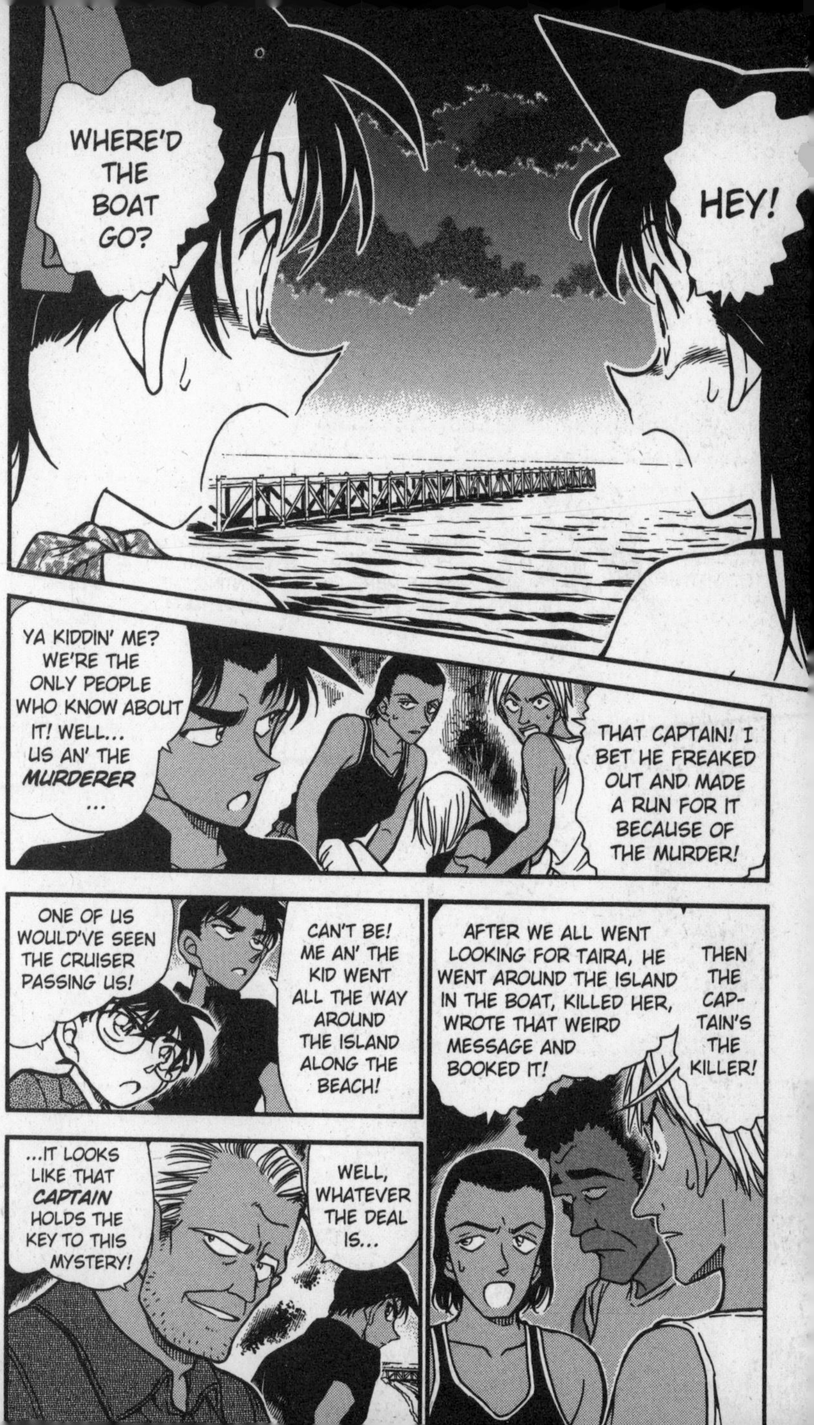
HEY!
WHERE'D THE BOAT GO?
THAT CAPTAIN! I BET HE FREAKED OUT AND MADE A RUN FOR IT BECAUSE OF THE MURDER!
YA KIDDIN' ME? WE'RE THE ONLY PEOPLE WHO KNOW ABOUT IT! WELL... US AN' THE MURDERER ...
THEN THE CAP-TAIN'S THE KILLER!
AFTER WE ALL WENT LOOKING FOR TAIRA, HE WENT AROUND THE ISLAND IN THE BOAT, KILLED HER, WROTE THAT WEIRD MESSAGE AND BOOKED IT!
CAN'T BE! ME AN' THE KID WENT ALL THE WAY AROUND THE ISLAND ALONG THE BEACH!
ONE OF US WOULD'VE SEEN THE CRUISER PASSING US!
WELL, WHATEVER THE DEAL IS...
...IT LOOKS LIKE THAT CAPTAIN HOLDS THE KEY TO THIS MYSTERY!

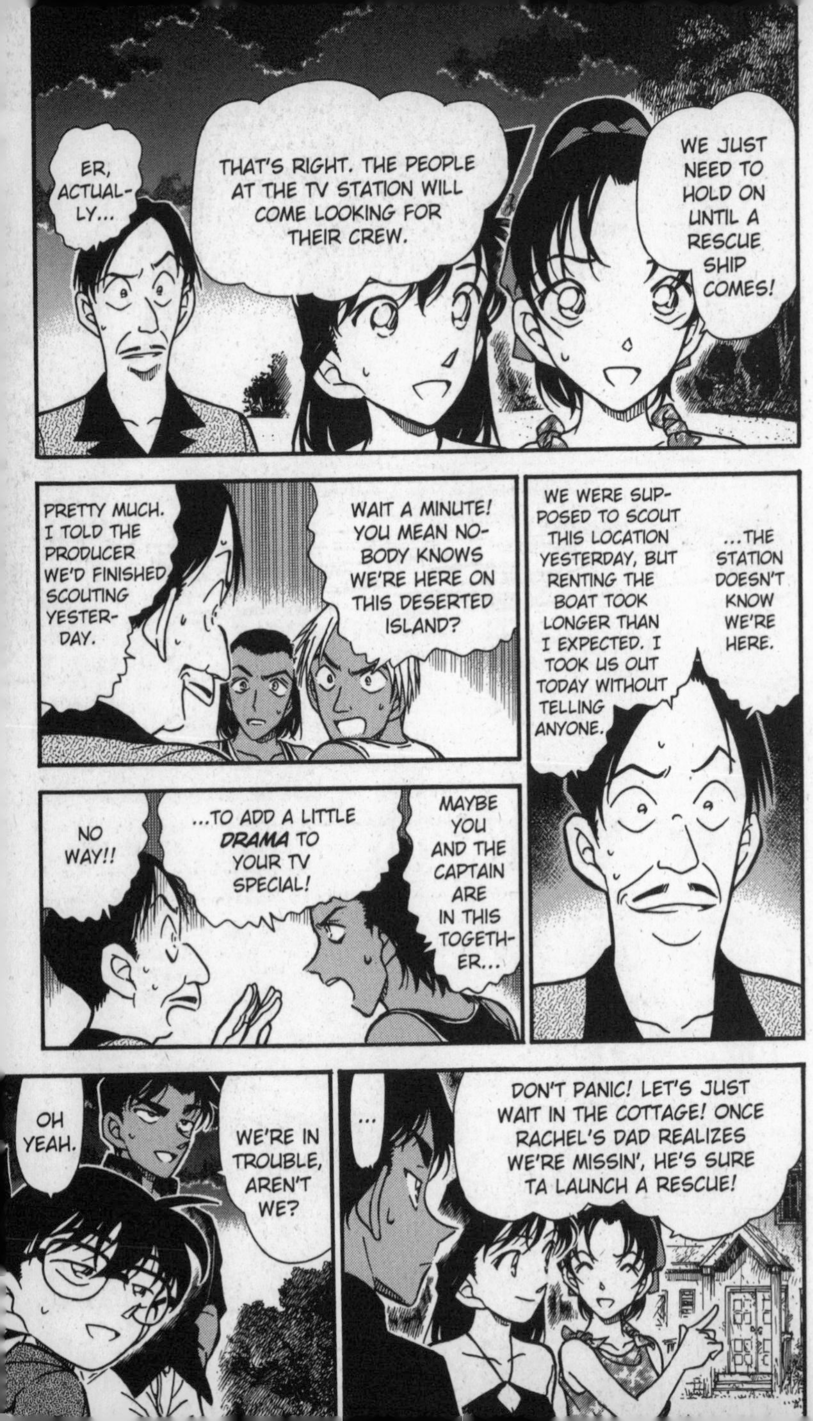
WE JUST NEED TO HOLD ON UNTIL A RESCUE SHIP COMES!
THAT'S RIGHT. THE PEOPLE AT THE TV STATION WILL COME LOOKING FOR THEIR CREW.
ER, ACTUALLY...
...THE STATION DOESN'T KNOW WE'RE HERE.
WE WERE SUP-POSED TO SCOUT THIS LOCATION YESTERDAY, BUT RENTING THE BOAT TOOK LONGER THAN I EXPECTED. I TOOK US OUT TODAY WITHOUT TELLING ANYONE.
WAIT A MINUTE! YOU MEAN NO-BODY KNOWS WE'RE HERE ON THIS DESERTED ISLAND?
PRETTY MUCH. I TOLD THE PRODUCER WE'D FINISHED SCOUTING YESTER-DAY.
MAYBE YOU AND THE CAPTAIN ARE IN THIS TOGETH-ER...
...TO ADD A LITTLE *DRAMA* TO YOUR TV SPECIAL!
NO WAY!!
DON'T PANIC! LET'S JUST WAIT IN THE COTTAGE! ONCE RACHEL'S DAD REALIZES WE'RE MISSIN', HE'S SURE TA LAUNCH A RESCUE!
...
WE'RE IN TROUBLE, AREN'T WE?
OH YEAH.

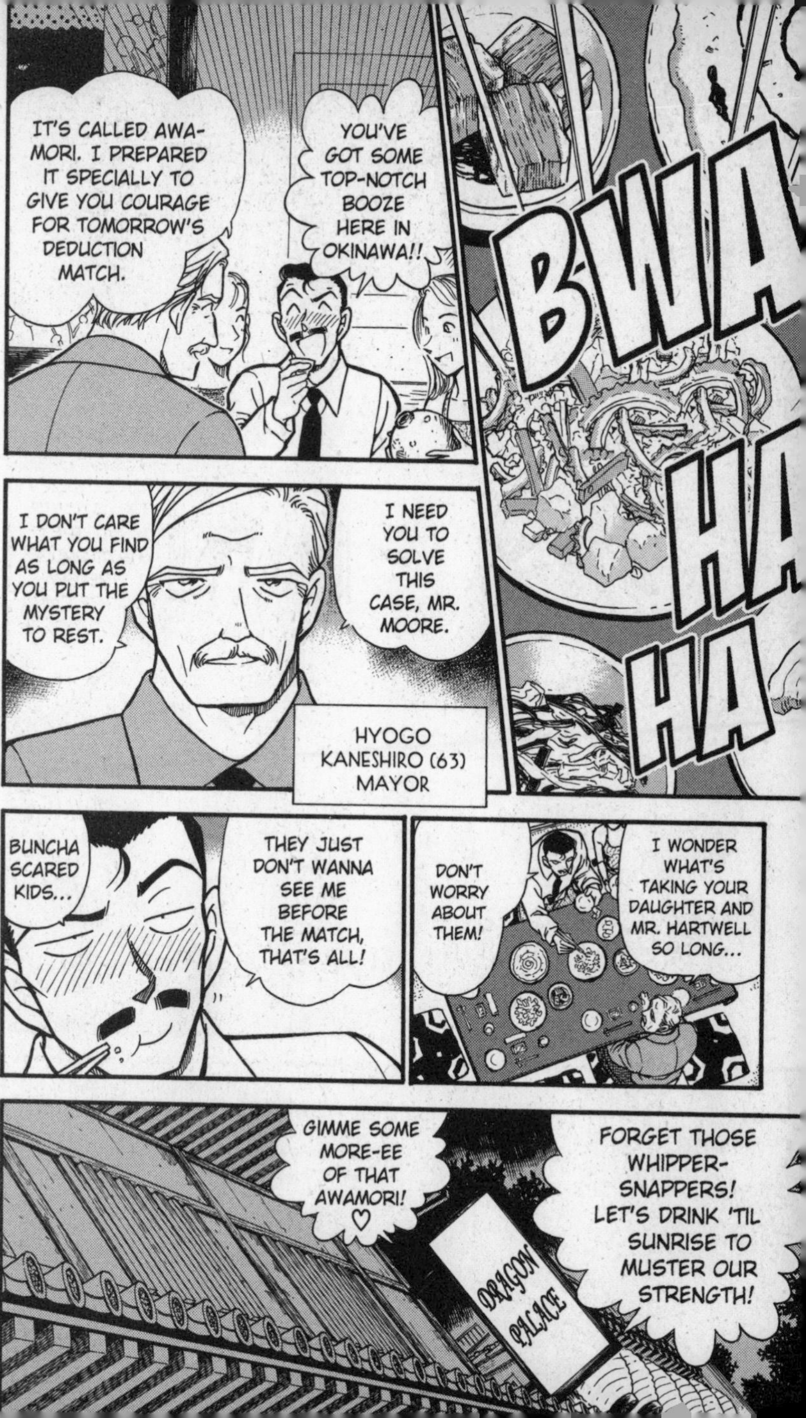
BWA HA HA
YOU'VE GOT SOME TOP-NOTCH BOOZE HERE IN OKINAWA!!
IT'S CALLED AWA-MORI. I PREPARED IT SPECIALLY TO GIVE YOU COURAGE FOR TOMORROW'S DEDUCTION MATCH.
I NEED YOU TO SOLVE THIS CASE, MR. MOORE.
I DON'T CARE WHAT YOU FIND AS LONG AS YOU PUT THE MYSTERY TO REST.
HYOGO KANESHIRO (63) MAYOR
I WONDER WHAT'S TAKING YOUR DAUGHTER AND MR. HARTWELL SO LONG...
DON'T WORRY ABOUT THEM!
THEY JUST DON'T WANNA SEE ME BEFORE THE MATCH, THAT'S ALL!
BUNCHA SCARED KIDS...
FORGET THOSE WHIPPER-SNAPPERS! LET'S DRINK 'TIL SUNRISE TO MUSTER OUR STRENGTH!
GIMME SOME MORE-EE OF THAT AWAMORI! ♡
DRAGON PALACE

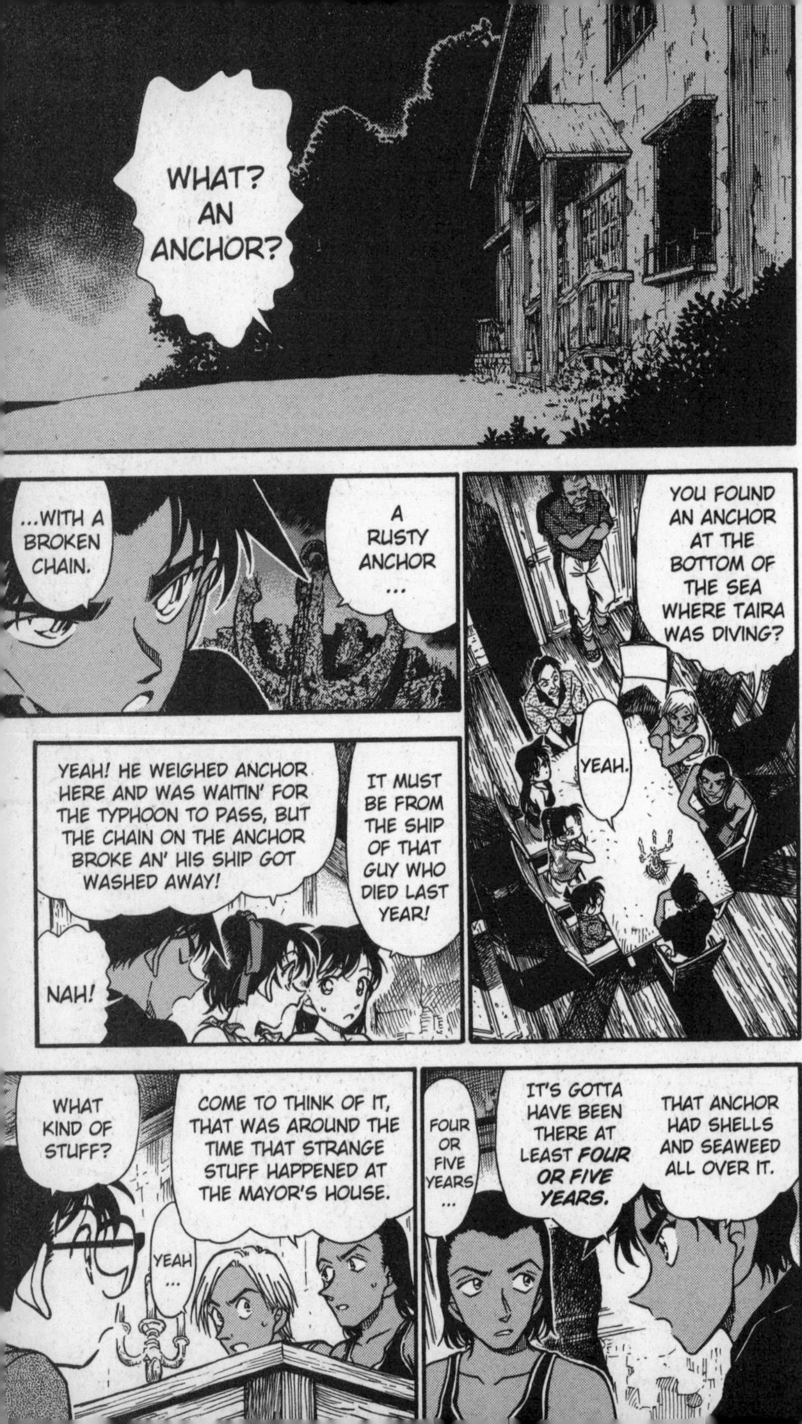

WHAT? AN ANCHOR?
YOU FOUND AN ANCHOR AT THE BOTTOM OF THE SEA WHERE TAIRA WAS DIVING?
YEAH.
A RUSTY ANCHOR ...
...WITH A BROKEN CHAIN.
IT MUST BE FROM THE SHIP OF THAT GUY WHO DIED LAST YEAR!
YEAH! HE WEIGHED ANCHOR HERE AND WAS WAITIN' FOR THE TYPHOON TO PASS, BUT THE CHAIN ON THE ANCHOR BROKE AN' HIS SHIP GOT WASHED AWAY!
NAH!
THAT ANCHOR HAD SHELLS AND SEAWEED ALL OVER IT.
IT'S GOTTA HAVE BEEN THERE AT LEAST *FOUR OR FIVE YEARS.*
FOUR OR FIVE YEARS ...
COME TO THINK OF IT, THAT WAS AROUND THE TIME THAT STRANGE STUFF HAPPENED AT THE MAYOR'S HOUSE.
WHAT KIND OF STUFF?
YEAH ...

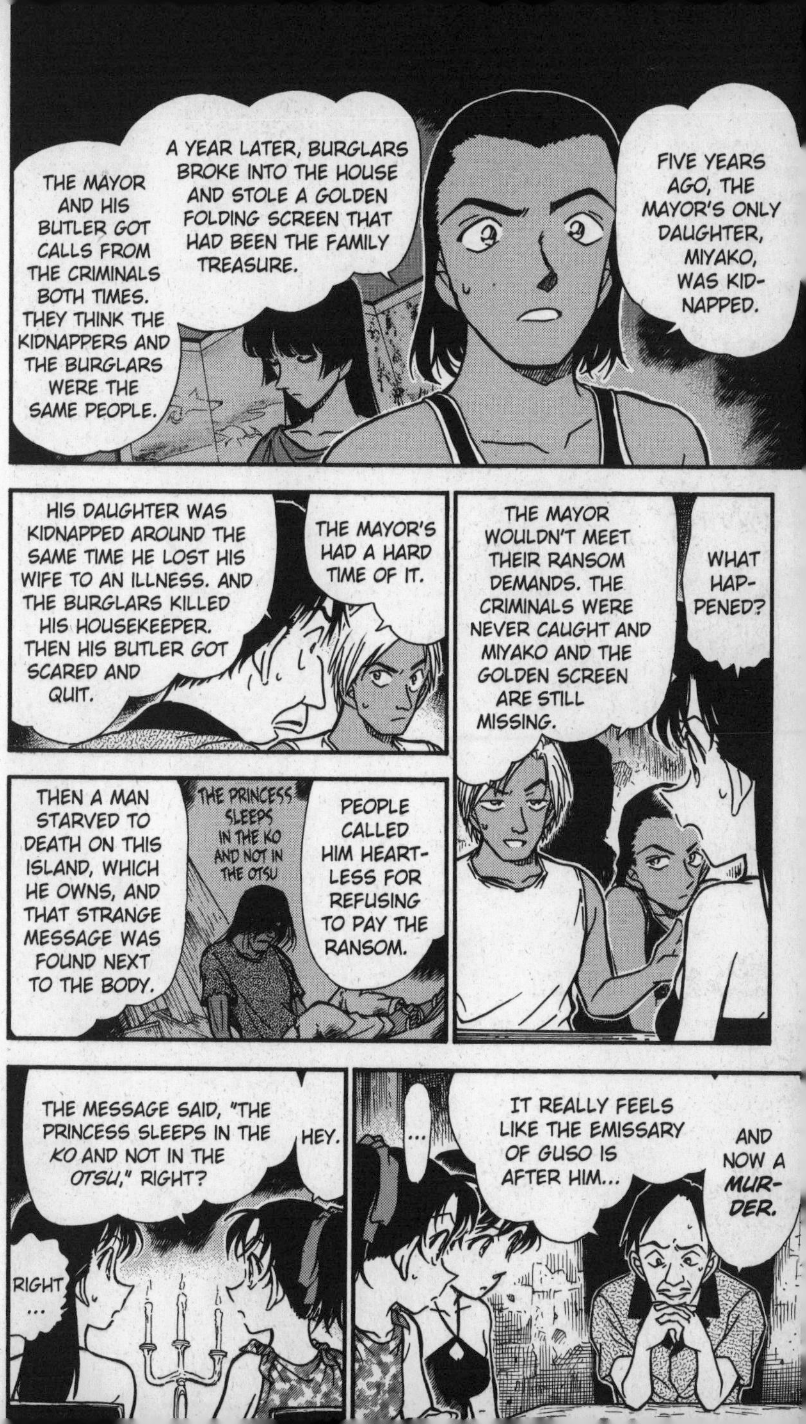
FIVE YEARS AGO, THE MAYOR'S ONLY DAUGHTER, MIYAKO, WAS KID-NAPPED.
A YEAR LATER, BURGLARS BROKE INTO THE HOUSE AND STOLE A GOLDEN FOLDING SCREEN THAT HAD BEEN THE FAMILY TREASURE.
THE MAYOR AND HIS BUTLER GOT CALLS FROM THE CRIMINALS BOTH TIMES. THEY THINK THE KIDNAPPERS AND THE BURGLARS WERE THE SAME PEOPLE.
WHAT HAP-PENED?
THE MAYOR WOULDN'T MEET THEIR RANSOM DEMANDS. THE CRIMINALS WERE NEVER CAUGHT AND MIYAKO AND THE GOLDEN SCREEN ARE STILL MISSING.
THE MAYOR'S HAD A HARD TIME OF IT.
HIS DAUGHTER WAS KIDNAPPED AROUND THE SAME TIME HE LOST HIS WIFE TO AN ILLNESS. AND THE BURGLARS KILLED HIS HOUSEKEEPER. THEN HIS BUTLER GOT SCARED AND QUIT.
PEOPLE CALLED HIM HEART-LESS FOR REFUSING TO PAY THE RANSOM.
THE PRINCESS SLEEPS IN THE KO AND NOT IN THE OTSU
THEN A MAN STARVED TO DEATH ON THIS ISLAND, WHICH HE OWNS, AND THAT STRANGE MESSAGE WAS FOUND NEXT TO THE BODY.
AND NOW A *MURDER.*
IT REALLY FEELS LIKE THE EMISSARY OF GUSO IS AFTER HIM...
...
HEY.
THE MESSAGE SAID, "THE PRINCESS SLEEPS IN THE *KO* AND NOT IN THE *OTSU*," RIGHT?
RIGHT...

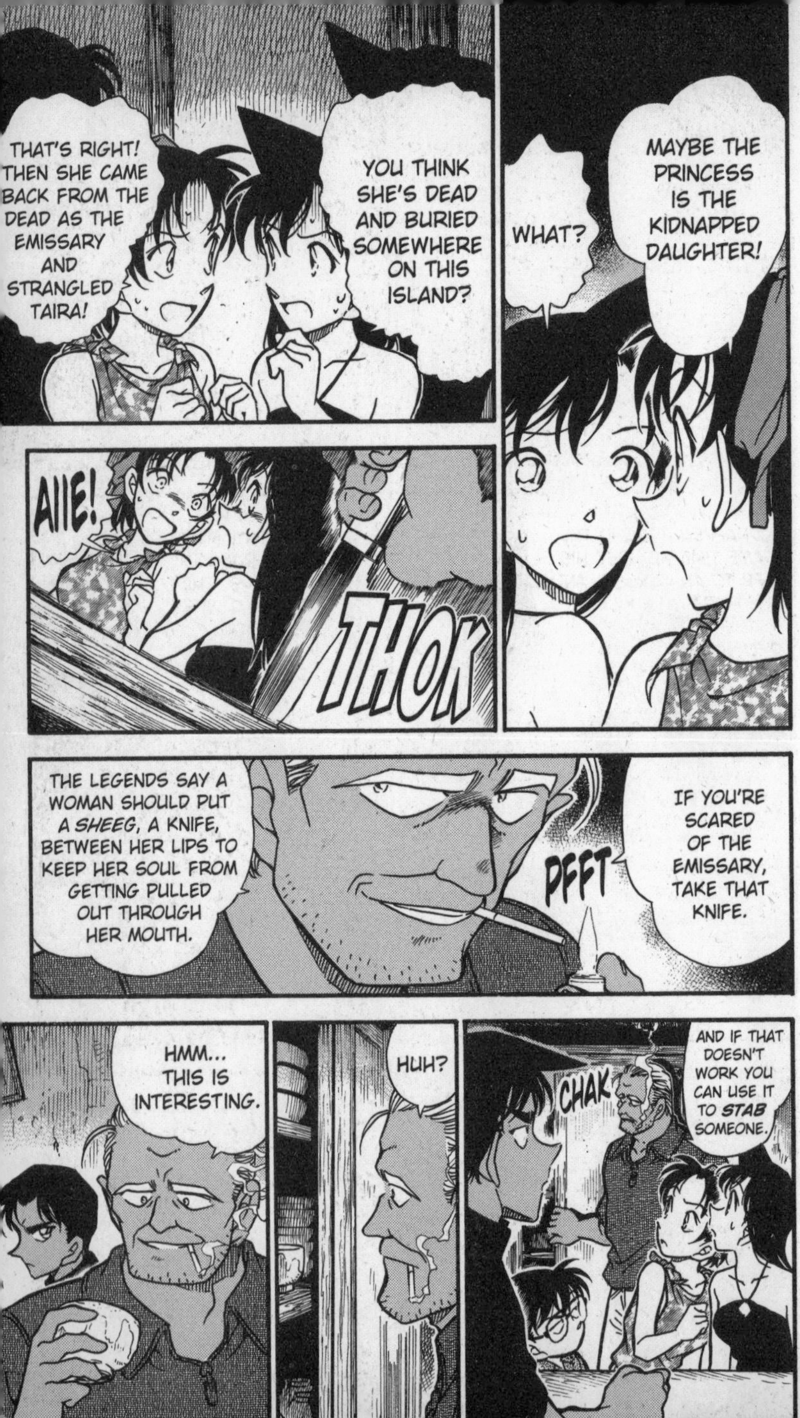
MAYBE THE PRINCESS IS THE KIDNAPPED DAUGHTER!
WHAT?
YOU THINK SHE'S DEAD AND BURIED SOMEWHERE ON THIS ISLAND?
THAT'S RIGHT! THEN SHE CAME BACK FROM THE DEAD AS THE EMISSARY AND STRANGLED TAIRA!
THOK
AIIE!
IF YOU'RE SCARED OF THE EMISSARY, TAKE THAT KNIFE.
PFFT
THE LEGENDS SAY A WOMAN SHOULD PUT A *SHEEG*, A KNIFE, BETWEEN HER LIPS TO KEEP HER SOUL FROM GETTING PULLED OUT THROUGH HER MOUTH.
AND IF THAT DOESN'T WORK YOU CAN USE IT TO ***STAB*** SOMEONE.
CHAK
HUH?
HMM... THIS IS INTERESTING.

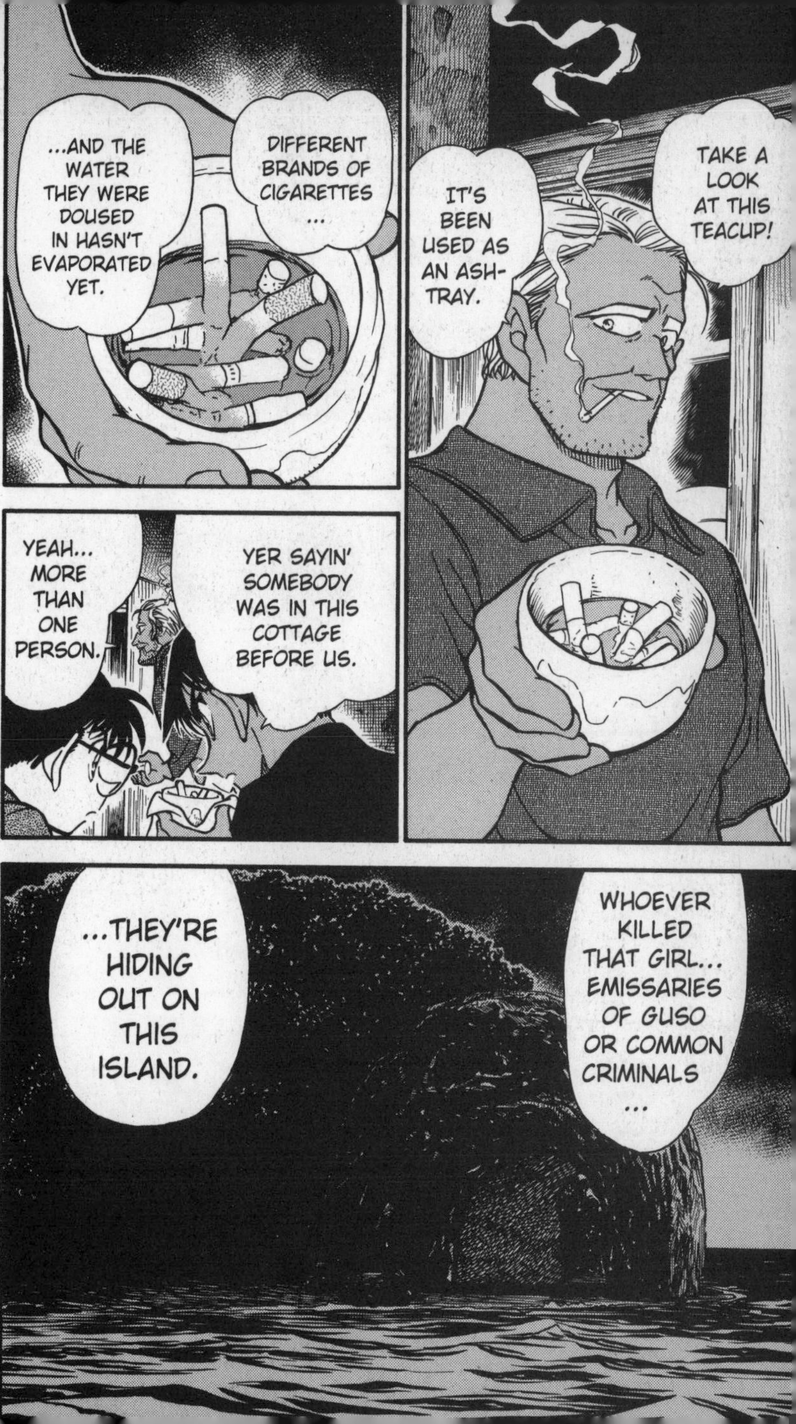
TAKE A LOOK AT THIS TEACUP!
IT'S BEEN USED AS AN ASH-TRAY.
DIFFERENT BRANDS OF CIGARETTES ...
...AND THE WATER THEY WERE DOUSED IN HASN'T EVAPORATED YET.
YER SAYIN' SOMEBODY WAS IN THIS COTTAGE BEFORE US.
YEAH... MORE THAN ONE PERSON.
WHOEVER KILLED THAT GIRL... EMISSARIES OF GUSO OR COMMON CRIMINALS ...
...THEY'RE HIDING OUT ON THIS ISLAND.

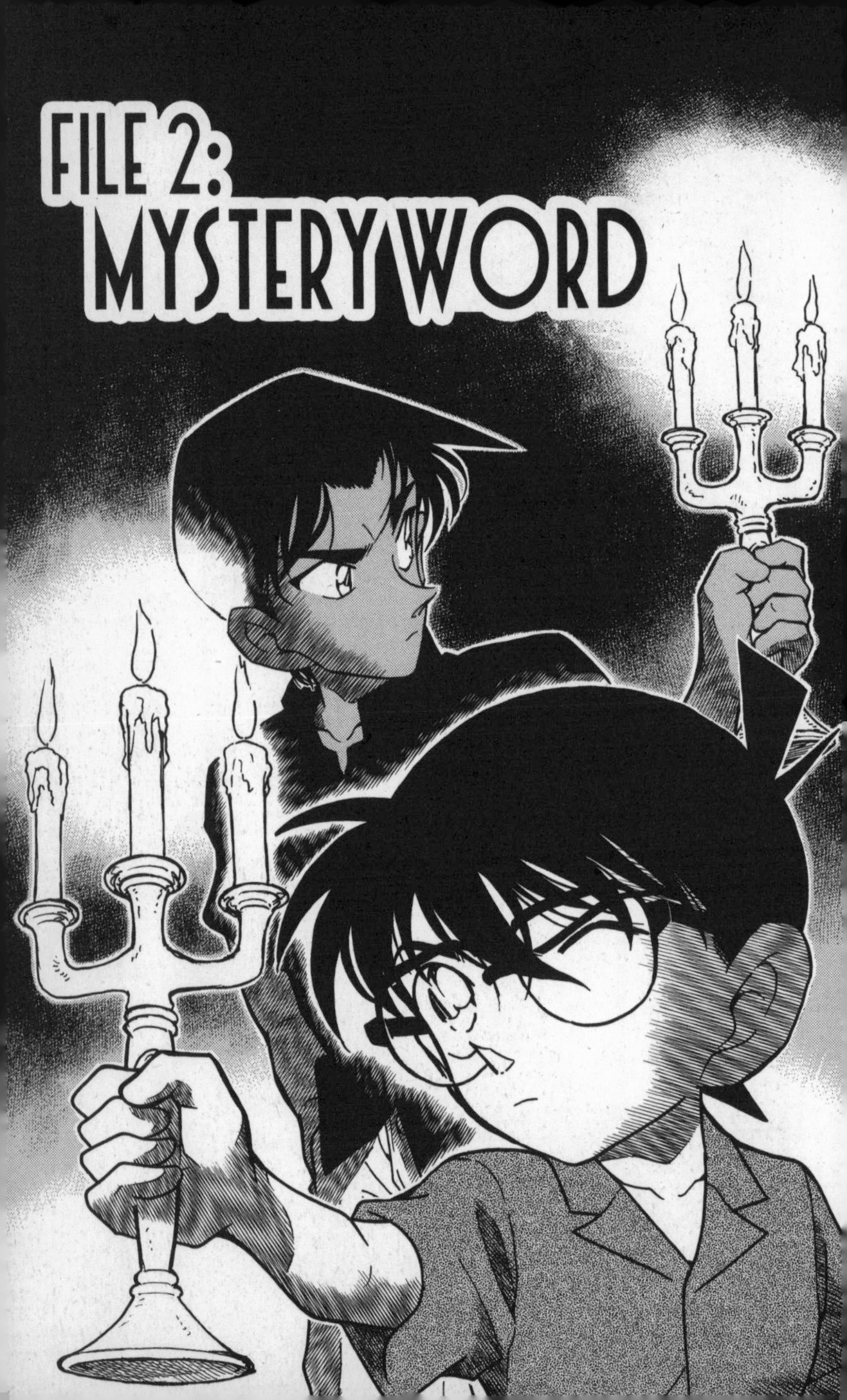
FILE 2:
MYSTERY WORD

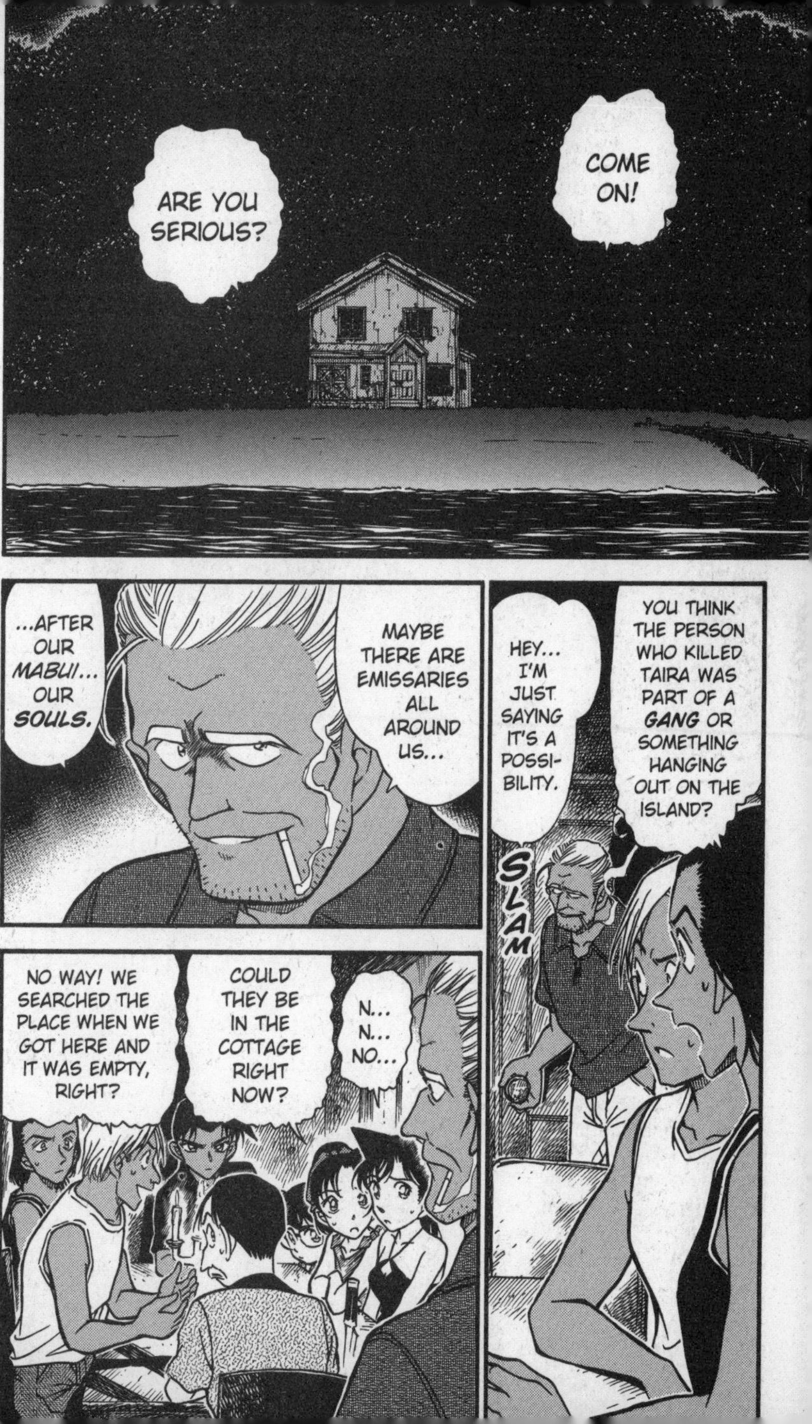
COME ON!
ARE YOU SERIOUS?
YOU THINK THE PERSON WHO KILLED TAIRA WAS PART OF A GANG OR SOMETHING HANGING OUT ON THE ISLAND?
HEY... I'M JUST SAYING IT'S A POSSIBILITY.
SLAM
MAYBE THERE ARE EMISSARIES ALL AROUND US...
...AFTER OUR MABUI... OUR SOULS.
N... N... NO...
COULD THEY BE IN THE COTTAGE RIGHT NOW?
NO WAY! WE SEARCHED THE PLACE WHEN WE GOT HERE AND IT WAS EMPTY, RIGHT?

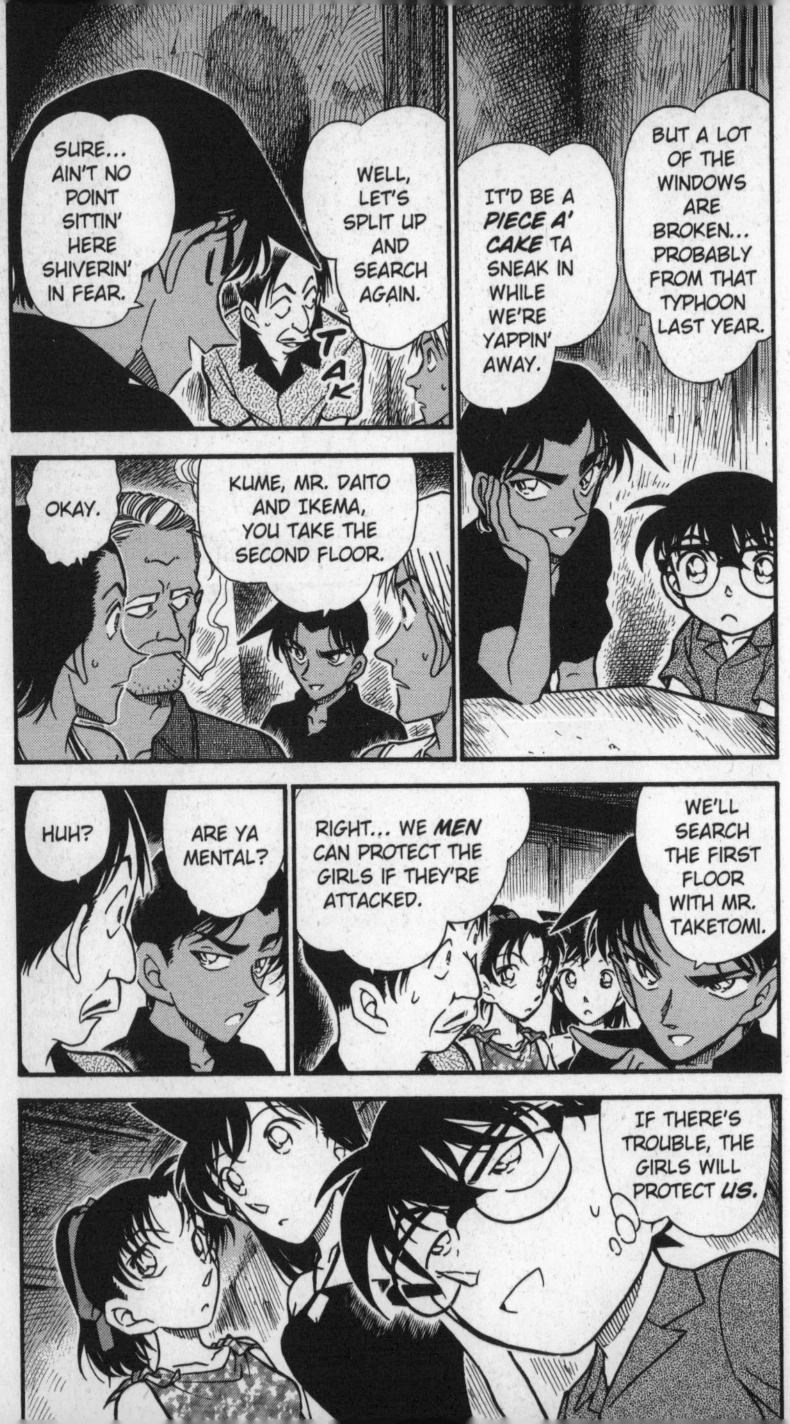
BUT A LOT OF THE WINDOWS ARE BROKEN... PROBABLY FROM THAT TYPHOON LAST YEAR.
IT'D BE A PIECE A' CAKE TA SNEAK IN WHILE WE'RE YAPPIN' AWAY.
WELL, LET'S SPLIT UP AND SEARCH AGAIN.
TAK
SURE... AIN'T NO POINT SITTIN' HERE SHIVERIN' IN FEAR.
KUME, MR. DAITO AND IKEMA, YOU TAKE THE SECOND FLOOR.
OKAY.
WE'LL SEARCH THE FIRST FLOOR WITH MR. TAKETOMI.
RIGHT... WE MEN CAN PROTECT THE GIRLS IF THEY'RE ATTACKED.
ARE YA MENTAL?
HUH?
IF THERE'S TROUBLE, THE GIRLS WILL PROTECT US.

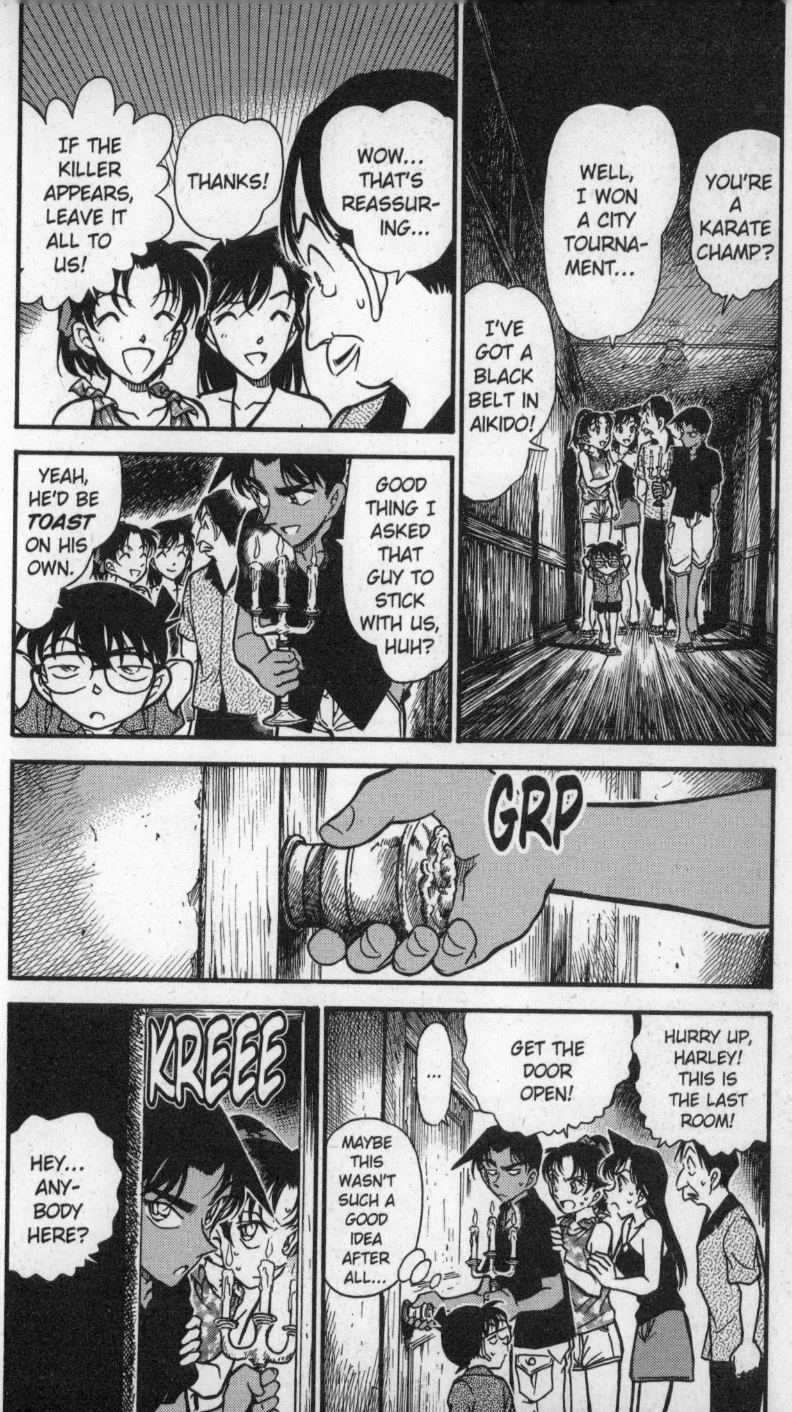
YOU'RE A KARATE CHAMP?
WELL, I WON A CITY TOURNAMENT...
I'VE GOT A BLACK BELT IN AIKIDO!
WOW... THAT'S REASSURING...
THANKS!
IF THE KILLER APPEARS, LEAVE IT ALL TO US!
GOOD THING I ASKED THAT GUY TO STICK WITH US, HUH?
YEAH, HE'D BE *TOAST* ON HIS OWN.
GRP
HURRY UP, HARLEY! THIS IS THE LAST ROOM!
GET THE DOOR OPEN!
...
MAYBE THIS WASN'T SUCH A GOOD IDEA AFTER ALL...
KREEE
HEY... ANYBODY HERE?

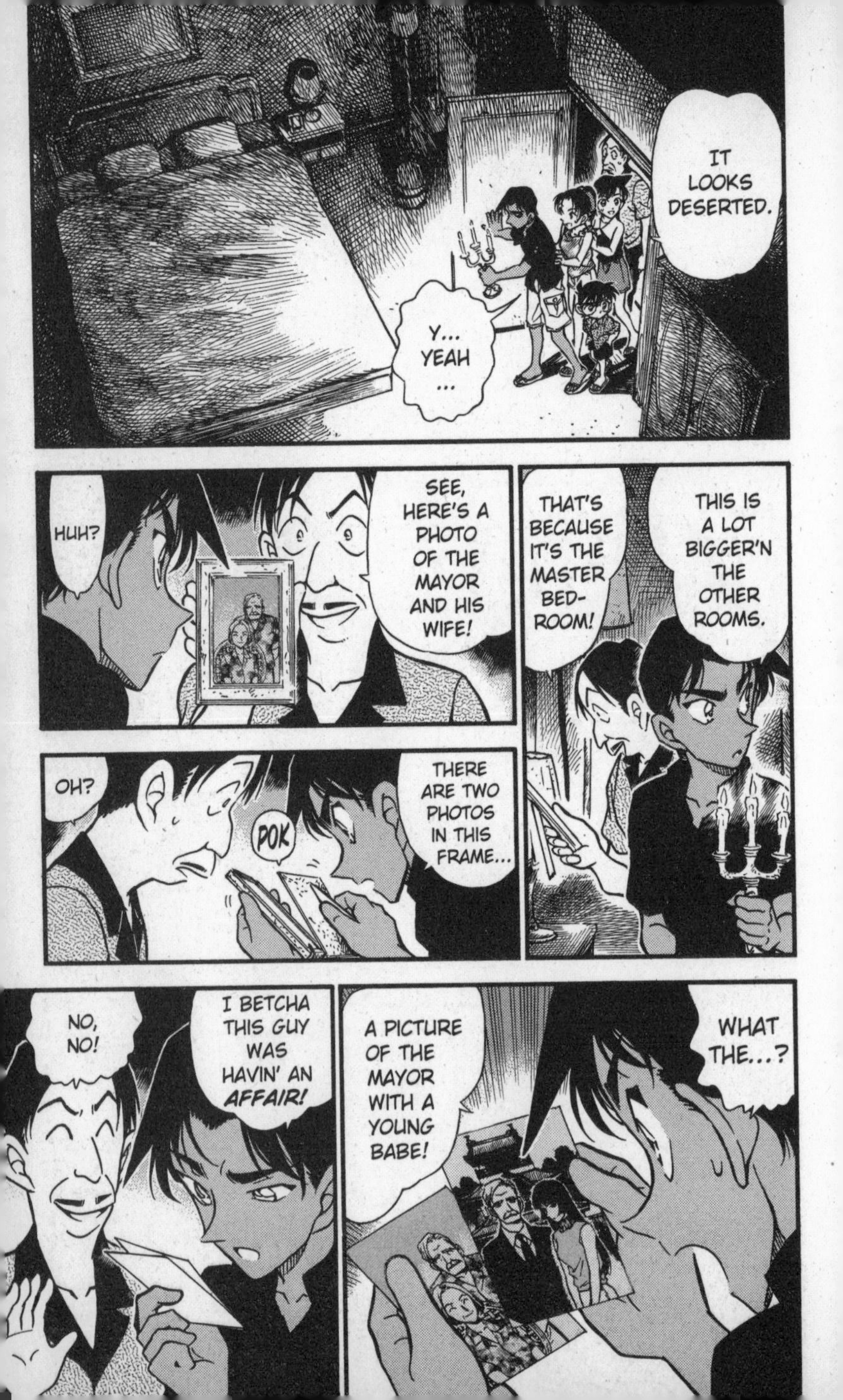
IT LOOKS DESERTED.
Y... YEAH ...
THIS IS A LOT BIGGER'N THE OTHER ROOMS.
THAT'S BECAUSE IT'S THE MASTER BED-ROOM!
SEE, HERE'S A PHOTO OF THE MAYOR AND HIS WIFE!
HUH?
THERE ARE TWO PHOTOS IN THIS FRAME...
POK
OH?
WHAT THE...?
A PICTURE OF THE MAYOR WITH A YOUNG BABE!
I BETCHA THIS GUY WAS HAVIN' AN *AFFAIR!*
NO, NO!

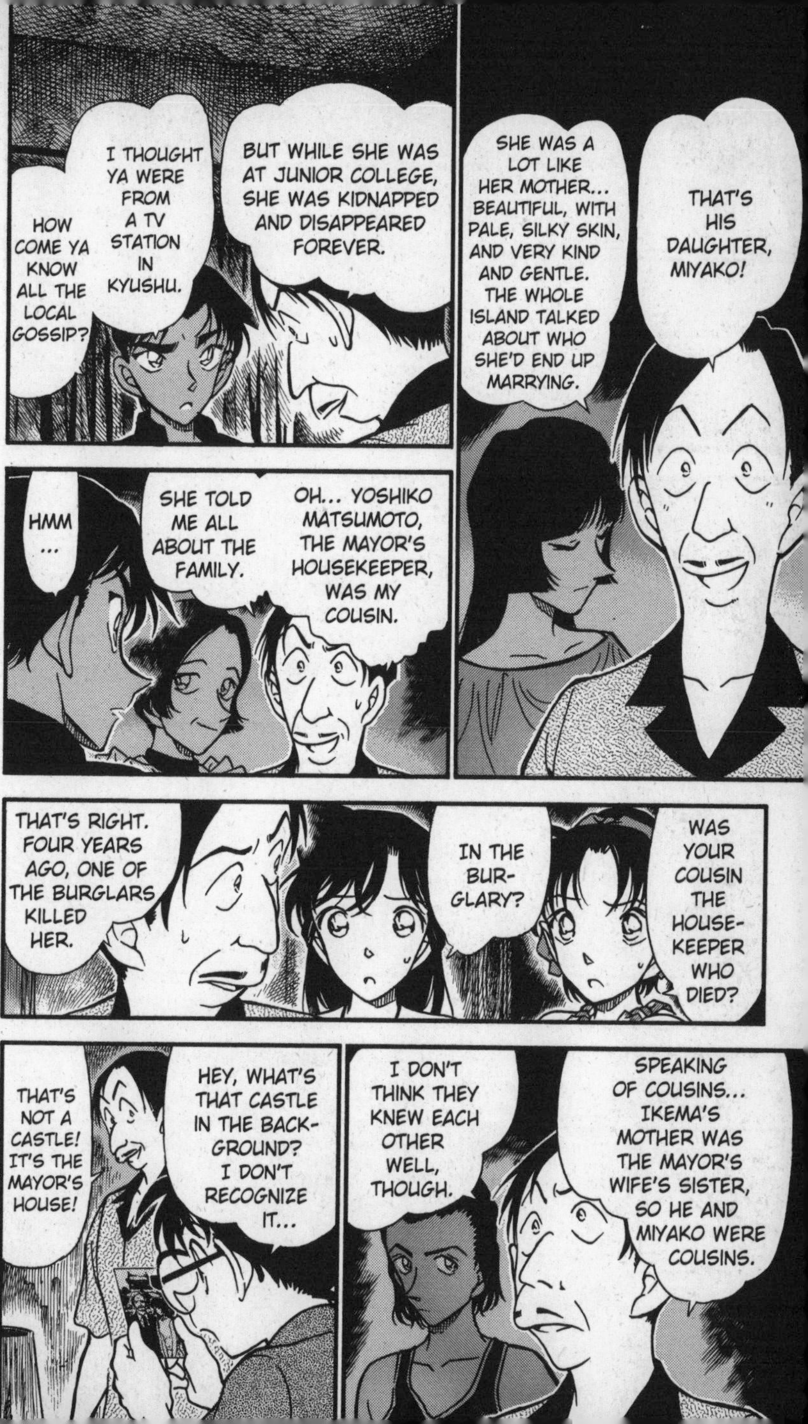
THAT'S HIS DAUGHTER, MIYAKO!
SHE WAS A LOT LIKE HER MOTHER... BEAUTIFUL, WITH PALE, SILKY SKIN, AND VERY KIND AND GENTLE. THE WHOLE ISLAND TALKED ABOUT WHO SHE'D END UP MARRYING.
BUT WHILE SHE WAS AT JUNIOR COLLEGE, SHE WAS KIDNAPPED AND DISAPPEARED FOREVER.
I THOUGHT YA WERE FROM A TV STATION IN KYUSHU.
HOW COME YA KNOW ALL THE LOCAL GOSSIP?
OH... YOSHIKO MATSUMOTO, THE MAYOR'S HOUSEKEEPER, WAS MY COUSIN.
SHE TOLD ME ALL ABOUT THE FAMILY.
HMM ...
WAS YOUR COUSIN THE HOUSE-KEEPER WHO DIED?
IN THE BUR-GLARY?
THAT'S RIGHT. FOUR YEARS AGO, ONE OF THE BURGLARS KILLED HER.
SPEAKING OF COUSINS... IKEMA'S MOTHER WAS THE MAYOR'S WIFE'S SISTER, SO HE AND MIYAKO WERE COUSINS.
I DON'T THINK THEY KNEW EACH OTHER WELL, THOUGH.
HEY, WHAT'S THAT CASTLE IN THE BACK-GROUND? I DON'T RECOGNIZE IT...
THAT'S NOT A CASTLE! IT'S THE MAYOR'S HOUSE!

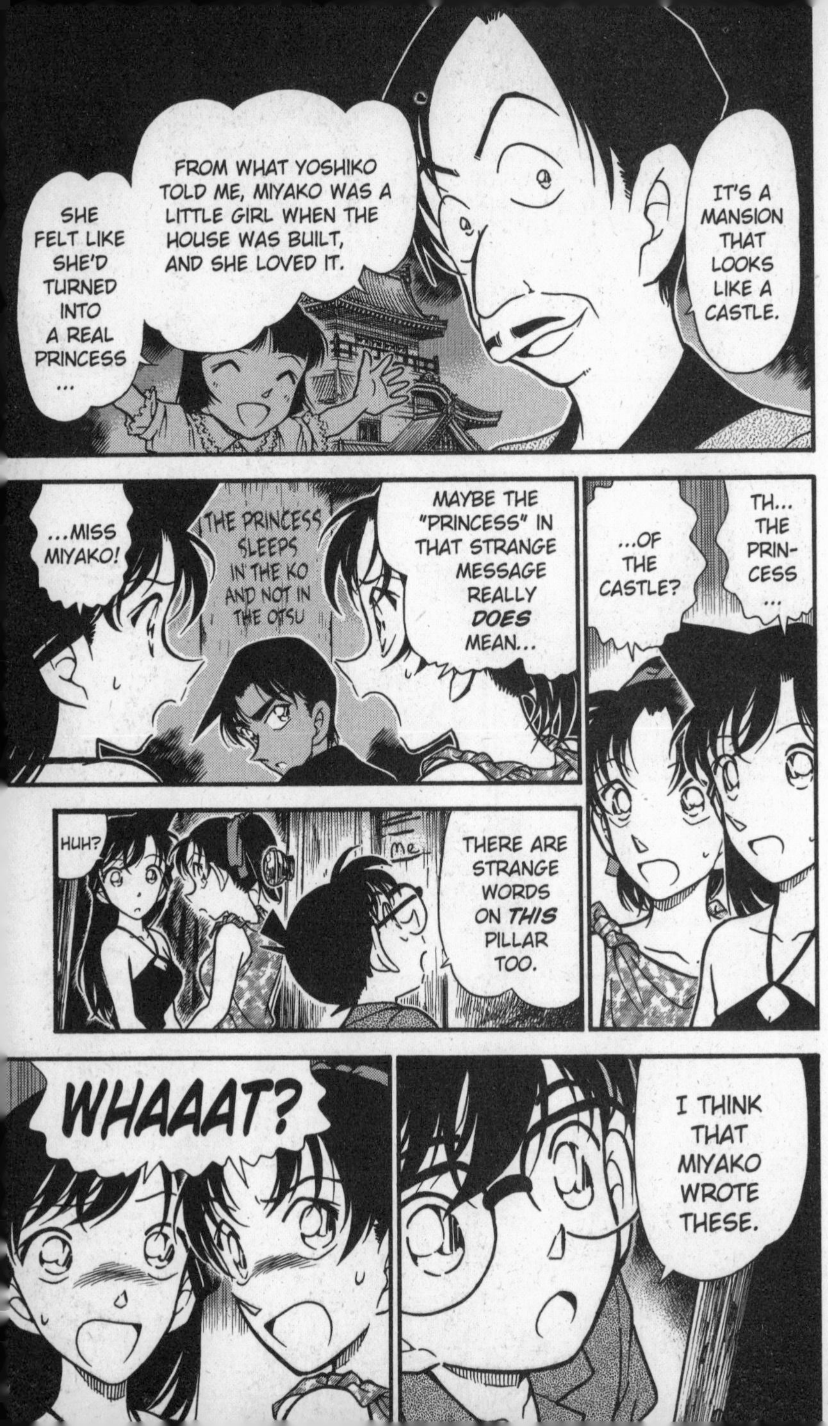

IT'S A MANSION THAT LOOKS LIKE A CASTLE.
FROM WHAT YOSHIKO TOLD ME, MIYAKO WAS A LITTLE GIRL WHEN THE HOUSE WAS BUILT, AND SHE LOVED IT.
SHE FELT LIKE SHE'D TURNED INTO A REAL PRINCESS ...
TH... THE PRIN-CESS ...
...OF THE CASTLE?
MAYBE THE "PRINCESS" IN THAT STRANGE MESSAGE REALLY *DOES* MEAN...
THE PRINCESS SLEEPS IN THE KO AND NOT IN THE OTSU
...MISS MIYAKO!
THERE ARE STRANGE WORDS ON *THIS* PILLAR TOO.
HUH?
I THINK THAT MIYAKO WROTE THESE.
WHAAAT?

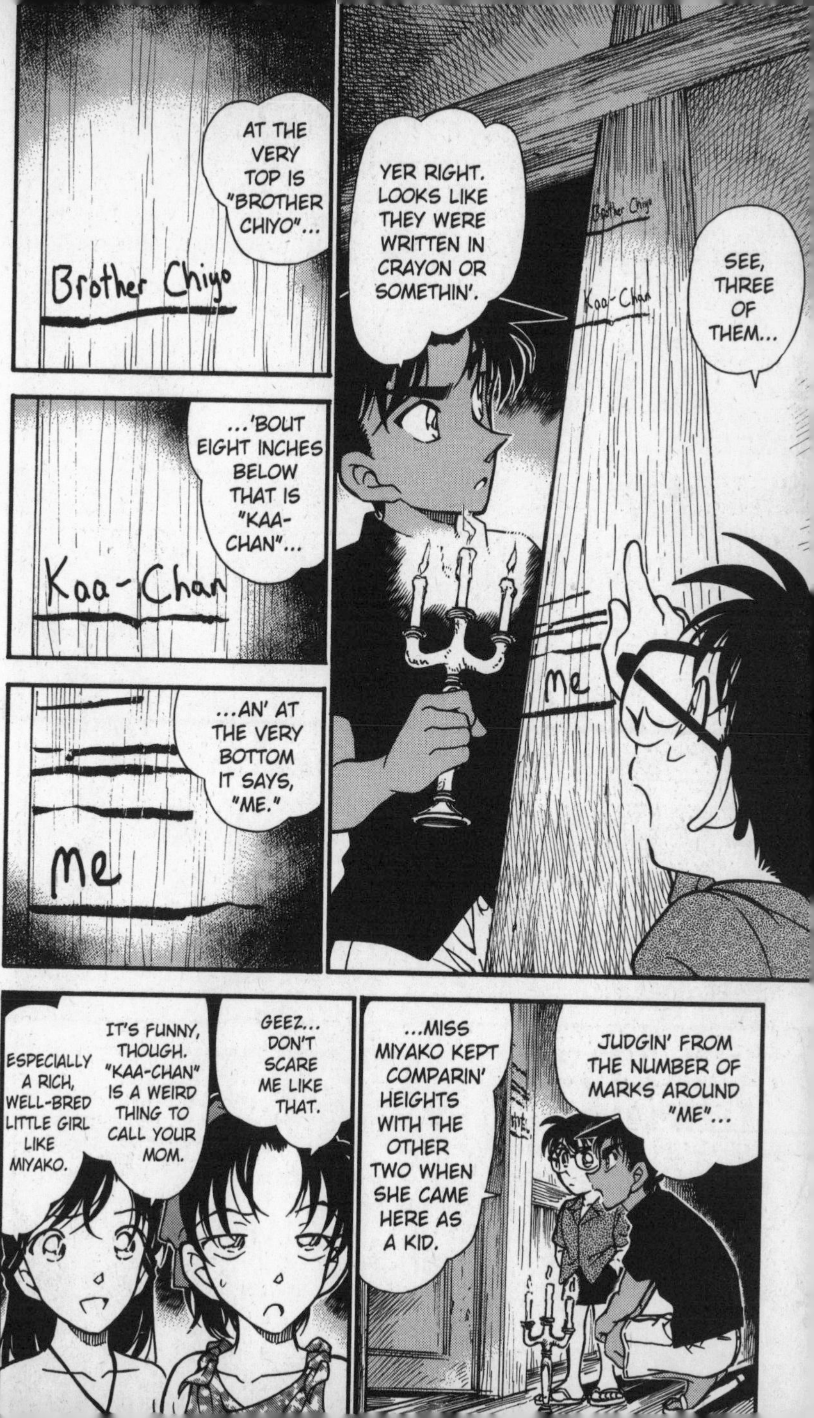
SEE, THREE OF THEM...
YER RIGHT. LOOKS LIKE THEY WERE WRITTEN IN CRAYON OR SOMETHIN'.
Brother Chiyo
Kaa-Chan
me
AT THE VERY TOP IS "BROTHER CHIYO"...
Brother Chiyo
...'BOUT EIGHT INCHES BELOW THAT IS "KAA-CHAN"...
Kaa-Chan
...AN' AT THE VERY BOTTOM IT SAYS, "ME."
me
JUDGIN' FROM THE NUMBER OF MARKS AROUND "ME"...
...MISS MIYAKO KEPT COMPARIN' HEIGHTS WITH THE OTHER TWO WHEN SHE CAME HERE AS A KID.
GEEZ... DON'T SCARE ME LIKE THAT.
IT'S FUNNY, THOUGH. "KAA-CHAN" IS A WEIRD THING TO CALL YOUR MOM.
ESPECIALLY A RICH, WELL-BRED LITTLE GIRL LIKE MIYAKO.

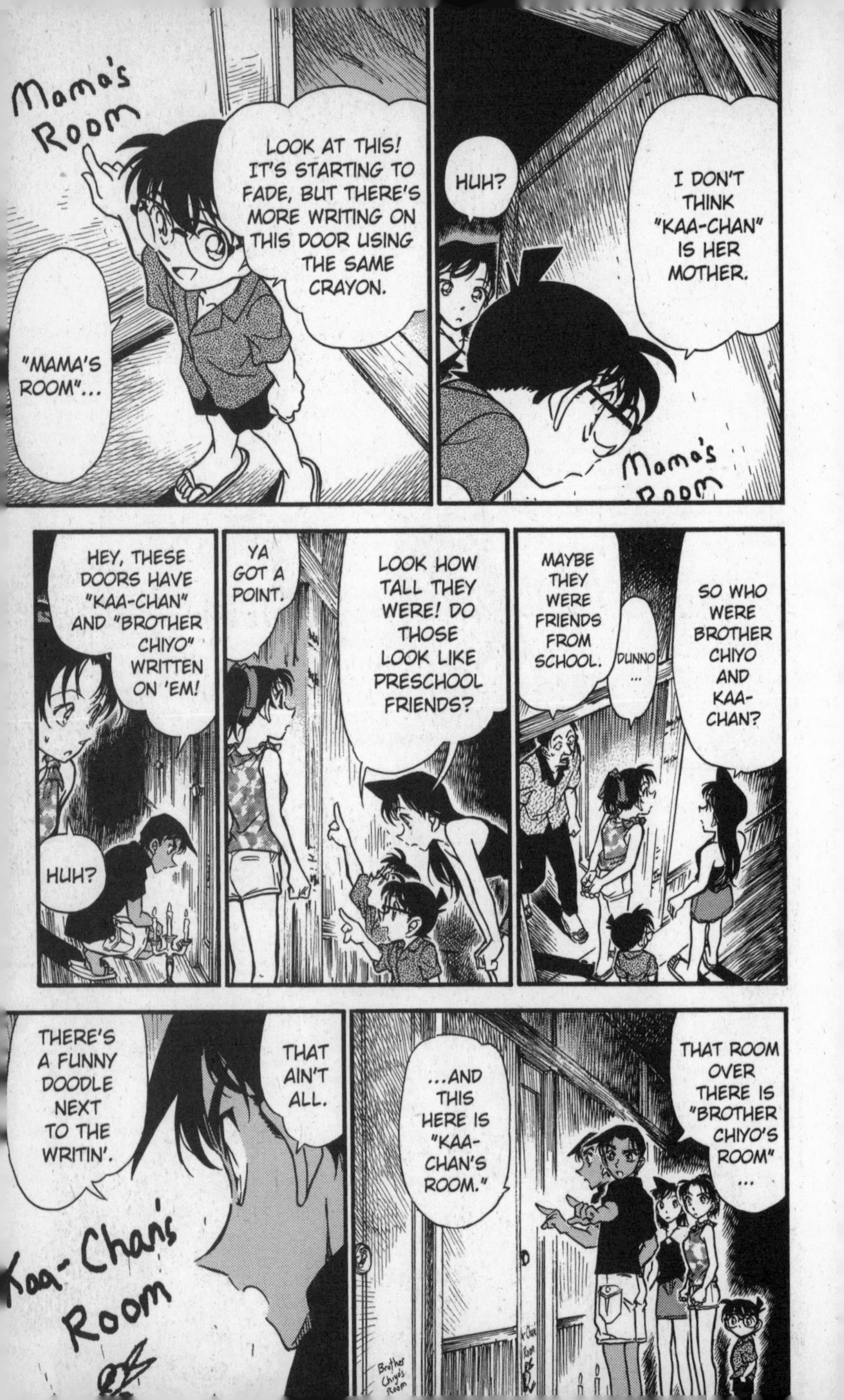
I DON'T THINK "KAA-CHAN" IS HER MOTHER.
HUH?
Mama's Room
LOOK AT THIS! IT'S STARTING TO FADE, BUT THERE'S MORE WRITING ON THIS DOOR USING THE SAME CRAYON.
Mama's Room
"MAMA'S ROOM"...
SO WHO WERE BROTHER CHIYO AND KAA-CHAN?
DUNNO...
MAYBE THEY WERE FRIENDS FROM SCHOOL.
LOOK HOW TALL THEY WERE! DO THOSE LOOK LIKE PRESCHOOL FRIENDS?
YA GOT A POINT.
HEY, THESE DOORS HAVE "KAA-CHAN" AND "BROTHER CHIYO" WRITTEN ON 'EM!
HUH?
THAT ROOM OVER THERE IS "BROTHER CHIYO'S ROOM"...
...AND THIS HERE IS "KAA-CHAN'S ROOM."
Brother Chiyo's Room
THAT AIN'T ALL.
THERE'S A FUNNY DOODLE NEXT TO THE WRITIN'.
Kaa-Chan's Room

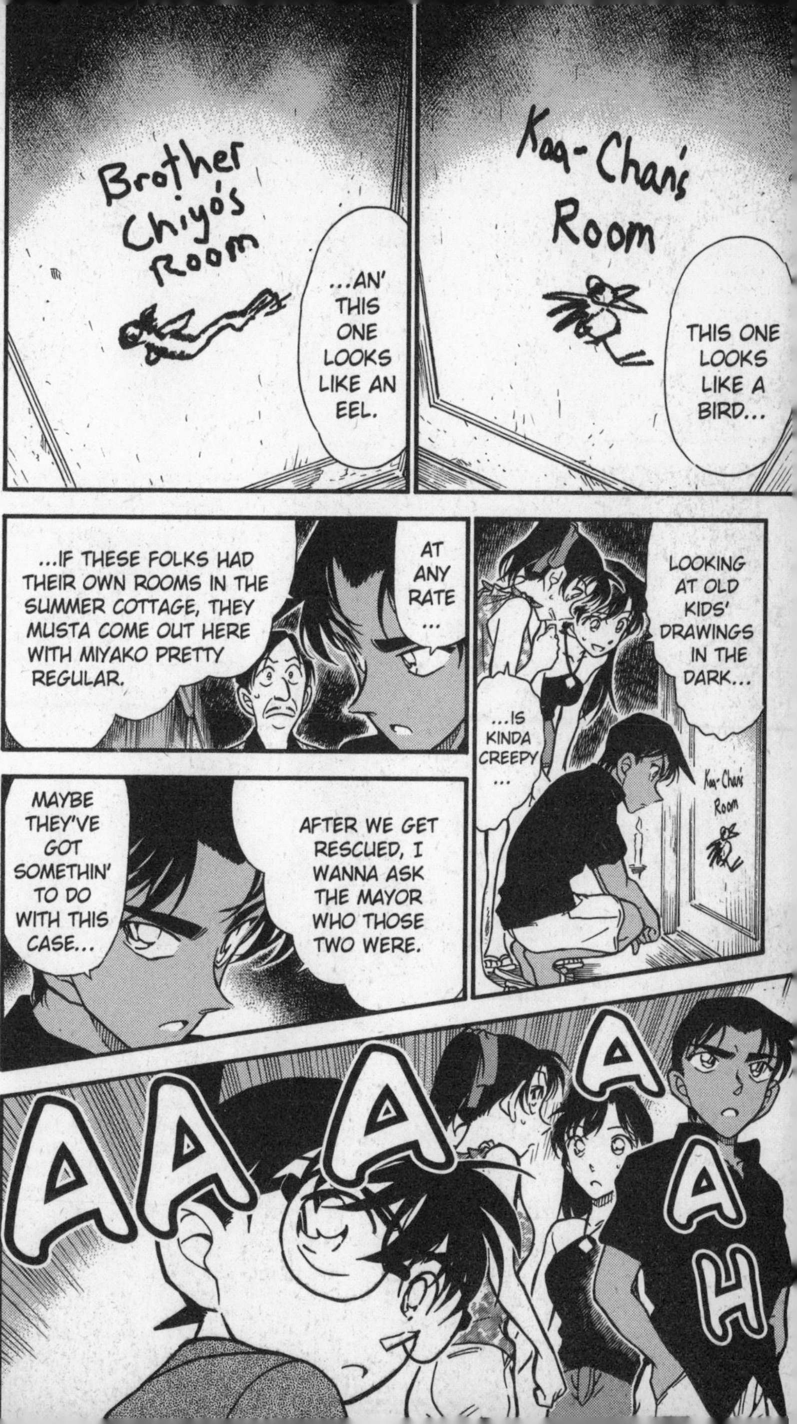
Kaa-Chan's Room
THIS ONE LOOKS LIKE A BIRD...
Brother Chiyo's Room
...AN' THIS ONE LOOKS LIKE AN EEL.
LOOKING AT OLD KIDS' DRAWINGS IN THE DARK...
...IS KINDA CREEPY...
Kaa-Chan's Room
AT ANY RATE...
...IF THESE FOLKS HAD THEIR OWN ROOMS IN THE SUMMER COTTAGE, THEY MUSTA COME OUT HERE WITH MIYAKO PRETTY REGULAR.
AFTER WE GET RESCUED, I WANNA ASK THE MAYOR WHO THOSE TWO WERE.
MAYBE THEY'VE GOT SOMETHIN' TO DO WITH THIS CASE...
AAAAAH

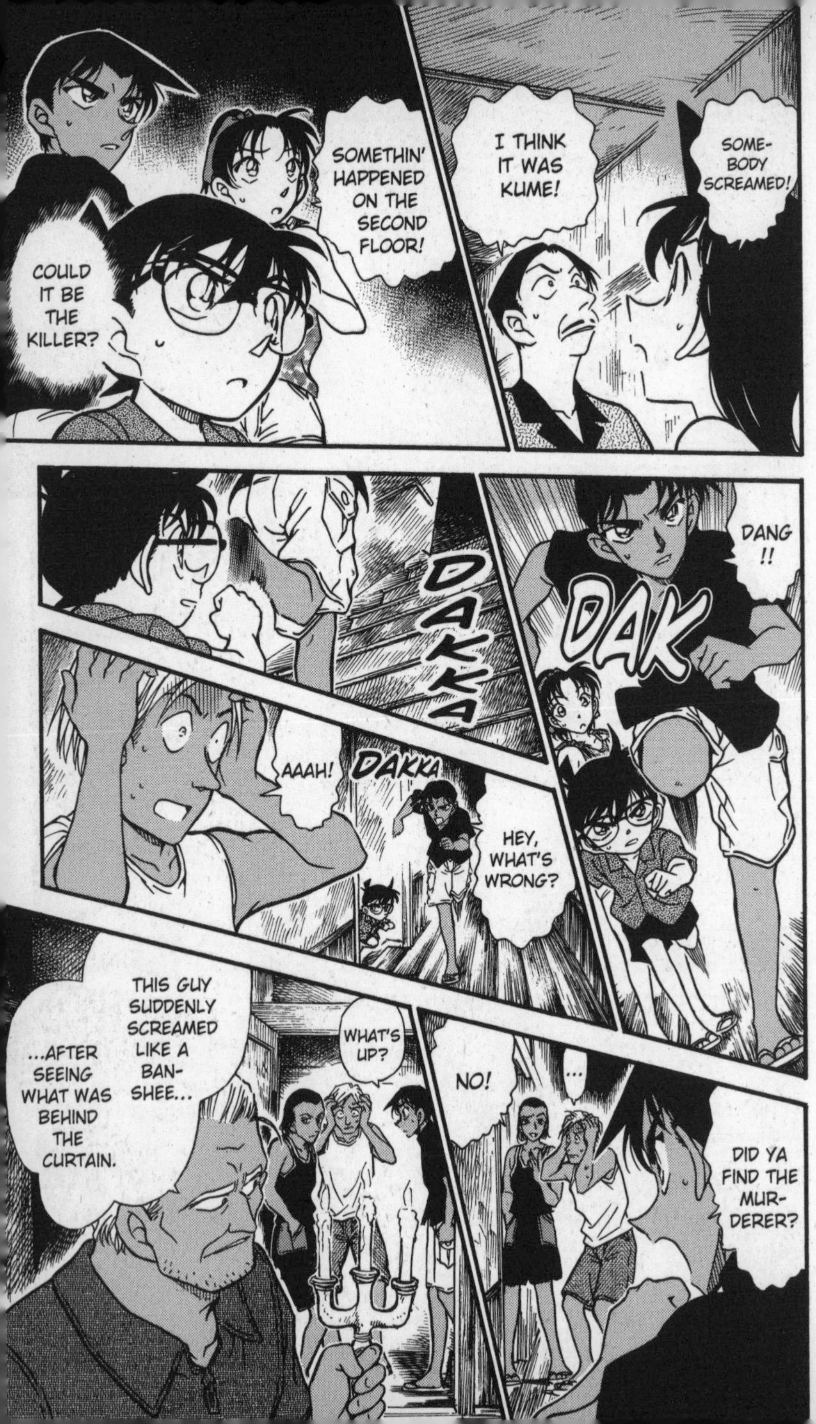

SOME-BODY SCREAMED!
I THINK IT WAS KUME!
SOMETHIN' HAPPENED ON THE SECOND FLOOR!
COULD IT BE THE KILLER?
DANG !!
DAK
DAKKA
AAAH!
DAKKA
HEY, WHAT'S WRONG?
DID YA FIND THE MUR-DERER?
...
NO!
WHAT'S UP?
THIS GUY SUDDENLY SCREAMED LIKE A BAN-SHEE...
...AFTER SEEING WHAT WAS BEHIND THE CURTAIN.

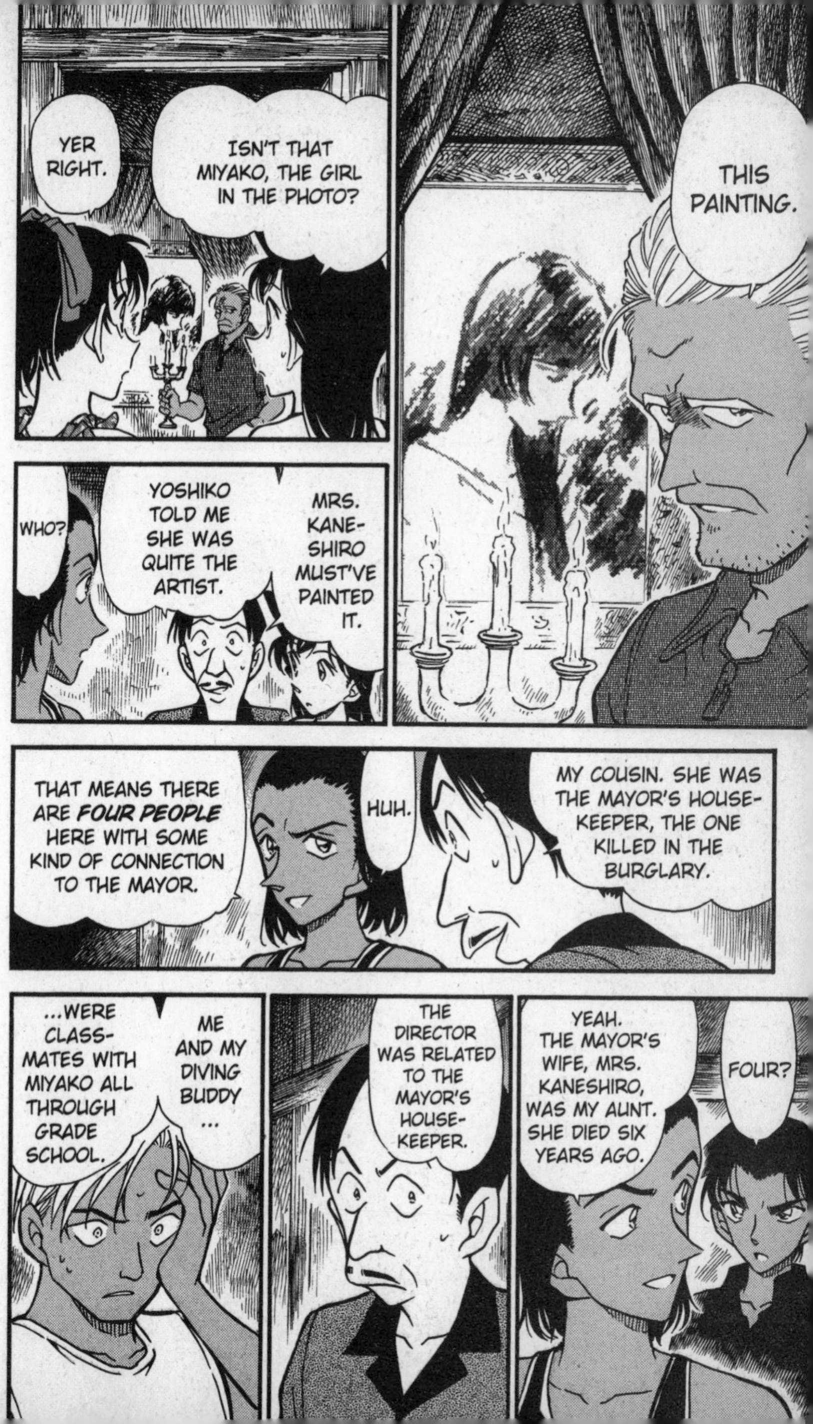
THIS PAINTING.
ISN'T THAT MIYAKO, THE GIRL IN THE PHOTO?
YER RIGHT.
MRS. KANE-SHIRO MUST'VE PAINTED IT.
YOSHIKO TOLD ME SHE WAS QUITE THE ARTIST.
WHO?
MY COUSIN. SHE WAS THE MAYOR'S HOUSE-KEEPER, THE ONE KILLED IN THE BURGLARY.
HUH.
THAT MEANS THERE ARE ***FOUR PEOPLE*** HERE WITH SOME KIND OF CONNECTION TO THE MAYOR.
FOUR?
YEAH. THE MAYOR'S WIFE, MRS. KANESHIRO, WAS MY AUNT. SHE DIED SIX YEARS AGO.
THE DIRECTOR WAS RELATED TO THE MAYOR'S HOUSE-KEEPER.
ME AND MY DIVING BUDDY ...
...WERE CLASS-MATES WITH MIYAKO ALL THROUGH GRADE SCHOOL.

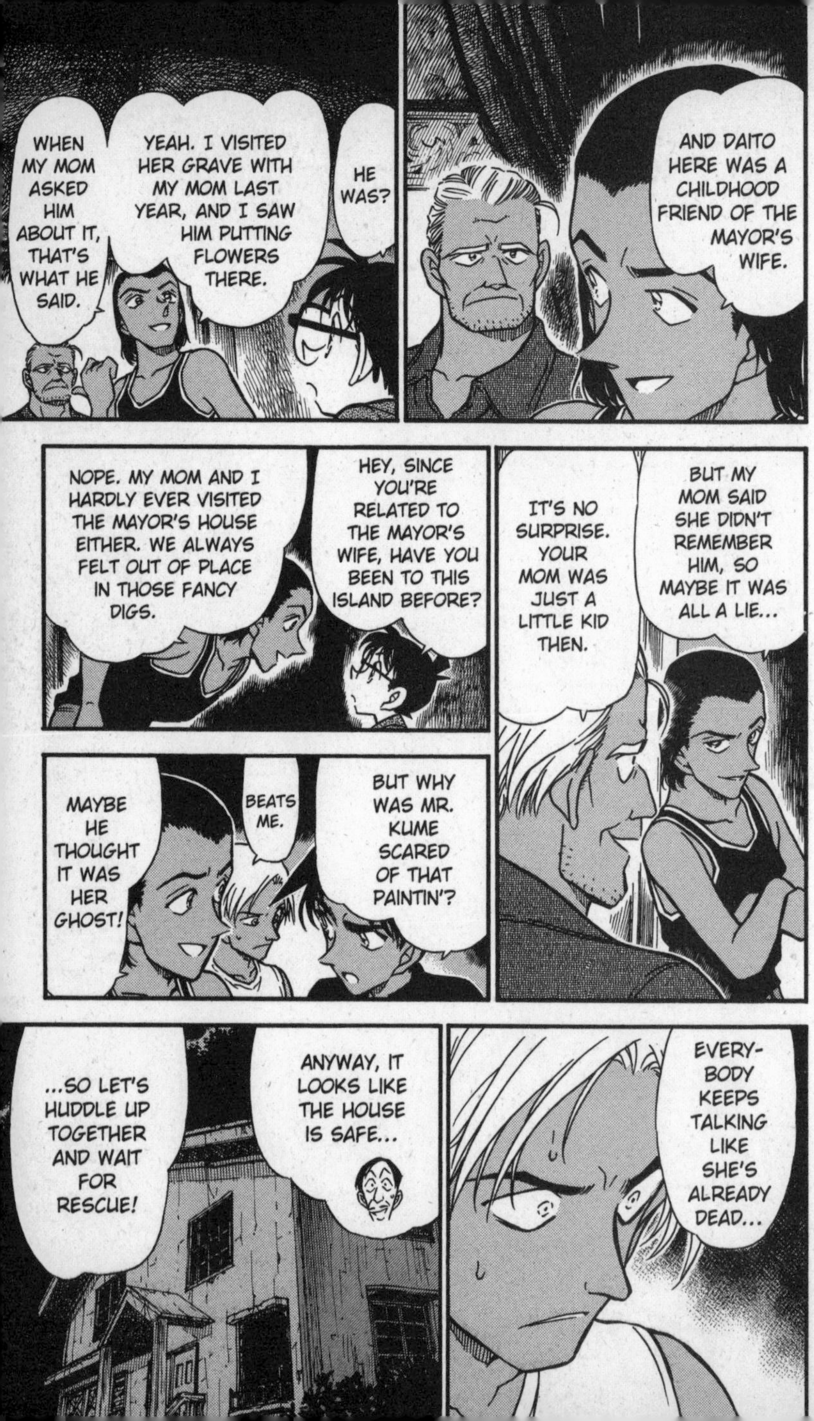
AND DAITO HERE WAS A CHILDHOOD FRIEND OF THE MAYOR'S WIFE.
HE WAS?
YEAH. I VISITED HER GRAVE WITH MY MOM LAST YEAR, AND I SAW HIM PUTTING FLOWERS THERE.
WHEN MY MOM ASKED HIM ABOUT IT, THAT'S WHAT HE SAID.
BUT MY MOM SAID SHE DIDN'T REMEMBER HIM, SO MAYBE IT WAS ALL A LIE...
IT'S NO SURPRISE. YOUR MOM WAS JUST A LITTLE KID THEN.
HEY, SINCE YOU'RE RELATED TO THE MAYOR'S WIFE, HAVE YOU BEEN TO THIS ISLAND BEFORE?
NOPE. MY MOM AND I HARDLY EVER VISITED THE MAYOR'S HOUSE EITHER. WE ALWAYS FELT OUT OF PLACE IN THOSE FANCY DIGS.
BUT WHY WAS MR. KUME SCARED OF THAT PAINTIN'?
BEATS ME.
MAYBE HE THOUGHT IT WAS HER GHOST!
EVERY-BODY KEEPS TALKING LIKE SHE'S ALREADY DEAD...
ANYWAY, IT LOOKS LIKE THE HOUSE IS SAFE...
...SO LET'S HUDDLE UP TOGETHER AND WAIT FOR RESCUE!

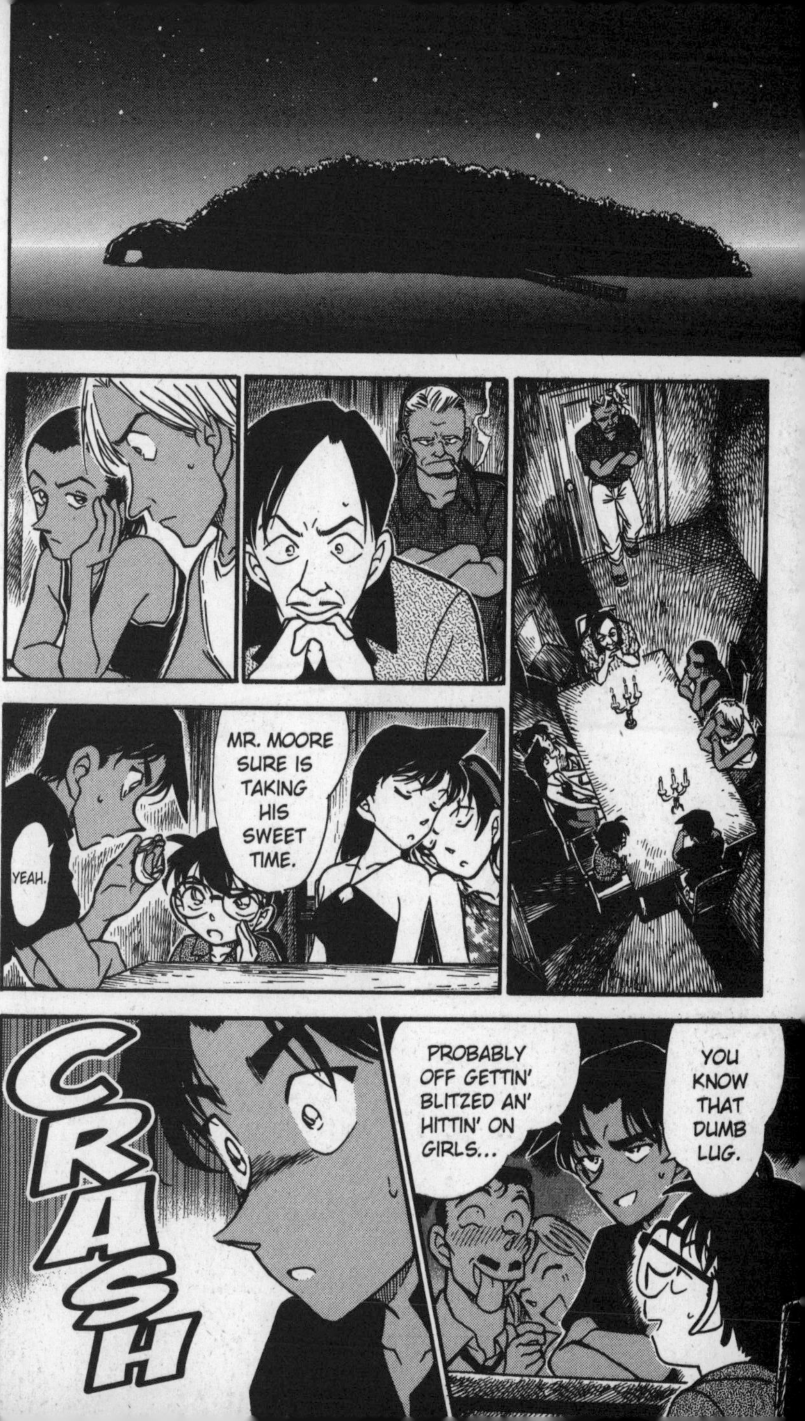
MR. MOORE SURE IS TAKING HIS SWEET TIME.
YEAH.
YOU KNOW THAT DUMB LUG.
PROBABLY OFF GETTIN' BLITZED AN' HITTIN' ON GIRLS...
CRASH

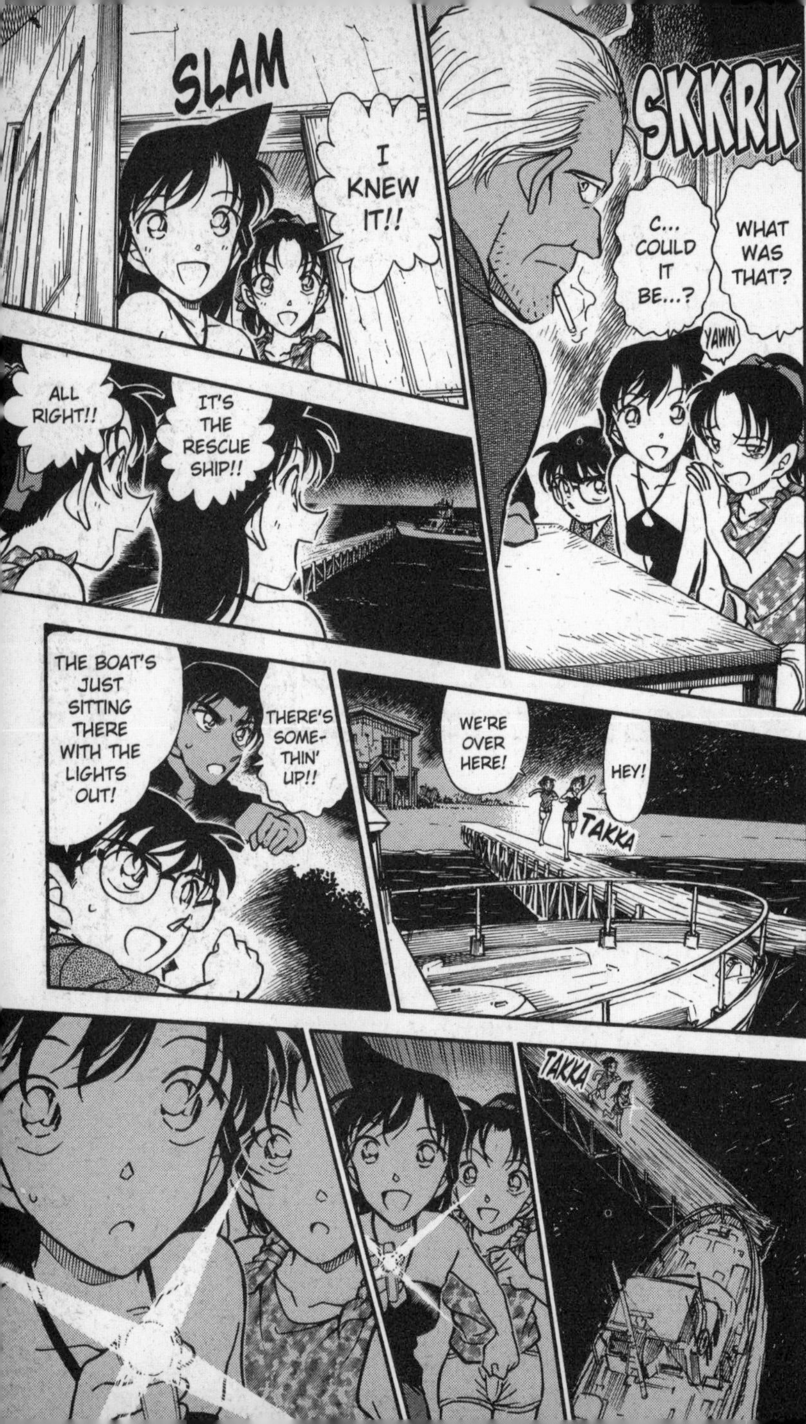
SKKRK
WHAT WAS THAT?
C... COULD IT BE...?
YAWN
SLAM
I KNEW IT!!
IT'S THE RESCUE SHIP!!
ALL RIGHT!!
HEY!
WE'RE OVER HERE!
TAKKA
THERE'S SOME-THIN' UP!!
THE BOAT'S JUST SITTING THERE WITH THE LIGHTS OUT!
TAKKA

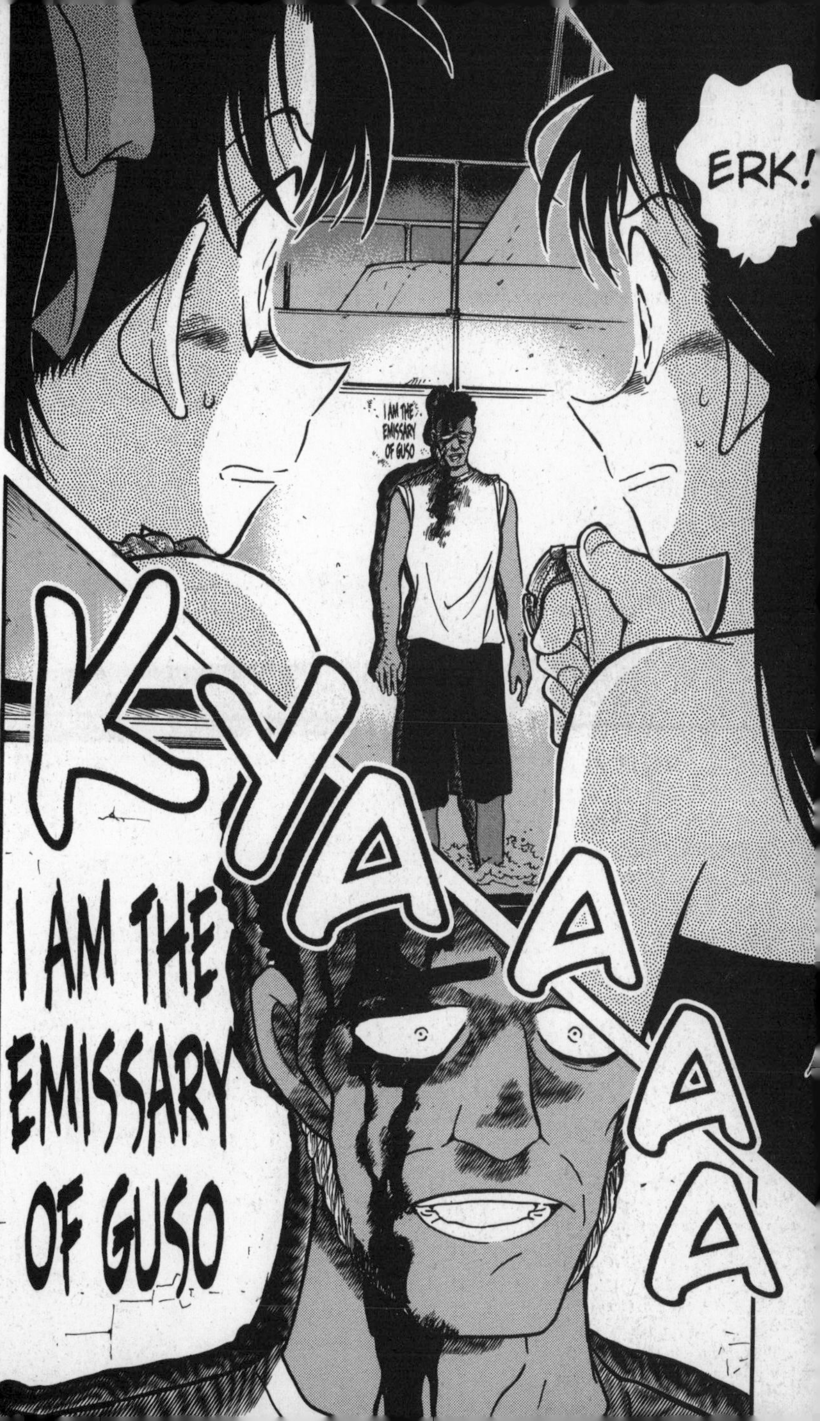
ERK!
I AM THE EMISSARY OF GUSO
KYAAAAA
I AM THE EMISSARY OF GUSO

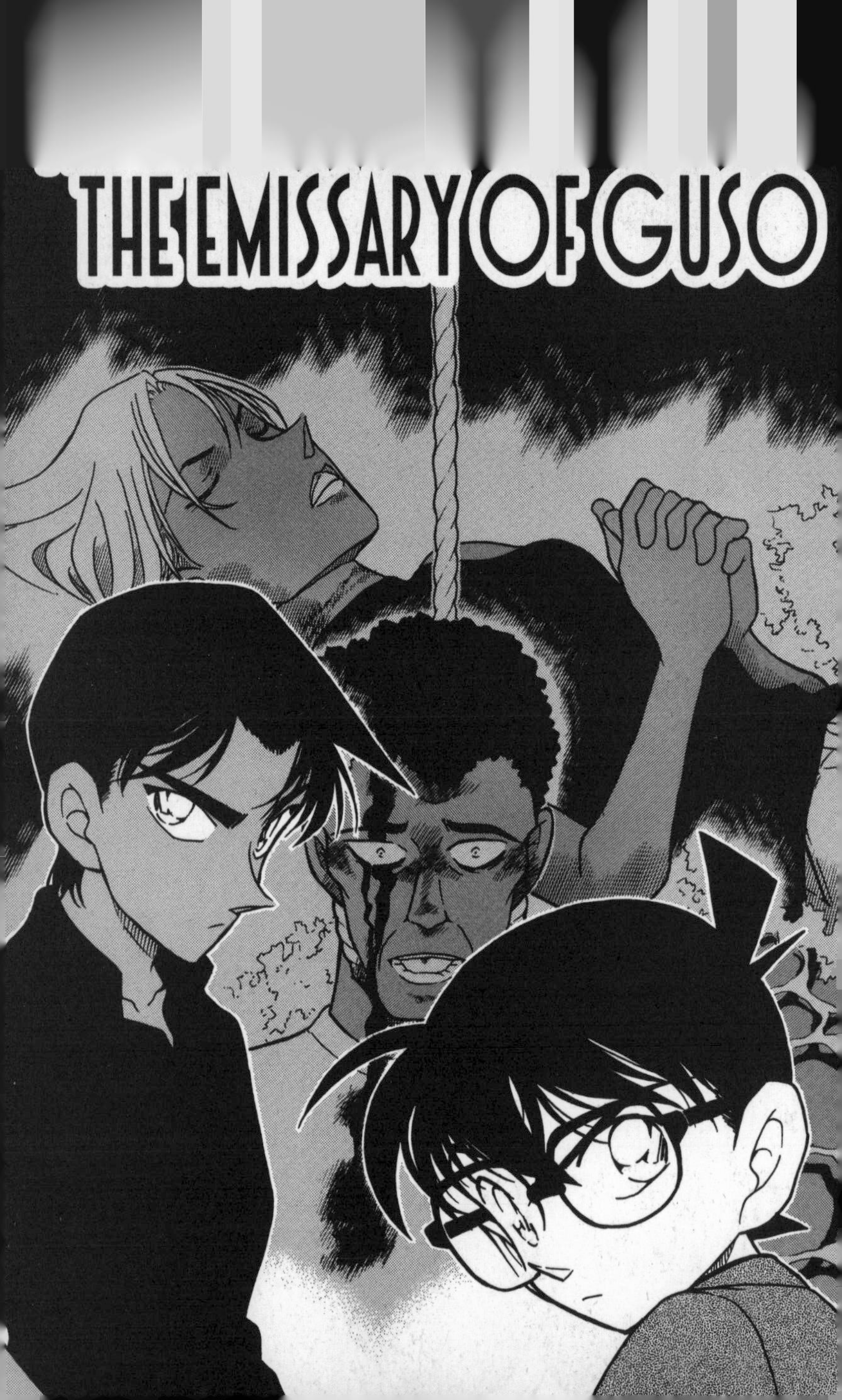
THE EMISSARY OF GUSO

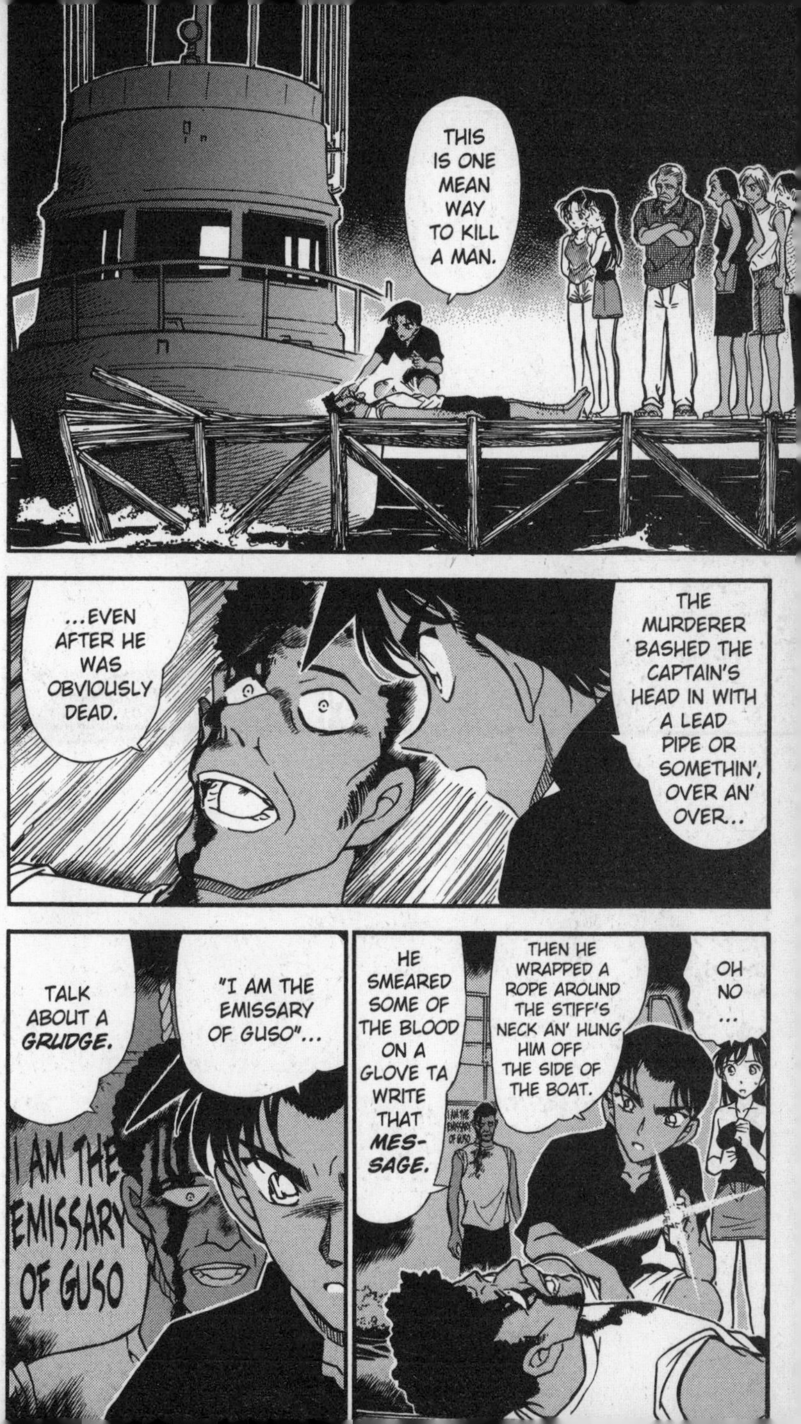
THIS IS ONE MEAN WAY TO KILL A MAN.
THE MURDERER BASHED THE CAPTAIN'S HEAD IN WITH A LEAD PIPE OR SOMETHIN', OVER AN' OVER...
...EVEN AFTER HE WAS OBVIOUSLY DEAD.
OH NO ...
THEN HE WRAPPED A ROPE AROUND THE STIFF'S NECK AN' HUNG HIM OFF THE SIDE OF THE BOAT.
HE SMEARED SOME OF THE BLOOD ON A GLOVE TA WRITE THAT *MESSAGE.*
I AM THE EMISSARY OF GUSO
"I AM THE EMISSARY OF GUSO"...
TALK ABOUT A *GRUDGE.*
I AM THE EMISSARY OF GUSO

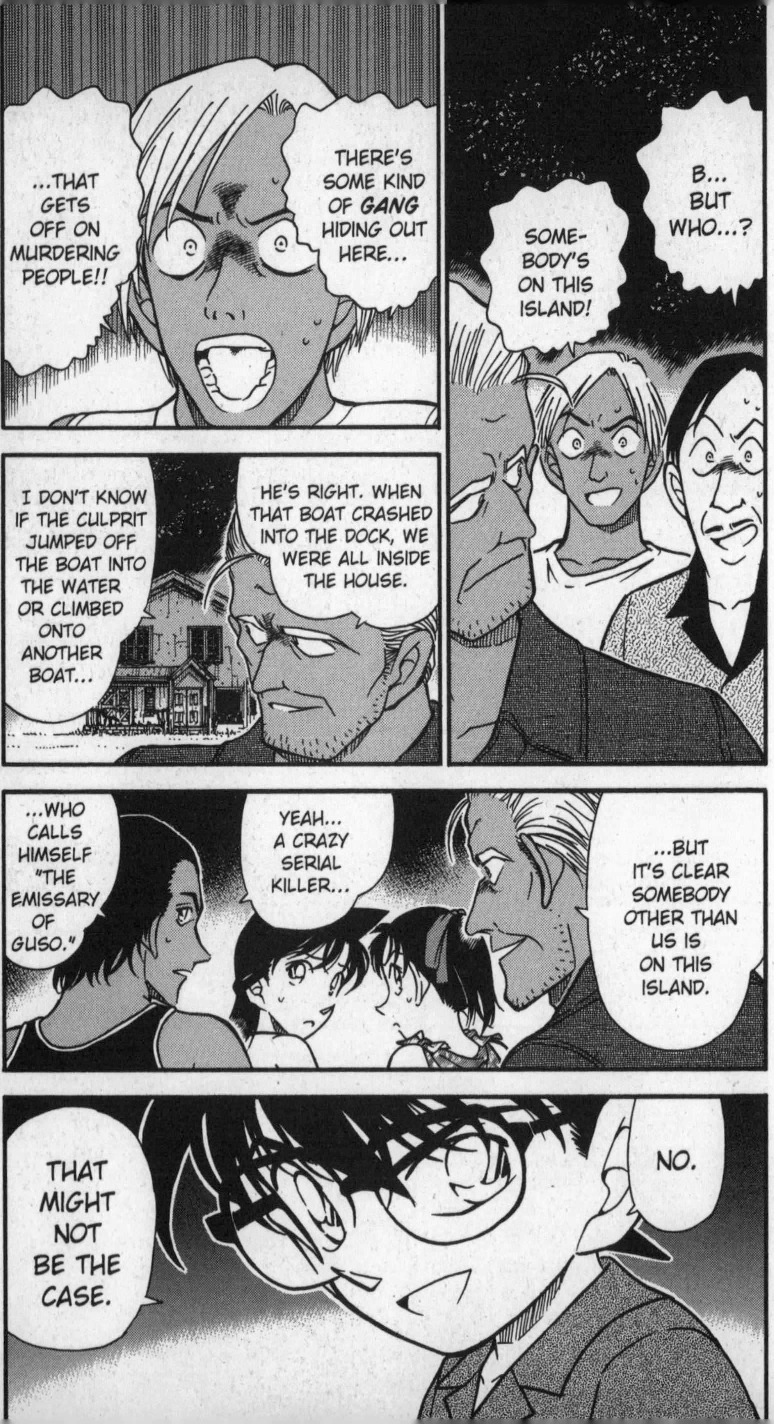
B... BUT WHO...?
SOME-BODY'S ON THIS ISLAND!
THERE'S SOME KIND OF GANG HIDING OUT HERE...
...THAT GETS OFF ON MURDERING PEOPLE!!
HE'S RIGHT. WHEN THAT BOAT CRASHED INTO THE DOCK, WE WERE ALL INSIDE THE HOUSE.
I DON'T KNOW IF THE CULPRIT JUMPED OFF THE BOAT INTO THE WATER OR CLIMBED ONTO ANOTHER BOAT...
...BUT IT'S CLEAR SOMEBODY OTHER THAN US IS ON THIS ISLAND.
YEAH... A CRAZY SERIAL KILLER...
...WHO CALLS HIMSELF "THE EMISSARY OF GUSO."
NO.
THAT MIGHT NOT BE THE CASE.

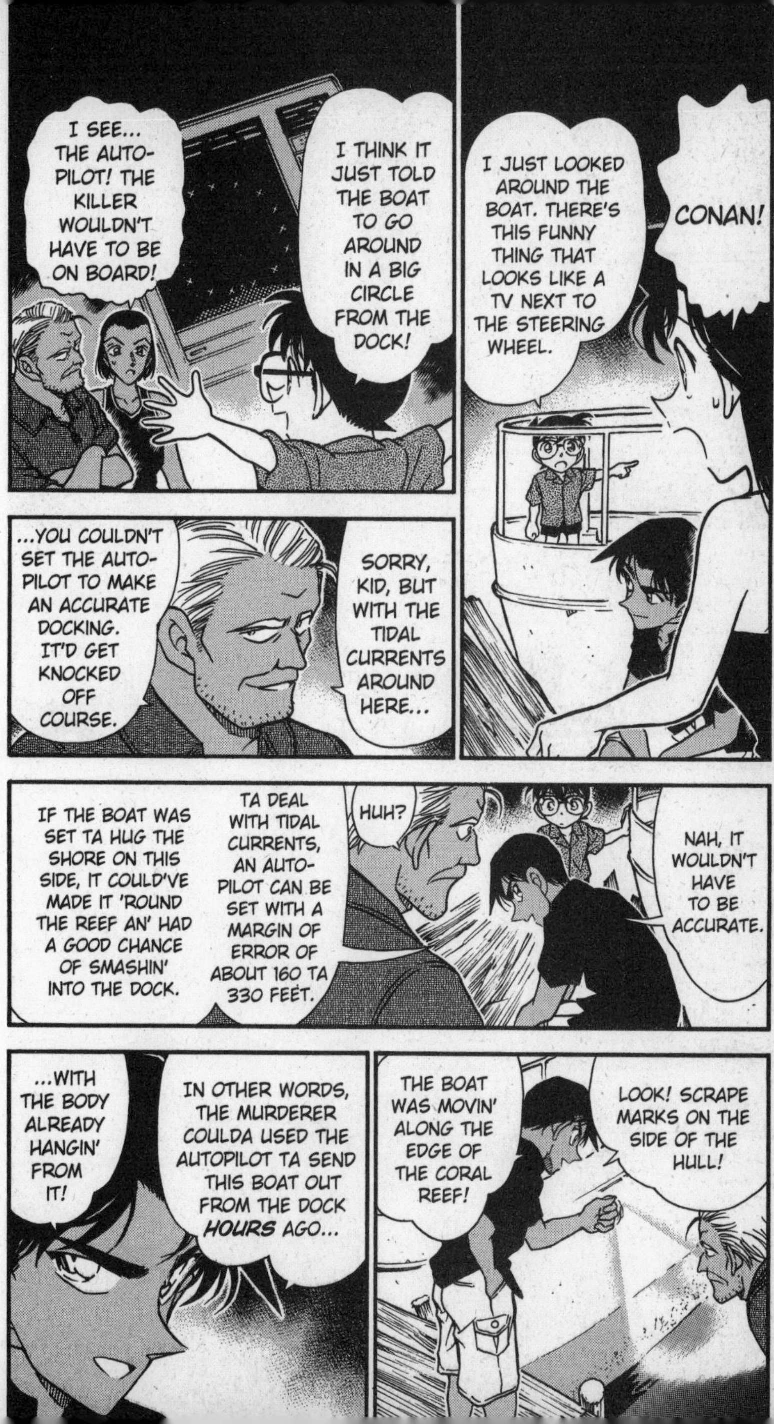
CONAN!
I JUST LOOKED AROUND THE BOAT. THERE'S THIS FUNNY THING THAT LOOKS LIKE A TV NEXT TO THE STEERING WHEEL.
I THINK IT JUST TOLD THE BOAT TO GO AROUND IN A BIG CIRCLE FROM THE DOCK!
I SEE... THE AUTO-PILOT! THE KILLER WOULDN'T HAVE TO BE ON BOARD!
SORRY, KID, BUT WITH THE TIDAL CURRENTS AROUND HERE...
...YOU COULDN'T SET THE AUTO-PILOT TO MAKE AN ACCURATE DOCKING. IT'D GET KNOCKED OFF COURSE.
NAH, IT WOULDN'T HAVE TO BE ACCURATE.
HUH?
TA DEAL WITH TIDAL CURRENTS, AN AUTO-PILOT CAN BE SET WITH A MARGIN OF ERROR OF ABOUT 160 TA 330 FEET.
IF THE BOAT WAS SET TA HUG THE SHORE ON THIS SIDE, IT COULD'VE MADE IT 'ROUND THE REEF AN' HAD A GOOD CHANCE OF SMASHIN' INTO THE DOCK.
LOOK! SCRAPE MARKS ON THE SIDE OF THE HULL!
THE BOAT WAS MOVIN' ALONG THE EDGE OF THE CORAL REEF!
IN OTHER WORDS, THE MURDERER COULDA USED THE AUTOPILOT TA SEND THIS BOAT OUT FROM THE DOCK ***HOURS*** AGO...
...WITH THE BODY ALREADY HANGIN' FROM IT!

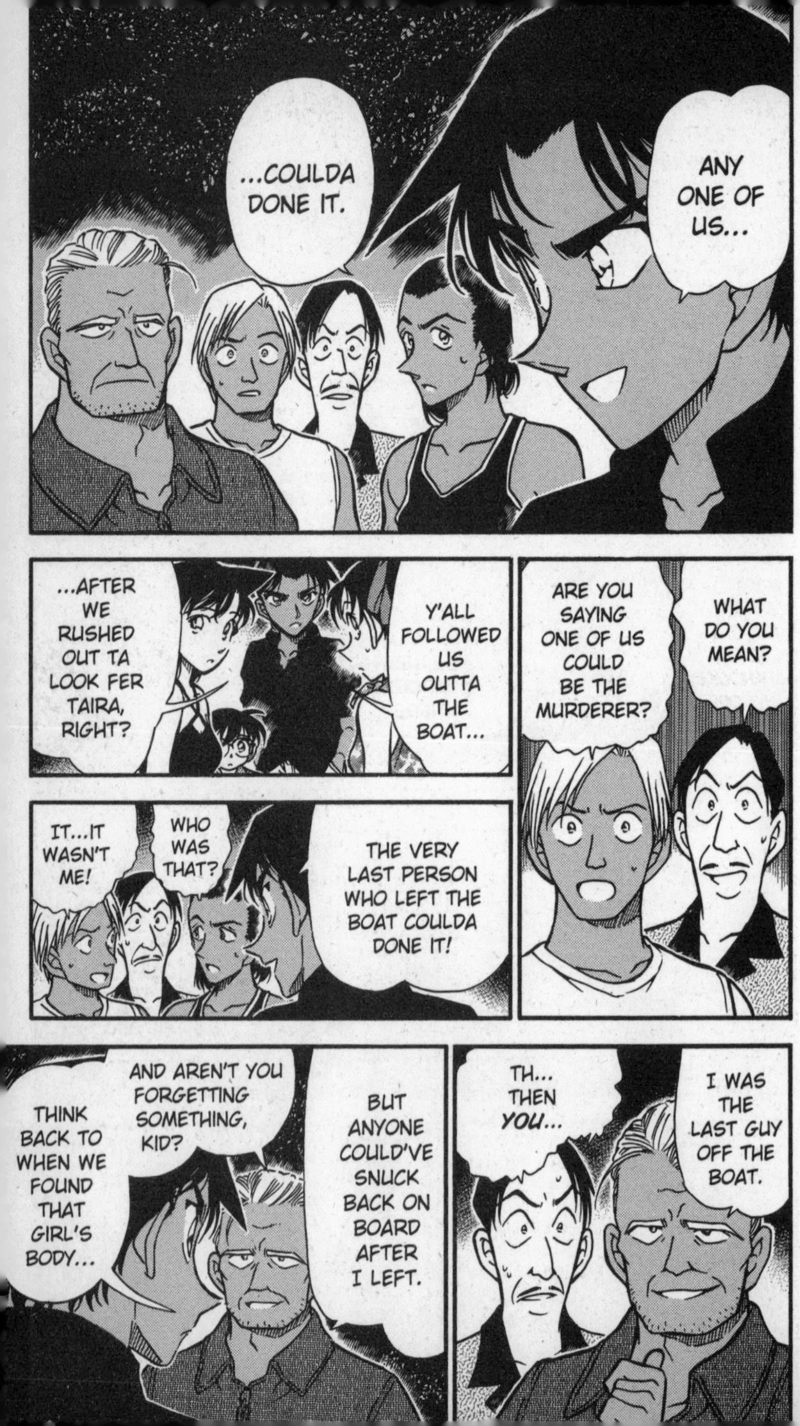
ANY ONE OF US...
...COULDA DONE IT.
WHAT DO YOU MEAN?
ARE YOU SAYING ONE OF US COULD BE THE MURDERER?
Y'ALL FOLLOWED US OUTTA THE BOAT...
...AFTER WE RUSHED OUT TA LOOK FER TAIRA, RIGHT?
THE VERY LAST PERSON WHO LEFT THE BOAT COULDA DONE IT!
WHO WAS THAT?
IT...IT WASN'T ME!
I WAS THE LAST GUY OFF THE BOAT.
TH... THEN *YOU*...
BUT ANYONE COULD'VE SNUCK BACK ON BOARD AFTER I LEFT.
AND AREN'T YOU FORGETTING SOMETHING, KID?
THINK BACK TO WHEN WE FOUND THAT GIRL'S BODY...

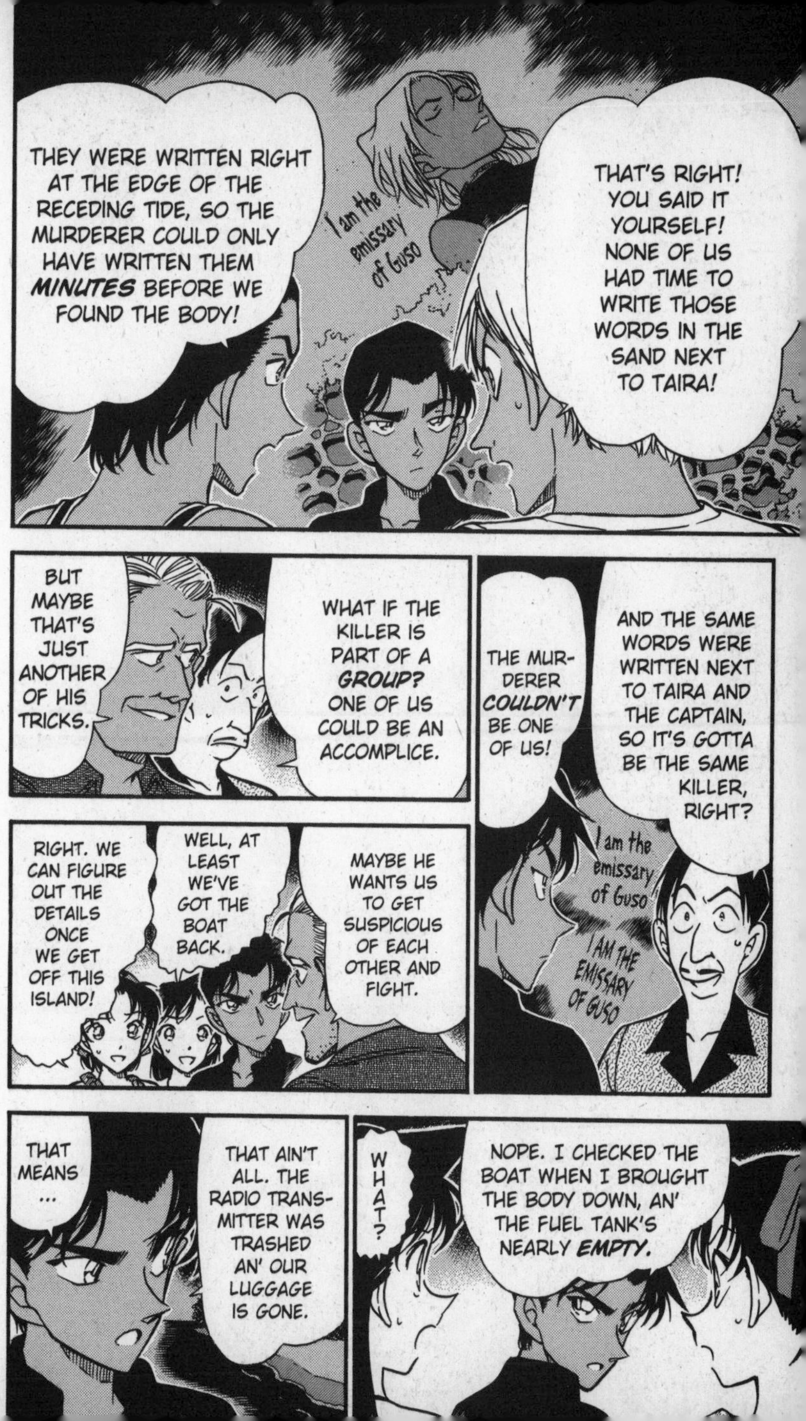
THAT'S RIGHT! YOU SAID IT YOURSELF! NONE OF US HAD TIME TO WRITE THOSE WORDS IN THE SAND NEXT TO TAIRA!
I am the emissary of Guso
THEY WERE WRITTEN RIGHT AT THE EDGE OF THE RECEDING TIDE, SO THE MURDERER COULD ONLY HAVE WRITTEN THEM **MINUTES** BEFORE WE FOUND THE BODY!
AND THE SAME WORDS WERE WRITTEN NEXT TO TAIRA AND THE CAPTAIN, SO IT'S GOTTA BE THE SAME KILLER, RIGHT?
THE MUR-DERER **COULDN'T** BE ONE OF US!
I am the emissary of Guso
I AM THE EMISSARY OF GUSO
WHAT IF THE KILLER IS PART OF A **GROUP?** ONE OF US COULD BE AN ACCOMPLICE.
BUT MAYBE THAT'S JUST ANOTHER OF HIS TRICKS.
MAYBE HE WANTS US TO GET SUSPICIOUS OF EACH OTHER AND FIGHT.
WELL, AT LEAST WE'VE GOT THE BOAT BACK.
RIGHT. WE CAN FIGURE OUT THE DETAILS ONCE WE GET OFF THIS ISLAND!
NOPE. I CHECKED THE BOAT WHEN I BROUGHT THE BODY DOWN, AN' THE FUEL TANK'S NEARLY **EMPTY.**
WHAT?
THAT AIN'T ALL. THE RADIO TRANS-MITTER WAS TRASHED AN' OUR LUGGAGE IS GONE.
THAT MEANS ...

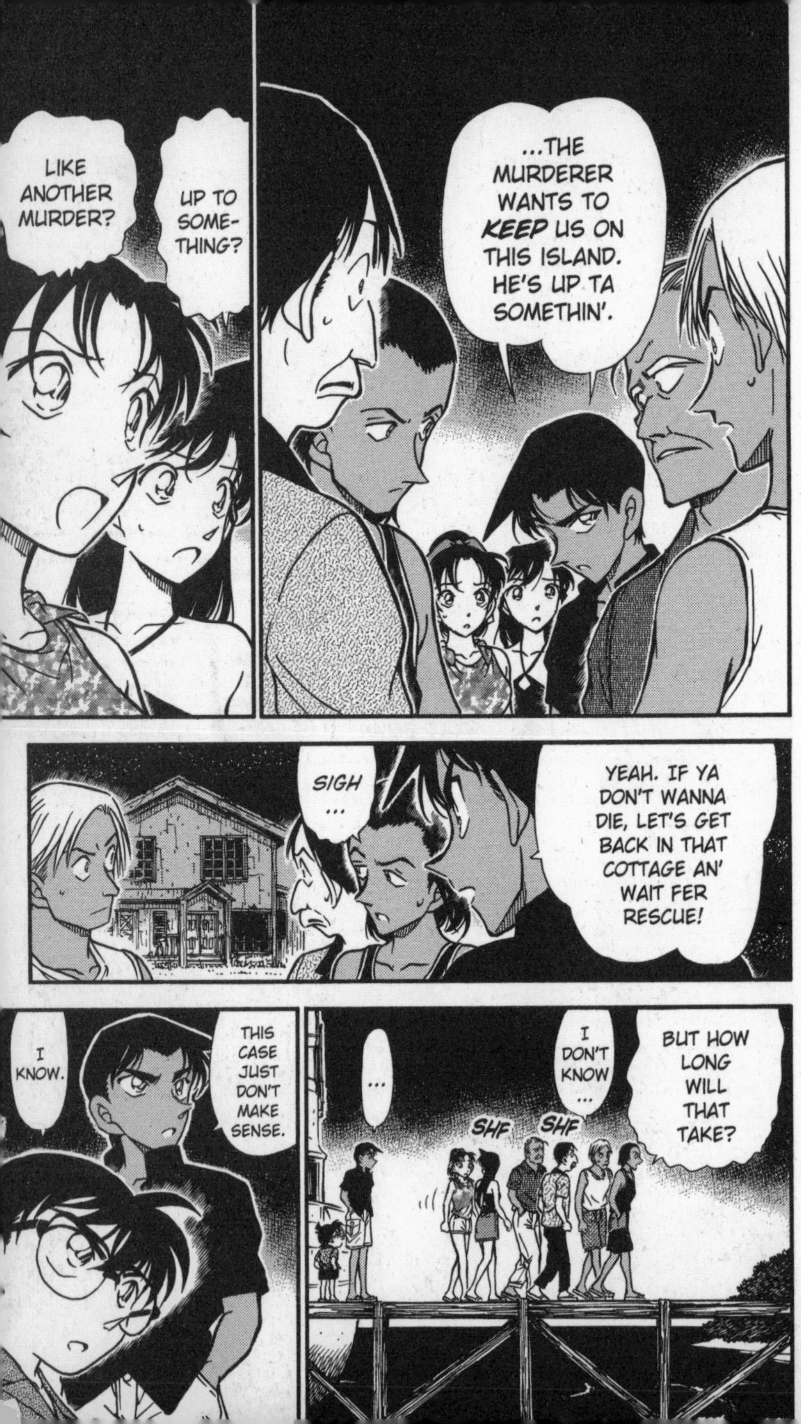
...THE MURDERER WANTS TO *KEEP* US ON THIS ISLAND. HE'S UP TA SOMETHIN'.
UP TO SOME-THING?
LIKE ANOTHER MURDER?
YEAH. IF YA DON'T WANNA DIE, LET'S GET BACK IN THAT COTTAGE AN' WAIT FER RESCUE!
SIGH ...
BUT HOW LONG WILL THAT TAKE?
I DON'T KNOW ...
SHF
SHF
...
THIS CASE JUST DON'T MAKE SENSE.
I KNOW.

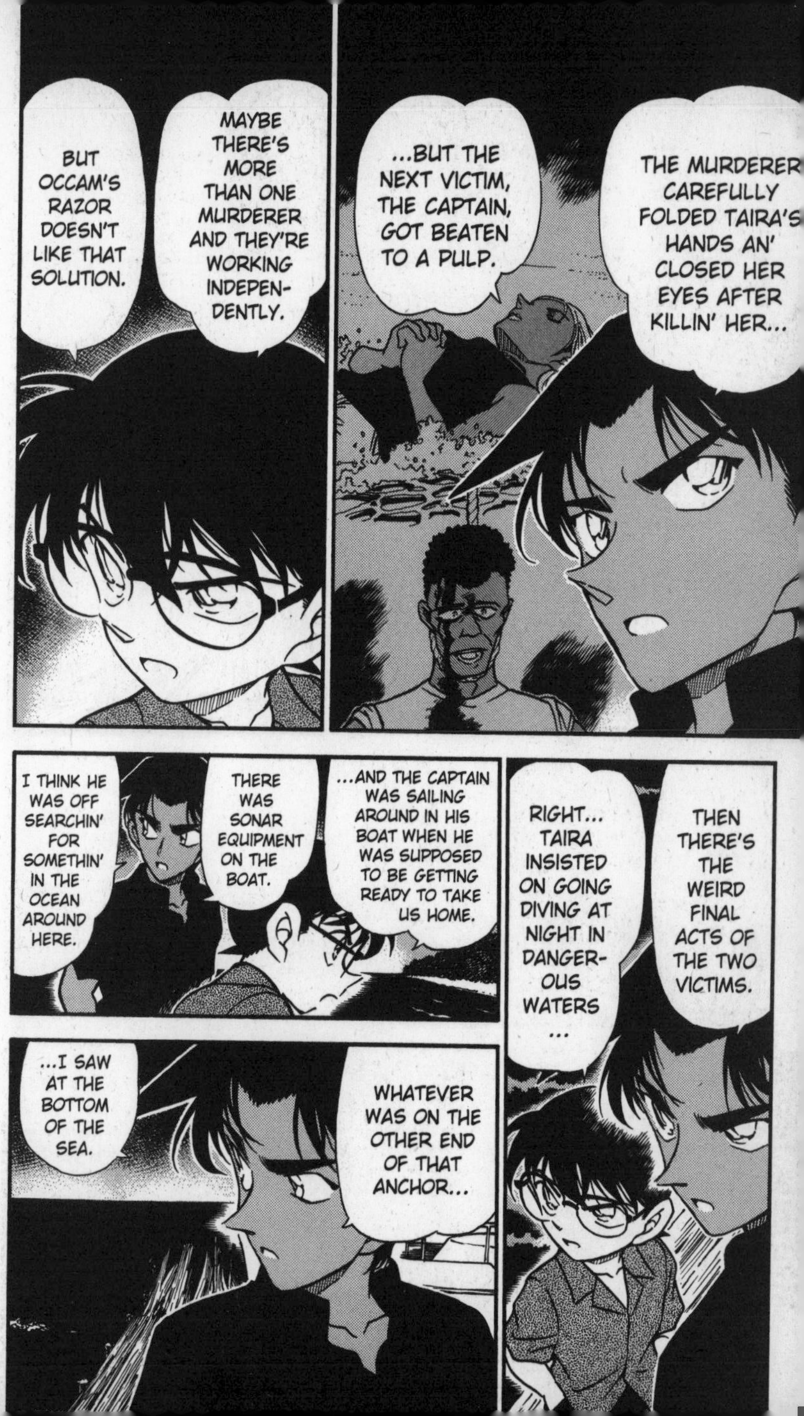
THE MURDERER CAREFULLY FOLDED TAIRA'S HANDS AN' CLOSED HER EYES AFTER KILLIN' HER...
...BUT THE NEXT VICTIM, THE CAPTAIN, GOT BEATEN TO A PULP.
MAYBE THERE'S MORE THAN ONE MURDERER AND THEY'RE WORKING INDEPENDENTLY.
BUT OCCAM'S RAZOR DOESN'T LIKE THAT SOLUTION.
THEN THERE'S THE WEIRD FINAL ACTS OF THE TWO VICTIMS.
RIGHT... TAIRA INSISTED ON GOING DIVING AT NIGHT IN DANGEROUS WATERS...
...AND THE CAPTAIN WAS SAILING AROUND IN HIS BOAT WHEN HE WAS SUPPOSED TO BE GETTING READY TO TAKE US HOME.
THERE WAS SONAR EQUIPMENT ON THE BOAT.
I THINK HE WAS OFF SEARCHIN' FOR SOMETHIN' IN THE OCEAN AROUND HERE.
WHATEVER WAS ON THE OTHER END OF THAT ANCHOR...
...I SAW AT THE BOTTOM OF THE SEA.

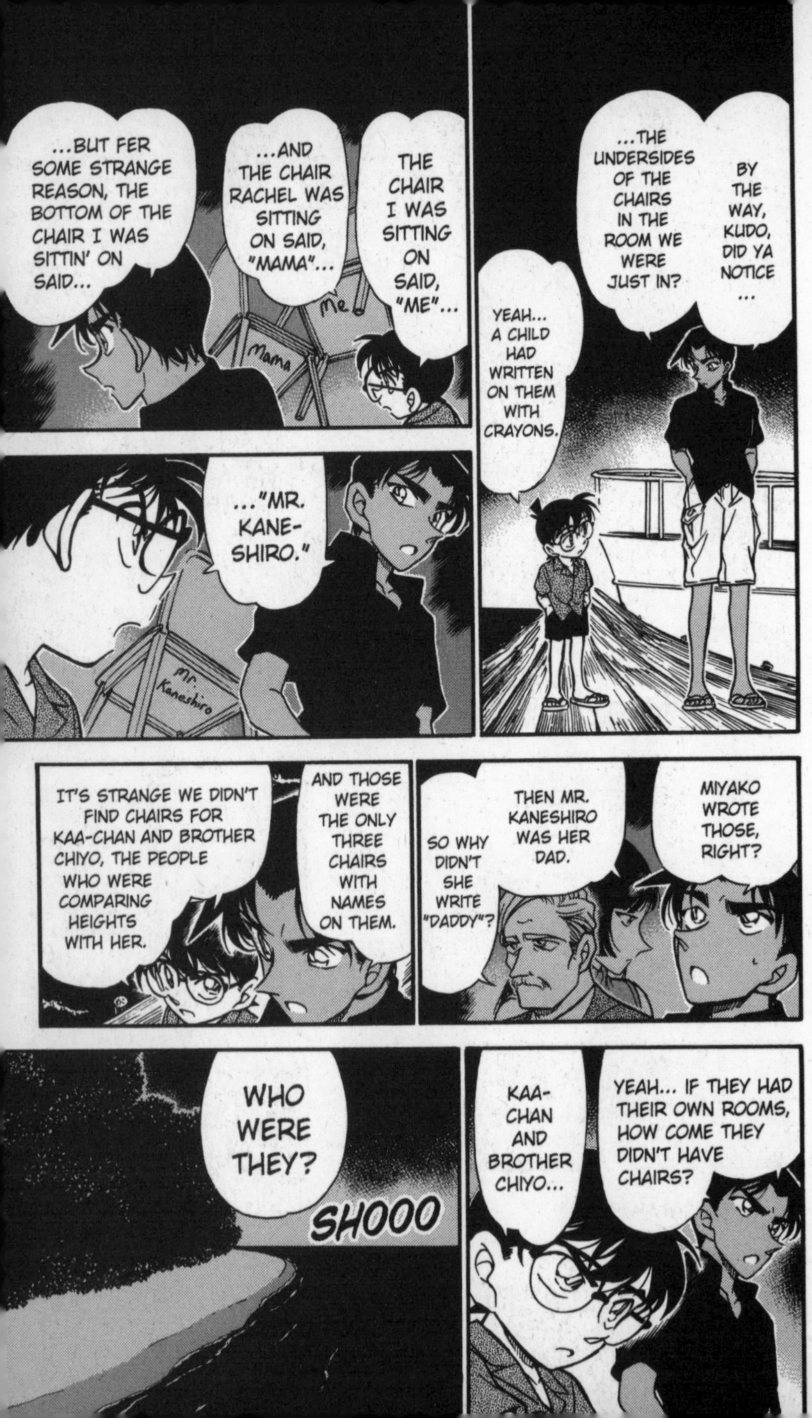
BY THE WAY, KUDO, DID YA NOTICE...
...THE UNDERSIDES OF THE CHAIRS IN THE ROOM WE WERE JUST IN?
YEAH... A CHILD HAD WRITTEN ON THEM WITH CRAYONS.
THE CHAIR I WAS SITTING ON SAID, "ME"...
...AND THE CHAIR RACHEL WAS SITTING ON SAID, "MAMA"...
...BUT FER SOME STRANGE REASON, THE BOTTOM OF THE CHAIR I WAS SITTIN' ON SAID...
Me
Mama
..."MR. KANESHIRO."
Mr. Kaneshiro
MIYAKO WROTE THOSE, RIGHT?
THEN MR. KANESHIRO WAS HER DAD.
SO WHY DIDN'T SHE WRITE "DADDY"?
AND THOSE WERE THE ONLY THREE CHAIRS WITH NAMES ON THEM.
IT'S STRANGE WE DIDN'T FIND CHAIRS FOR KAA-CHAN AND BROTHER CHIYO, THE PEOPLE WHO WERE COMPARING HEIGHTS WITH HER.
YEAH... IF THEY HAD THEIR OWN ROOMS, HOW COME THEY DIDN'T HAVE CHAIRS?
KAA-CHAN AND BROTHER CHIYO...
WHO WERE THEY?
SHOOO

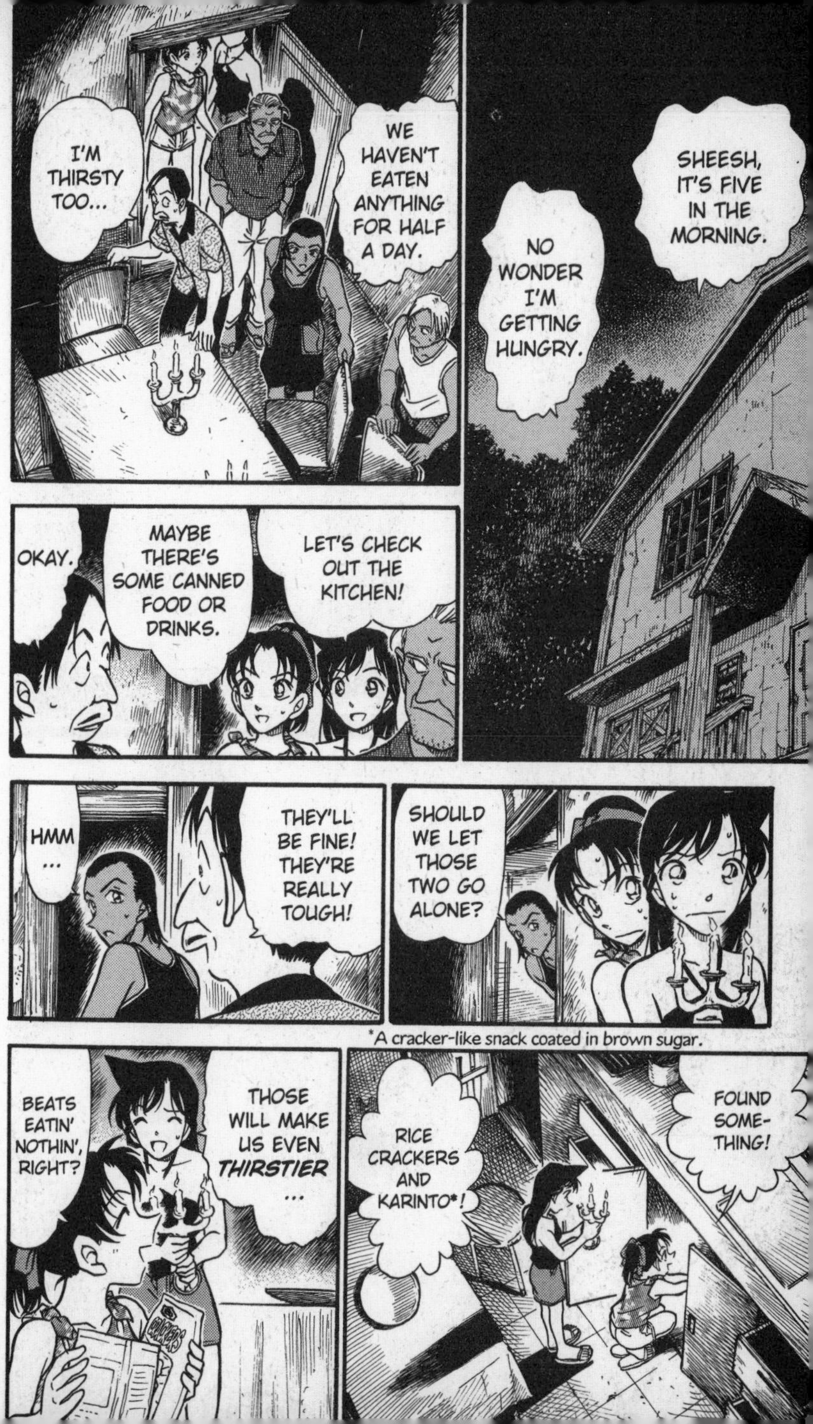
SHEESH, IT'S FIVE IN THE MORNING.
NO WONDER I'M GETTING HUNGRY.
WE HAVEN'T EATEN ANYTHING FOR HALF A DAY.
I'M THIRSTY TOO...
LET'S CHECK OUT THE KITCHEN!
MAYBE THERE'S SOME CANNED FOOD OR DRINKS.
OKAY.
SHOULD WE LET THOSE TWO GO ALONE?
THEY'LL BE FINE! THEY'RE REALLY TOUGH!
HMM ...
FOUND SOME-THING!
RICE CRACKERS AND KARINTO*!
THOSE WILL MAKE US EVEN *THIRSTIER* ...
BEATS EATIN' NOTHIN', RIGHT?

*A cracker-like snack coated in brown sugar.

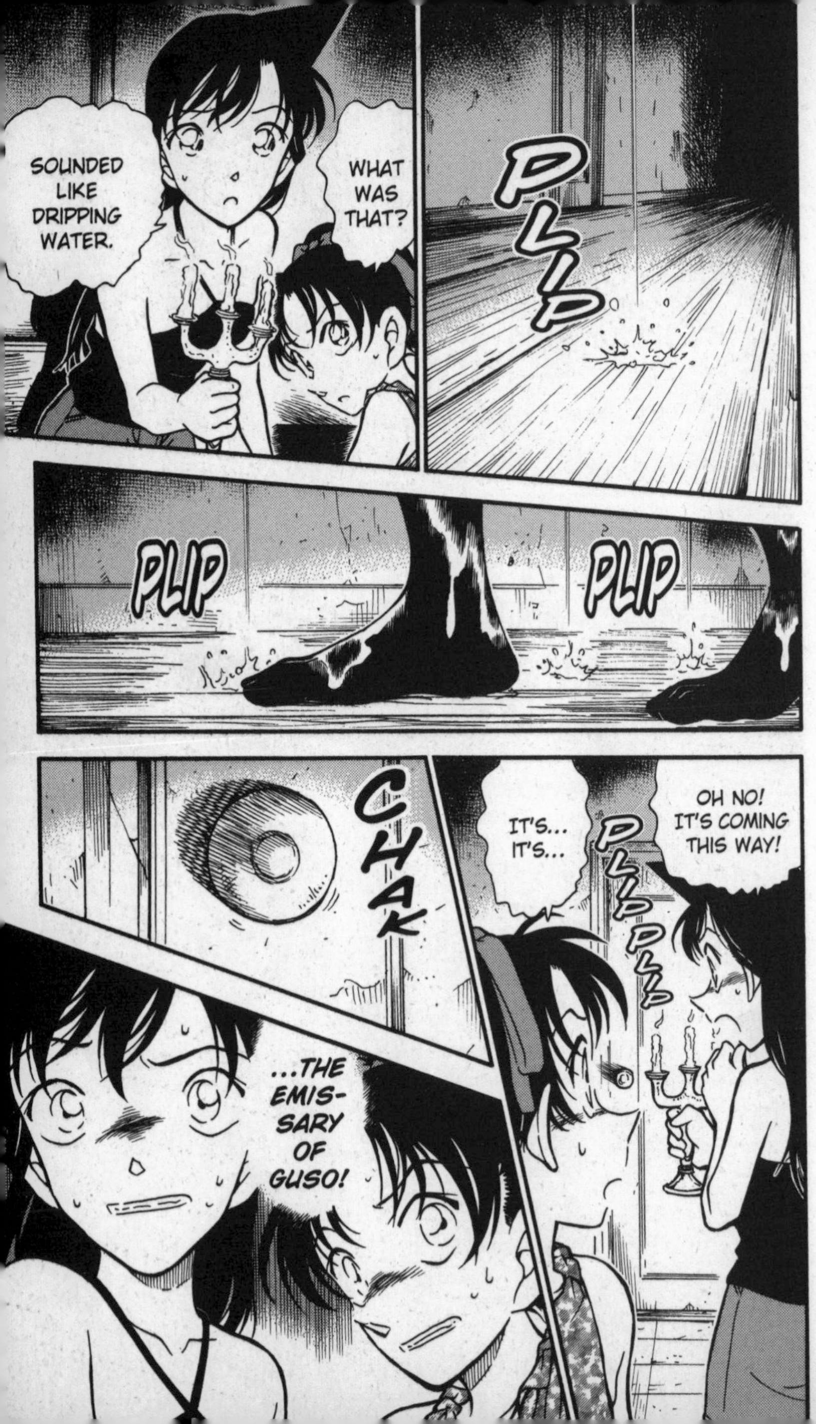
PLIP
WHAT WAS THAT?
SOUNDED LIKE DRIPPING WATER.
PLIP
PLIP
OH NO! IT'S COMING THIS WAY!
PLIPPLIP
IT'S... IT'S...
CHAK
...THE EMISSARY OF GUSO!

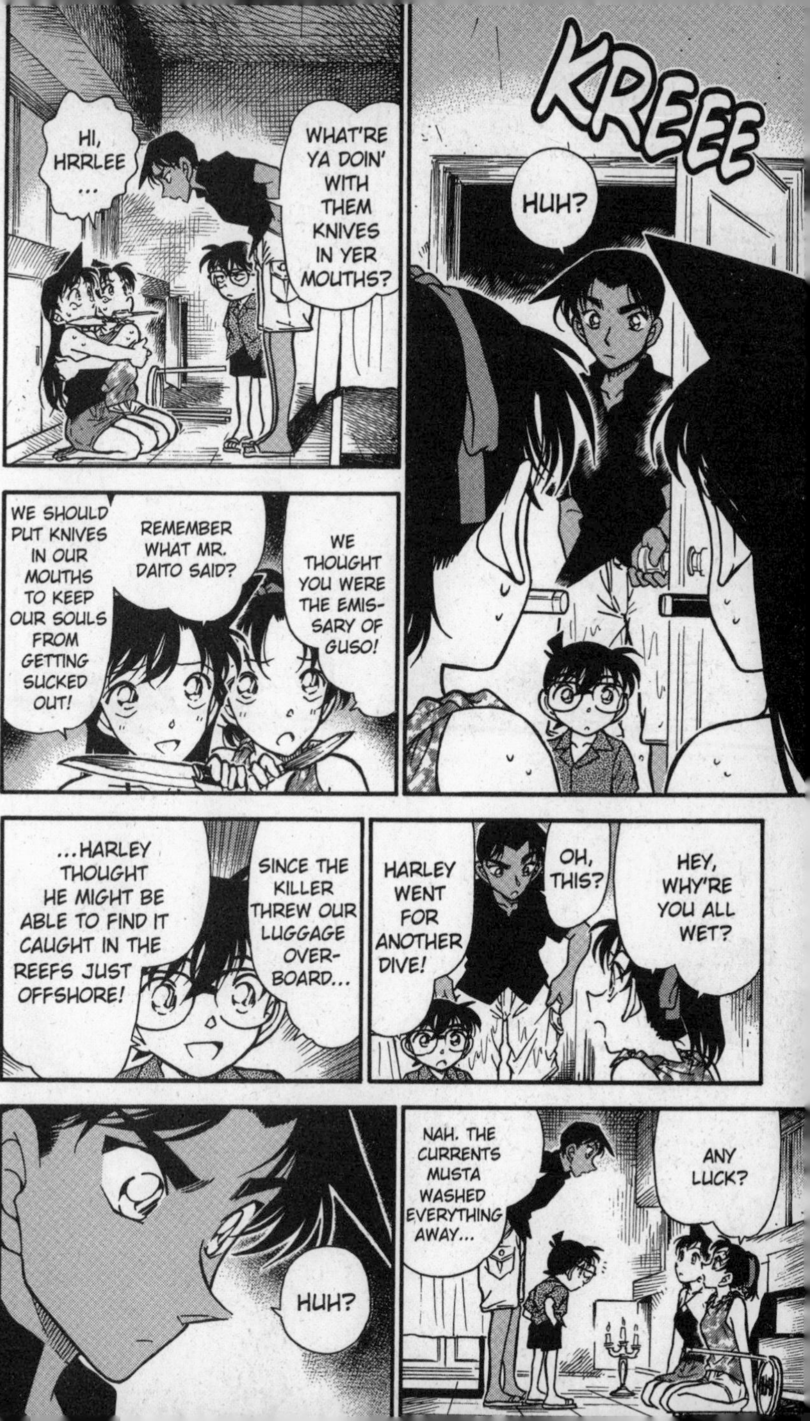
KREEE
HUH?
WHAT'RE YA DOIN' WITH THEM KNIVES IN YER MOUTHS?
HI, HRRLEE ...
WE THOUGHT YOU WERE THE EMISSARY OF GUSO!
REMEMBER WHAT MR. DAITO SAID?
WE SHOULD PUT KNIVES IN OUR MOUTHS TO KEEP OUR SOULS FROM GETTING SUCKED OUT!
HEY, WHY'RE YOU ALL WET?
OH, THIS?
HARLEY WENT FOR ANOTHER DIVE!
SINCE THE KILLER THREW OUR LUGGAGE OVERBOARD...
...HARLEY THOUGHT HE MIGHT BE ABLE TO FIND IT CAUGHT IN THE REEFS JUST OFFSHORE!
ANY LUCK?
NAH. THE CURRENTS MUSTA WASHED EVERYTHING AWAY...
HUH?

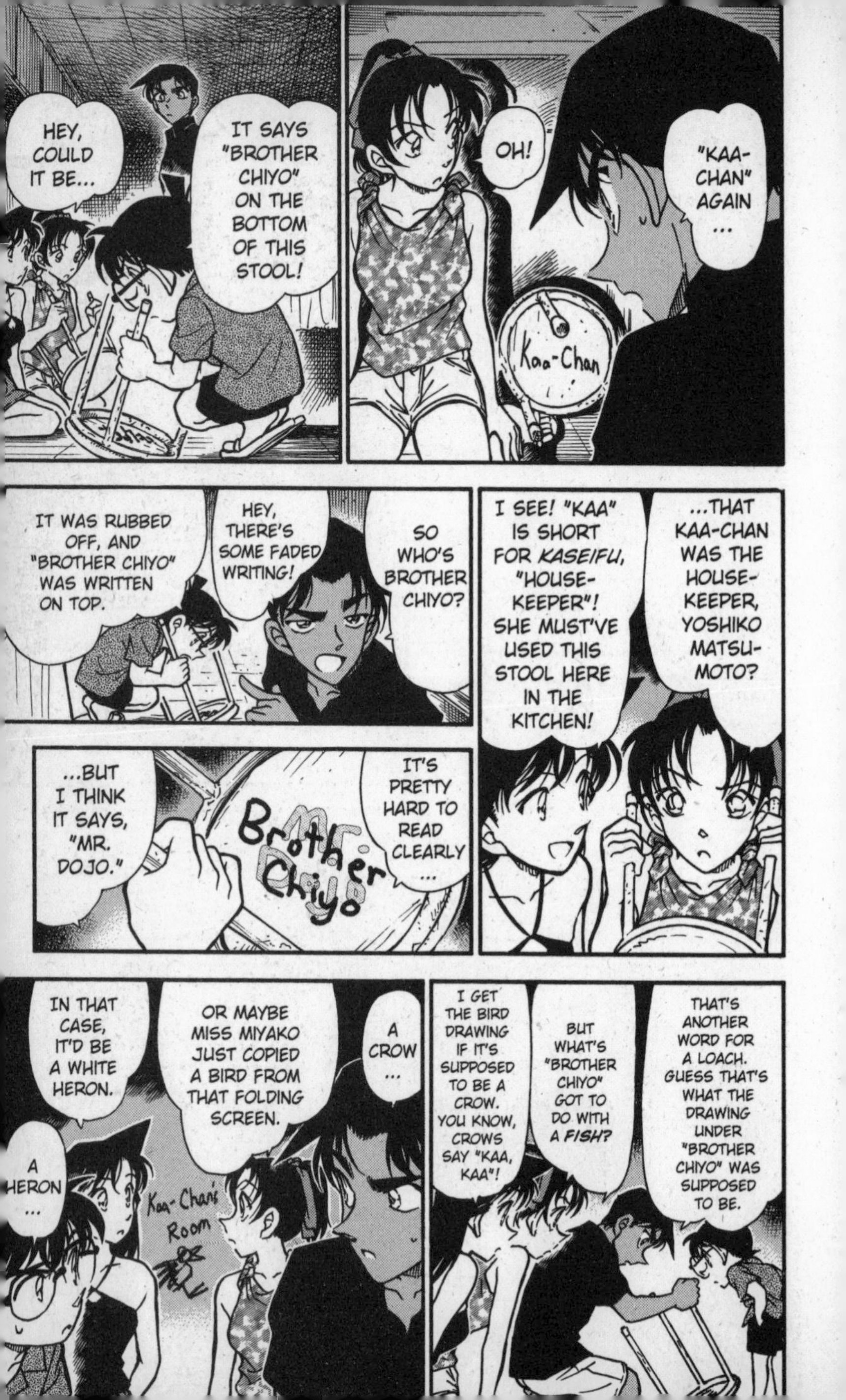
"KAA-CHAN" AGAIN ...
OH!
Kaa-Chan
IT SAYS "BROTHER CHIYO" ON THE BOTTOM OF THIS STOOL!
HEY, COULD IT BE...
...THAT KAA-CHAN WAS THE HOUSE-KEEPER, YOSHIKO MATSU-MOTO?
I SEE! "KAA" IS SHORT FOR *KASEIFU*, "HOUSE-KEEPER"! SHE MUST'VE USED THIS STOOL HERE IN THE KITCHEN!
SO WHO'S BROTHER CHIYO?
HEY, THERE'S SOME FADED WRITING!
IT WAS RUBBED OFF, AND "BROTHER CHIYO" WAS WRITTEN ON TOP.
IT'S PRETTY HARD TO READ CLEARLY ...
Brother Chiyo
...BUT I THINK IT SAYS, "MR. DOJO."
THAT'S ANOTHER WORD FOR A LOACH. GUESS THAT'S WHAT THE DRAWING UNDER "BROTHER CHIYO" WAS SUPPOSED TO BE.
BUT WHAT'S "BROTHER CHIYO" GOT TO DO WITH A *FISH?*
I GET THE BIRD DRAWING IF IT'S SUPPOSED TO BE A CROW. YOU KNOW, CROWS SAY "KAA, KAA"!
A CROW ...
OR MAYBE MISS MIYAKO JUST COPIED A BIRD FROM THAT FOLDING SCREEN.
IN THAT CASE, IT'D BE A WHITE HERON.
A HERON ...
Kaa-Chan's Room

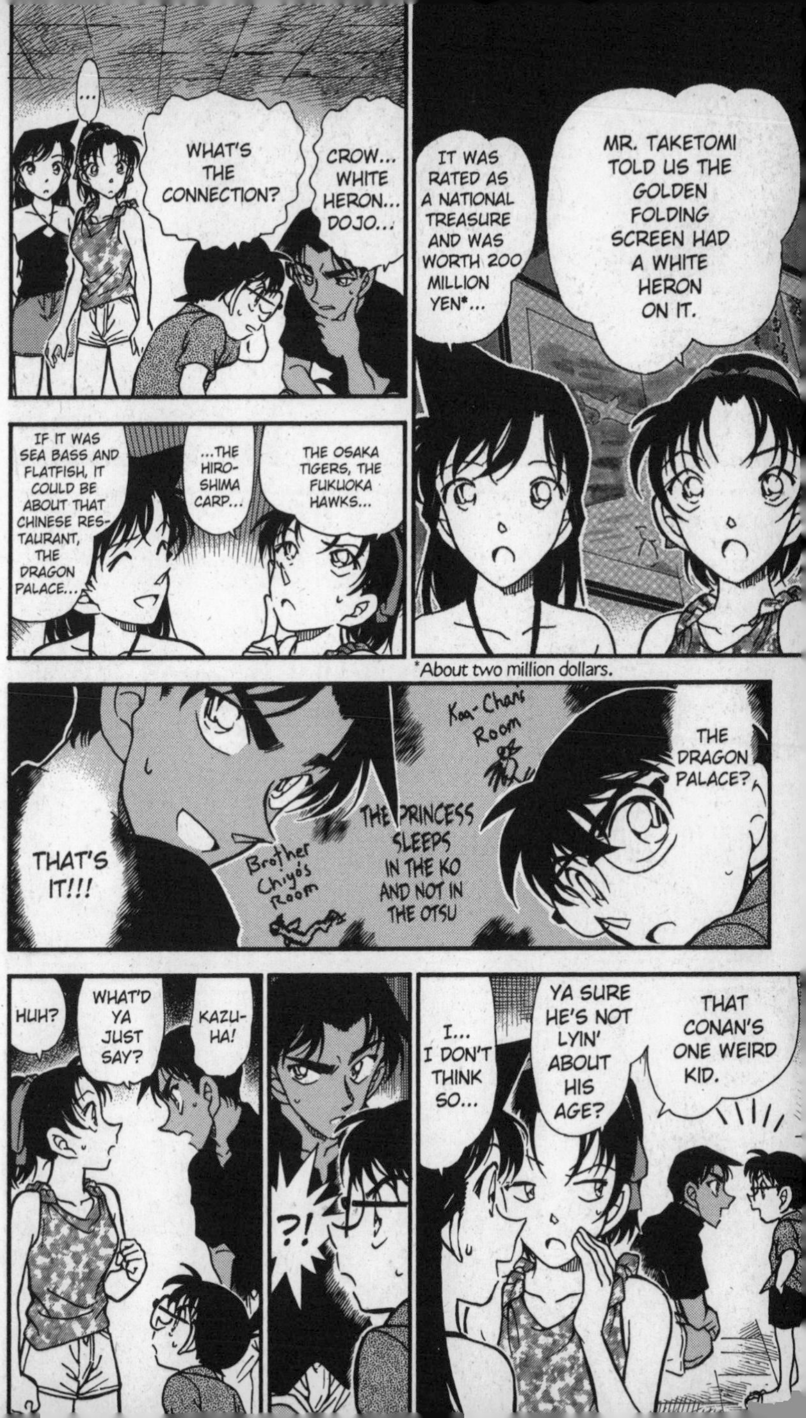
MR. TAKETOMI TOLD US THE GOLDEN FOLDING SCREEN HAD A WHITE HERON ON IT.
IT WAS RATED AS A NATIONAL TREASURE AND WAS WORTH 200 MILLION YEN*...
CROW... WHITE HERON... DOJO...
WHAT'S THE CONNECTION?
...
THE OSAKA TIGERS, THE FUKUOKA HAWKS...
...THE HIROSHIMA CARP...
IF IT WAS SEA BASS AND FLATFISH, IT COULD BE ABOUT THAT CHINESE RESTAURANT, THE DRAGON PALACE...
THE DRAGON PALACE?
Koa-Chan's Room
THE PRINCESS SLEEPS IN THE KO AND NOT IN THE OTSU
Brother Chiyo's Room
THAT'S IT!!!
THAT CONAN'S ONE WEIRD KID.
YA SURE HE'S NOT LYIN' ABOUT HIS AGE?
I... I DON'T THINK SO...
?!
KAZU-HA!
WHAT'D YA JUST SAY?
HUH?
*About two million dollars.

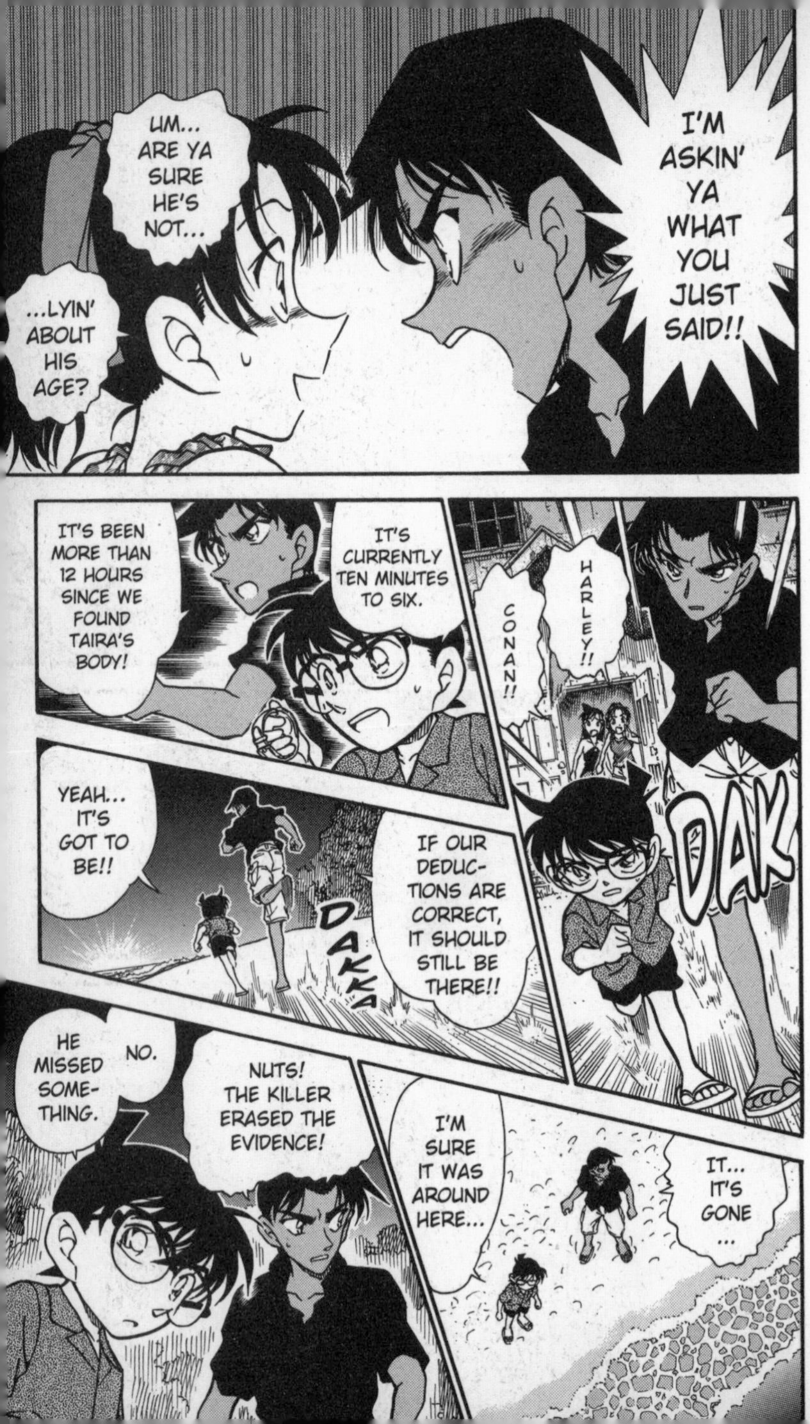
I'M ASKIN' YA WHAT YOU JUST SAID!!
UM... ARE YA SURE HE'S NOT...
...LYIN' ABOUT HIS AGE?
HARLEY!!
CONAN!!
DAK
IT'S CURRENTLY TEN MINUTES TO SIX.
IT'S BEEN MORE THAN 12 HOURS SINCE WE FOUND TAIRA'S BODY!
IF OUR DEDUCTIONS ARE CORRECT, IT SHOULD STILL BE THERE!!
DAKKA
YEAH... IT'S GOT TO BE!!
IT... IT'S GONE ...
I'M SURE IT WAS AROUND HERE...
NUTS! THE KILLER ERASED THE EVIDENCE!
NO.
HE MISSED SOMETHING.

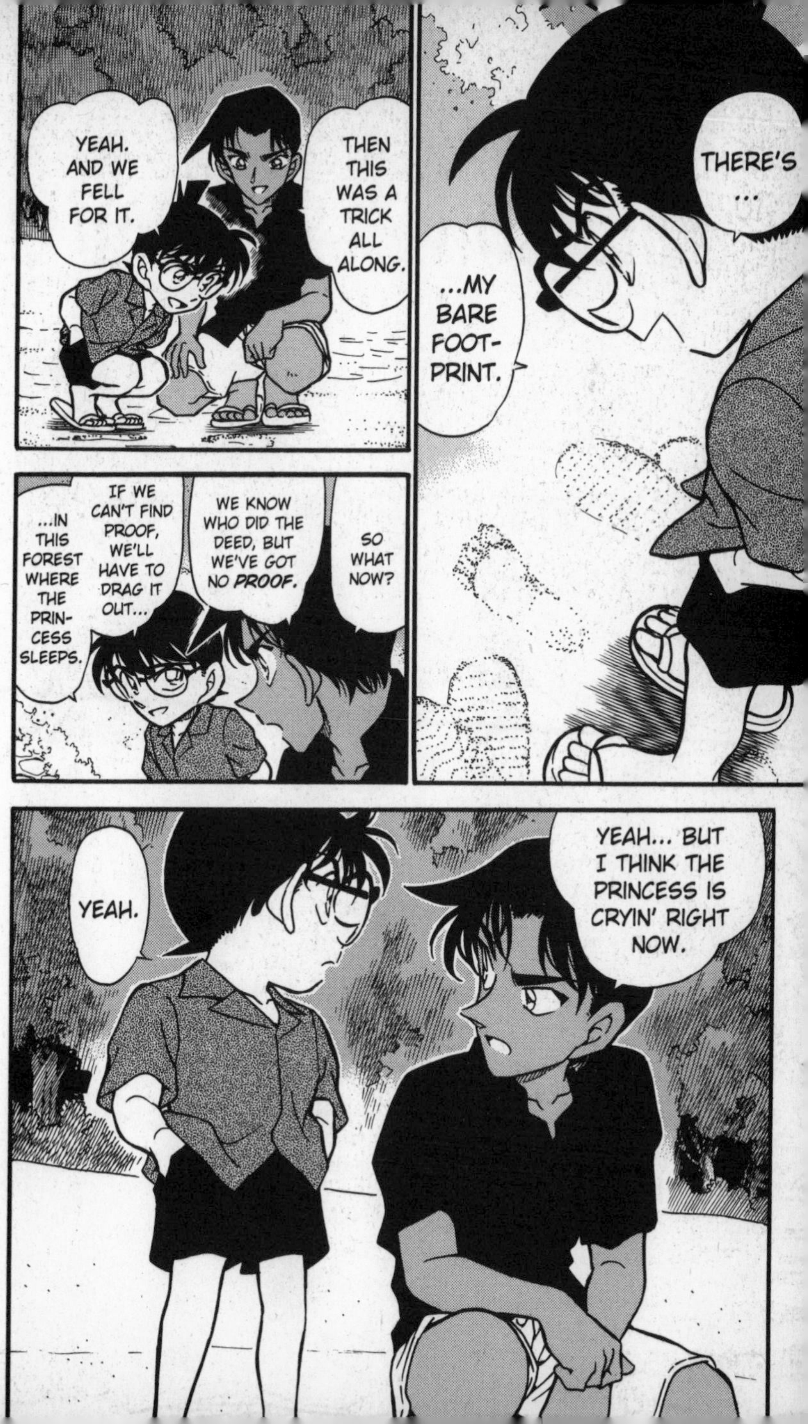
THERE'S ...
...MY BARE FOOT-PRINT.
THEN THIS WAS A TRICK ALL ALONG.
YEAH. AND WE FELL FOR IT.
SO WHAT NOW?
WE KNOW WHO DID THE DEED, BUT WE'VE GOT NO *PROOF*.
IF WE CAN'T FIND PROOF, WE'LL HAVE TO DRAG IT OUT...
...IN THIS FOREST WHERE THE PRINCESS SLEEPS.
YEAH... BUT I THINK THE PRINCESS IS CRYIN' RIGHT NOW.
YEAH.

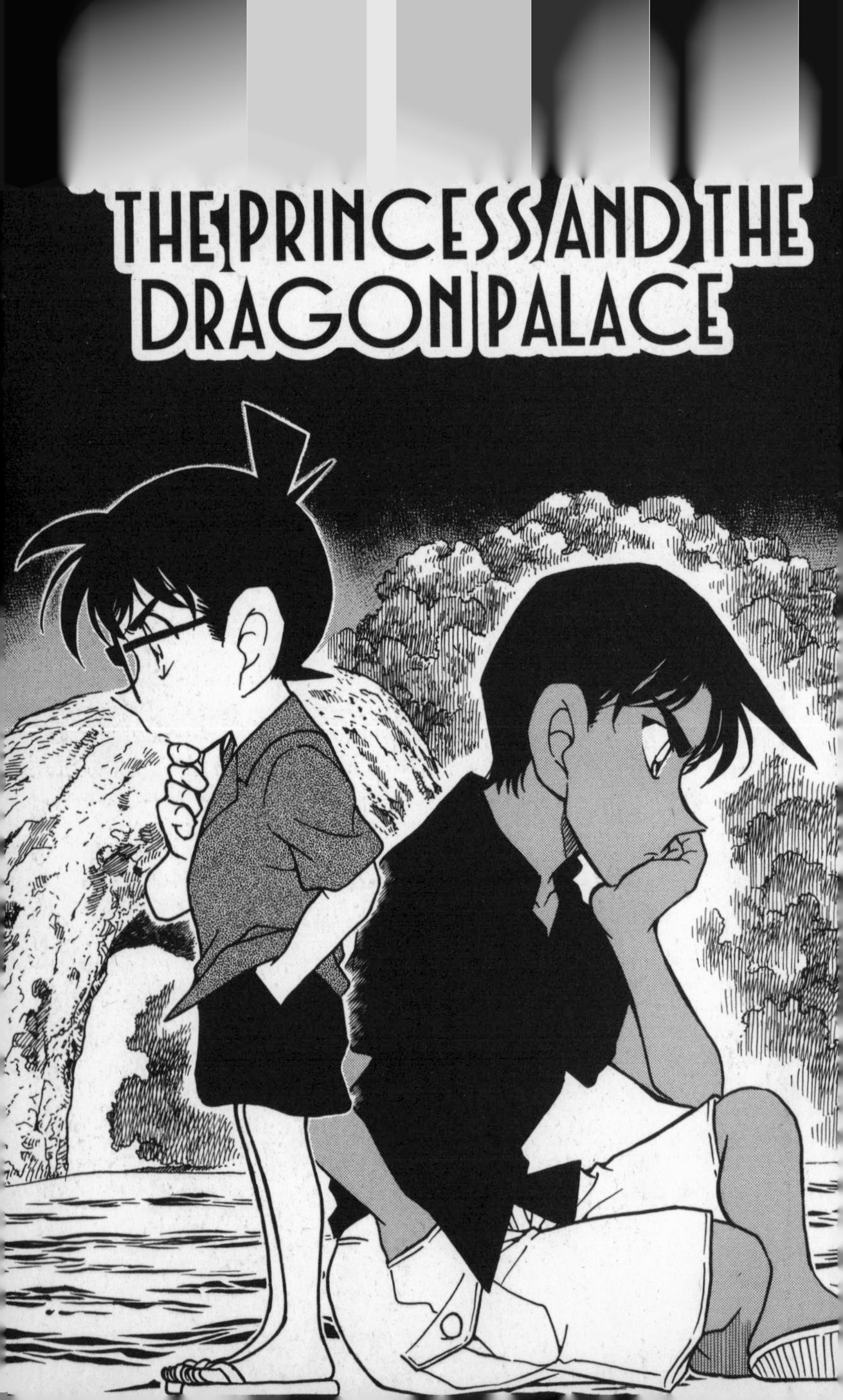
THE PRINCESS AND THE DRAGON PALACE

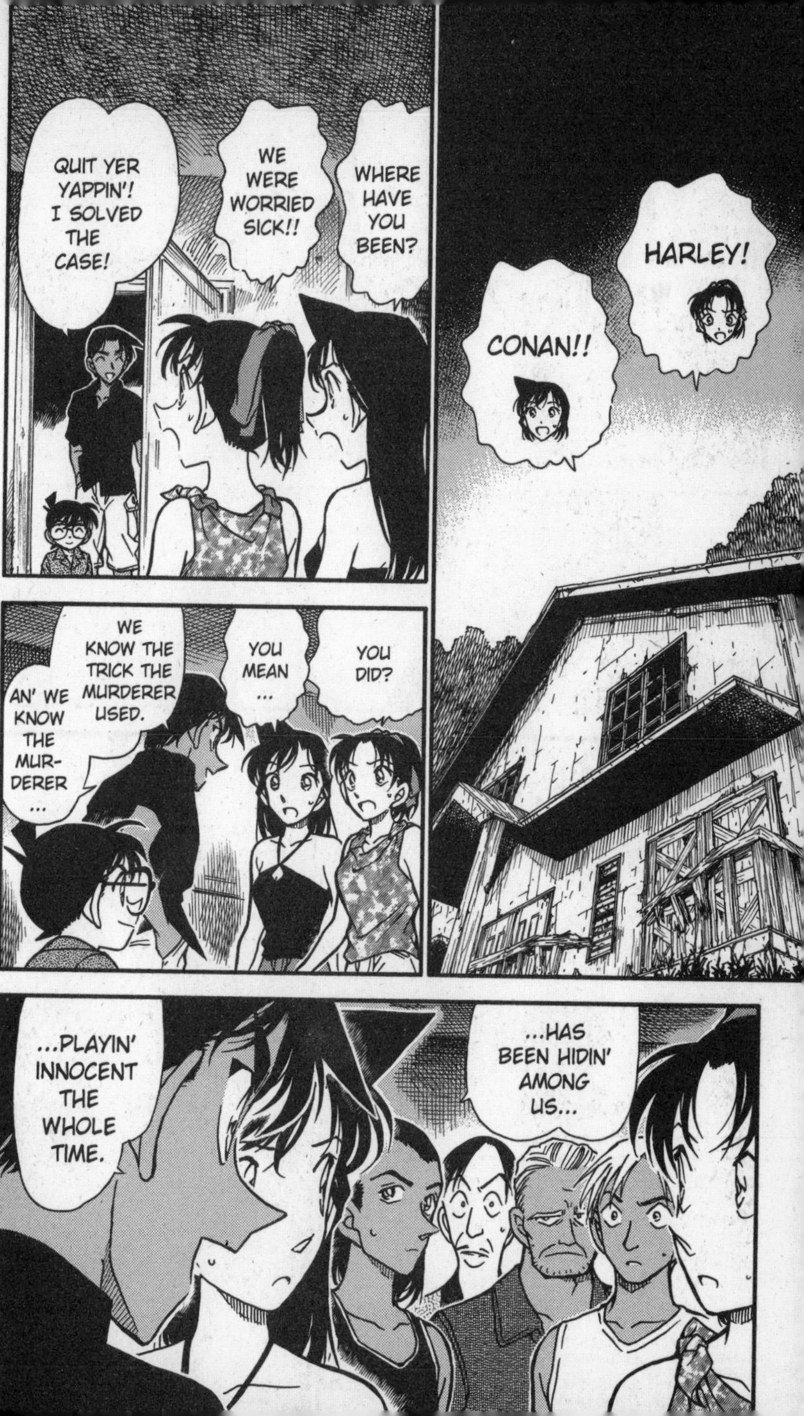
HARLEY!
CONAN!!
WHERE HAVE YOU BEEN?
WE WERE WORRIED SICK!!
QUIT YER YAPPIN'! I SOLVED THE CASE!
YOU DID?
YOU MEAN ...
WE KNOW THE TRICK THE MURDERER USED.
AN' WE KNOW THE MURDERER ...
...HAS BEEN HIDIN' AMONG US...
...PLAYIN' INNOCENT THE WHOLE TIME.

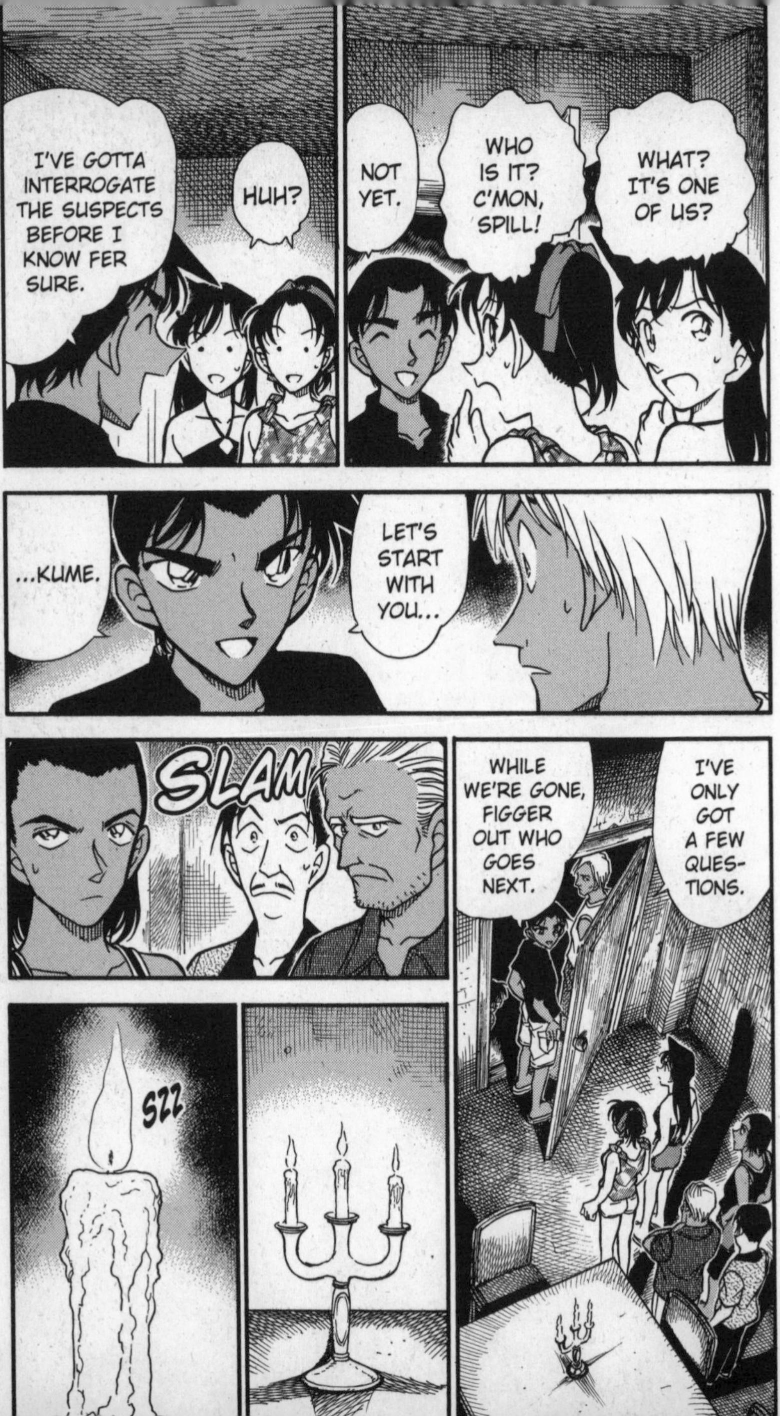
WHAT? IT'S ONE OF US?
WHO IS IT? C'MON, SPILL!
NOT YET.
HUH?
I'VE GOTTA INTERROGATE THE SUSPECTS BEFORE I KNOW FER SURE.
LET'S START WITH YOU...
...KUME.
I'VE ONLY GOT A FEW QUES-TIONS.
WHILE WE'RE GONE, FIGGER OUT WHO GOES NEXT.
SLAM
SZZ

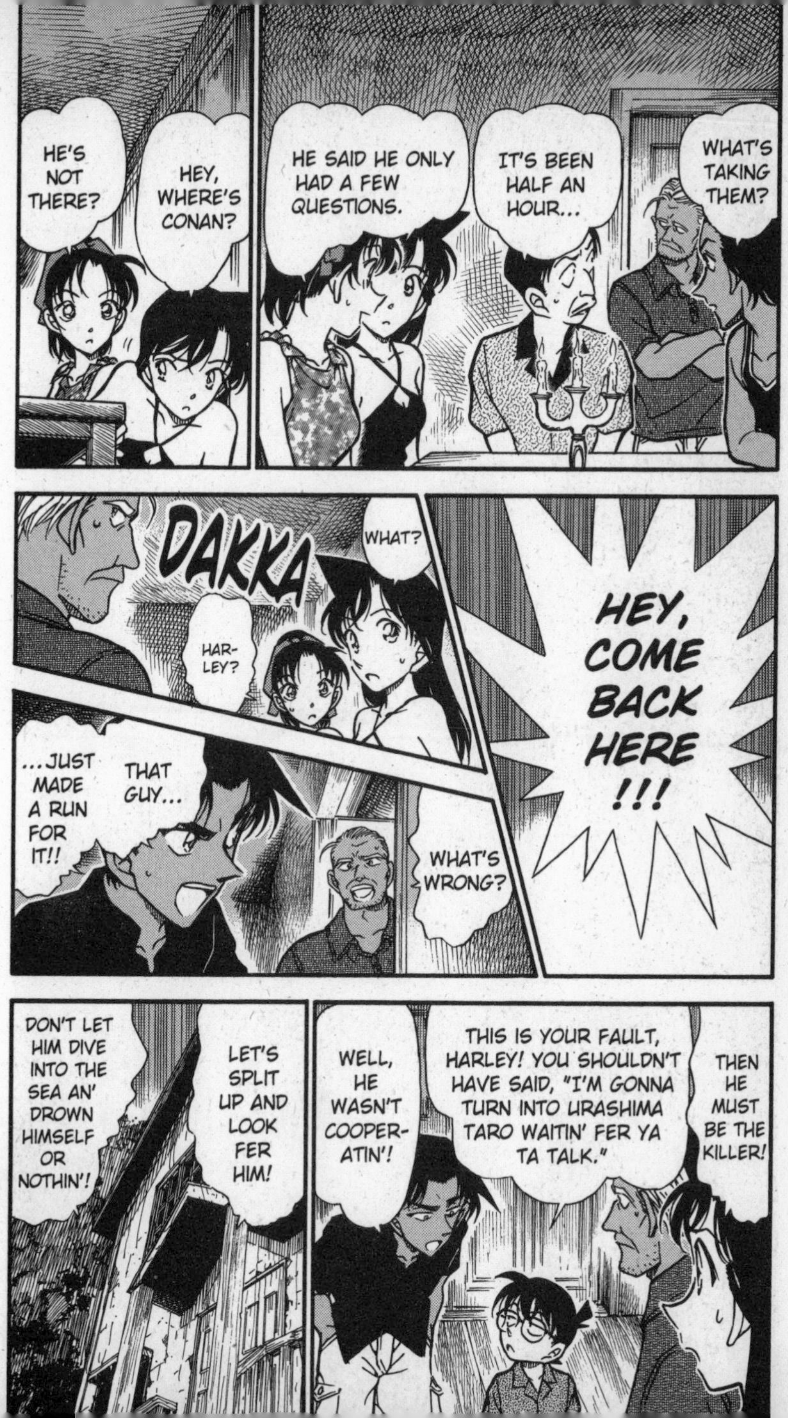
WHAT'S TAKING THEM?
IT'S BEEN HALF AN HOUR...
HE SAID HE ONLY HAD A FEW QUESTIONS.
HEY, WHERE'S CONAN?
HE'S NOT THERE?
HEY, COME BACK HERE!!!
WHAT?
DAKKA
HAR-LEY?
WHAT'S WRONG?
THAT GUY...
...JUST MADE A RUN FOR IT!!
THEN HE MUST BE THE KILLER!
THIS IS YOUR FAULT, HARLEY! YOU SHOULDN'T HAVE SAID, "I'M GONNA TURN INTO URASHIMA TARO WAITIN' FER YA TA TALK."
WELL, HE WASN'T COOPER-ATIN'!
LET'S SPLIT UP AND LOOK FER HIM!
DON'T LET HIM DIVE INTO THE SEA AN' DROWN HIMSELF OR NOTHIN'!

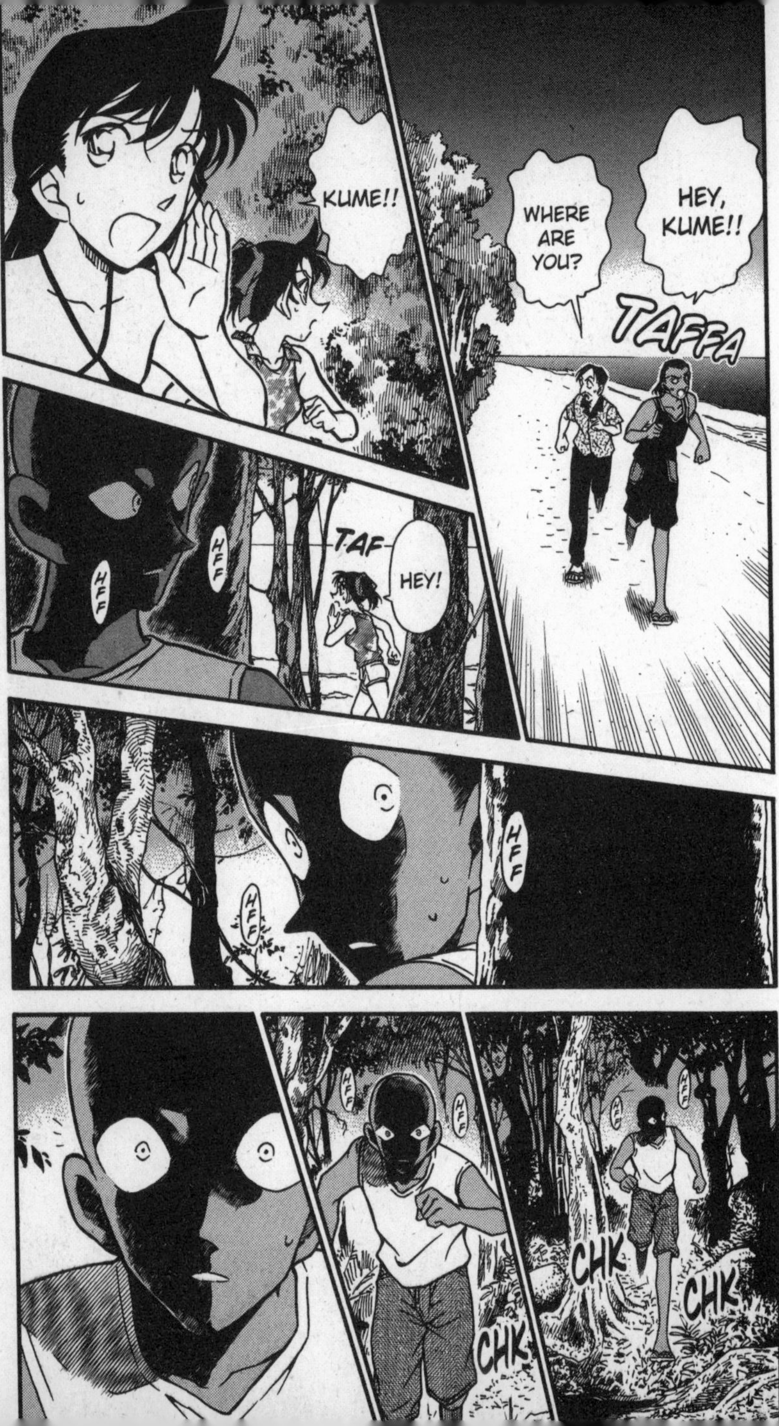
HEY, KUME!!
WHERE ARE YOU?
TAFFA
KUME!!
HEY!
TAF
HFF
HFF
HFF
HFF
HFF
CHK
CHK
CHK
HFF
HFF

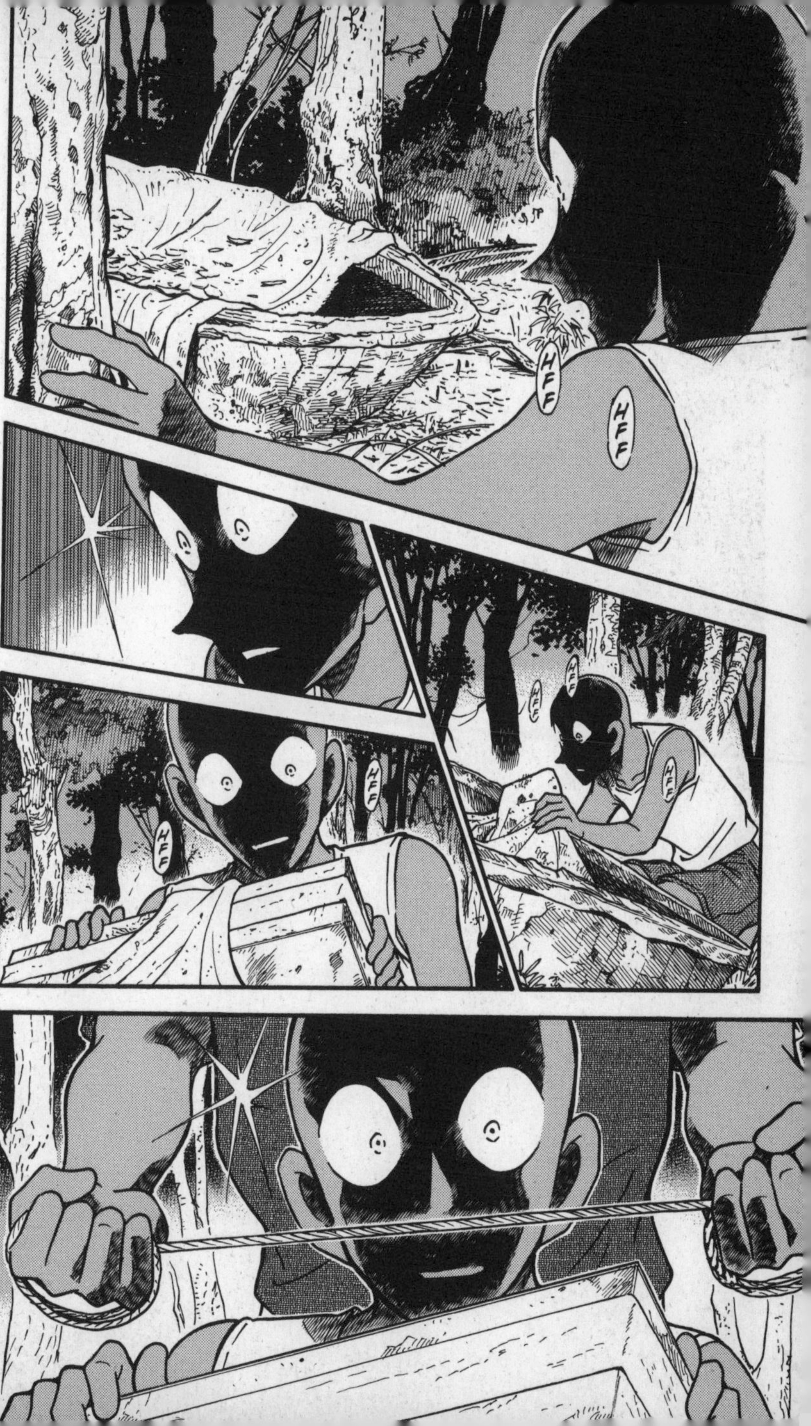
HFF
HFF
HFF
HFF
HFF
HFF
HFF

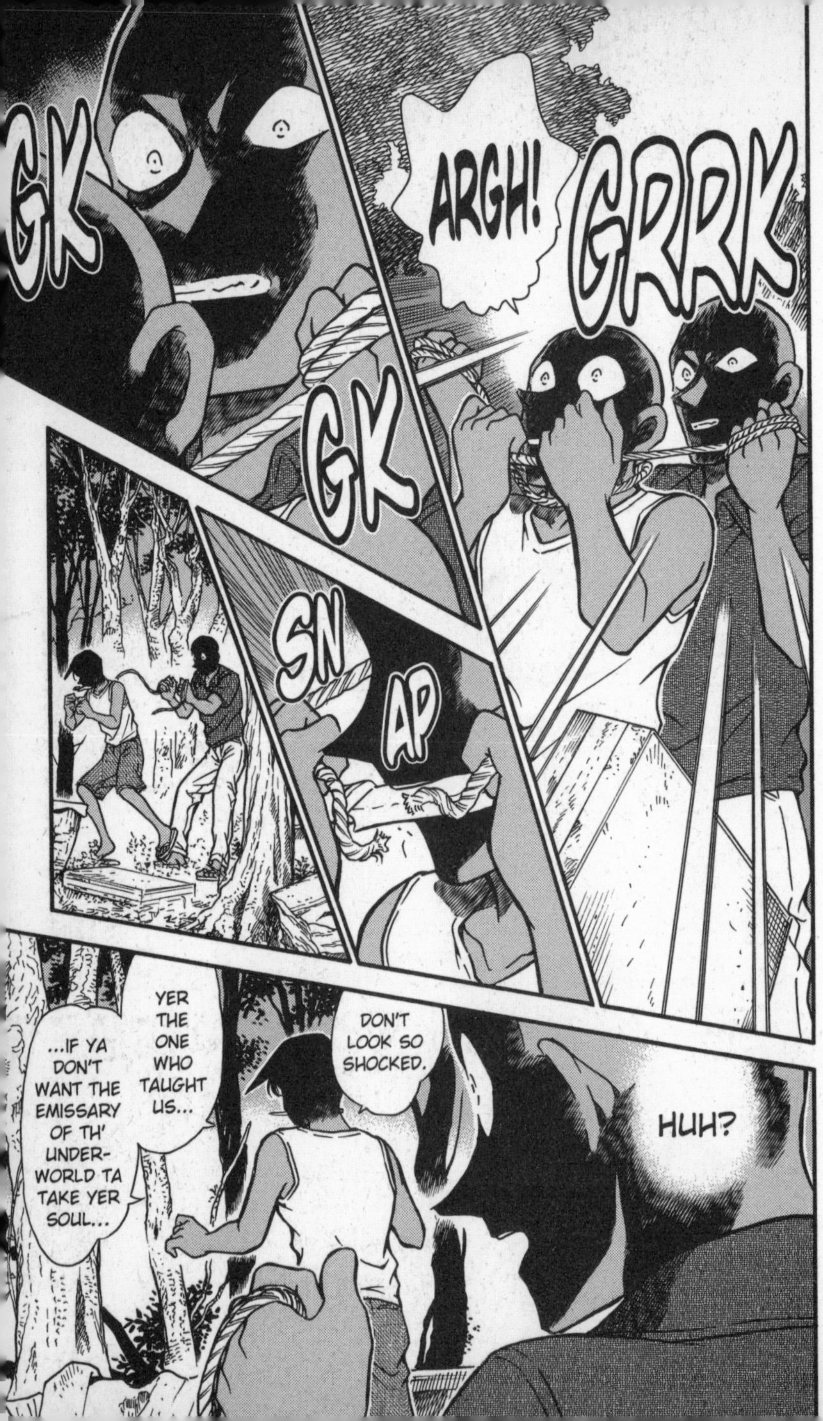
ARGH!
GRRK
GK
GK
SNAP
HUH?
DON'T LOOK SO SHOCKED.
YER THE ONE WHO TAUGHT US...
...IF YA DON'T WANT THE EMISSARY OF TH' UNDER-WORLD TA TAKE YER SOUL...

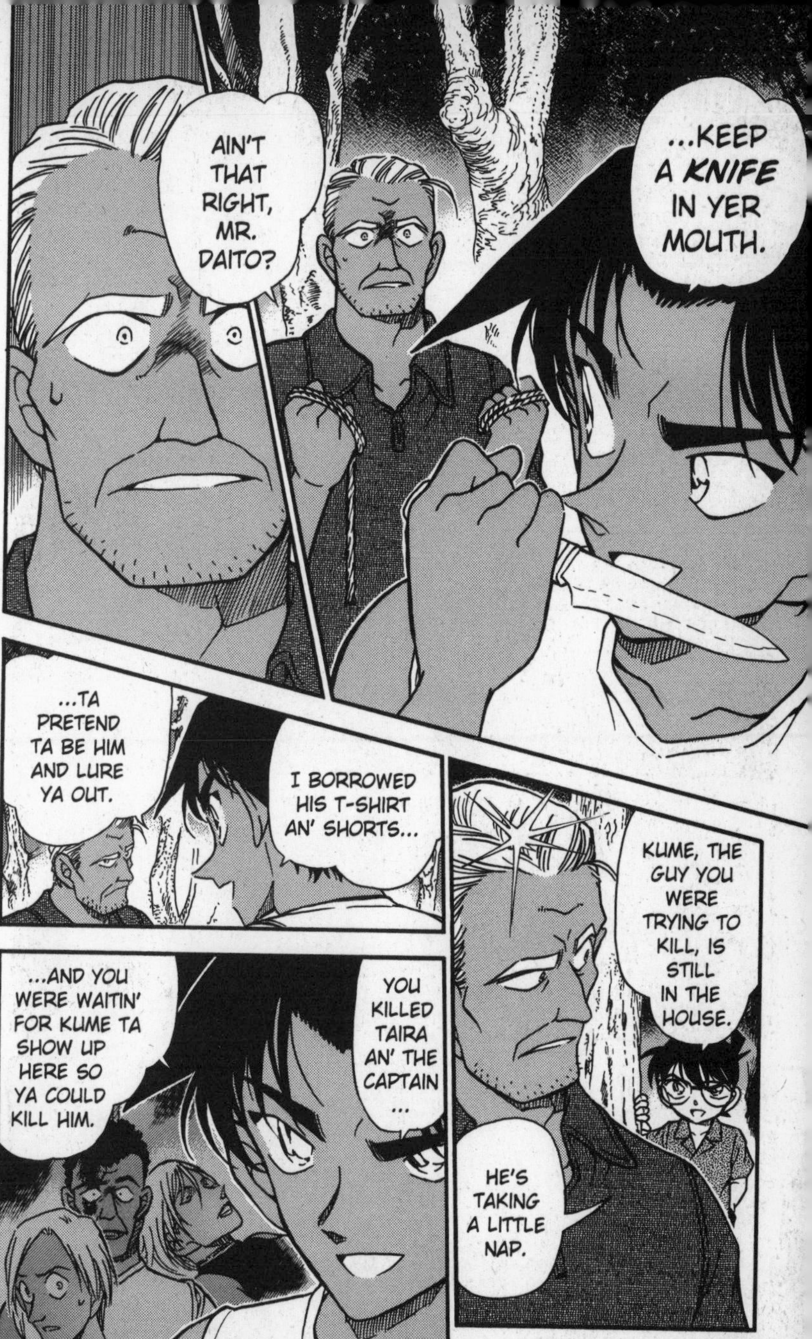
...KEEP A KNIFE IN YER MOUTH.
AIN'T THAT RIGHT, MR. DAITO?
KUME, THE GUY YOU WERE TRYING TO KILL, IS STILL IN THE HOUSE.
HE'S TAKING A LITTLE NAP.
I BORROWED HIS T-SHIRT AN' SHORTS...
...TA PRETEND TA BE HIM AND LURE YA OUT.
YOU KILLED TAIRA AN' THE CAPTAIN...
...AND YOU WERE WAITIN' FOR KUME TA SHOW UP HERE SO YA COULD KILL HIM.

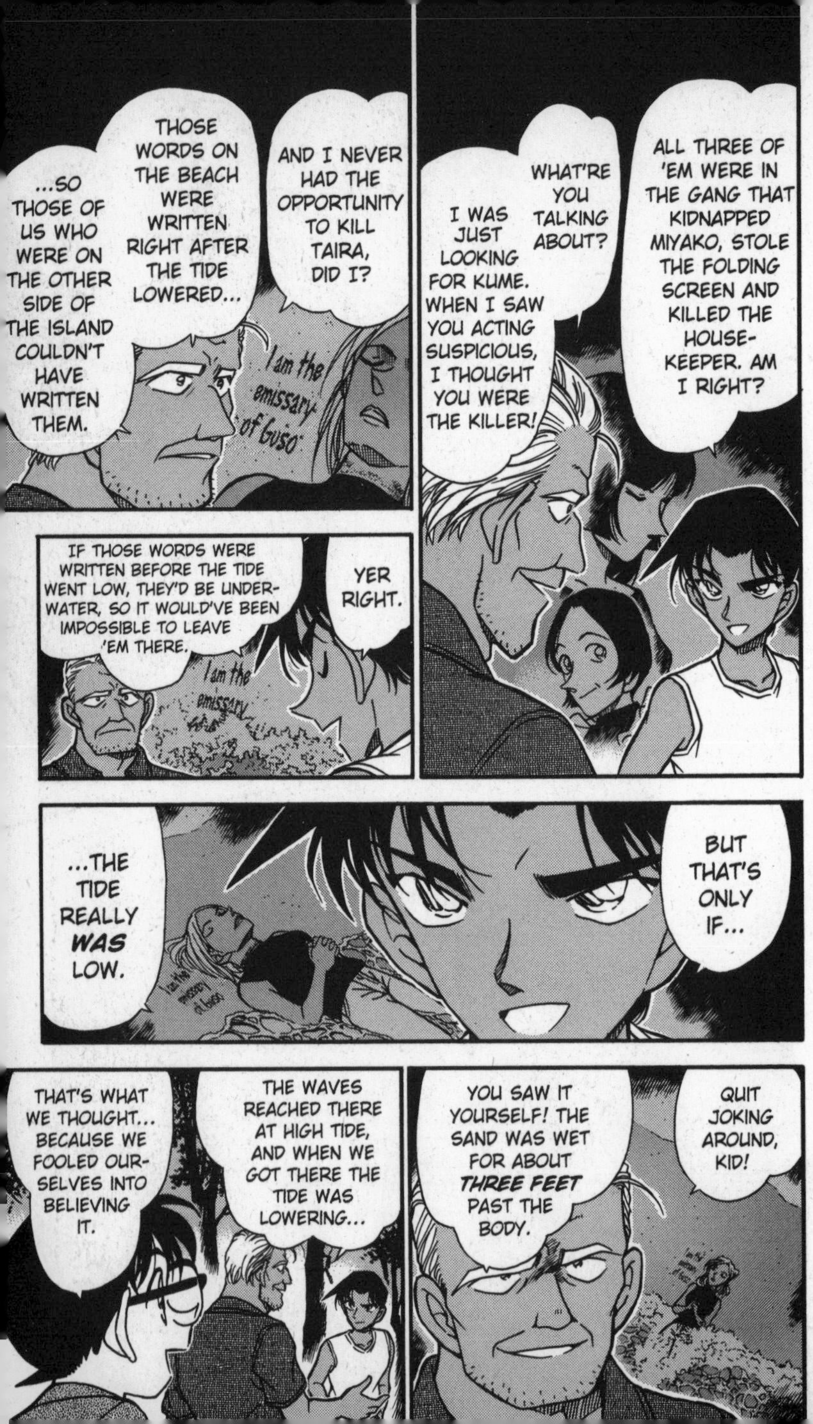

ALL THREE OF 'EM WERE IN THE GANG THAT KIDNAPPED MIYAKO, STOLE THE FOLDING SCREEN AND KILLED THE HOUSE-KEEPER. AM I RIGHT?
WHAT'RE YOU TALKING ABOUT?
I WAS JUST LOOKING FOR KUME. WHEN I SAW YOU ACTING SUSPICIOUS, I THOUGHT YOU WERE THE KILLER!
AND I NEVER HAD THE OPPORTUNITY TO KILL TAIRA, DID I?
THOSE WORDS ON THE BEACH WERE WRITTEN RIGHT AFTER THE TIDE LOWERED...
...SO THOSE OF US WHO WERE ON THE OTHER SIDE OF THE ISLAND COULDN'T HAVE WRITTEN THEM.
I am the emissary of Guso
YER RIGHT.
IF THOSE WORDS WERE WRITTEN BEFORE THE TIDE WENT LOW, THEY'D BE UNDER-WATER, SO IT WOULD'VE BEEN IMPOSSIBLE TO LEAVE 'EM THERE.
I am the emissary
BUT THAT'S ONLY IF...
...THE TIDE REALLY ***WAS*** LOW.
QUIT JOKING AROUND, KID!
YOU SAW IT YOURSELF! THE SAND WAS WET FOR ABOUT ***THREE FEET*** PAST THE BODY.
THE WAVES REACHED THERE AT HIGH TIDE, AND WHEN WE GOT THERE THE TIDE WAS LOWERING...
THAT'S WHAT WE THOUGHT... BECAUSE WE FOOLED OUR-SELVES INTO BELIEVING IT.

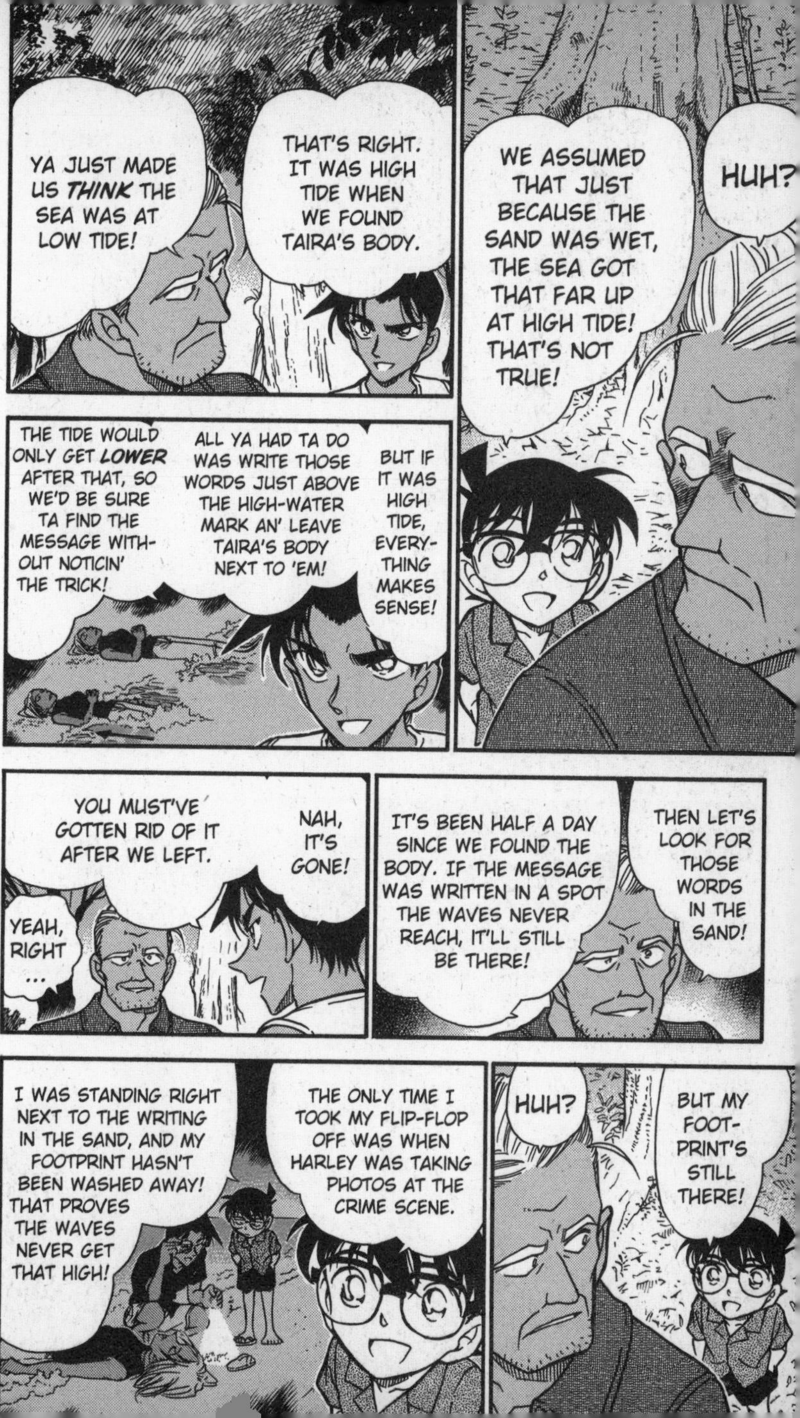

HUH?
WE ASSUMED THAT JUST BECAUSE THE SAND WAS WET, THE SEA GOT THAT FAR UP AT HIGH TIDE! THAT'S NOT TRUE!
THAT'S RIGHT. IT WAS HIGH TIDE WHEN WE FOUND TAIRA'S BODY.
YA JUST MADE US *THINK* THE SEA WAS AT LOW TIDE!
BUT IF IT WAS HIGH TIDE, EVERYTHING MAKES SENSE!
ALL YA HAD TA DO WAS WRITE THOSE WORDS JUST ABOVE THE HIGH-WATER MARK AN' LEAVE TAIRA'S BODY NEXT TO 'EM!
THE TIDE WOULD ONLY GET *LOWER* AFTER THAT, SO WE'D BE SURE TA FIND THE MESSAGE WITHOUT NOTICIN' THE TRICK!
THEN LET'S LOOK FOR THOSE WORDS IN THE SAND!
IT'S BEEN HALF A DAY SINCE WE FOUND THE BODY. IF THE MESSAGE WAS WRITTEN IN A SPOT THE WAVES NEVER REACH, IT'LL STILL BE THERE!
NAH, IT'S GONE!
YOU MUST'VE GOTTEN RID OF IT AFTER WE LEFT.
YEAH, RIGHT ...
BUT MY FOOTPRINT'S STILL THERE!
HUH?
THE ONLY TIME I TOOK MY FLIP-FLOP OFF WAS WHEN HARLEY WAS TAKING PHOTOS AT THE CRIME SCENE.
I WAS STANDING RIGHT NEXT TO THE WRITING IN THE SAND, AND MY FOOTPRINT HASN'T BEEN WASHED AWAY! THAT PROVES THE WAVES NEVER GET THAT HIGH!

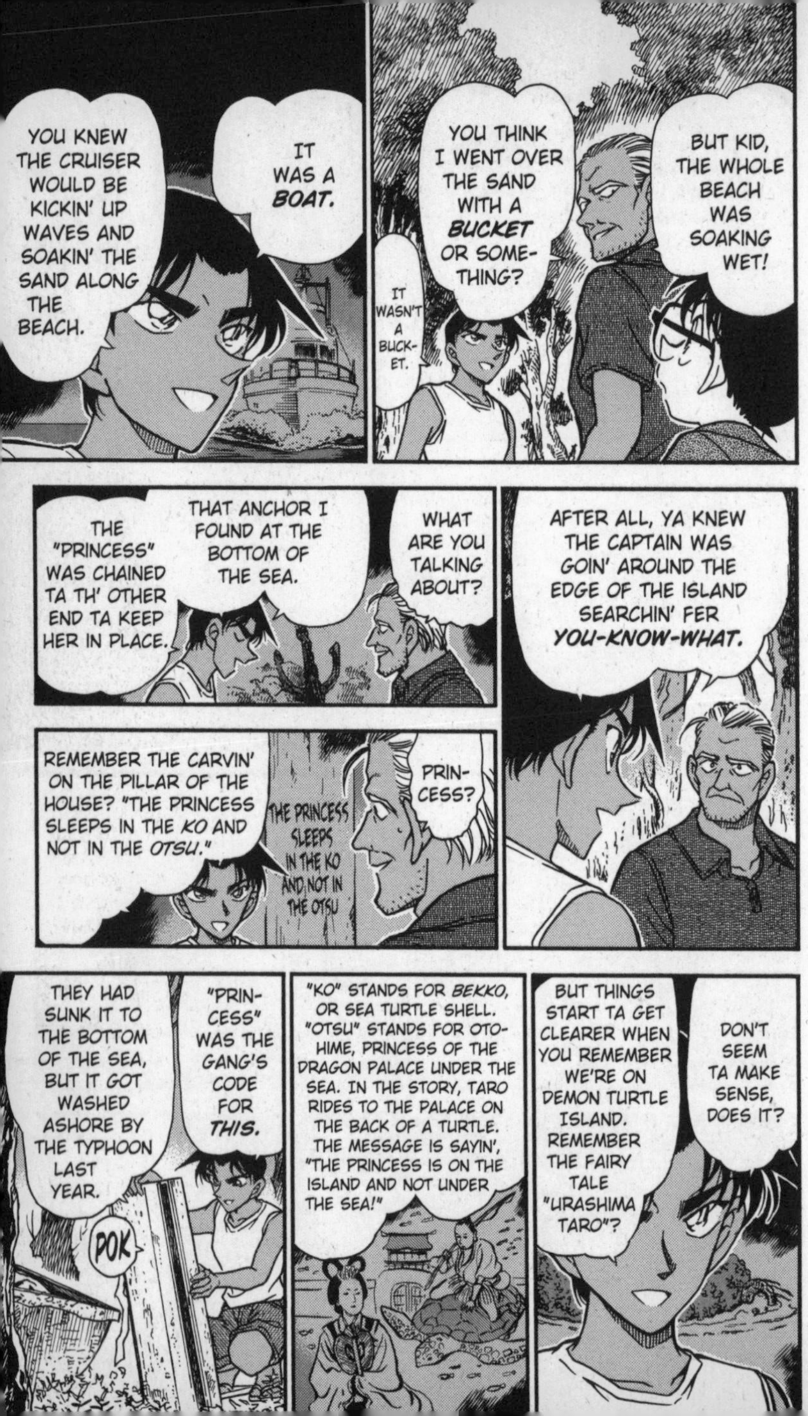
BUT KID, THE WHOLE BEACH WAS SOAKING WET!
YOU THINK I WENT OVER THE SAND WITH A BUCKET OR SOME-THING?
IT WASN'T A BUCK-ET.
IT WAS A BOAT.
YOU KNEW THE CRUISER WOULD BE KICKIN' UP WAVES AND SOAKIN' THE SAND ALONG THE BEACH.
AFTER ALL, YA KNEW THE CAPTAIN WAS GOIN' AROUND THE EDGE OF THE ISLAND SEARCHIN' FER YOU-KNOW-WHAT.
WHAT ARE YOU TALKING ABOUT?
THAT ANCHOR I FOUND AT THE BOTTOM OF THE SEA.
THE "PRINCESS" WAS CHAINED TA TH' OTHER END TA KEEP HER IN PLACE.
PRIN-CESS?
REMEMBER THE CARVIN' ON THE PILLAR OF THE HOUSE? "THE PRINCESS SLEEPS IN THE KO AND NOT IN THE OTSU."
THE PRINCESS SLEEPS IN THE KO AND NOT IN THE OTSU
DON'T SEEM TA MAKE SENSE, DOES IT?
BUT THINGS START TA GET CLEARER WHEN YOU REMEMBER WE'RE ON DEMON TURTLE ISLAND. REMEMBER THE FAIRY TALE "URASHIMA TARO"?
"KO" STANDS FOR BEKKO, OR SEA TURTLE SHELL. "OTSU" STANDS FOR OTO-HIME, PRINCESS OF THE DRAGON PALACE UNDER THE SEA. IN THE STORY, TARO RIDES TO THE PALACE ON THE BACK OF A TURTLE. THE MESSAGE IS SAYIN', "THE PRINCESS IS ON THE ISLAND AND NOT UNDER THE SEA!"
"PRIN-CESS" WAS THE GANG'S CODE FOR THIS.
THEY HAD SUNK IT TO THE BOTTOM OF THE SEA, BUT IT GOT WASHED ASHORE BY THE TYPHOON LAST YEAR.
POK

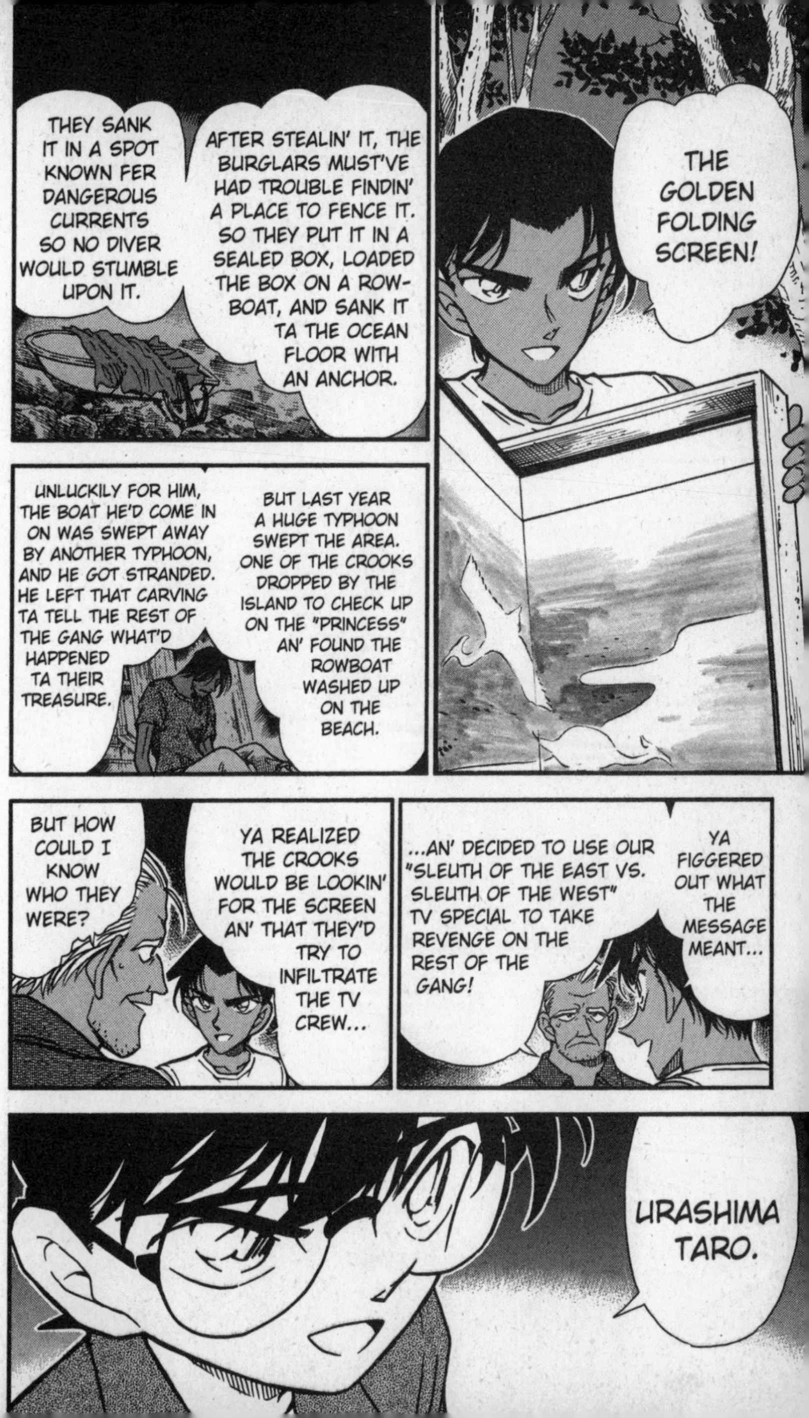
THE GOLDEN FOLDING SCREEN!
AFTER STEALIN' IT, THE BURGLARS MUST'VE HAD TROUBLE FINDIN' A PLACE TO FENCE IT. SO THEY PUT IT IN A SEALED BOX, LOADED THE BOX ON A ROW-BOAT, AND SANK IT TA THE OCEAN FLOOR WITH AN ANCHOR.
THEY SANK IT IN A SPOT KNOWN FER DANGEROUS CURRENTS SO NO DIVER WOULD STUMBLE UPON IT.
BUT LAST YEAR A HUGE TYPHOON SWEPT THE AREA. ONE OF THE CROOKS DROPPED BY THE ISLAND TO CHECK UP ON THE "PRINCESS" AN' FOUND THE ROWBOAT WASHED UP ON THE BEACH.
UNLUCKILY FOR HIM, THE BOAT HE'D COME IN ON WAS SWEPT AWAY BY ANOTHER TYPHOON, AND HE GOT STRANDED. HE LEFT THAT CARVING TA TELL THE REST OF THE GANG WHAT'D HAPPENED TA THEIR TREASURE.
YA FIGGERED OUT WHAT THE MESSAGE MEANT...
...AN' DECIDED TO USE OUR "SLEUTH OF THE EAST VS. SLEUTH OF THE WEST" TV SPECIAL TO TAKE REVENGE ON THE REST OF THE GANG!
YA REALIZED THE CROOKS WOULD BE LOOKIN' FOR THE SCREEN AN' THAT THEY'D TRY TO INFILTRATE THE TV CREW...
BUT HOW COULD I KNOW WHO THEY WERE?
URASHIMA TARO.

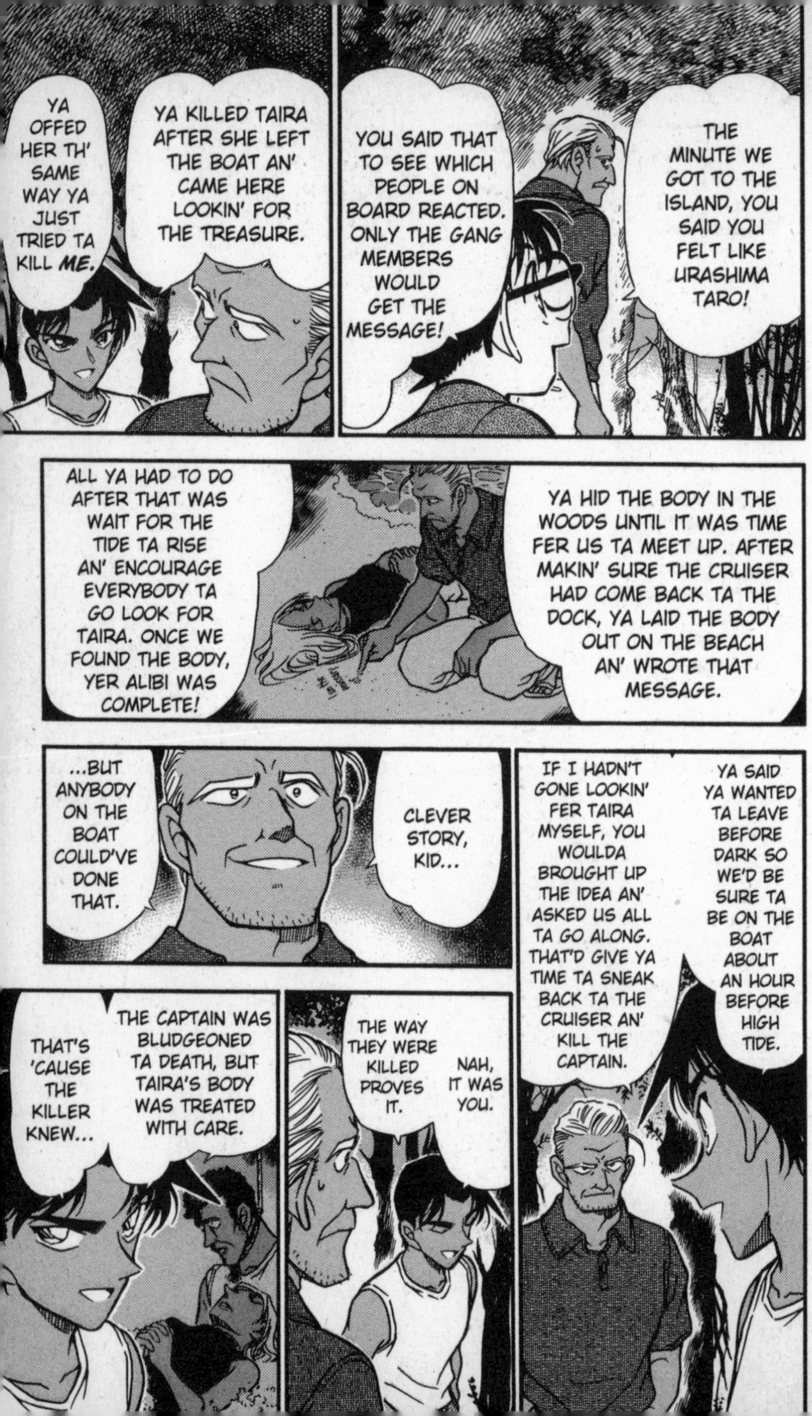
THE MINUTE WE GOT TO THE ISLAND, YOU SAID YOU FELT LIKE URASHIMA TARO!
YOU SAID THAT TO SEE WHICH PEOPLE ON BOARD REACTED. ONLY THE GANG MEMBERS WOULD GET THE MESSAGE!
YA KILLED TAIRA AFTER SHE LEFT THE BOAT AN' CAME HERE LOOKIN' FOR THE TREASURE.
YA OFFED HER TH' SAME WAY YA JUST TRIED TA KILL *ME*.
YA HID THE BODY IN THE WOODS UNTIL IT WAS TIME FER US TA MEET UP. AFTER MAKIN' SURE THE CRUISER HAD COME BACK TA THE DOCK, YA LAID THE BODY OUT ON THE BEACH AN' WROTE THAT MESSAGE.
ALL YA HAD TO DO AFTER THAT WAS WAIT FOR THE TIDE TA RISE AN' ENCOURAGE EVERYBODY TA GO LOOK FOR TAIRA. ONCE WE FOUND THE BODY, YER ALIBI WAS COMPLETE!
YA SAID YA WANTED TA LEAVE BEFORE DARK SO WE'D BE SURE TA BE ON THE BOAT ABOUT AN HOUR BEFORE HIGH TIDE.
IF I HADN'T GONE LOOKIN' FER TAIRA MYSELF, YOU WOULDA BROUGHT UP THE IDEA AN' ASKED US ALL TA GO ALONG. THAT'D GIVE YA TIME TA SNEAK BACK TA THE CRUISER AN' KILL THE CAPTAIN.
CLEVER STORY, KID...
...BUT ANYBODY ON THE BOAT COULD'VE DONE THAT.
NAH, IT WAS YOU.
THE WAY THEY WERE KILLED PROVES IT.
THE CAPTAIN WAS BLUDGEONED TA DEATH, BUT TAIRA'S BODY WAS TREATED WITH CARE.
THAT'S 'CAUSE THE KILLER KNEW...

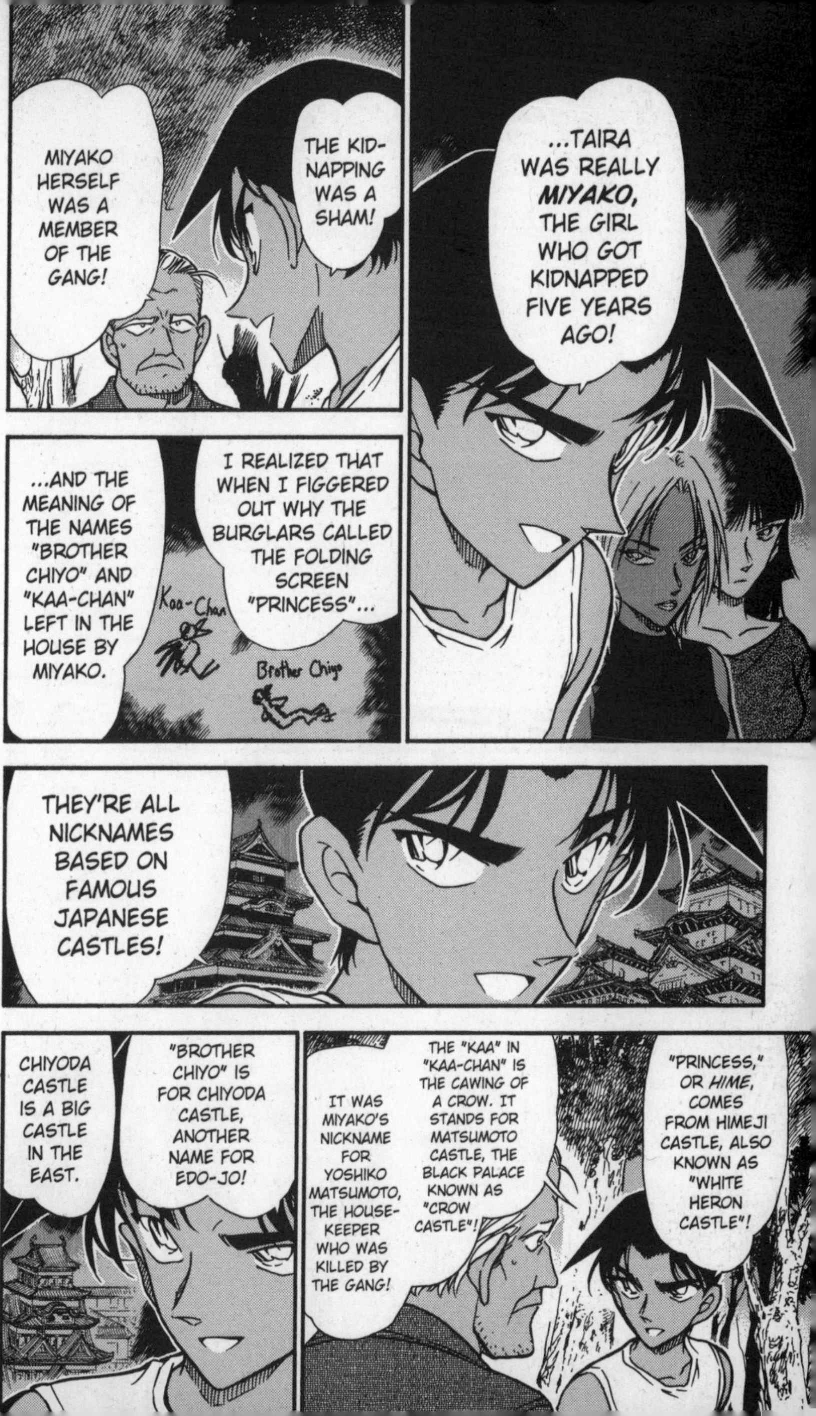
...TAIRA WAS REALLY *MIYAKO,* THE GIRL WHO GOT KIDNAPPED FIVE YEARS AGO!
THE KIDNAPPING WAS A SHAM!
MIYAKO HERSELF WAS A MEMBER OF THE GANG!
I REALIZED THAT WHEN I FIGGERED OUT WHY THE BURGLARS CALLED THE FOLDING SCREEN "PRINCESS"...
...AND THE MEANING OF THE NAMES "BROTHER CHIYO" AND "KAA-CHAN" LEFT IN THE HOUSE BY MIYAKO.
Kaa-Chan
Brother Chiyo
THEY'RE ALL NICKNAMES BASED ON FAMOUS JAPANESE CASTLES!
"PRINCESS," OR *HIME*, COMES FROM HIMEJI CASTLE, ALSO KNOWN AS "WHITE HERON CASTLE"!
THE "KAA" IN "KAA-CHAN" IS THE CAWING OF A CROW. IT STANDS FOR MATSUMOTO CASTLE, THE BLACK PALACE KNOWN AS "CROW CASTLE"!
IT WAS MIYAKO'S NICKNAME FOR YOSHIKO MATSUMOTO, THE HOUSE-KEEPER WHO WAS KILLED BY THE GANG!
"BROTHER CHIYO" IS FOR CHIYODA CASTLE, ANOTHER NAME FOR EDO-JO!
CHIYODA CASTLE IS A BIG CASTLE IN THE EAST.

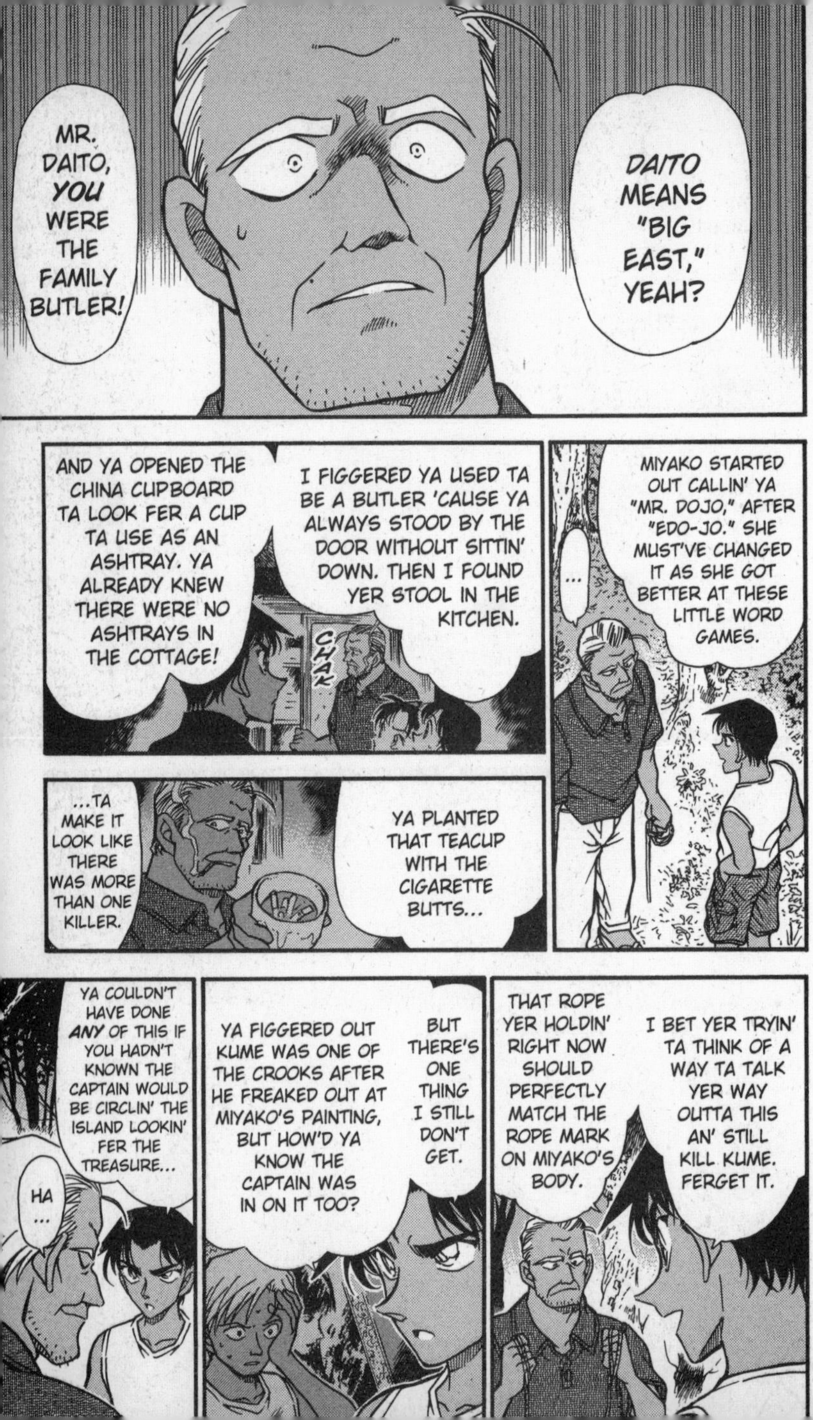
DAITO MEANS "BIG EAST," YEAH?
MR. DAITO, YOU WERE THE FAMILY BUTLER!
MIYAKO STARTED OUT CALLIN' YA "MR. DOJO," AFTER "EDO-JO." SHE MUST'VE CHANGED IT AS SHE GOT BETTER AT THESE LITTLE WORD GAMES.
...
I FIGGERED YA USED TA BE A BUTLER 'CAUSE YA ALWAYS STOOD BY THE DOOR WITHOUT SITTIN' DOWN. THEN I FOUND YER STOOL IN THE KITCHEN.
AND YA OPENED THE CHINA CUPBOARD TA LOOK FER A CUP TA USE AS AN ASHTRAY. YA ALREADY KNEW THERE WERE NO ASHTRAYS IN THE COTTAGE!
CHAK
YA PLANTED THAT TEACUP WITH THE CIGARETTE BUTTS...
...TA MAKE IT LOOK LIKE THERE WAS MORE THAN ONE KILLER.
I BET YER TRYIN' TA THINK OF A WAY TA TALK YER WAY OUTTA THIS AN' STILL KILL KUME. FERGET IT.
THAT ROPE YER HOLDIN' RIGHT NOW SHOULD PERFECTLY MATCH THE ROPE MARK ON MIYAKO'S BODY.
BUT THERE'S ONE THING I STILL DON'T GET.
YA FIGGERED OUT KUME WAS ONE OF THE CROOKS AFTER HE FREAKED OUT AT MIYAKO'S PAINTING, BUT HOW'D YA KNOW THE CAPTAIN WAS IN ON IT TOO?
YA COULDN'T HAVE DONE ANY OF THIS IF YOU HADN'T KNOWN THE CAPTAIN WOULD BE CIRCLIN' THE ISLAND LOOKIN' FER THE TREASURE...
HA ...

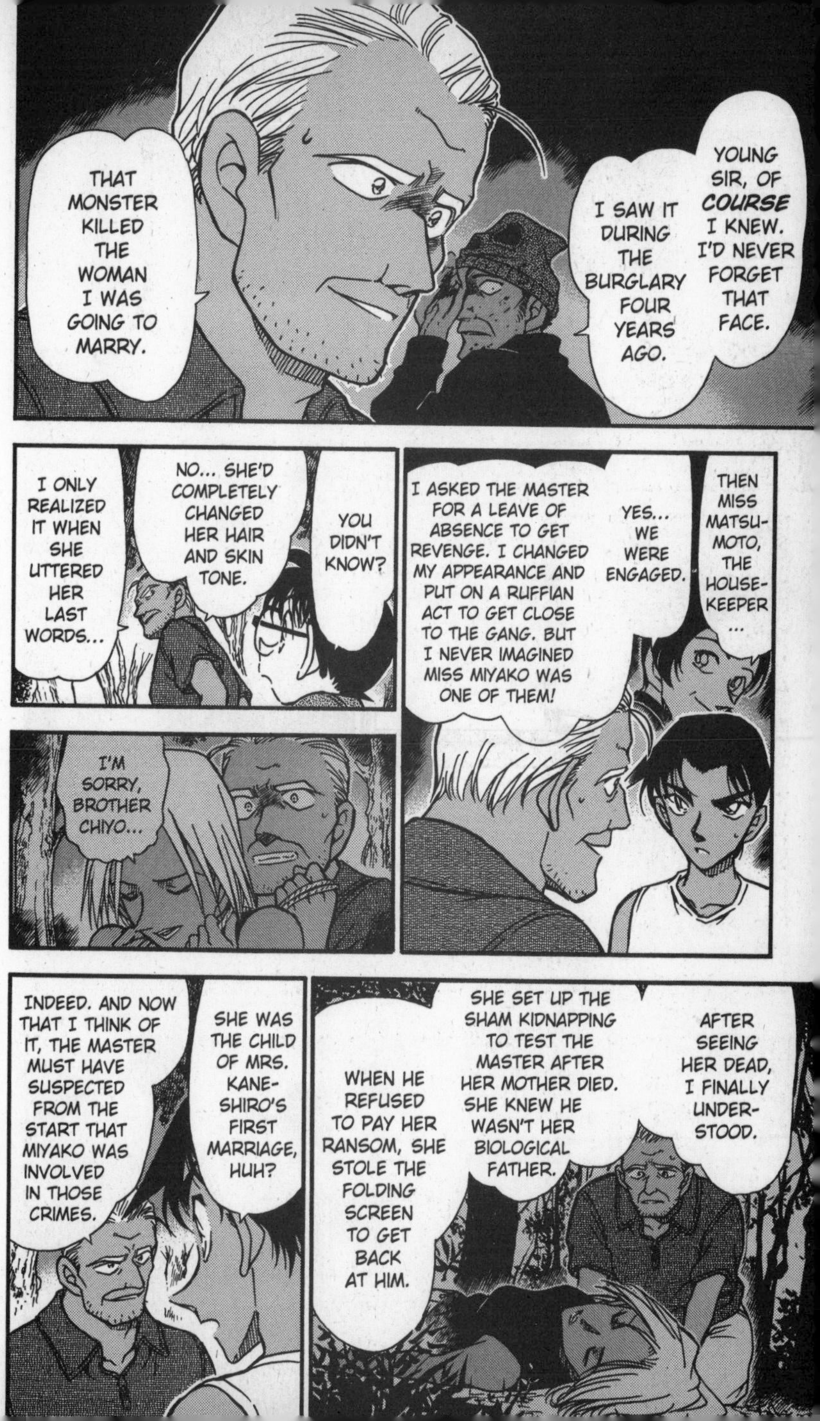
YOUNG SIR, OF COURSE I KNEW. I'D NEVER FORGET THAT FACE.
I SAW IT DURING THE BURGLARY FOUR YEARS AGO.
THAT MONSTER KILLED THE WOMAN I WAS GOING TO MARRY.
THEN MISS MATSU-MOTO, THE HOUSE-KEEPER...
YES... WE WERE ENGAGED.
I ASKED THE MASTER FOR A LEAVE OF ABSENCE TO GET REVENGE. I CHANGED MY APPEARANCE AND PUT ON A RUFFIAN ACT TO GET CLOSE TO THE GANG. BUT I NEVER IMAGINED MISS MIYAKO WAS ONE OF THEM!
YOU DIDN'T KNOW?
NO... SHE'D COMPLETELY CHANGED HER HAIR AND SKIN TONE.
I ONLY REALIZED IT WHEN SHE UTTERED HER LAST WORDS...
I'M SORRY, BROTHER CHIYO...
AFTER SEEING HER DEAD, I FINALLY UNDER-STOOD.
SHE SET UP THE SHAM KIDNAPPING TO TEST THE MASTER AFTER HER MOTHER DIED. SHE KNEW HE WASN'T HER BIOLOGICAL FATHER.
WHEN HE REFUSED TO PAY HER RANSOM, SHE STOLE THE FOLDING SCREEN TO GET BACK AT HIM.
SHE WAS THE CHILD OF MRS. KANE-SHIRO'S FIRST MARRIAGE, HUH?
INDEED. AND NOW THAT I THINK OF IT, THE MASTER MUST HAVE SUSPECTED FROM THE START THAT MIYAKO WAS INVOLVED IN THOSE CRIMES.

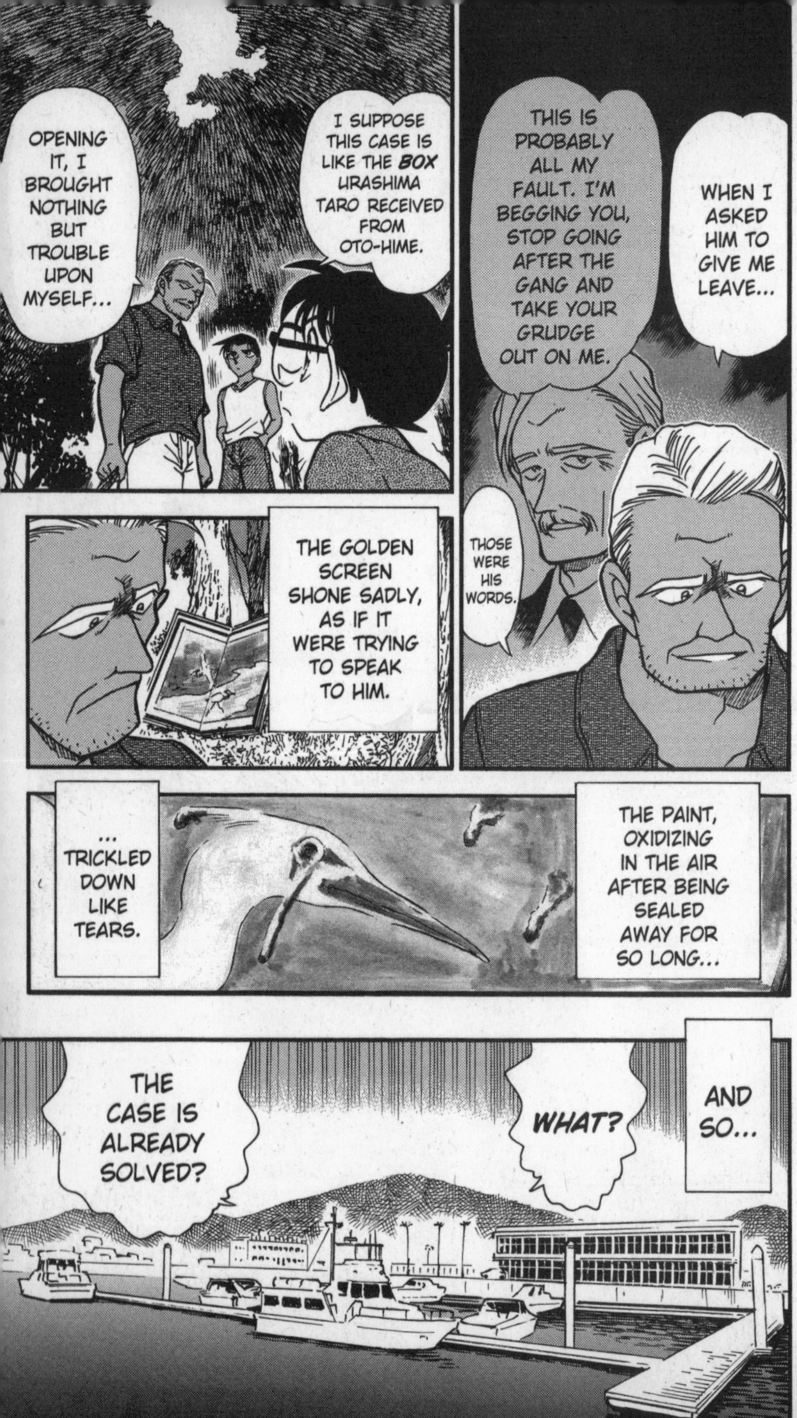
WHEN I ASKED HIM TO GIVE ME LEAVE...
THIS IS PROBABLY ALL MY FAULT. I'M BEGGING YOU, STOP GOING AFTER THE GANG AND TAKE YOUR GRUDGE OUT ON ME.
THOSE WERE HIS WORDS.
I SUPPOSE THIS CASE IS LIKE THE *BOX* URASHIMA TARO RECEIVED FROM OTO-HIME.
OPENING IT, I BROUGHT NOTHING BUT TROUBLE UPON MYSELF...
THE GOLDEN SCREEN SHONE SADLY, AS IF IT WERE TRYING TO SPEAK TO HIM.
THE PAINT, OXIDIZING IN THE AIR AFTER BEING SEALED AWAY FOR SO LONG...
...TRICKLED DOWN LIKE TEARS.
AND SO...
WHAT?
THE CASE IS ALREADY SOLVED?

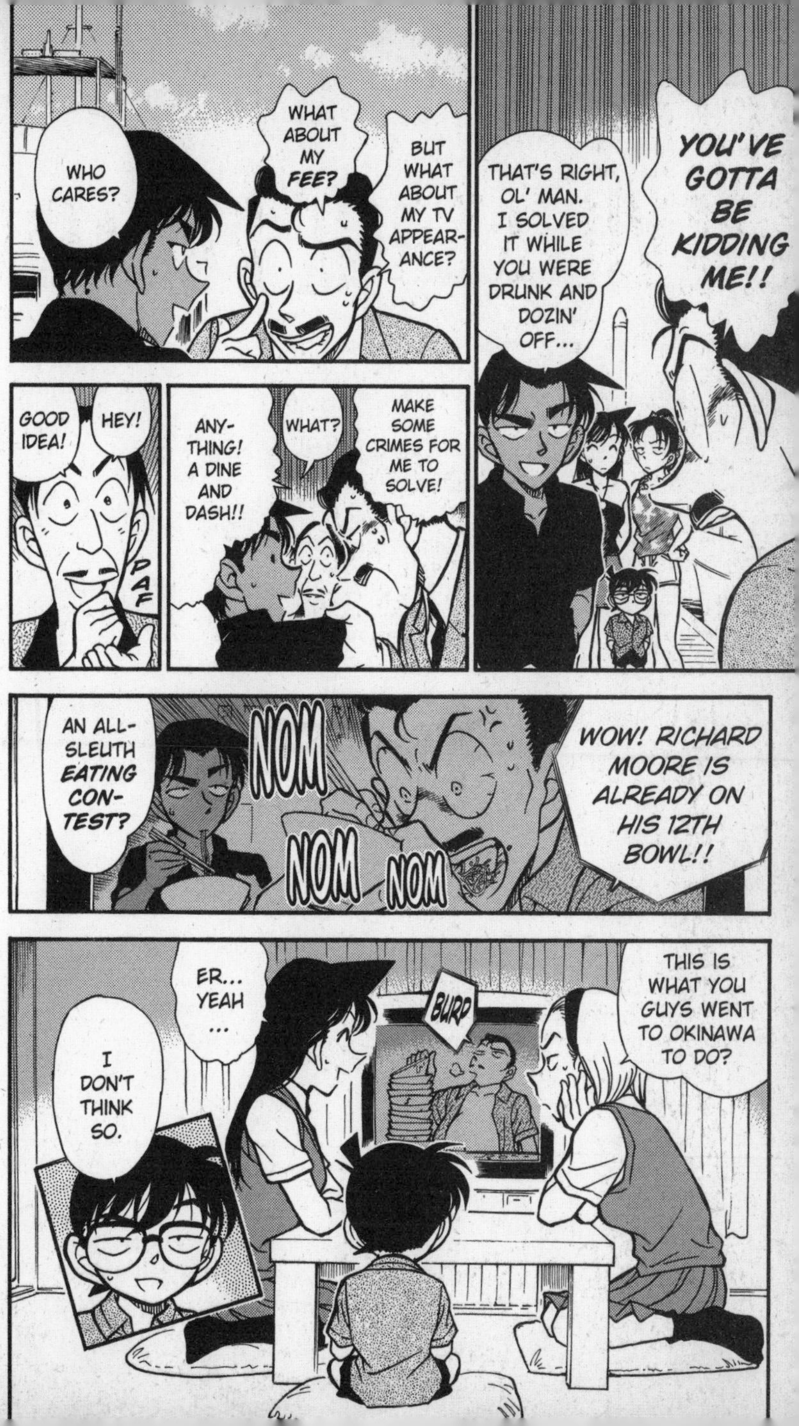
YOU'VE GOTTA BE KIDDING ME!!
THAT'S RIGHT, OL' MAN. I SOLVED IT WHILE YOU WERE DRUNK AND DOZIN' OFF...
BUT WHAT ABOUT MY TV APPEARANCE?
WHAT ABOUT MY FEE?
WHO CARES?
MAKE SOME CRIMES FOR ME TO SOLVE!
WHAT?
ANYTHING! A DINE AND DASH!!
HEY!
GOOD IDEA!
PAF
WOW! RICHARD MOORE IS ALREADY ON HIS 12TH BOWL!!
NOM
NOM
NOM
AN ALL-SLEUTH EATING CONTEST?
THIS IS WHAT YOU GUYS WENT TO OKINAWA TO DO?
BURP
ER... YEAH ...
I DON'T THINK SO.

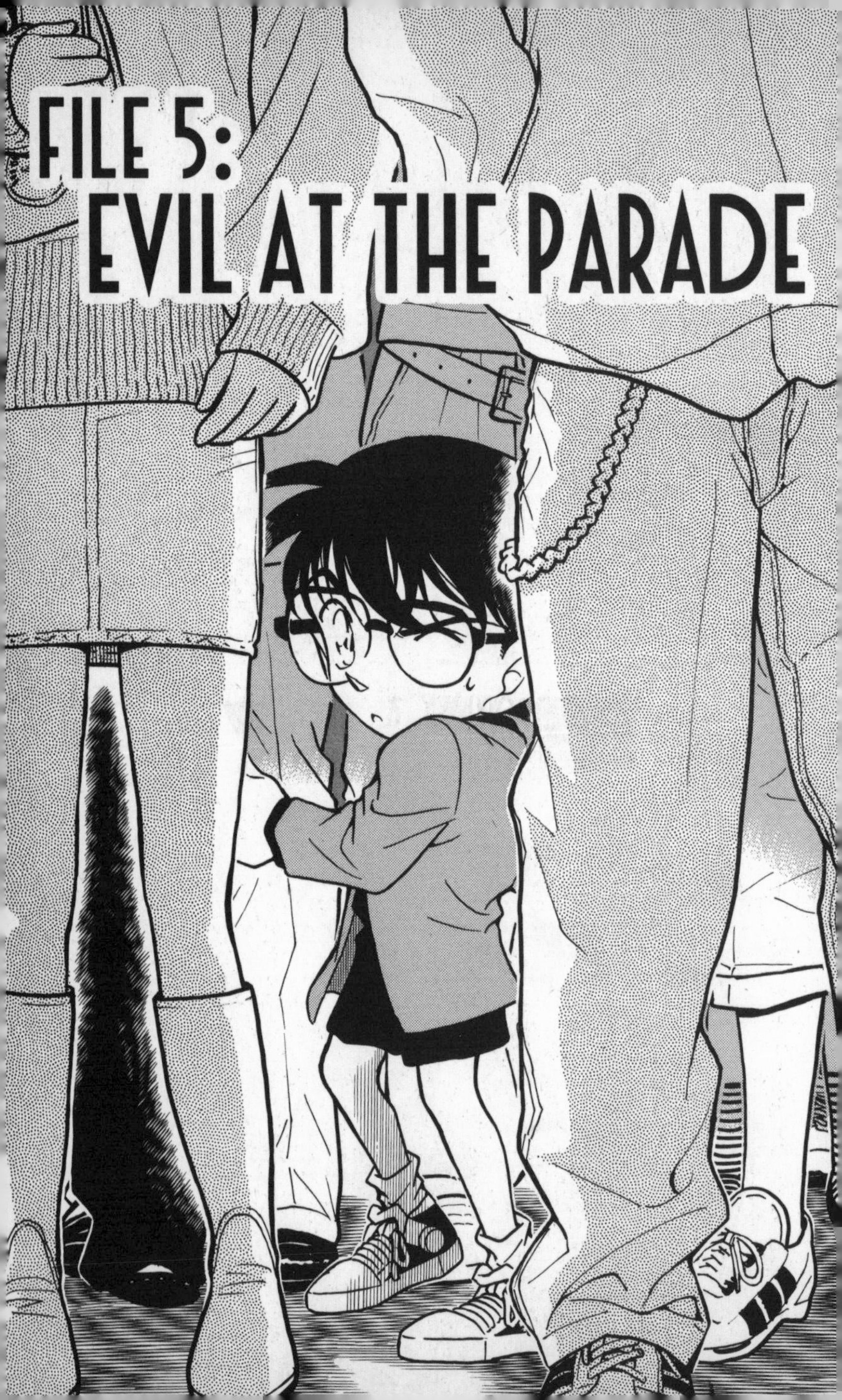
FILE 5:
EVIL AT THE PARADE

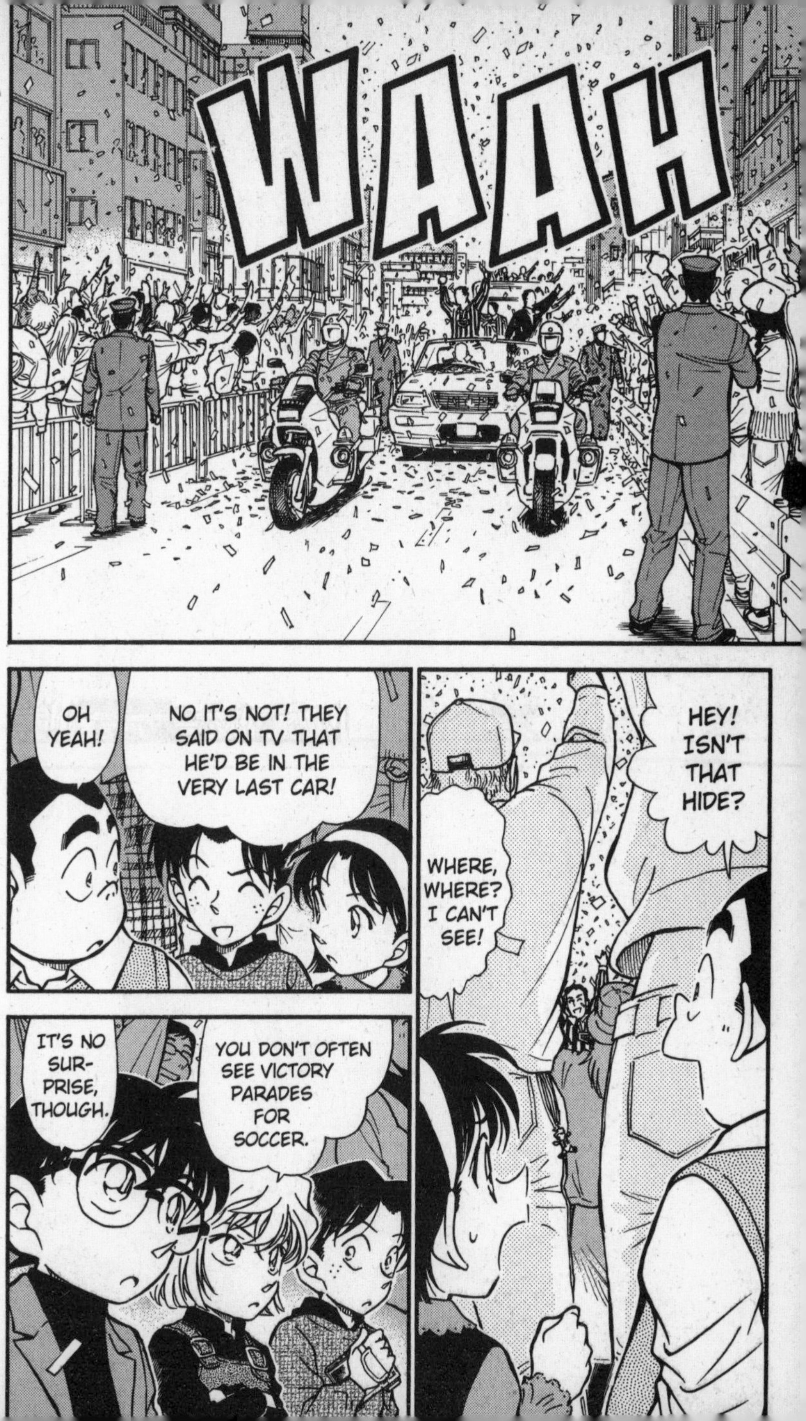
WAAH
HEY! ISN'T THAT HIDE?
WHERE, WHERE? I CAN'T SEE!
OH YEAH!
NO IT'S NOT! THEY SAID ON TV THAT HE'D BE IN THE VERY LAST CAR!
YOU DON'T OFTEN SEE VICTORY PARADES FOR SOCCER.
IT'S NO SUR-PRISE, THOUGH.

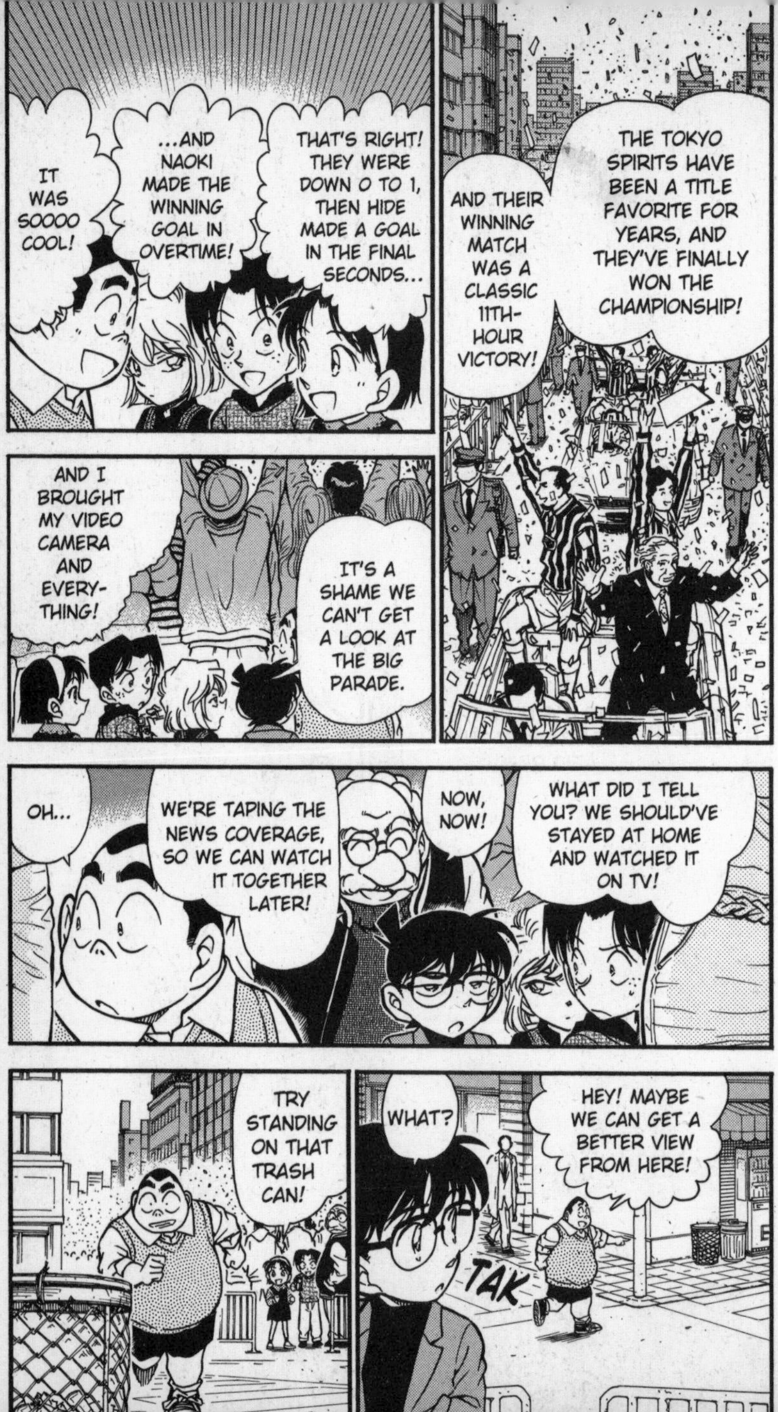
THE TOKYO SPIRITS HAVE BEEN A TITLE FAVORITE FOR YEARS, AND THEY'VE FINALLY WON THE CHAMPIONSHIP!
AND THEIR WINNING MATCH WAS A CLASSIC 11TH-HOUR VICTORY!
THAT'S RIGHT! THEY WERE DOWN 0 TO 1, THEN HIDE MADE A GOAL IN THE FINAL SECONDS...
...AND NAOKI MADE THE WINNING GOAL IN OVERTIME!
IT WAS SOOOO COOL!
IT'S A SHAME WE CAN'T GET A LOOK AT THE BIG PARADE.
AND I BROUGHT MY VIDEO CAMERA AND EVERY-THING!
WHAT DID I TELL YOU? WE SHOULD'VE STAYED AT HOME AND WATCHED IT ON TV!
NOW, NOW!
WE'RE TAPING THE NEWS COVERAGE, SO WE CAN WATCH IT TOGETHER LATER!
OH...
HEY! MAYBE WE CAN GET A BETTER VIEW FROM HERE!
WHAT?
TAK
TRY STANDING ON THAT TRASH CAN!

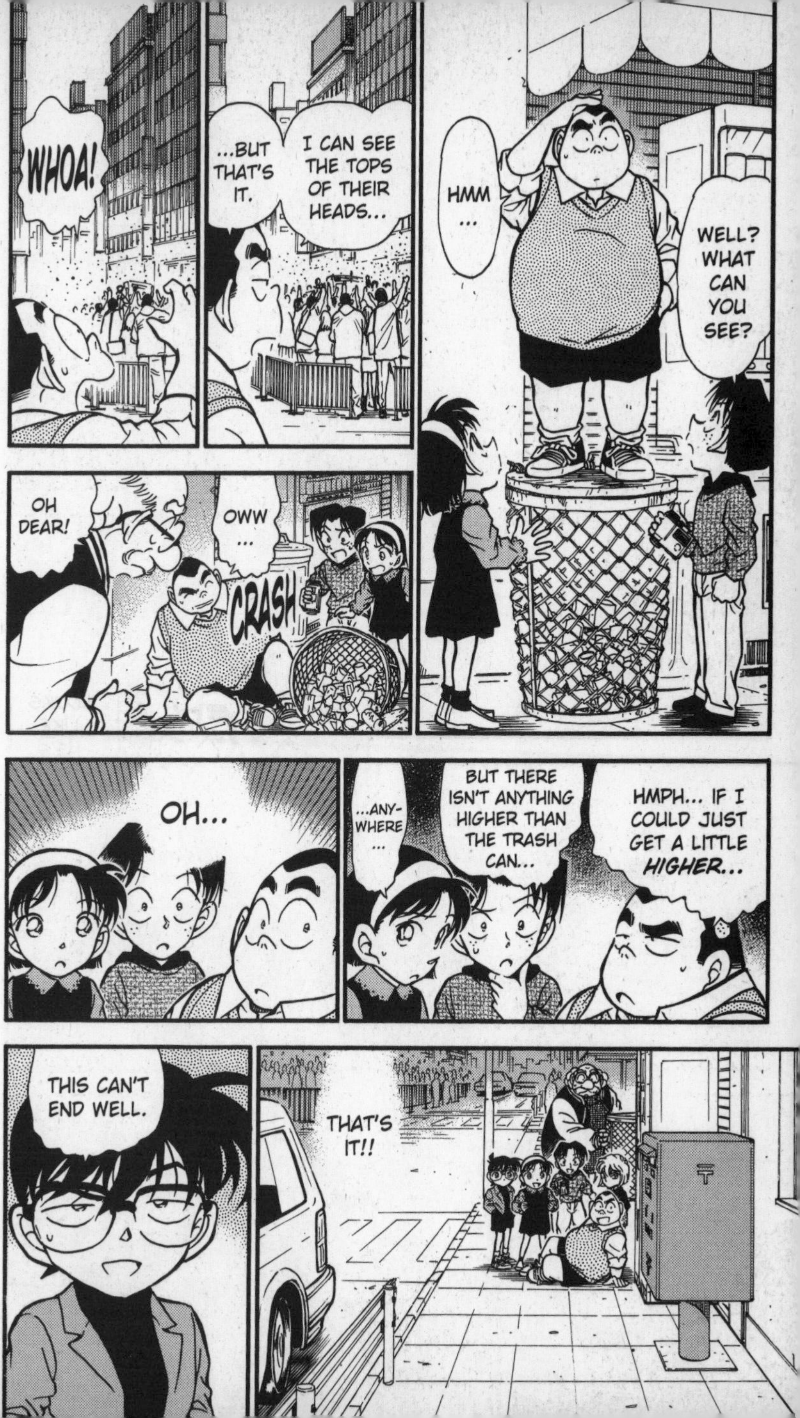
WELL? WHAT CAN YOU SEE?
HMM...
I CAN SEE THE TOPS OF THEIR HEADS...
...BUT THAT'S IT.
WHOA!
OWW...
CRASH
OH DEAR!
HMPH... IF I COULD JUST GET A LITTLE *HIGHER*...
BUT THERE ISN'T ANYTHING HIGHER THAN THE TRASH CAN...
...ANYWHERE...
OH...
THAT'S IT!!
THIS CAN'T END WELL.

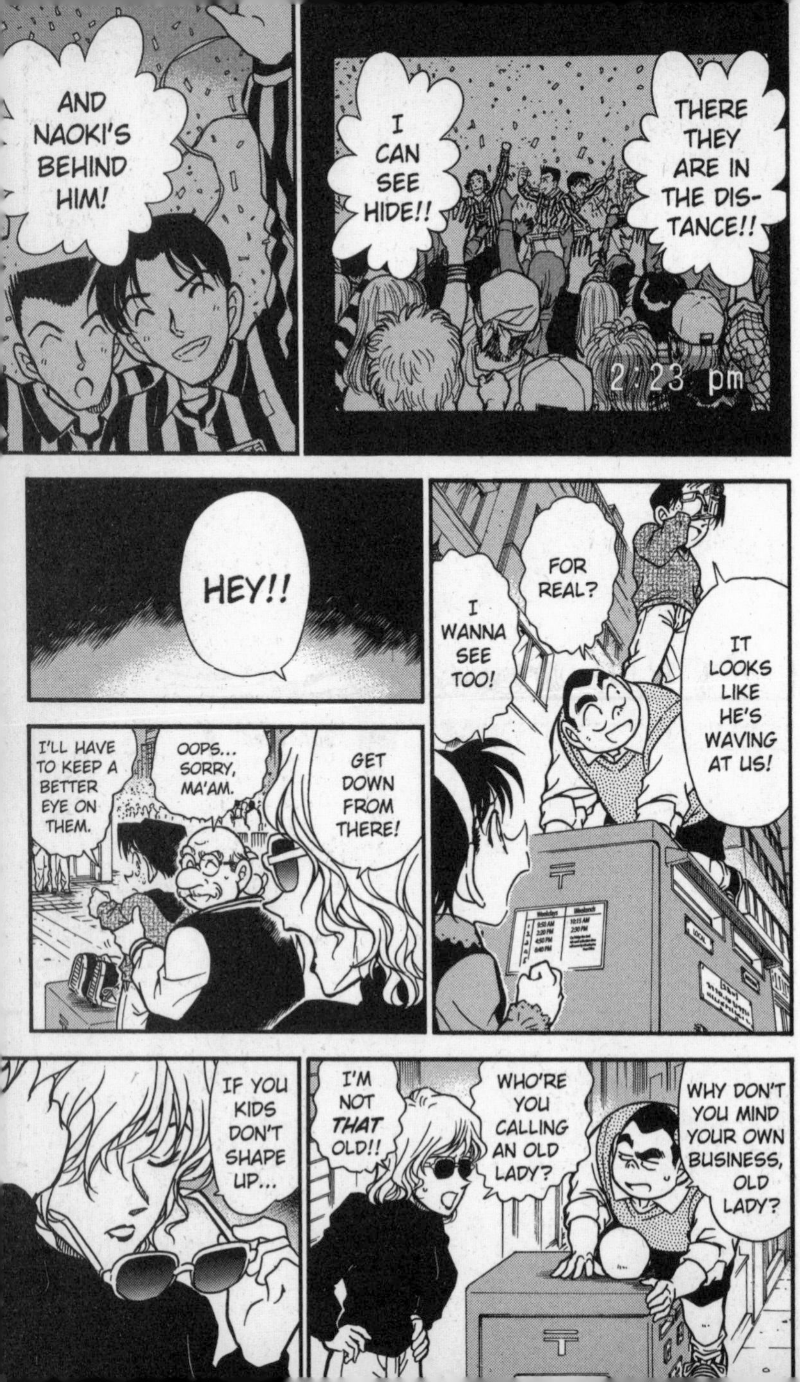
THERE THEY ARE IN THE DIS-TANCE!!
I CAN SEE HIDE!!
2:23 pm
AND NAOKI'S BEHIND HIM!
IT LOOKS LIKE HE'S WAVING AT US!
FOR REAL?
I WANNA SEE TOO!
HEY!!
GET DOWN FROM THERE!
OOPS... SORRY, MA'AM.
I'LL HAVE TO KEEP A BETTER EYE ON THEM.
WHY DON'T YOU MIND YOUR OWN BUSINESS, OLD LADY?
WHO'RE YOU CALLING AN OLD LADY?
I'M NOT *THAT* OLD!!
IF YOU KIDS DON'T SHAPE UP...

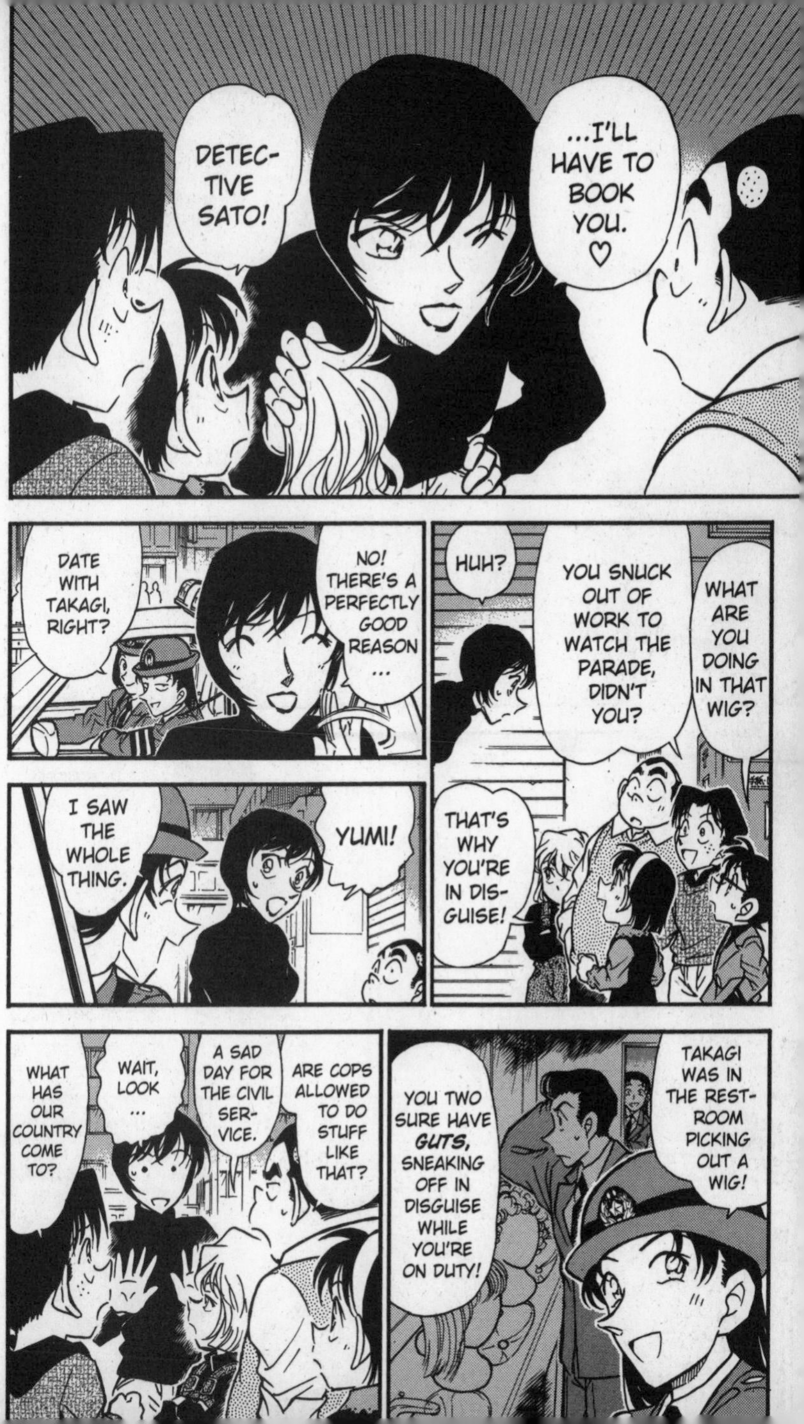
...I'LL HAVE TO BOOK YOU. ♡
DETECTIVE SATO!
WHAT ARE YOU DOING IN THAT WIG?
YOU SNUCK OUT OF WORK TO WATCH THE PARADE, DIDN'T YOU?
HUH?
NO! THERE'S A PERFECTLY GOOD REASON ...
DATE WITH TAKAGI, RIGHT?
THAT'S WHY YOU'RE IN DISGUISE!
YUMI!
I SAW THE WHOLE THING.
TAKAGI WAS IN THE RESTROOM PICKING OUT A WIG!
YOU TWO SURE HAVE **GUTS**, SNEAKING OFF IN DISGUISE WHILE YOU'RE ON DUTY!
ARE COPS ALLOWED TO DO STUFF LIKE THAT?
A SAD DAY FOR THE CIVIL SERVICE.
WAIT, LOOK ...
WHAT HAS OUR COUNTRY COME TO?

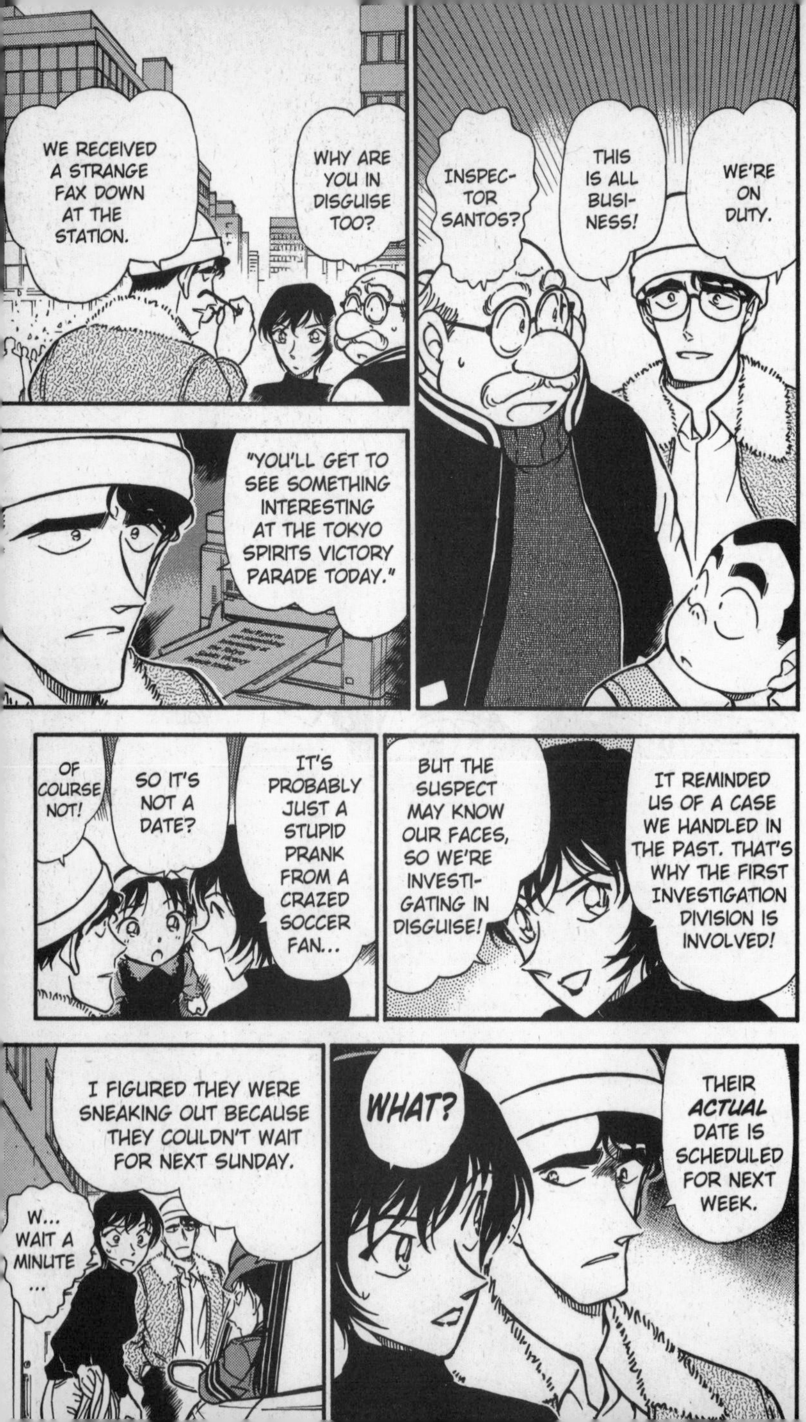
WE'RE ON DUTY.
THIS IS ALL BUSINESS!
INSPECTOR SANTOS?
WHY ARE YOU IN DISGUISE TOO?
WE RECEIVED A STRANGE FAX DOWN AT THE STATION.
"YOU'LL GET TO SEE SOMETHING INTERESTING AT THE TOKYO SPIRITS VICTORY PARADE TODAY."
IT REMINDED US OF A CASE WE HANDLED IN THE PAST. THAT'S WHY THE FIRST INVESTIGATION DIVISION IS INVOLVED!
BUT THE SUSPECT MAY KNOW OUR FACES, SO WE'RE INVESTIGATING IN DISGUISE!
IT'S PROBABLY JUST A STUPID PRANK FROM A CRAZED SOCCER FAN...
SO IT'S NOT A DATE?
OF COURSE NOT!
THEIR *ACTUAL* DATE IS SCHEDULED FOR NEXT WEEK.
WHAT?
I FIGURED THEY WERE SNEAKING OUT BECAUSE THEY COULDN'T WAIT FOR NEXT SUNDAY.
W... WAIT A MINUTE ...

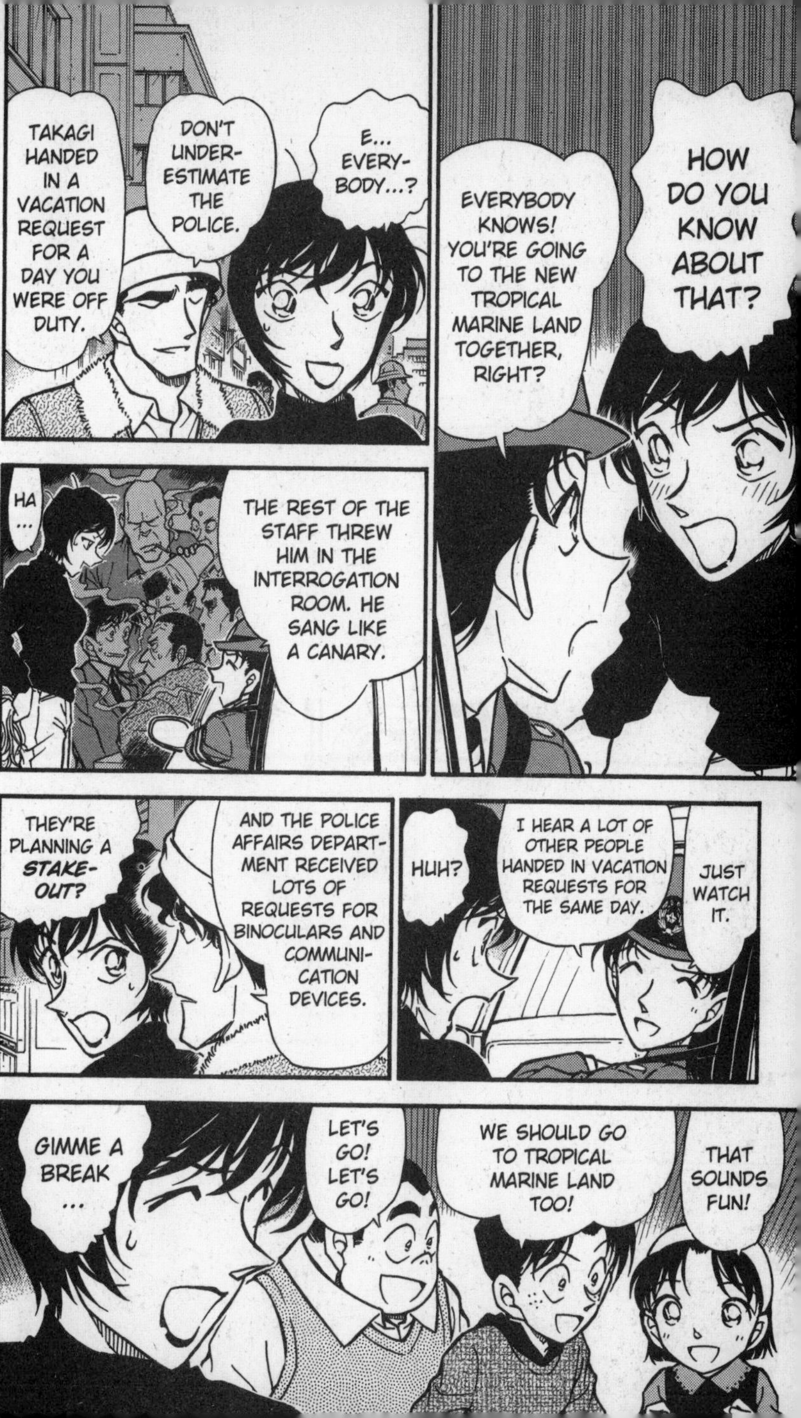
HOW DO YOU KNOW ABOUT THAT?
EVERYBODY KNOWS! YOU'RE GOING TO THE NEW TROPICAL MARINE LAND TOGETHER, RIGHT?
E... EVERYBODY...?
DON'T UNDERESTIMATE THE POLICE.
TAKAGI HANDED IN A VACATION REQUEST FOR A DAY YOU WERE OFF DUTY.
THE REST OF THE STAFF THREW HIM IN THE INTERROGATION ROOM. HE SANG LIKE A CANARY.
HA ...
JUST WATCH IT.
I HEAR A LOT OF OTHER PEOPLE HANDED IN VACATION REQUESTS FOR THE SAME DAY.
HUH?
AND THE POLICE AFFAIRS DEPARTMENT RECEIVED LOTS OF REQUESTS FOR BINOCULARS AND COMMUNICATION DEVICES.
THEY'RE PLANNING A ***STAKE-OUT***?
THAT SOUNDS FUN!
WE SHOULD GO TO TROPICAL MARINE LAND TOO!
LET'S GO! LET'S GO!
GIMME A BREAK ...

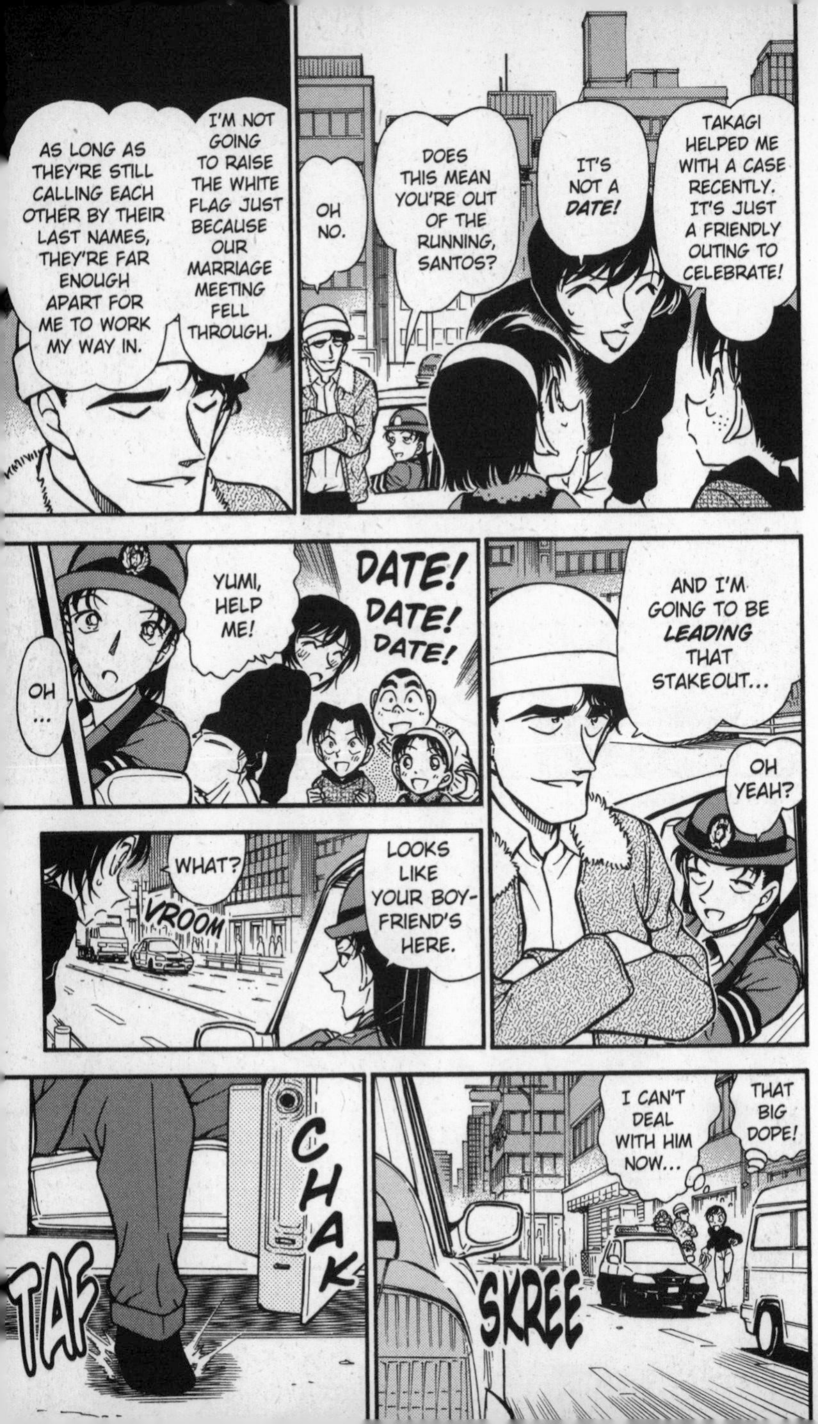
TAKAGI HELPED ME WITH A CASE RECENTLY. IT'S JUST A FRIENDLY OUTING TO CELEBRATE!
IT'S NOT A *DATE!*
DOES THIS MEAN YOU'RE OUT OF THE RUNNING, SANTOS?
OH NO.
I'M NOT GOING TO RAISE THE WHITE FLAG JUST BECAUSE OUR MARRIAGE MEETING FELL THROUGH.
AS LONG AS THEY'RE STILL CALLING EACH OTHER BY THEIR LAST NAMES, THEY'RE FAR ENOUGH APART FOR ME TO WORK MY WAY IN.
AND I'M GOING TO BE *LEADING* THAT STAKEOUT...
OH YEAH?
DATE! DATE! DATE!
YUMI, HELP ME!
OH ...
LOOKS LIKE YOUR BOY-FRIEND'S HERE.
WHAT?
VROOM
THAT BIG DOPE!
I CAN'T DEAL WITH HIM NOW...
SKREE
CHAK
TAF

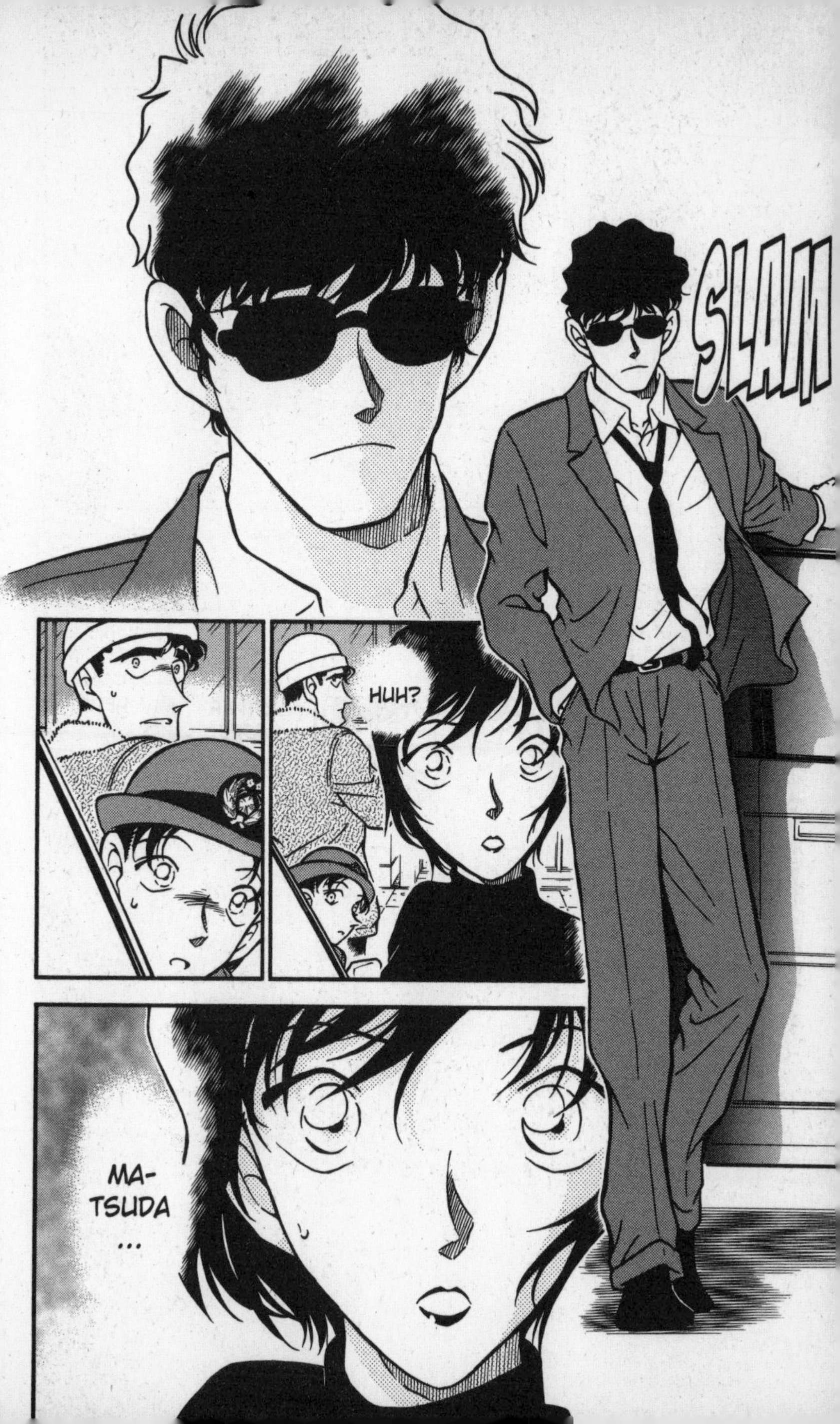
SLAM
HUH?
MA-
TSUDA
...

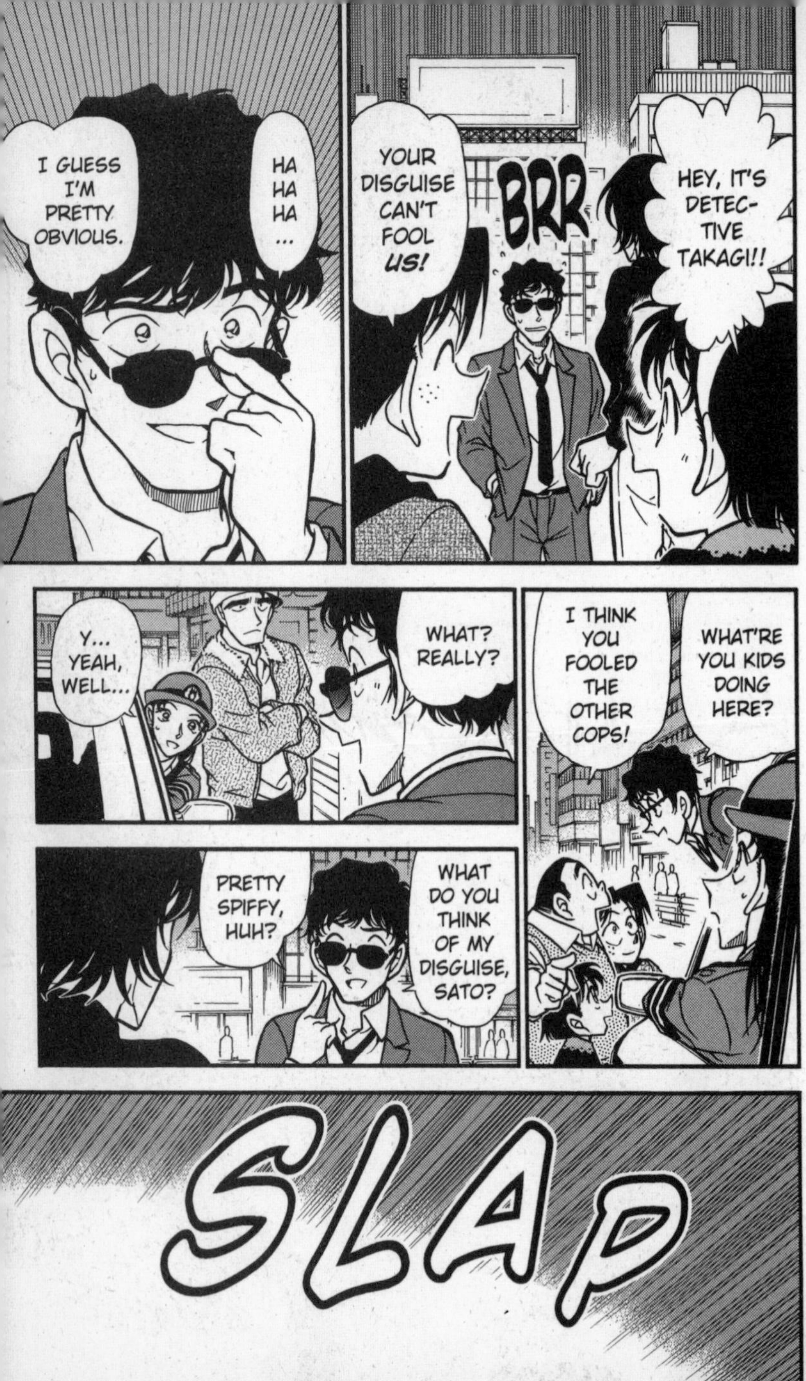
HEY, IT'S DETEC-TIVE TAKAGI!!
BRR
YOUR DISGUISE CAN'T FOOL US!
HA HA HA ...
I GUESS I'M PRETTY OBVIOUS.
WHAT'RE YOU KIDS DOING HERE?
I THINK YOU FOOLED THE OTHER COPS!
WHAT? REALLY?
Y... YEAH, WELL...
WHAT DO YOU THINK OF MY DISGUISE, SATO?
PRETTY SPIFFY, HUH?
SLAP

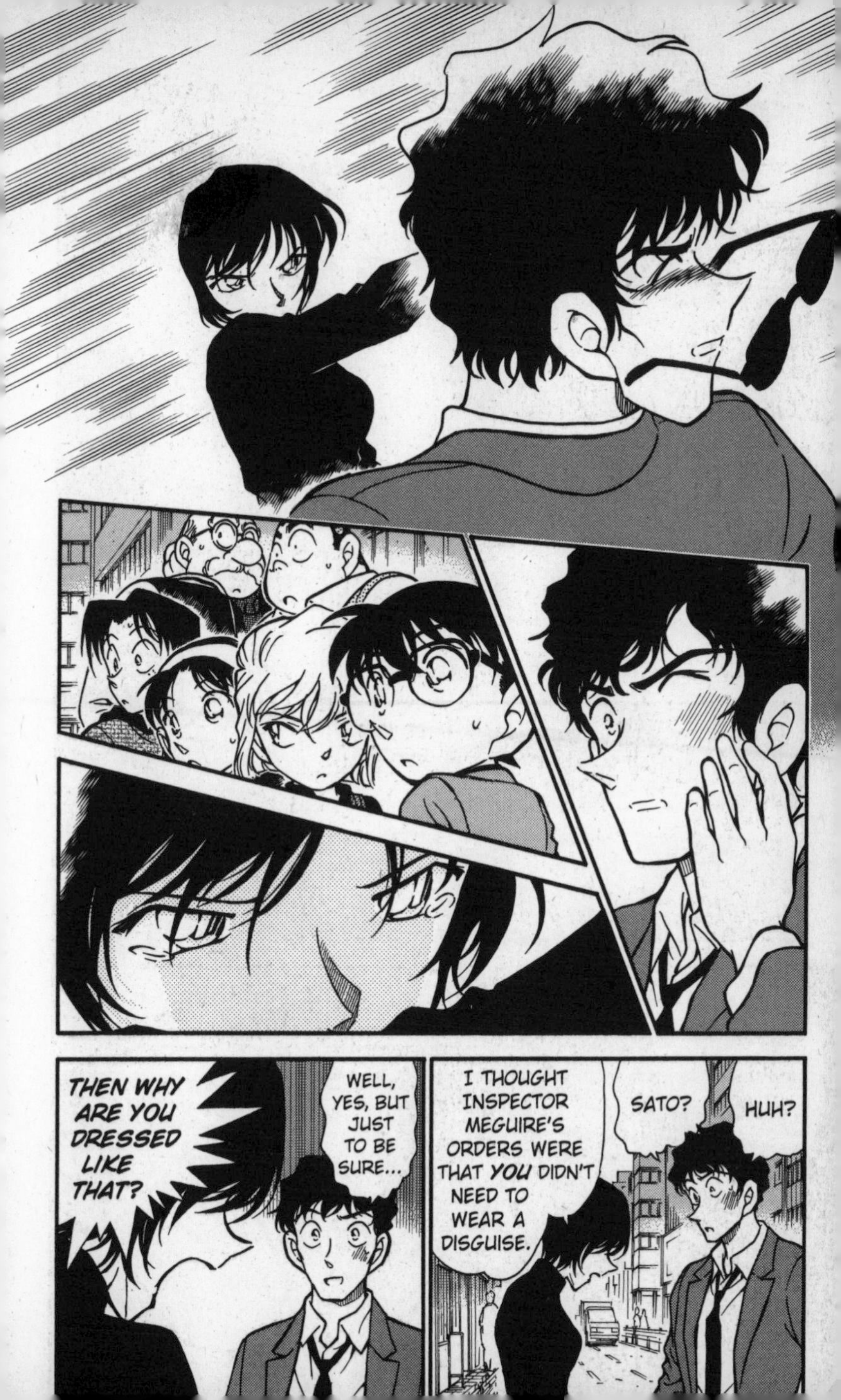
HUH?
SATO?
I THOUGHT INSPECTOR MEGUIRE'S ORDERS WERE THAT YOU DIDN'T NEED TO WEAR A DISGUISE.
WELL, YES, BUT JUST TO BE SURE...
THEN WHY ARE YOU DRESSED LIKE THAT?

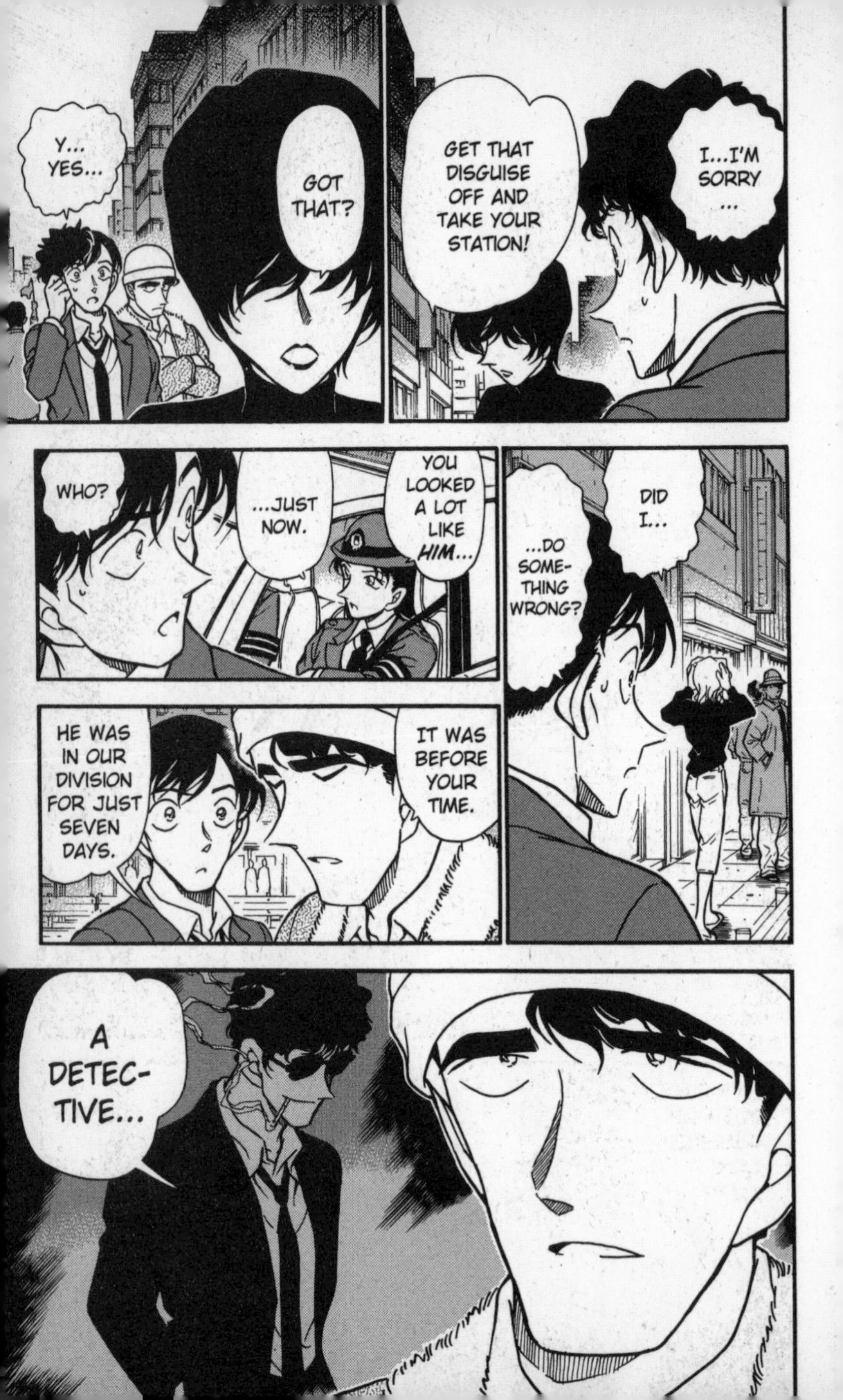
I...I'M SORRY ...
GET THAT DISGUISE OFF AND TAKE YOUR STATION!
GOT THAT?
Y... YES...
DID I...
...DO SOME-THING WRONG?
YOU LOOKED A LOT LIKE *HIM*...
...JUST NOW.
WHO?
IT WAS BEFORE YOUR TIME.
HE WAS IN OUR DIVISION FOR JUST SEVEN DAYS.
A DETEC-TIVE...

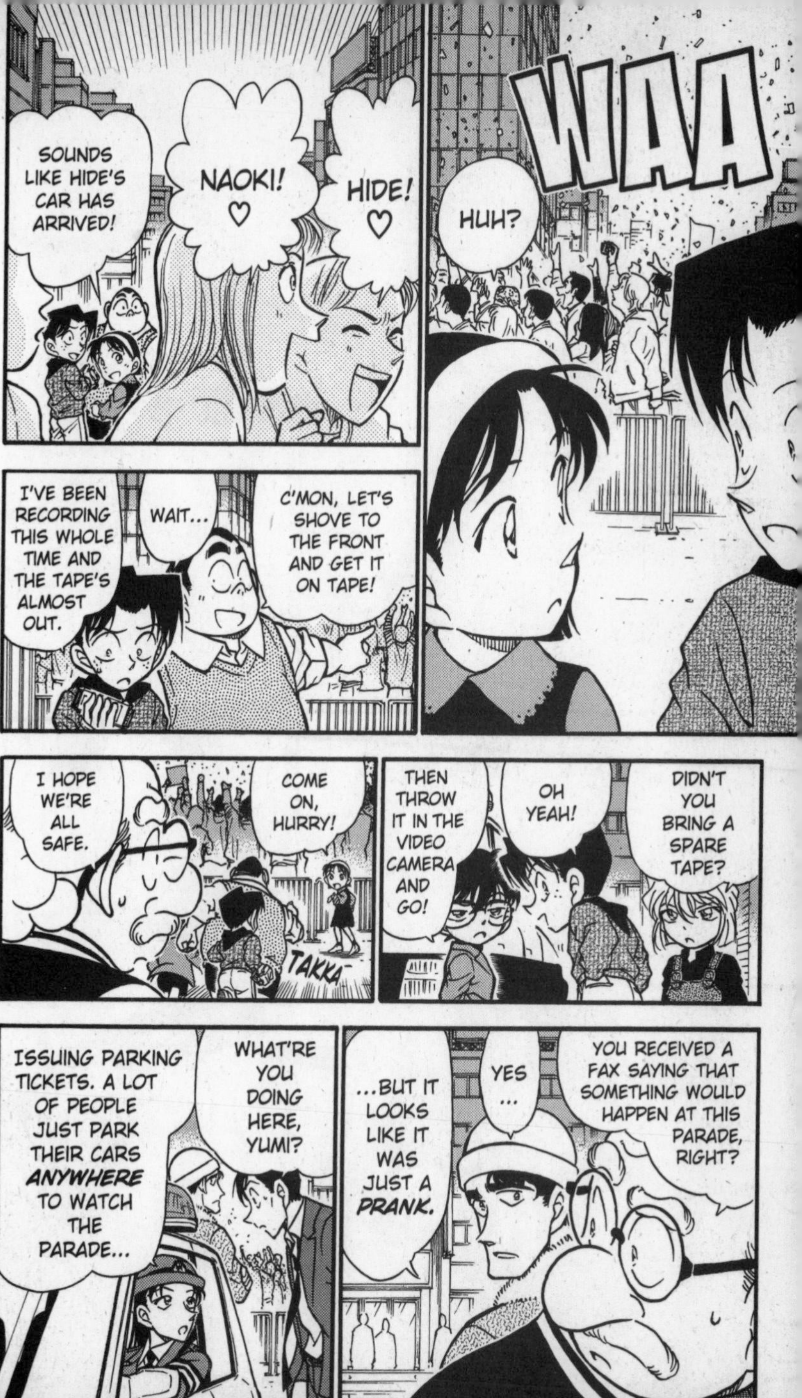
WAA
HUH?
HIDE! ♡
NAOKI! ♡
SOUNDS LIKE HIDE'S CAR HAS ARRIVED!
C'MON, LET'S SHOVE TO THE FRONT AND GET IT ON TAPE!
WAIT...
I'VE BEEN RECORDING THIS WHOLE TIME AND THE TAPE'S ALMOST OUT.
DIDN'T YOU BRING A SPARE TAPE?
OH YEAH!
THEN THROW IT IN THE VIDEO CAMERA AND GO!
COME ON, HURRY!
I HOPE WE'RE ALL SAFE.
TAKKA
YOU RECEIVED A FAX SAYING THAT SOMETHING WOULD HAPPEN AT THIS PARADE, RIGHT?
YES...
...BUT IT LOOKS LIKE IT WAS JUST A PRANK.
WHAT'RE YOU DOING HERE, YUMI?
ISSUING PARKING TICKETS. A LOT OF PEOPLE JUST PARK THEIR CARS ANYWHERE TO WATCH THE PARADE...

SORRY...

IF YOU DON'T MOVE YOUR CAR, I'LL GIVE *YOU* A TICKET TOO!

HEY!

THUP

THUP

TOK TOK

WHERE ARE YOU?

GUYS? UM, GUYS?

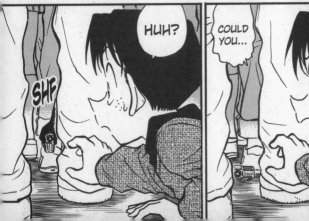

SHF

HUH?

COULD YOU...

UM, EXCUSE ME...

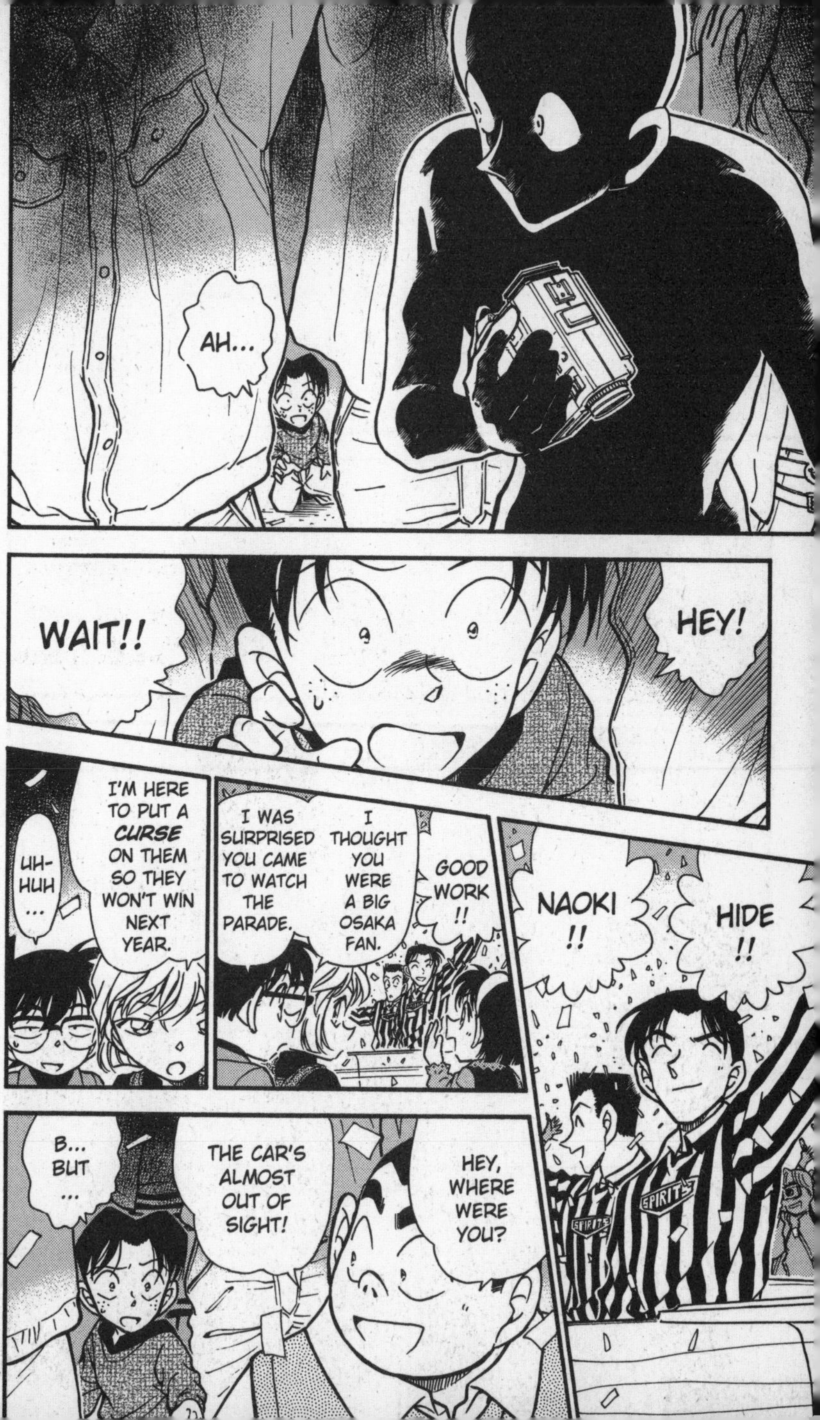

AH...
HEY!
WAIT!!
HIDE!!
NAOKI!!
GOOD WORK!!
I THOUGHT YOU WERE A BIG OSAKA FAN.
I WAS SURPRISED YOU CAME TO WATCH THE PARADE.
I'M HERE TO PUT A ***CURSE*** ON THEM SO THEY WON'T WIN NEXT YEAR.
UH-HUH...
HEY, WHERE WERE YOU?
THE CAR'S ALMOST OUT OF SIGHT!
B... BUT...

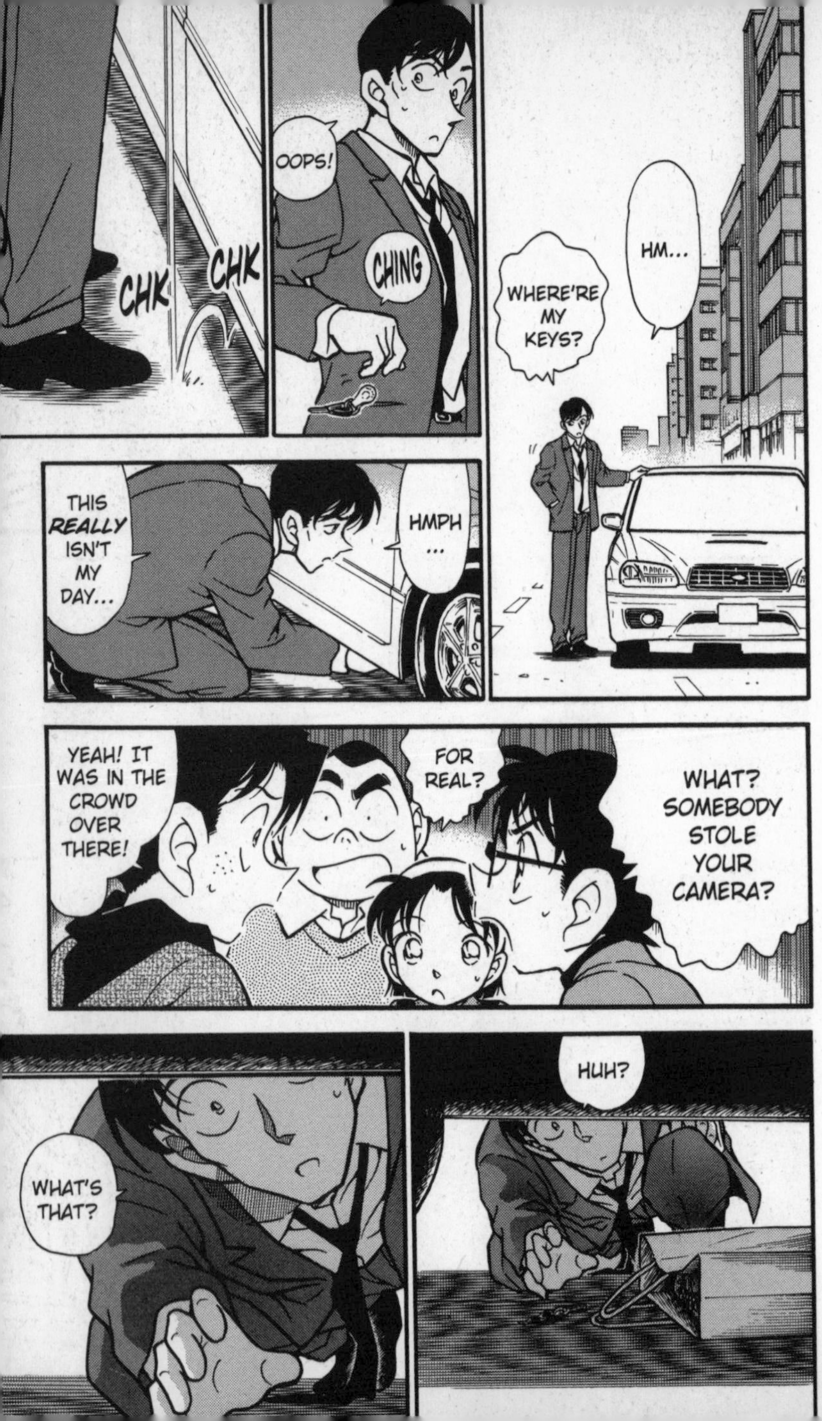
HM...
WHERE'RE MY KEYS?
OOPS!
CHING
CHK CHK
HMPH ...
THIS *REALLY* ISN'T MY DAY...
WHAT? SOMEBODY STOLE YOUR CAMERA?
FOR REAL?
YEAH! IT WAS IN THE CROWD OVER THERE!
HUH?
WHAT'S THAT?

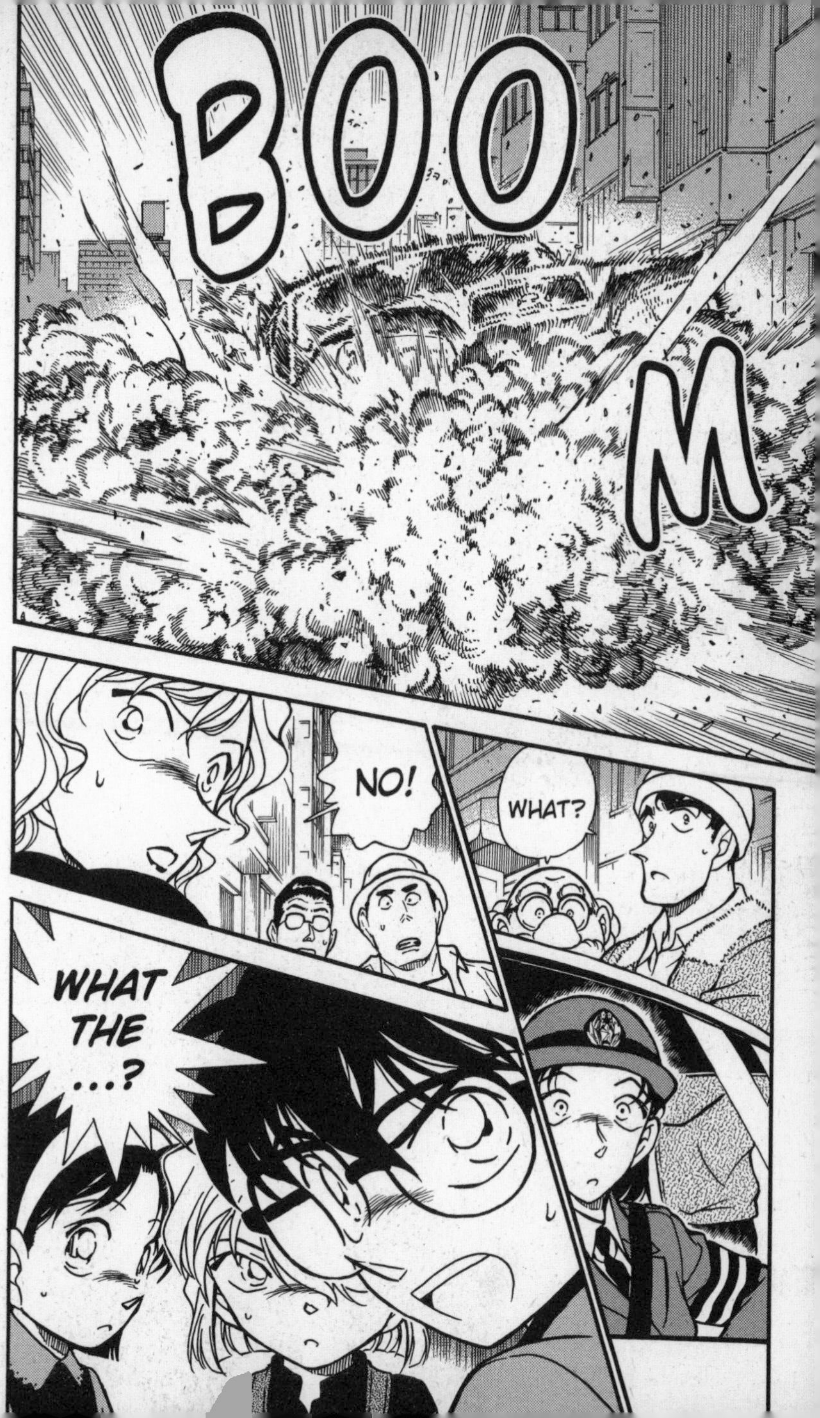
BOOOM
WHAT?
NO!
WHAT THE ...?

FILE 6: VIDEO EVIDENCE

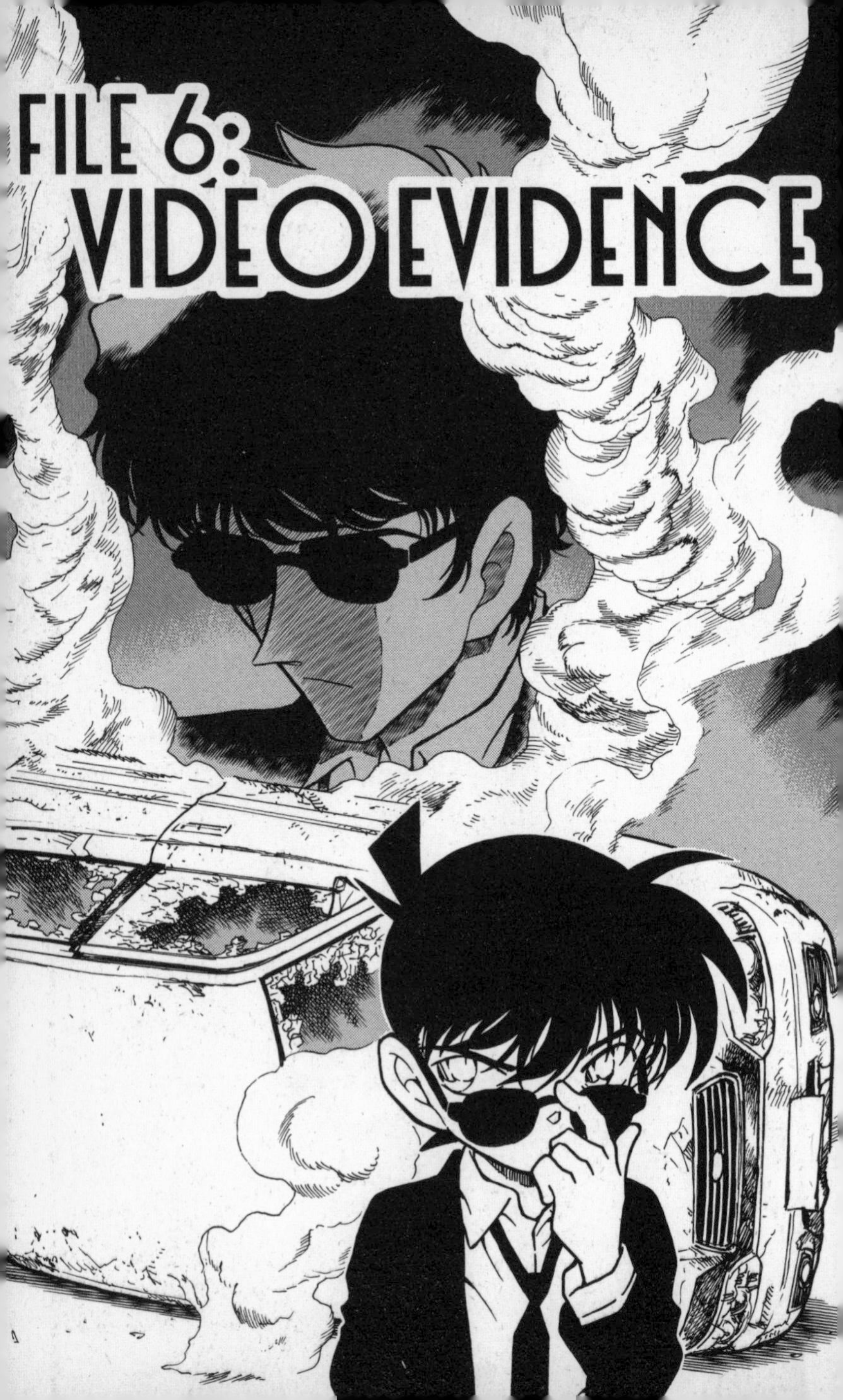

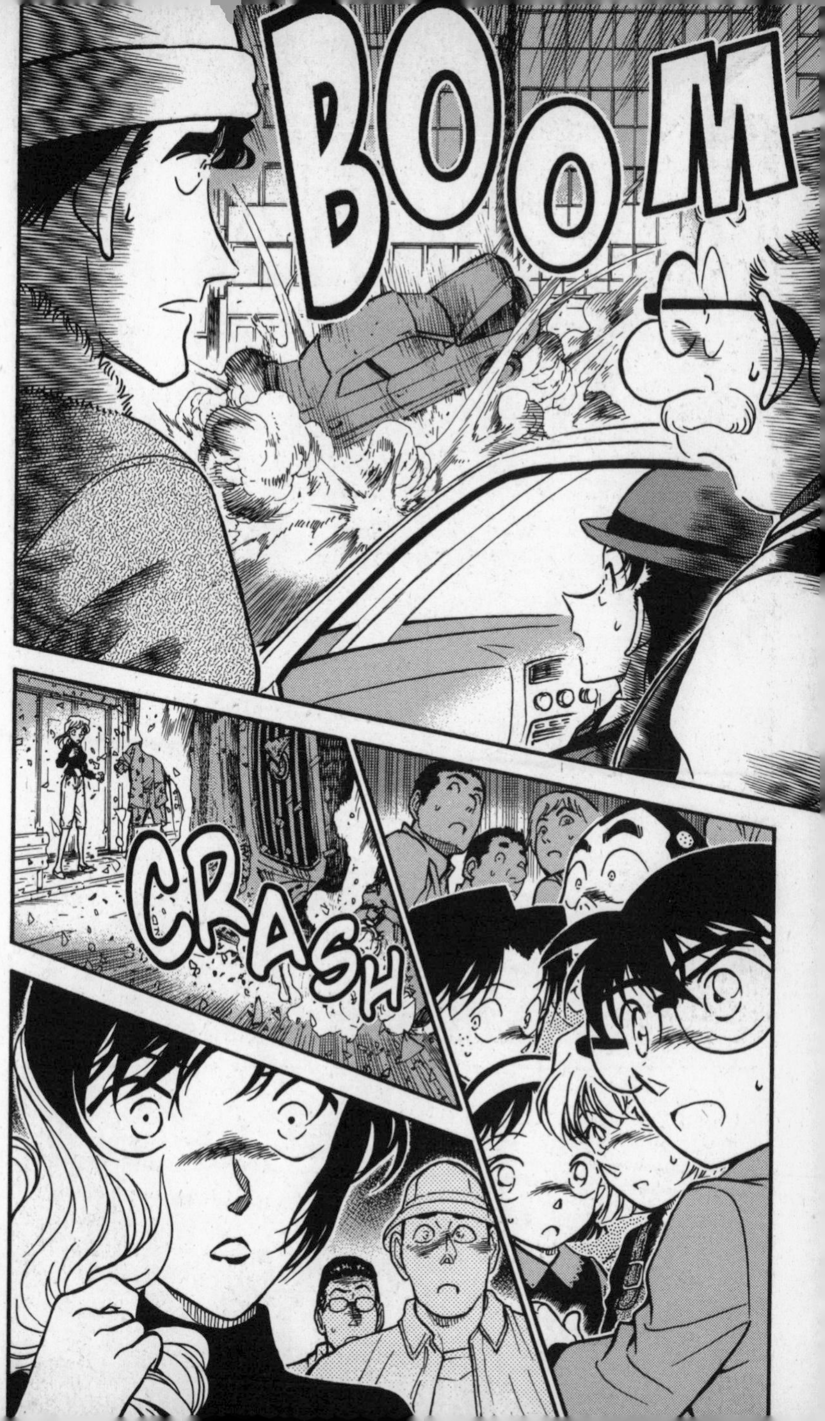
BOOM
CRASH

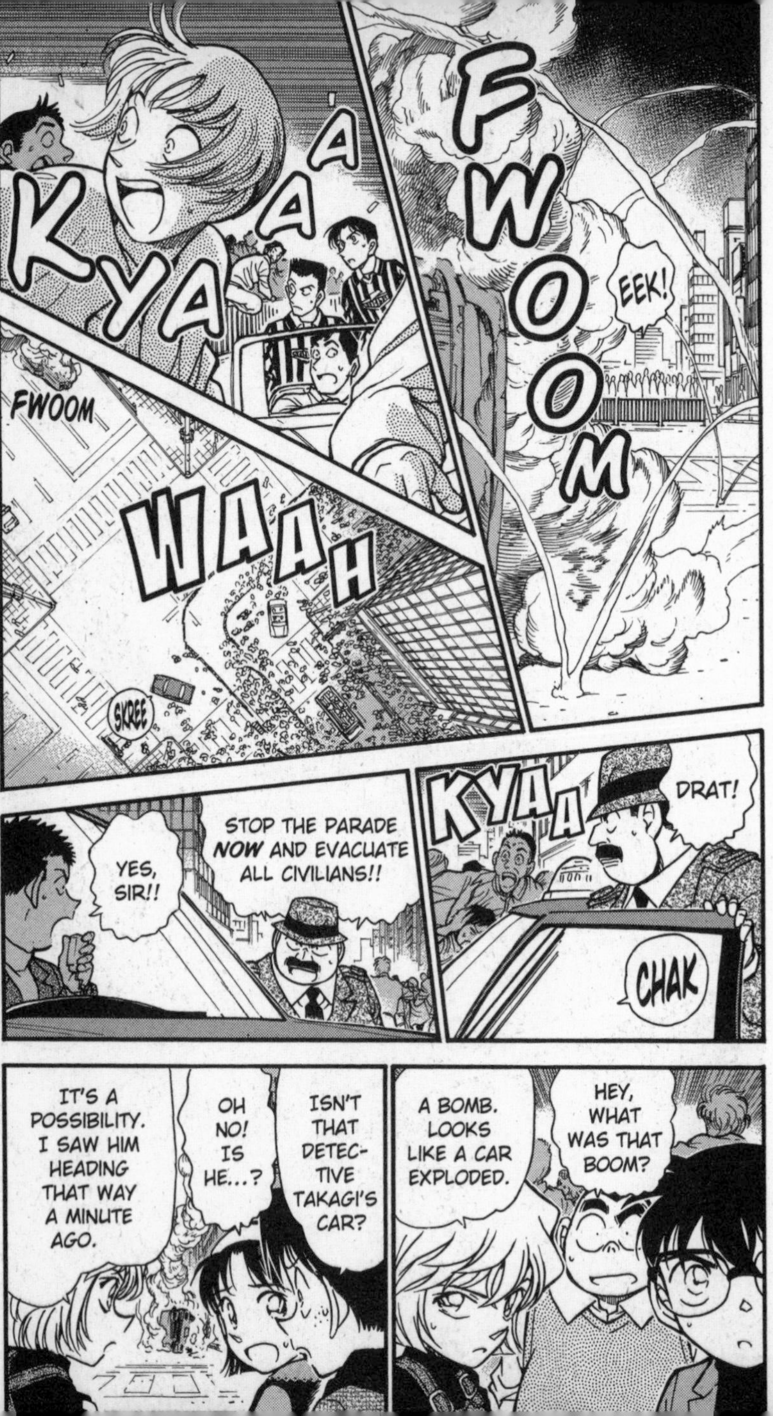
FWOOOM
EEK!
KYAAAA
FWOOM
WAAAH
SKREE
KYAAA
DRAT!
CHAK
STOP THE PARADE NOW AND EVACUATE ALL CIVILIANS!!
YES, SIR!!
HEY, WHAT WAS THAT BOOM?
A BOMB. LOOKS LIKE A CAR EXPLODED.
ISN'T THAT DETECTIVE TAKAGI'S CAR?
OH NO! IS HE...?
IT'S A POSSIBILITY. I SAW HIM HEADING THAT WAY A MINUTE AGO.

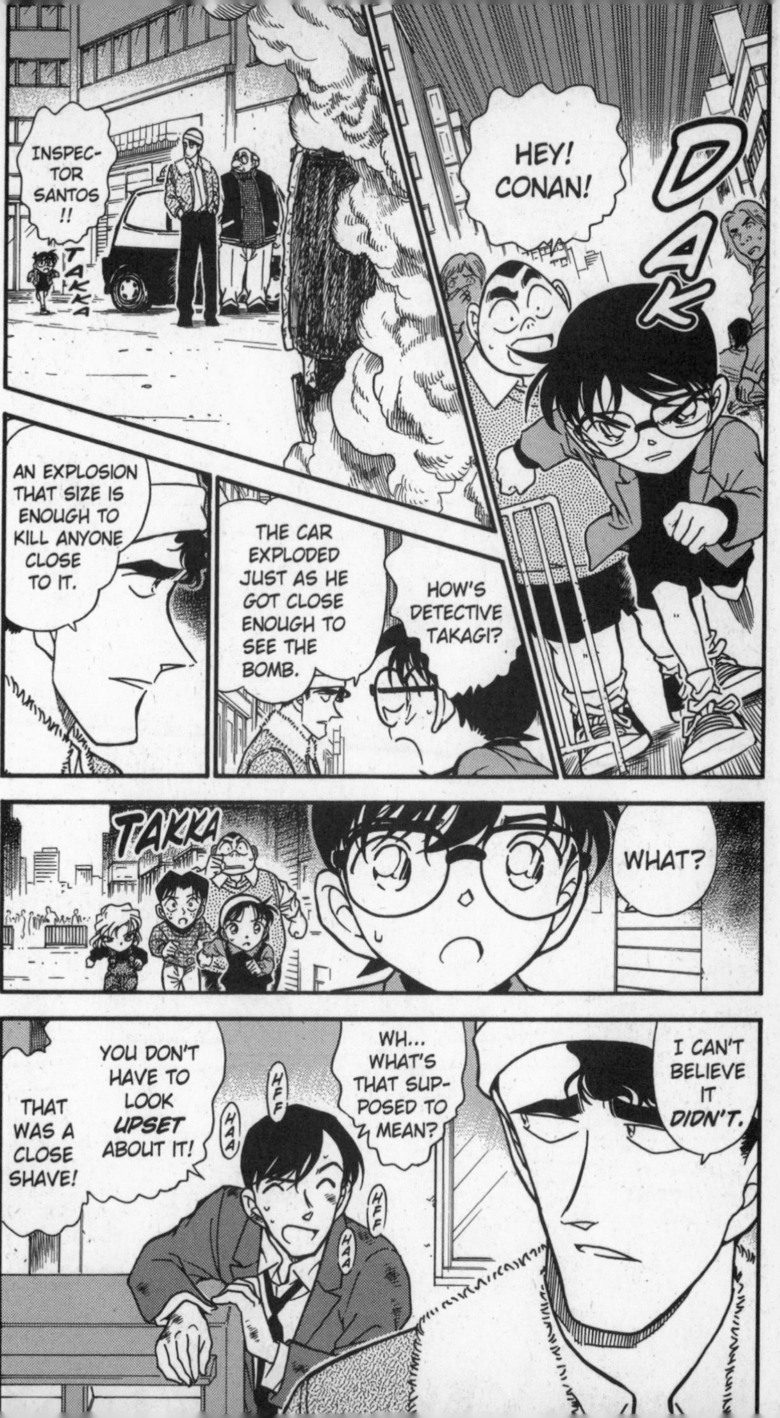
DAK
HEY! CONAN!
INSPECTOR SANTOS !!
TAKKA
HOW'S DETECTIVE TAKAGI?
THE CAR EXPLODED JUST AS HE GOT CLOSE ENOUGH TO SEE THE BOMB.
AN EXPLOSION THAT SIZE IS ENOUGH TO KILL ANYONE CLOSE TO IT.
WHAT?
TAKKA
I CAN'T BELIEVE IT *DIDN'T.*
WH... WHAT'S THAT SUPPOSED TO MEAN?
HFF
HAA
HFF
HAA
YOU DON'T HAVE TO LOOK **UPSET** ABOUT IT!
THAT WAS A CLOSE SHAVE!

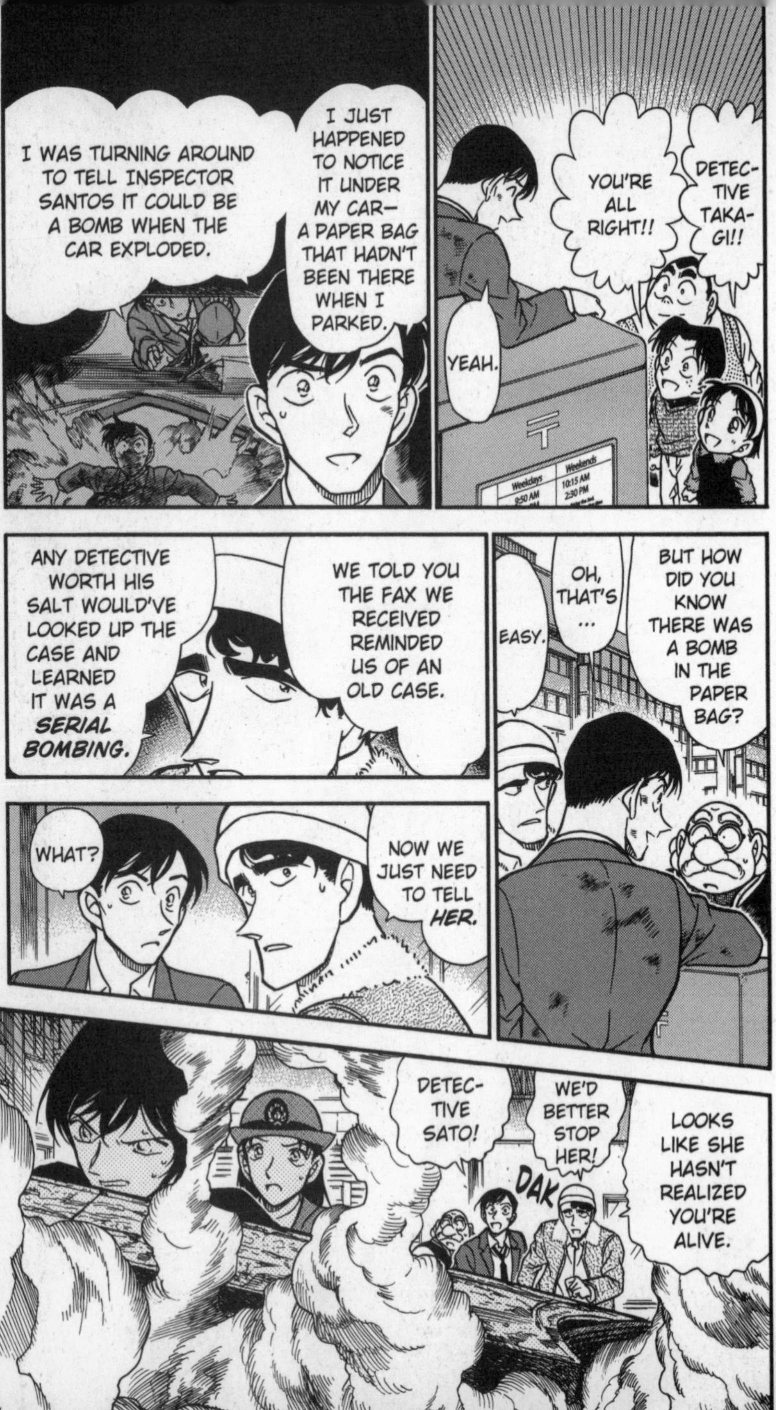

DETEC-TIVE TAKA-GI!!
YOU'RE ALL RIGHT!!
YEAH.
Weekdays
9:50 AM
Weekends
10:15 AM
2:30 PM
I JUST HAPPENED TO NOTICE IT UNDER MY CAR— A PAPER BAG THAT HADN'T BEEN THERE WHEN I PARKED.
I WAS TURNING AROUND TO TELL INSPECTOR SANTOS IT COULD BE A BOMB WHEN THE CAR EXPLODED.
BUT HOW DID YOU KNOW THERE WAS A BOMB IN THE PAPER BAG?
OH, THAT'S ...
EASY.
WE TOLD YOU THE FAX WE RECEIVED REMINDED US OF AN OLD CASE.
ANY DETECTIVE WORTH HIS SALT WOULD'VE LOOKED UP THE CASE AND LEARNED IT WAS A ***SERIAL BOMBING.***
NOW WE JUST NEED TO TELL ***HER.***
WHAT?
LOOKS LIKE SHE HASN'T REALIZED YOU'RE ALIVE.
WE'D BETTER STOP HER!
DETEC-TIVE SATO!
DAK

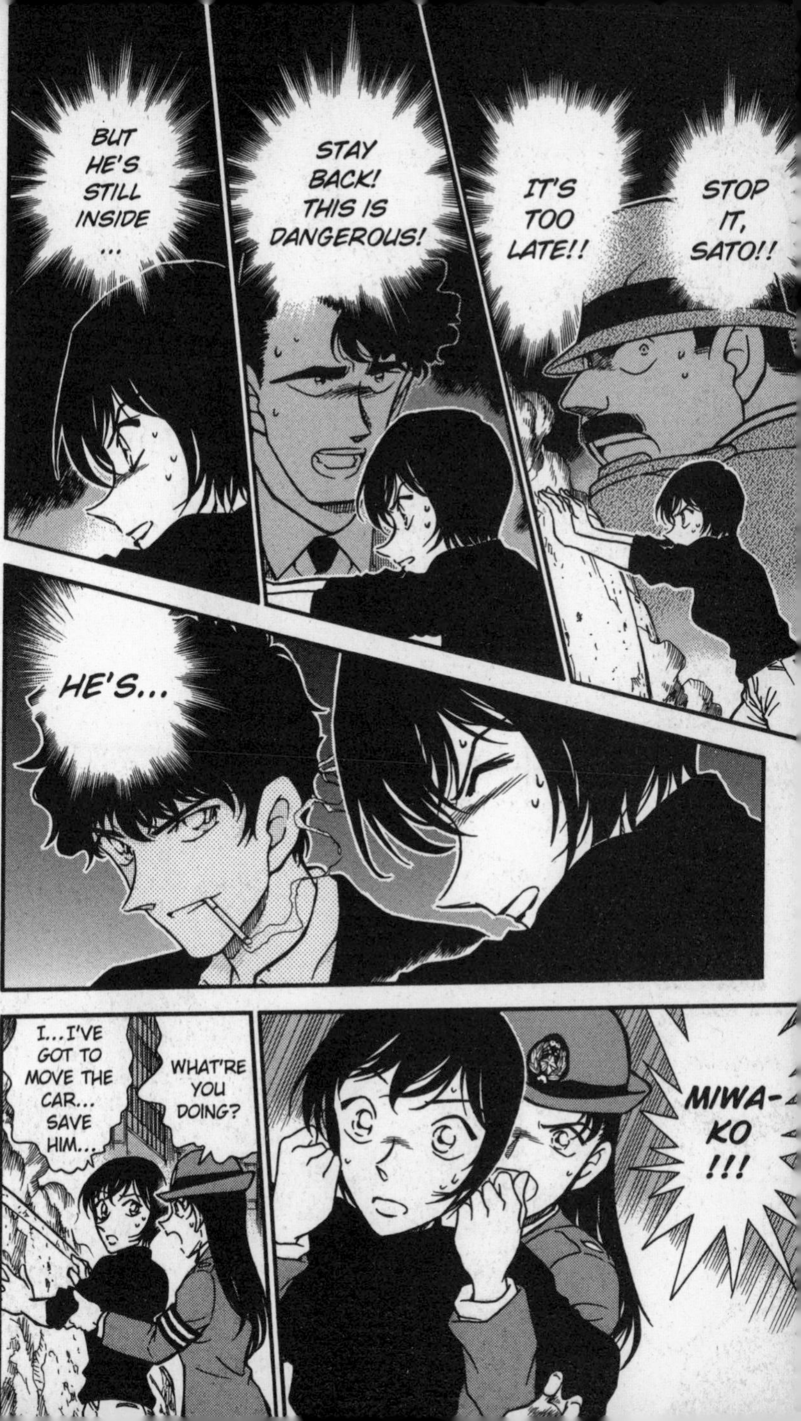
STOP IT, SATO!!
IT'S TOO LATE!!
STAY BACK! THIS IS DANGEROUS!
BUT HE'S STILL INSIDE...
HE'S...
MIWAKO!!!
WHAT'RE YOU DOING?
I...I'VE GOT TO MOVE THE CAR... SAVE HIM...

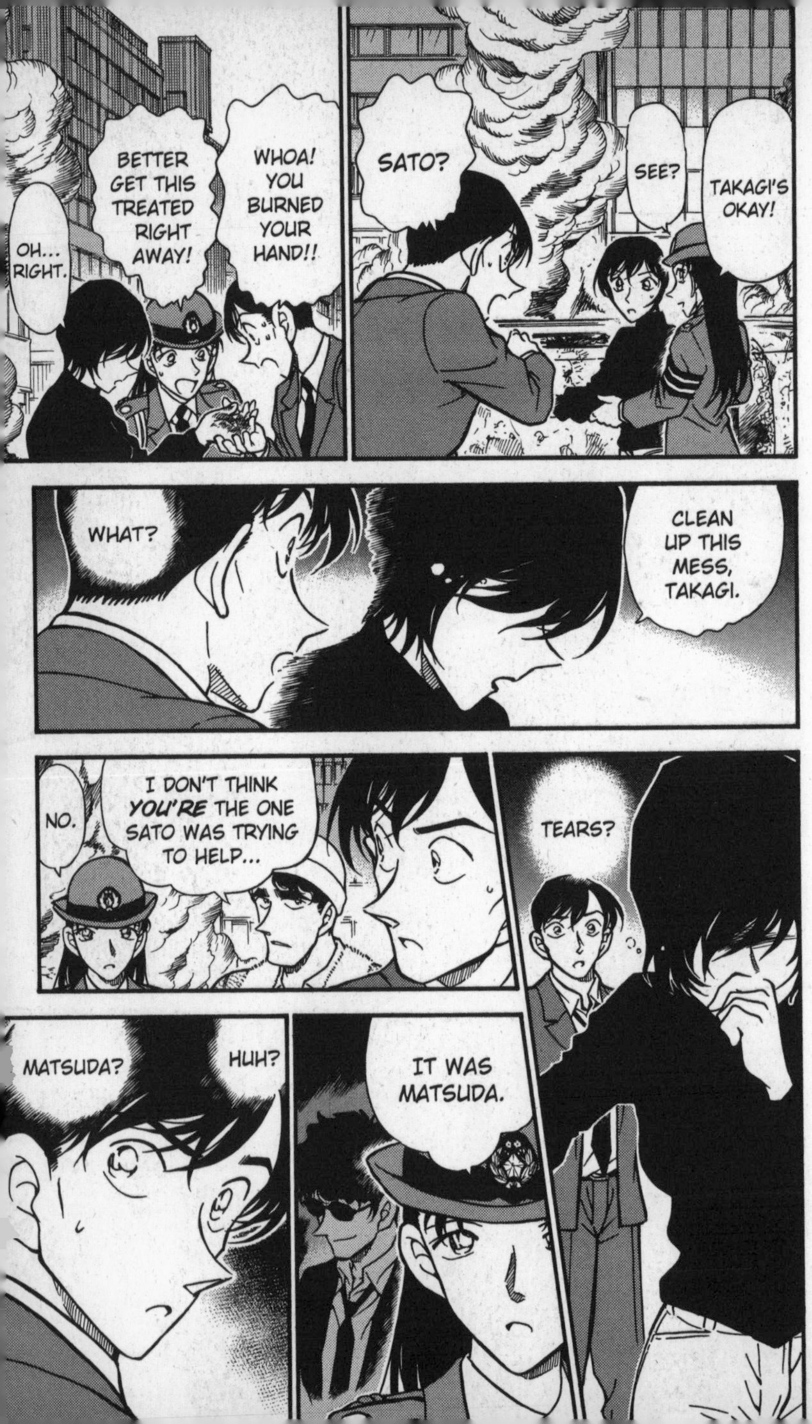
TAKAGI'S OKAY!
SEE?
SATO?
WHOA! YOU BURNED YOUR HAND!!
BETTER GET THIS TREATED RIGHT AWAY!
OH... RIGHT.
CLEAN UP THIS MESS, TAKAGI.
WHAT?
TEARS?
I DON'T THINK *YOU'RE* THE ONE SATO WAS TRYING TO HELP...
NO.
IT WAS MATSUDA.
HUH?
MATSUDA?

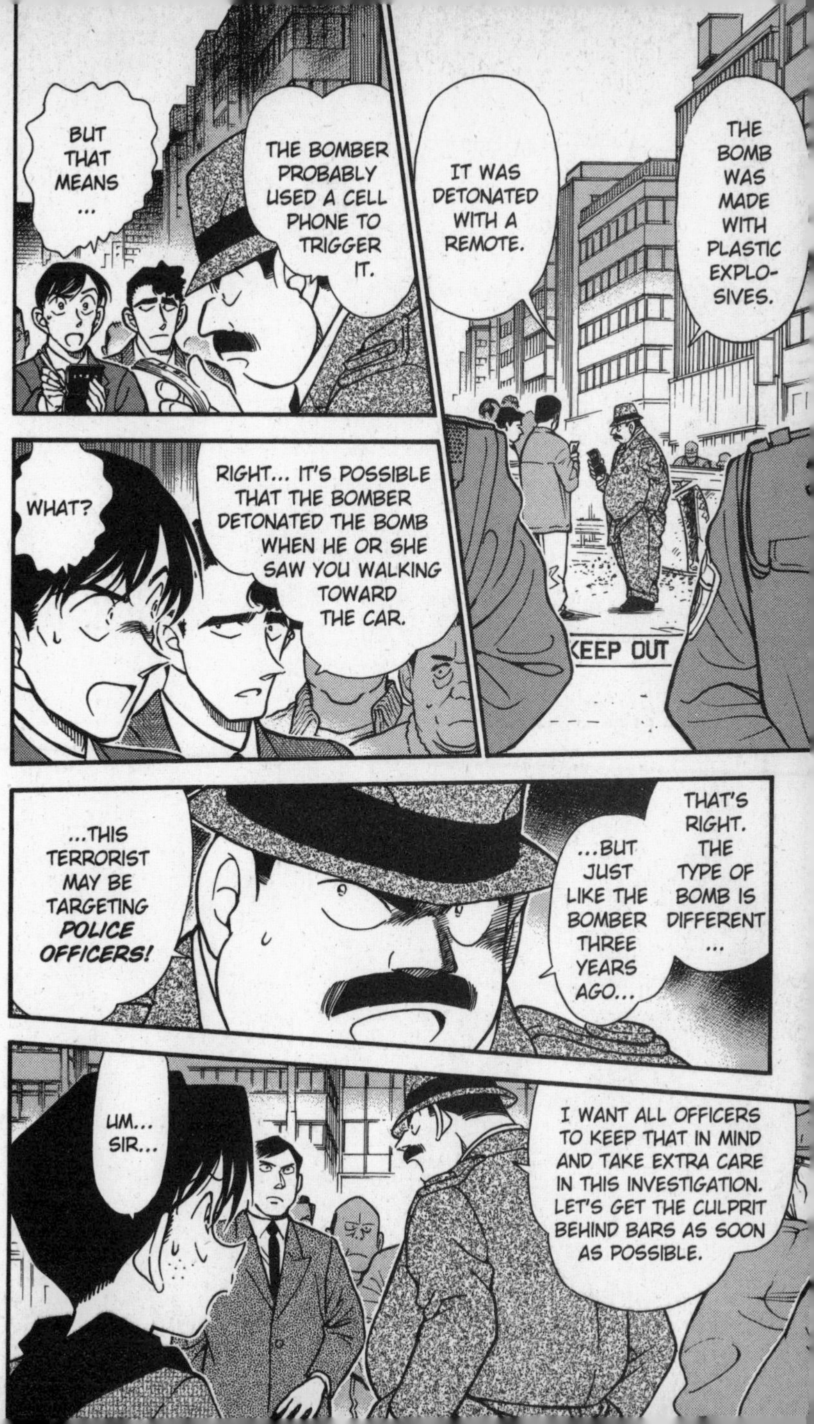
THE BOMB WAS MADE WITH PLASTIC EXPLO-SIVES.
IT WAS DETONATED WITH A REMOTE.
KEEP OUT
THE BOMBER PROBABLY USED A CELL PHONE TO TRIGGER IT.
BUT THAT MEANS ...
RIGHT... IT'S POSSIBLE THAT THE BOMBER DETONATED THE BOMB WHEN HE OR SHE SAW YOU WALKING TOWARD THE CAR.
WHAT?
THAT'S RIGHT. THE TYPE OF BOMB IS DIFFERENT ...
...BUT JUST LIKE THE BOMBER THREE YEARS AGO...
...THIS TERRORIST MAY BE TARGETING POLICE OFFICERS!
I WANT ALL OFFICERS TO KEEP THAT IN MIND AND TAKE EXTRA CARE IN THIS INVESTIGATION. LET'S GET THE CULPRIT BEHIND BARS AS SOON AS POSSIBLE.
UM... SIR...

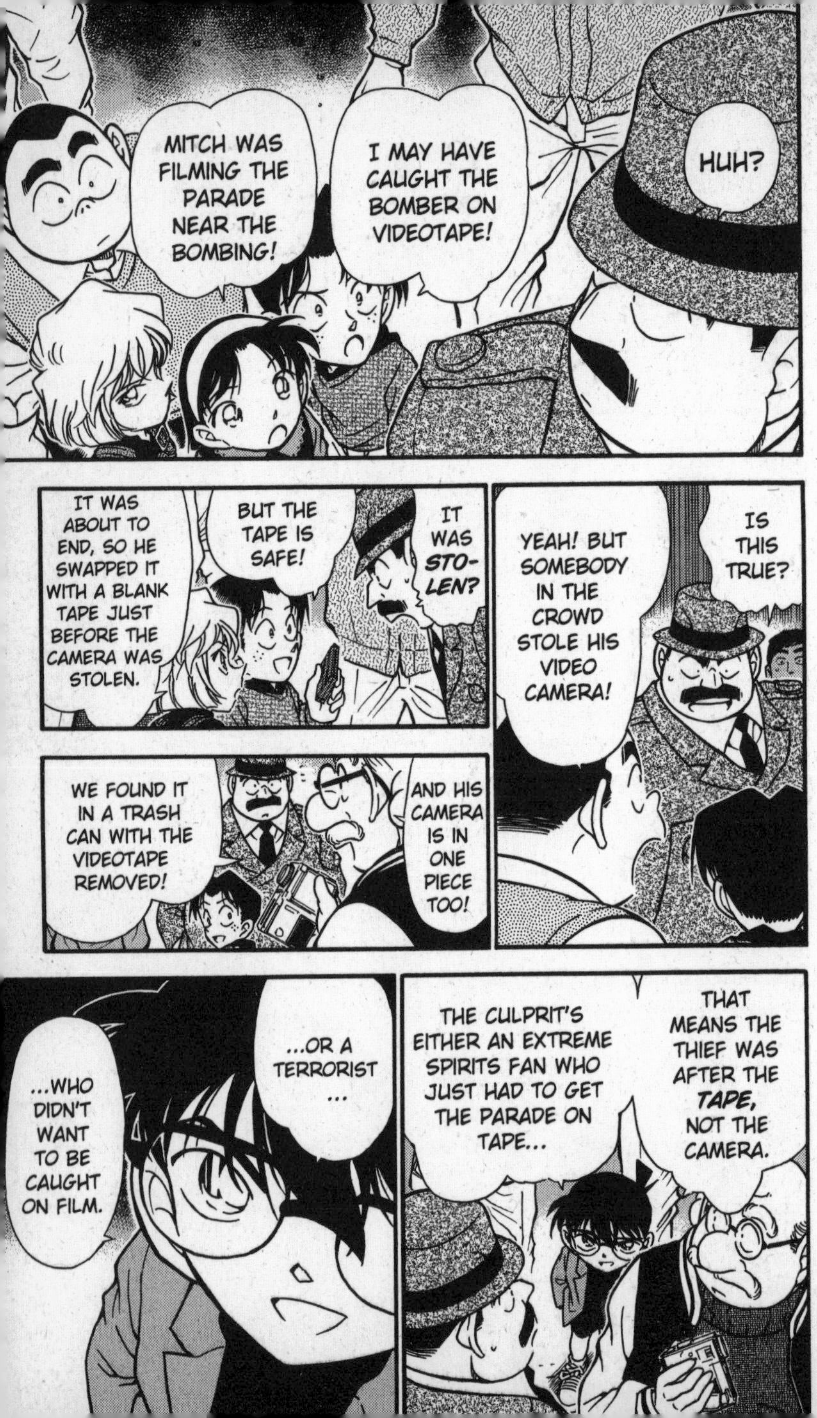
HUH?
I MAY HAVE CAUGHT THE BOMBER ON VIDEOTAPE!
MITCH WAS FILMING THE PARADE NEAR THE BOMBING!
IS THIS TRUE?
YEAH! BUT SOMEBODY IN THE CROWD STOLE HIS VIDEO CAMERA!
IT WAS *STOLEN?*
BUT THE TAPE IS SAFE!
IT WAS ABOUT TO END, SO HE SWAPPED IT WITH A BLANK TAPE JUST BEFORE THE CAMERA WAS STOLEN.
AND HIS CAMERA IS IN ONE PIECE TOO!
WE FOUND IT IN A TRASH CAN WITH THE VIDEOTAPE REMOVED!
THAT MEANS THE THIEF WAS AFTER THE *TAPE,* NOT THE CAMERA.
THE CULPRIT'S EITHER AN EXTREME SPIRITS FAN WHO JUST HAD TO GET THE PARADE ON TAPE...
...OR A TERRORIST ...
...WHO DIDN'T WANT TO BE CAUGHT ON FILM.

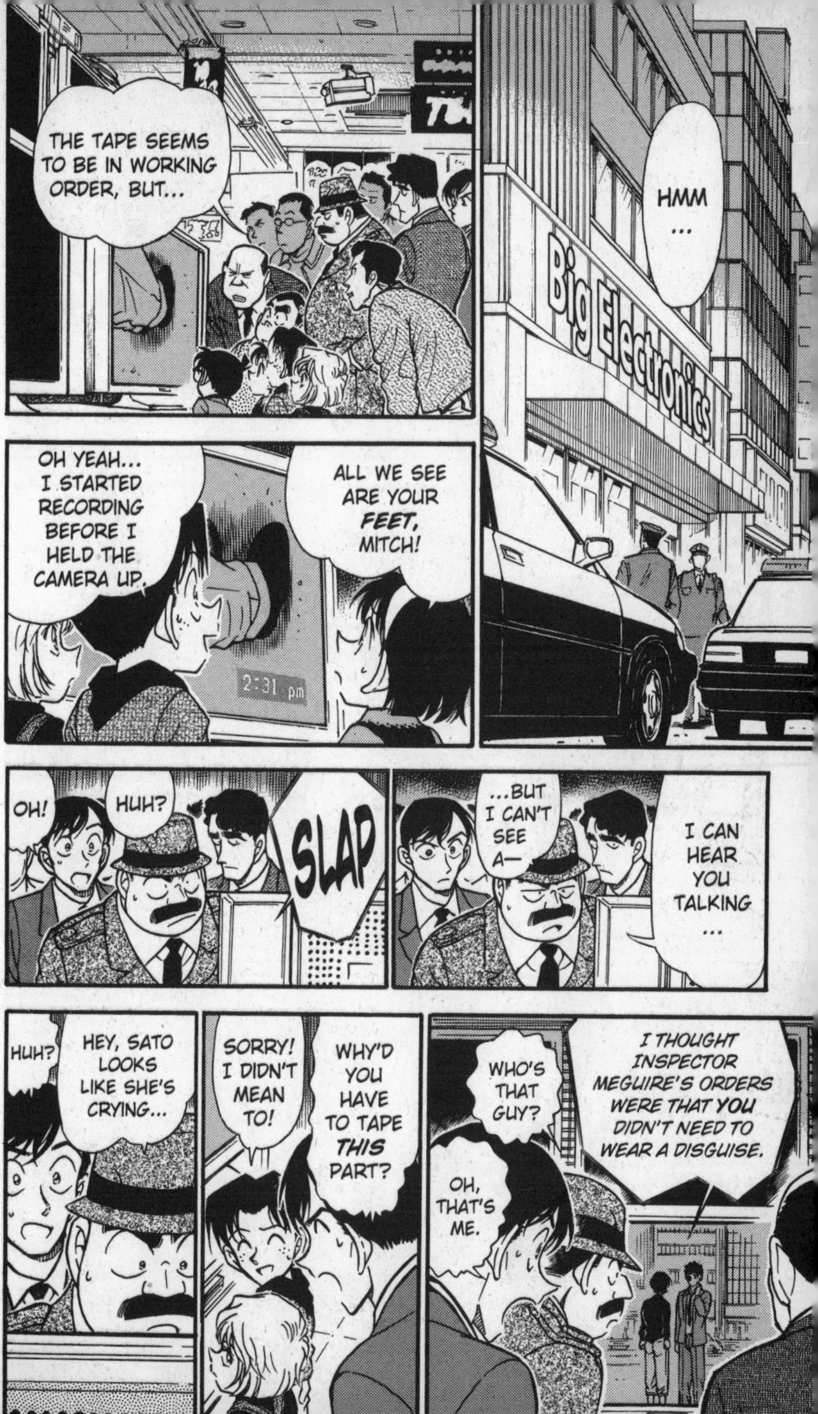
HMM ...
Big Electronics
THE TAPE SEEMS TO BE IN WORKING ORDER, BUT...
ALL WE SEE ARE YOUR *FEET*, MITCH!
OH YEAH... I STARTED RECORDING BEFORE I HELD THE CAMERA UP.
2:31 pm
I CAN HEAR YOU TALKING ...
...BUT I CAN'T SEE A—
SLAP
HUH?
OH!
I THOUGHT INSPECTOR MEGUIRE'S ORDERS WERE THAT **YOU** *DIDN'T NEED TO WEAR A DISGUISE.*
WHO'S THAT GUY?
OH, THAT'S ME.
WHY'D YOU HAVE TO TAPE *THIS* PART?
SORRY! I DIDN'T MEAN TO!
HEY, SATO LOOKS LIKE SHE'S CRYING...
HUH?

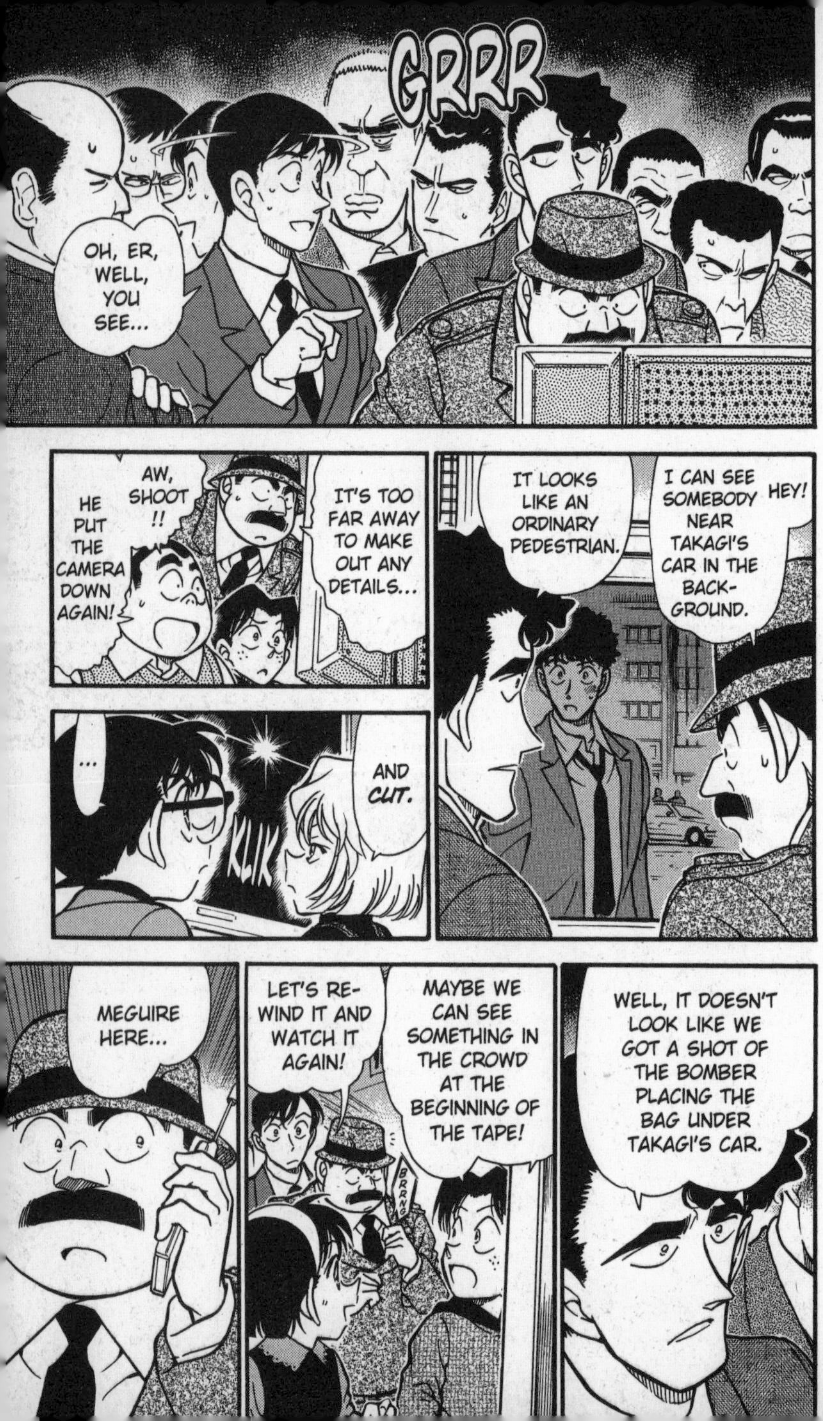
GRRR
OH, ER, WELL, YOU SEE...
HEY!
I CAN SEE SOMEBODY NEAR TAKAGI'S CAR IN THE BACK-GROUND.
IT LOOKS LIKE AN ORDINARY PEDESTRIAN.
IT'S TOO FAR AWAY TO MAKE OUT ANY DETAILS...
AW, SHOOT !!
HE PUT THE CAMERA DOWN AGAIN!
AND CUT.
KLIK
...
WELL, IT DOESN'T LOOK LIKE WE GOT A SHOT OF THE BOMBER PLACING THE BAG UNDER TAKAGI'S CAR.
MAYBE WE CAN SEE SOMETHING IN THE CROWD AT THE BEGINNING OF THE TAPE!
LET'S RE-WIND IT AND WATCH IT AGAIN!
BRRNG
MEGUIRE HERE...

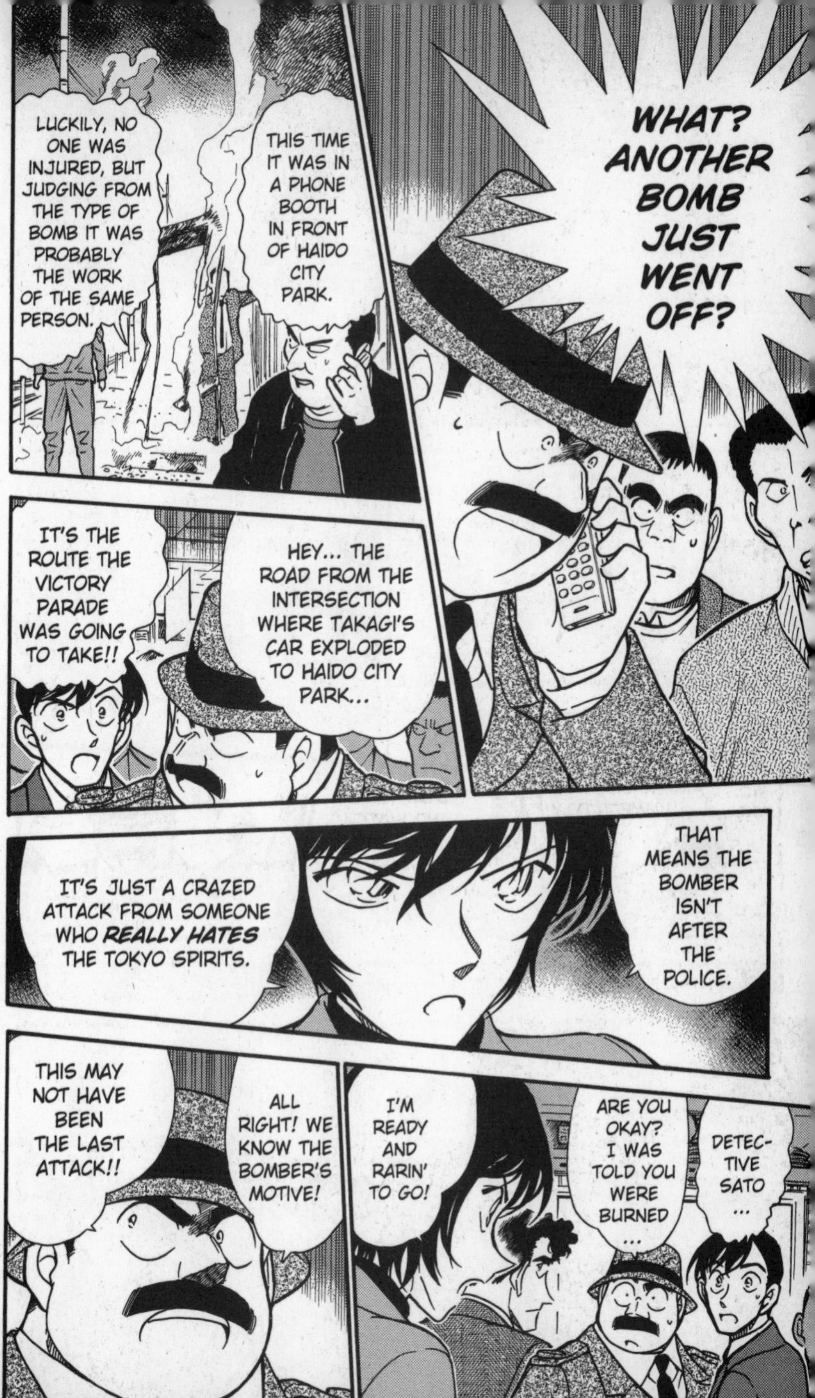
WHAT? ANOTHER BOMB JUST WENT OFF?
THIS TIME IT WAS IN A PHONE BOOTH IN FRONT OF HAIDO CITY PARK.
LUCKILY, NO ONE WAS INJURED, BUT JUDGING FROM THE TYPE OF BOMB IT WAS PROBABLY THE WORK OF THE SAME PERSON.
HEY... THE ROAD FROM THE INTERSECTION WHERE TAKAGI'S CAR EXPLODED TO HAIDO CITY PARK...
IT'S THE ROUTE THE VICTORY PARADE WAS GOING TO TAKE!!
THAT MEANS THE BOMBER ISN'T AFTER THE POLICE.
IT'S JUST A CRAZED ATTACK FROM SOMEONE WHO ***REALLY HATES*** THE TOKYO SPIRITS.
DETEC-TIVE SATO ...
ARE YOU OKAY? I WAS TOLD YOU WERE BURNED ...
I'M READY AND RARIN' TO GO!
ALL RIGHT! WE KNOW THE BOMBER'S MOTIVE!
THIS MAY NOT HAVE BEEN THE LAST ATTACK!!

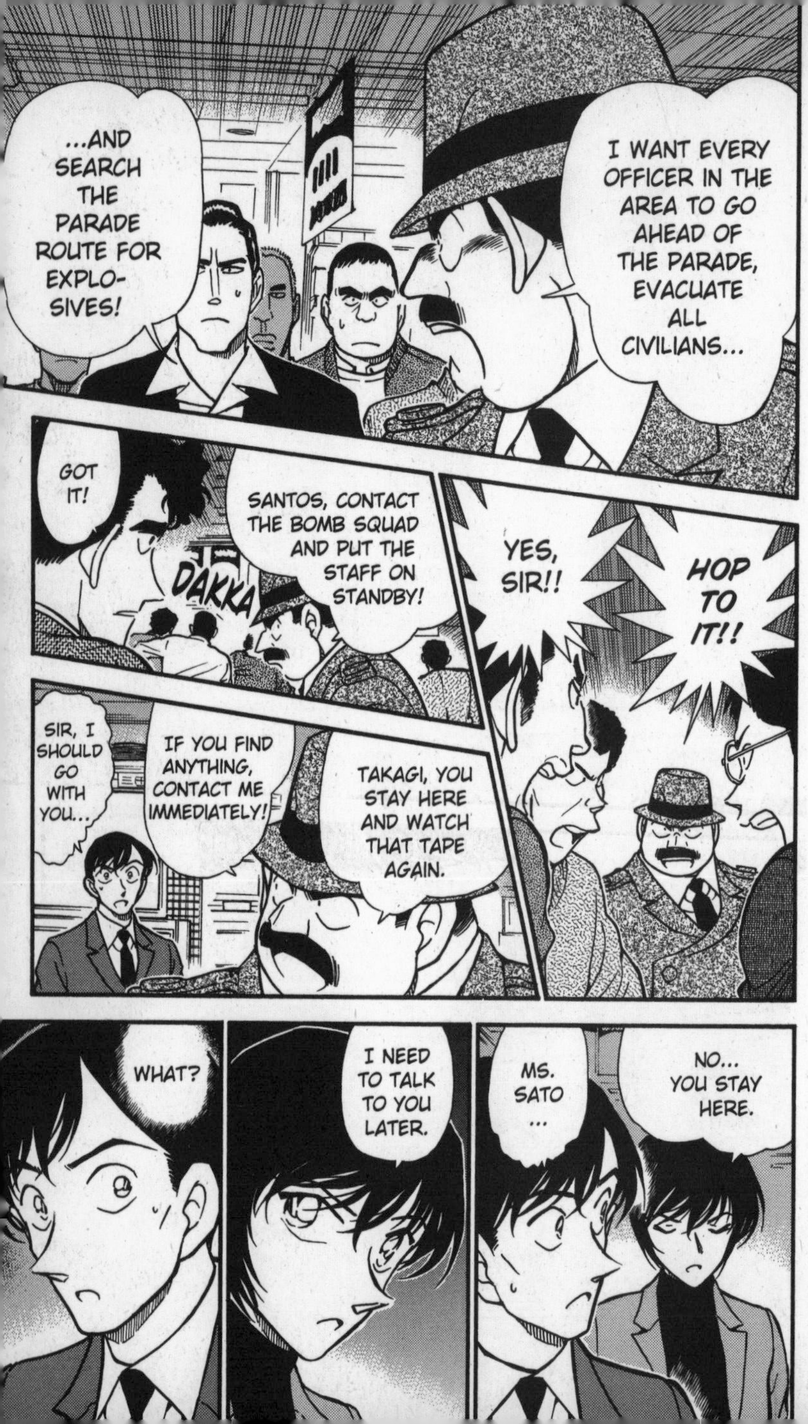
I WANT EVERY OFFICER IN THE AREA TO GO AHEAD OF THE PARADE, EVACUATE ALL CIVILIANS...
...AND SEARCH THE PARADE ROUTE FOR EXPLO-SIVES!
HOP TO IT!!
YES, SIR!!
SANTOS, CONTACT THE BOMB SQUAD AND PUT THE STAFF ON STANDBY!
DAKKA
GOT IT!
TAKAGI, YOU STAY HERE AND WATCH THAT TAPE AGAIN.
IF YOU FIND ANYTHING, CONTACT ME IMMEDIATELY!
SIR, I SHOULD GO WITH YOU...
NO... YOU STAY HERE.
MS. SATO ...
I NEED TO TALK TO YOU LATER.
WHAT?

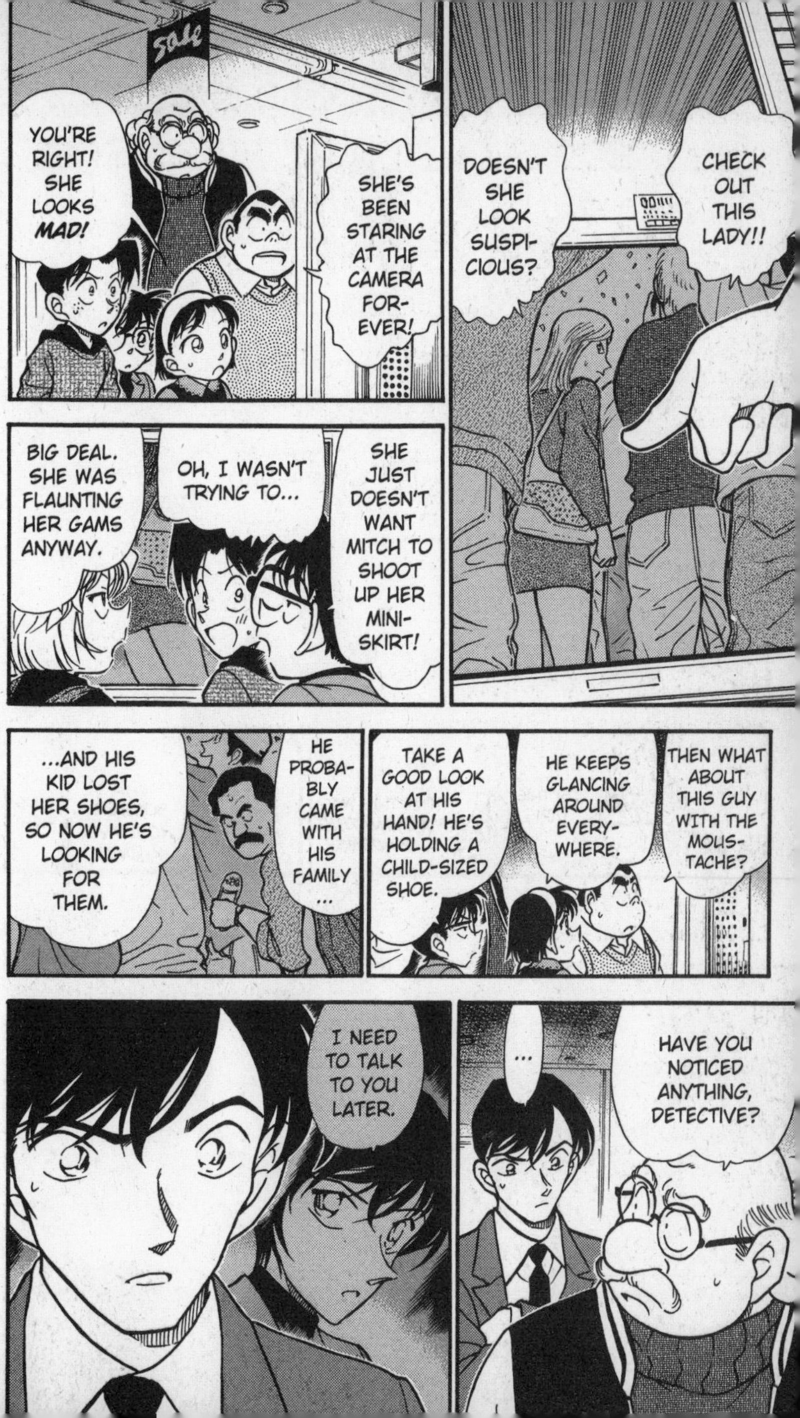
CHECK OUT THIS LADY!!
DOESN'T SHE LOOK SUSPICIOUS?
SHE'S BEEN STARING AT THE CAMERA FOREVER!
YOU'RE RIGHT! SHE LOOKS *MAD!*
SHE JUST DOESN'T WANT MITCH TO SHOOT UP HER MINISKIRT!
OH, I WASN'T TRYING TO...
BIG DEAL. SHE WAS FLAUNTING HER GAMS ANYWAY.
THEN WHAT ABOUT THIS GUY WITH THE MOUSTACHE?
HE KEEPS GLANCING AROUND EVERYWHERE.
TAKE A GOOD LOOK AT HIS HAND! HE'S HOLDING A CHILD-SIZED SHOE.
HE PROBABLY CAME WITH HIS FAMILY...
...AND HIS KID LOST HER SHOES, SO NOW HE'S LOOKING FOR THEM.
HAVE YOU NOTICED ANYTHING, DETECTIVE?
...
I NEED TO TALK TO YOU LATER.

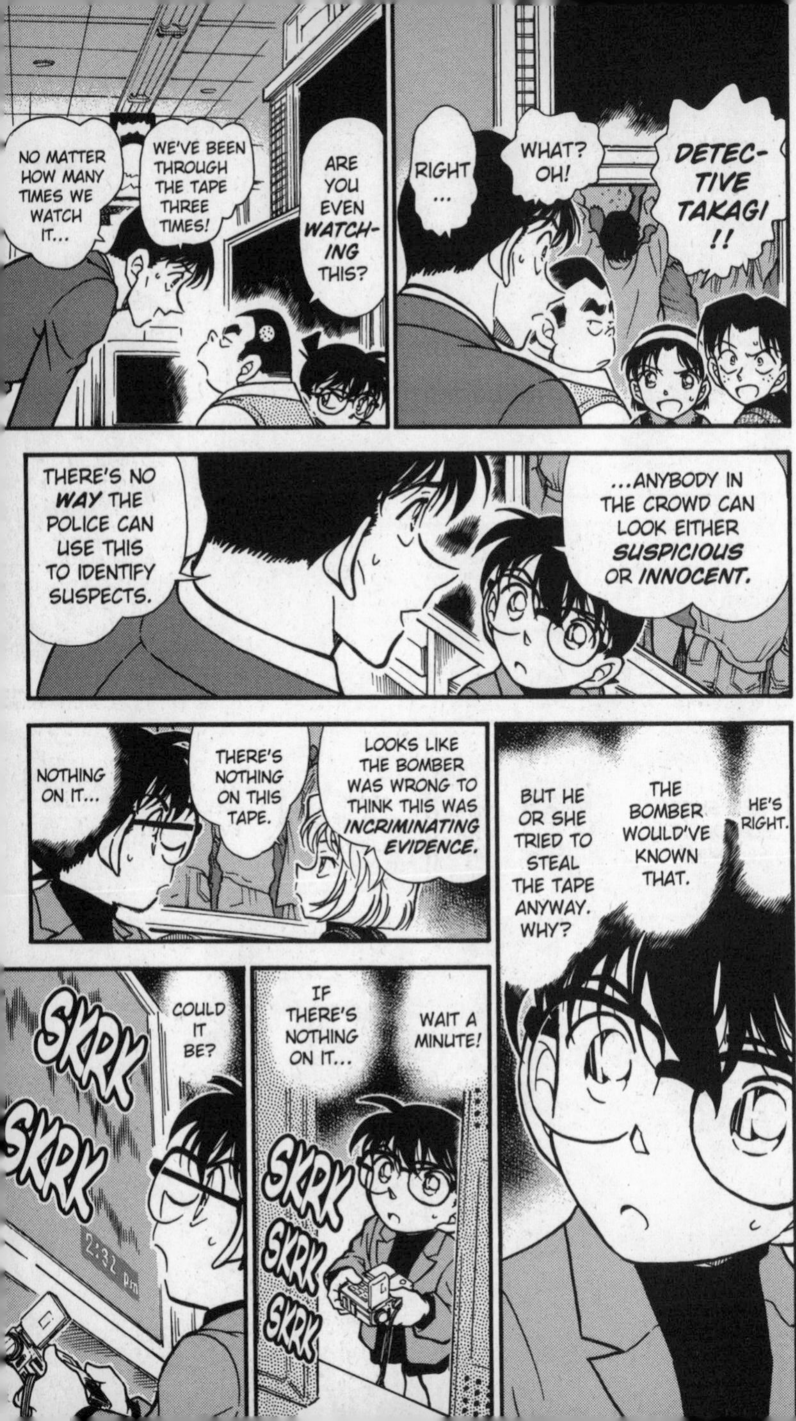
DETECTIVE TAKAGI!!
WHAT? OH!
RIGHT...
ARE YOU EVEN WATCHING THIS?
WE'VE BEEN THROUGH THE TAPE THREE TIMES!
NO MATTER HOW MANY TIMES WE WATCH IT...
...ANYBODY IN THE CROWD CAN LOOK EITHER SUSPICIOUS OR INNOCENT.
THERE'S NO WAY THE POLICE CAN USE THIS TO IDENTIFY SUSPECTS.
HE'S RIGHT.
THE BOMBER WOULD'VE KNOWN THAT.
BUT HE OR SHE TRIED TO STEAL THE TAPE ANYWAY. WHY?
LOOKS LIKE THE BOMBER WAS WRONG TO THINK THIS WAS INCRIMINATING EVIDENCE.
THERE'S NOTHING ON THIS TAPE.
NOTHING ON IT...
WAIT A MINUTE!
IF THERE'S NOTHING ON IT...
SKRK
SKRK
SKRK
COULD IT BE?
SKRK
SKRK
2:32 pm

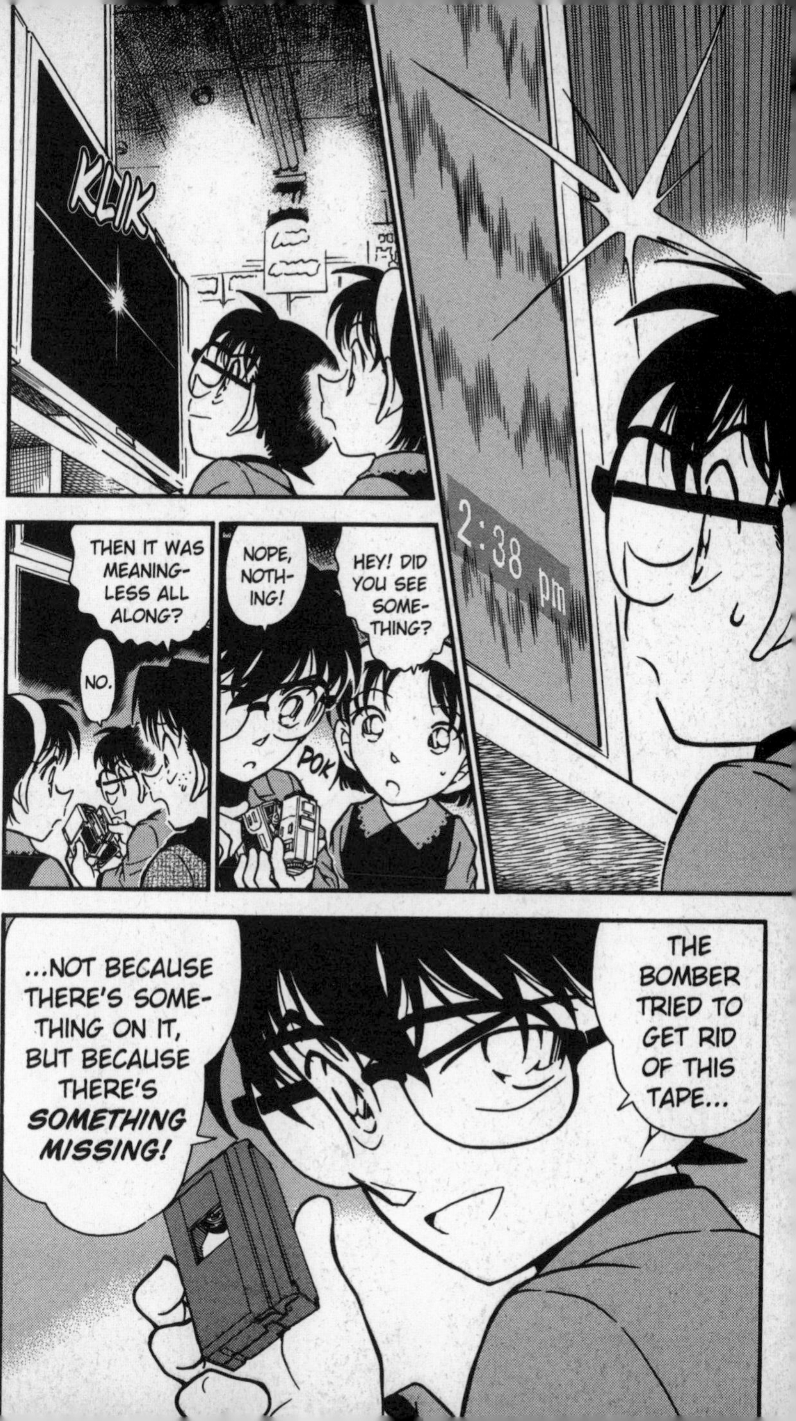
2:38 pm
KLIK
HEY! DID YOU SEE SOME-THING?
NOPE, NOTH-ING!
POK
THEN IT WAS MEANING-LESS ALL ALONG?
NO.
THE BOMBER TRIED TO GET RID OF THIS TAPE...
...NOT BECAUSE THERE'S SOME-THING ON IT, BUT BECAUSE THERE'S *SOMETHING MISSING!*

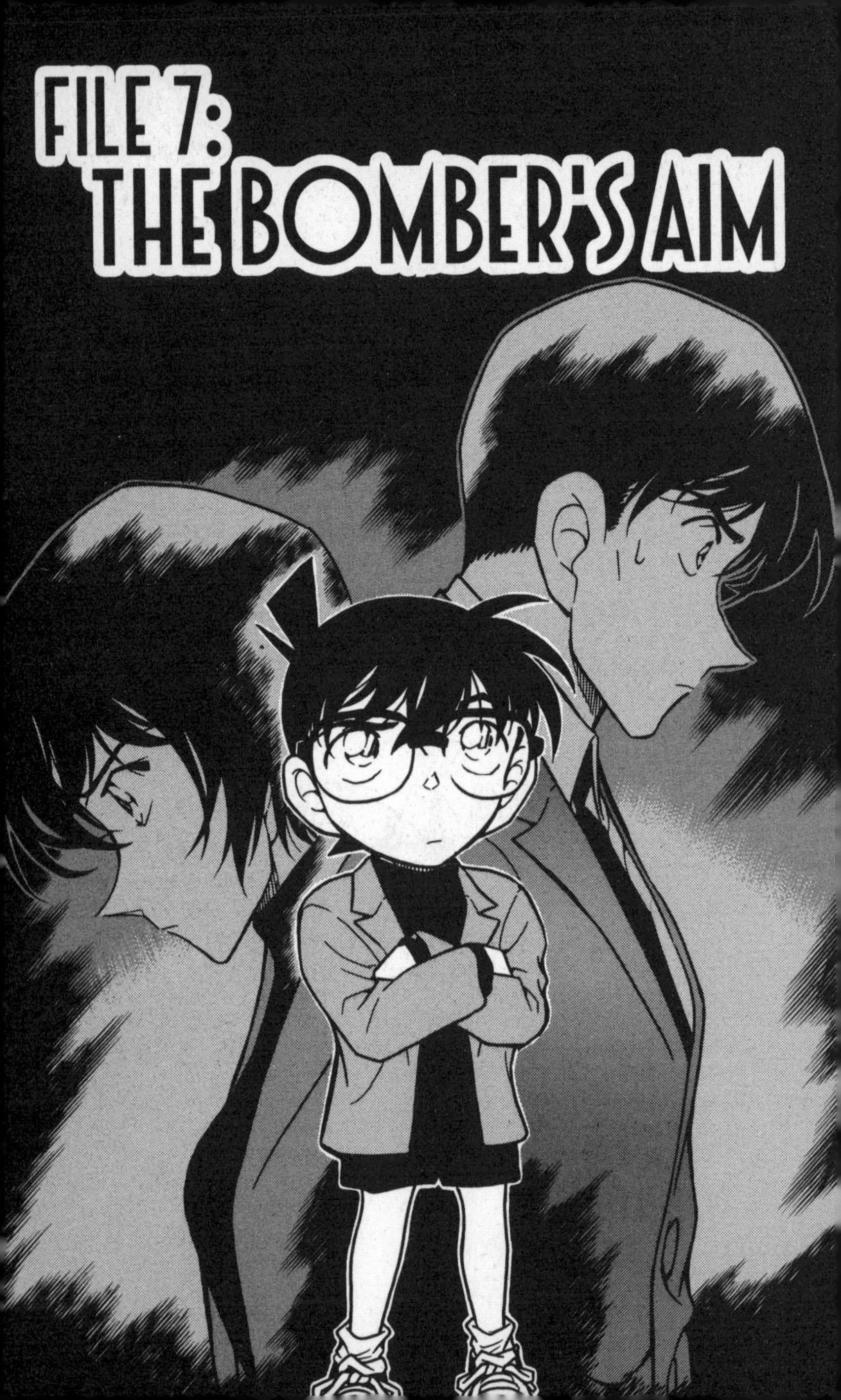
FILE 7:
THE BOMBER'S AIM

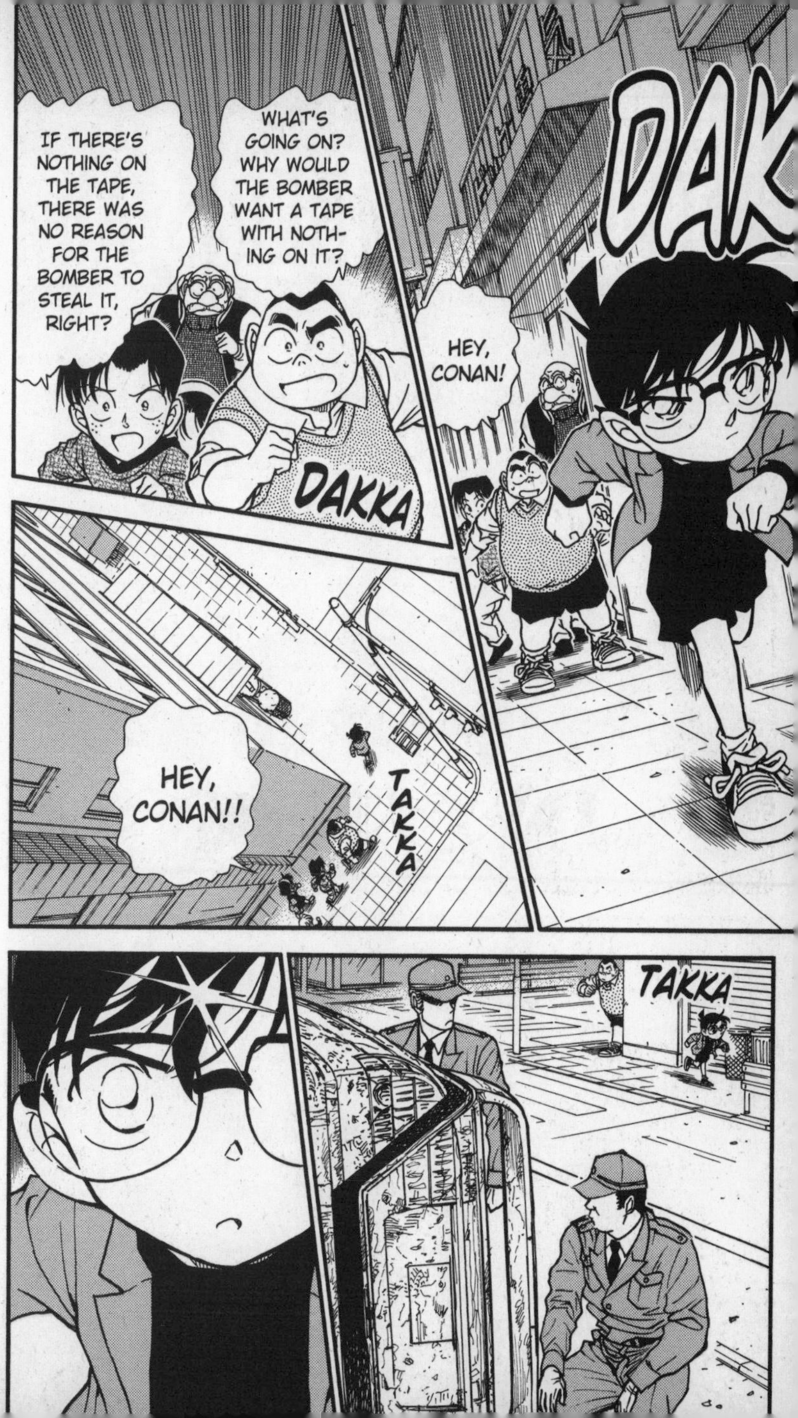
DAK
HEY, CONAN!
WHAT'S GOING ON? WHY WOULD THE BOMBER WANT A TAPE WITH NOTHING ON IT?
IF THERE'S NOTHING ON THE TAPE, THERE WAS NO REASON FOR THE BOMBER TO STEAL IT, RIGHT?
DAKKA
TAKKA
HEY, CONAN!!
TAKKA

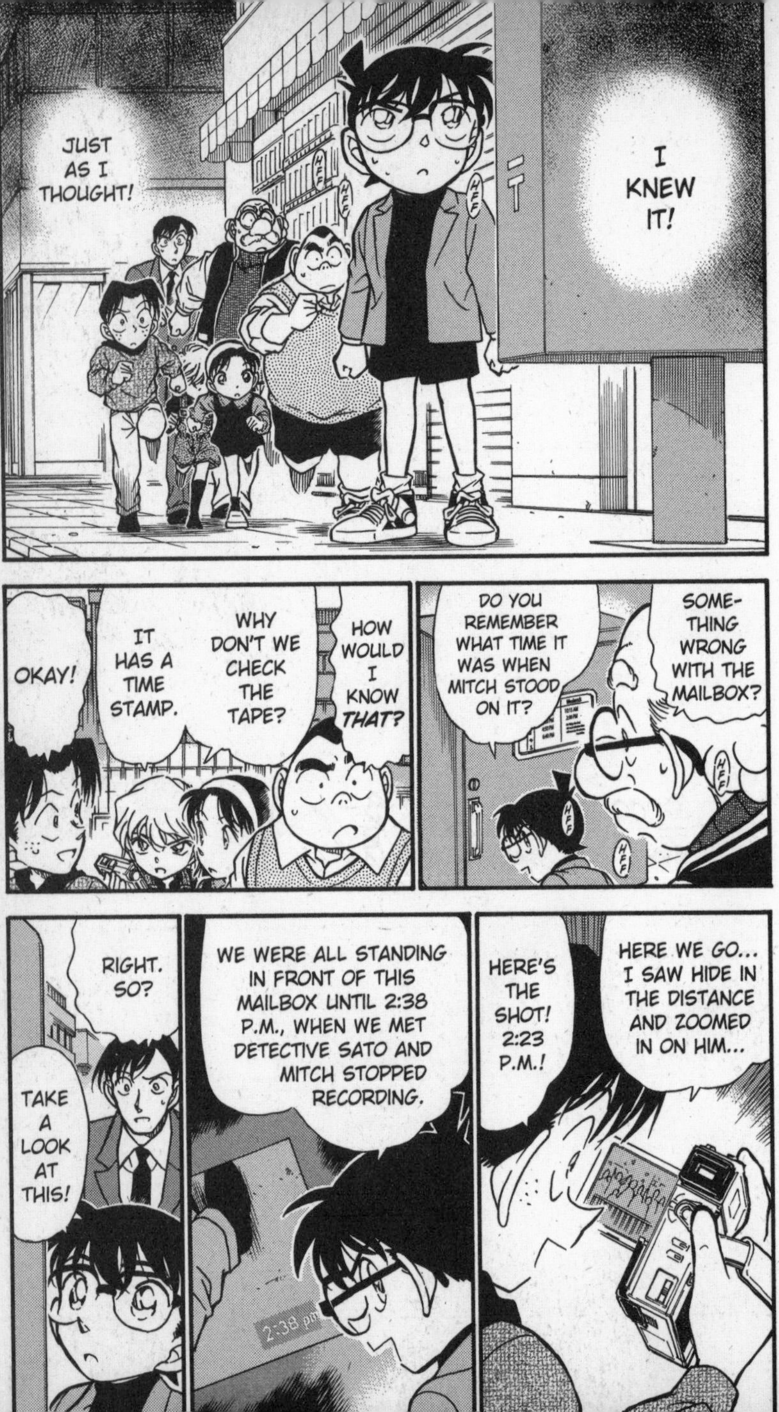

I KNEW IT!
HFF
HFF
HFF
JUST AS I THOUGHT!
SOME-THING WRONG WITH THE MAILBOX?
DO YOU REMEMBER WHAT TIME IT WAS WHEN MITCH STOOD ON IT?
HFF
HFF
HFF
HOW WOULD I KNOW *THAT?*
WHY DON'T WE CHECK THE TAPE?
IT HAS A TIME STAMP.
OKAY!
HERE WE GO... I SAW HIDE IN THE DISTANCE AND ZOOMED IN ON HIM...
HERE'S THE SHOT! 2:23 P.M.!
WE WERE ALL STANDING IN FRONT OF THIS MAILBOX UNTIL 2:38 P.M., WHEN WE MET DETECTIVE SATO AND MITCH STOPPED RECORDING.
2:38 pm
RIGHT. SO?
TAKE A LOOK AT THIS!

ON WEEKENDS THEY COLLECT THE MAIL AROUND 2:30 P.M.

	Weekdays	Weekends
1	9:50 AM	10:15 AM
2	2:20 PM	2:30 PM
3		
4	4:50 PM	
5	6:40 PM	

On Friday the 2nd, 4th mail collection time will move by 60 minutes.
Post Office

THE TIME-TABLE FOR THE MAIL COLLEC-TION!!

WHICH MEANS WE DIDN'T SEE SOMETHING WE SHOULD'VE SEEN, RIGHT?

RIGHT...

IT NEVER CAME TO COLLECT THE MAIL!!

I KNOW! THE MAIL TRUCK!

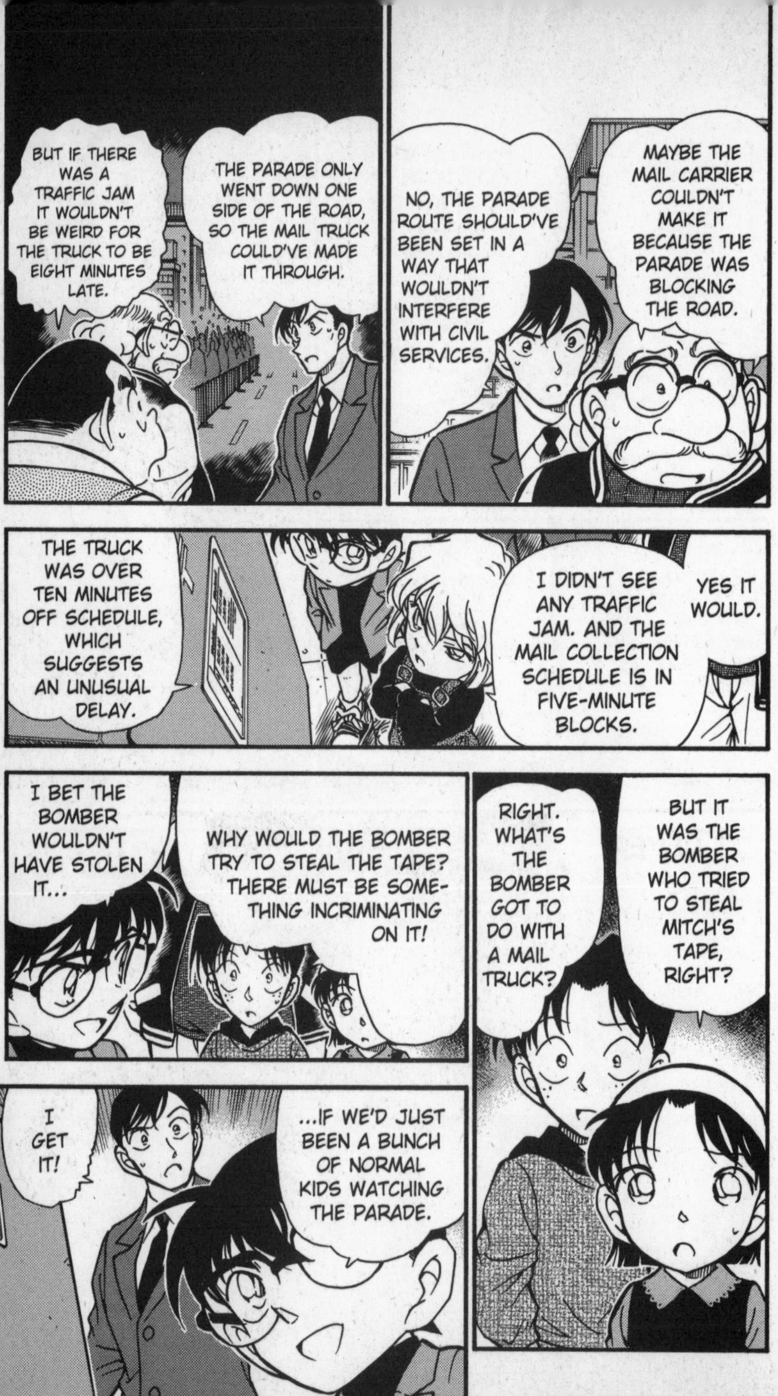
MAYBE THE MAIL CARRIER COULDN'T MAKE IT BECAUSE THE PARADE WAS BLOCKING THE ROAD.
NO, THE PARADE ROUTE SHOULD'VE BEEN SET IN A WAY THAT WOULDN'T INTERFERE WITH CIVIL SERVICES.
THE PARADE ONLY WENT DOWN ONE SIDE OF THE ROAD, SO THE MAIL TRUCK COULD'VE MADE IT THROUGH.
BUT IF THERE WAS A TRAFFIC JAM IT WOULDN'T BE WEIRD FOR THE TRUCK TO BE EIGHT MINUTES LATE.
YES IT WOULD.
I DIDN'T SEE ANY TRAFFIC JAM. AND THE MAIL COLLECTION SCHEDULE IS IN FIVE-MINUTE BLOCKS.
THE TRUCK WAS OVER TEN MINUTES OFF SCHEDULE, WHICH SUGGESTS AN UNUSUAL DELAY.
BUT IT WAS THE BOMBER WHO TRIED TO STEAL MITCH'S TAPE, RIGHT?
RIGHT. WHAT'S THE BOMBER GOT TO DO WITH A MAIL TRUCK?
WHY WOULD THE BOMBER TRY TO STEAL THE TAPE? THERE MUST BE SOMETHING INCRIMINATING ON IT!
I BET THE BOMBER WOULDN'T HAVE STOLEN IT...
...IF WE'D JUST BEEN A BUNCH OF NORMAL KIDS WATCHING THE PARADE.
I GET IT!

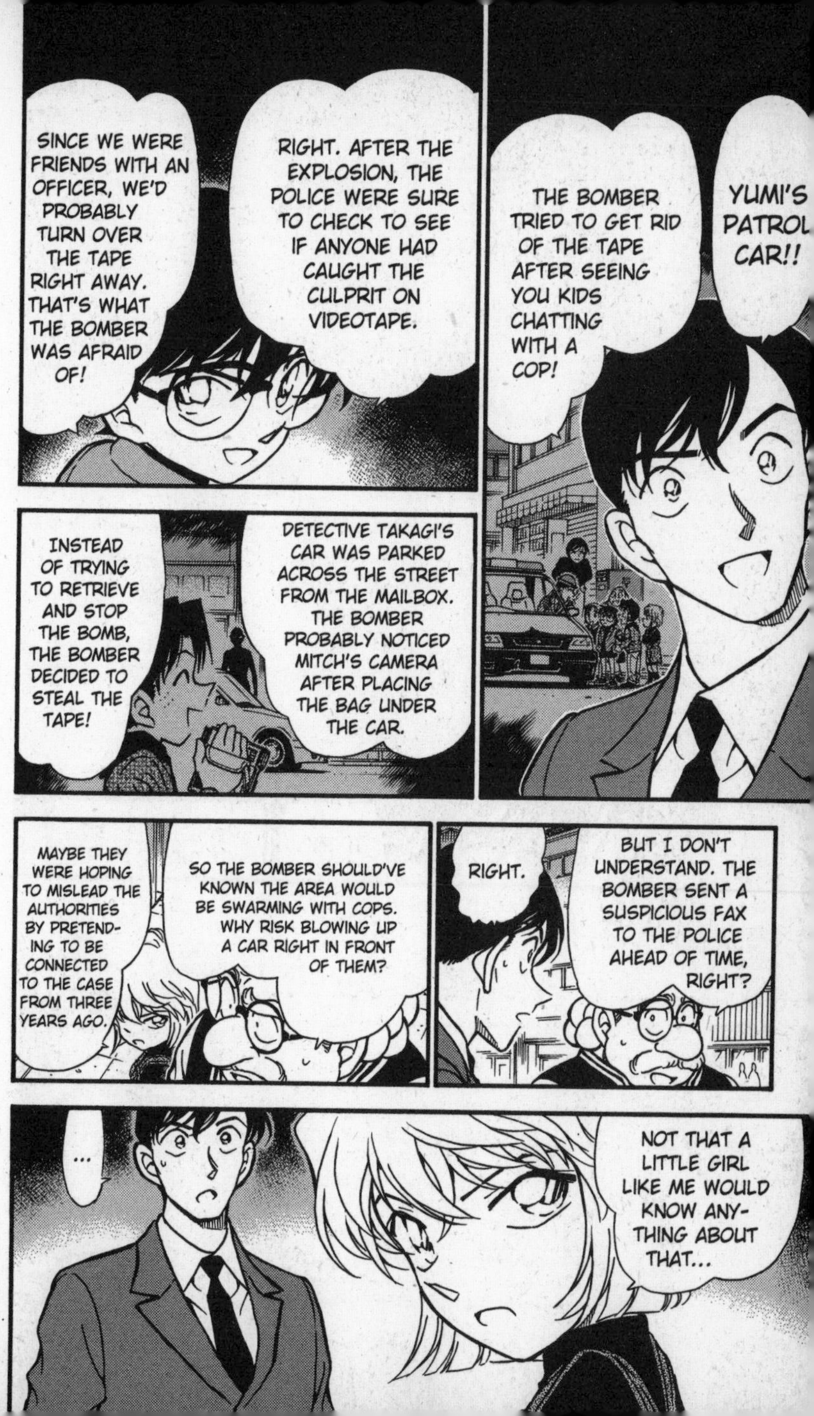
YUMI'S PATROL CAR!!
THE BOMBER TRIED TO GET RID OF THE TAPE AFTER SEEING YOU KIDS CHATTING WITH A COP!
RIGHT. AFTER THE EXPLOSION, THE POLICE WERE SURE TO CHECK TO SEE IF ANYONE HAD CAUGHT THE CULPRIT ON VIDEOTAPE.
SINCE WE WERE FRIENDS WITH AN OFFICER, WE'D PROBABLY TURN OVER THE TAPE RIGHT AWAY. THAT'S WHAT THE BOMBER WAS AFRAID OF!
DETECTIVE TAKAGI'S CAR WAS PARKED ACROSS THE STREET FROM THE MAILBOX. THE BOMBER PROBABLY NOTICED MITCH'S CAMERA AFTER PLACING THE BAG UNDER THE CAR.
INSTEAD OF TRYING TO RETRIEVE AND STOP THE BOMB, THE BOMBER DECIDED TO STEAL THE TAPE!
BUT I DON'T UNDERSTAND. THE BOMBER SENT A SUSPICIOUS FAX TO THE POLICE AHEAD OF TIME, RIGHT?
RIGHT.
SO THE BOMBER SHOULD'VE KNOWN THE AREA WOULD BE SWARMING WITH COPS. WHY RISK BLOWING UP A CAR RIGHT IN FRONT OF THEM?
MAYBE THEY WERE HOPING TO MISLEAD THE AUTHORITIES BY PRETEND-ING TO BE CONNECTED TO THE CASE FROM THREE YEARS AGO.
NOT THAT A LITTLE GIRL LIKE ME WOULD KNOW ANY-THING ABOUT THAT...
...

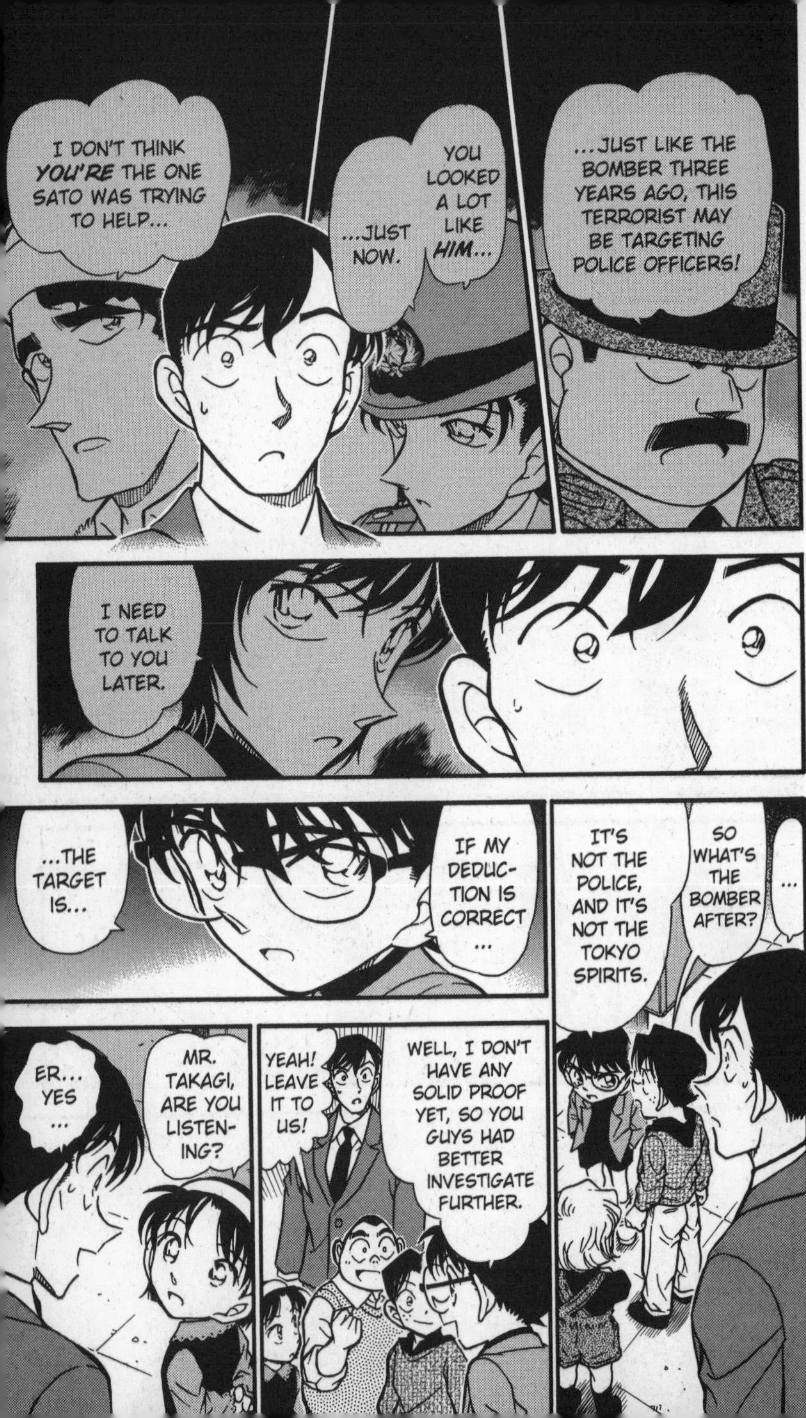
...JUST LIKE THE BOMBER THREE YEARS AGO, THIS TERRORIST MAY BE TARGETING POLICE OFFICERS!
YOU LOOKED A LOT LIKE *HIM*...
...JUST NOW.
I DON'T THINK *YOU'RE* THE ONE SATO WAS TRYING TO HELP...
I NEED TO TALK TO YOU LATER.
...
SO WHAT'S THE BOMBER AFTER?
IT'S NOT THE POLICE, AND IT'S NOT THE TOKYO SPIRITS.
IF MY DEDUCTION IS CORRECT...
...THE TARGET IS...
WELL, I DON'T HAVE ANY SOLID PROOF YET, SO YOU GUYS HAD BETTER INVESTIGATE FURTHER.
YEAH! LEAVE IT TO US!
MR. TAKAGI, ARE YOU LISTENING?
ER... YES...

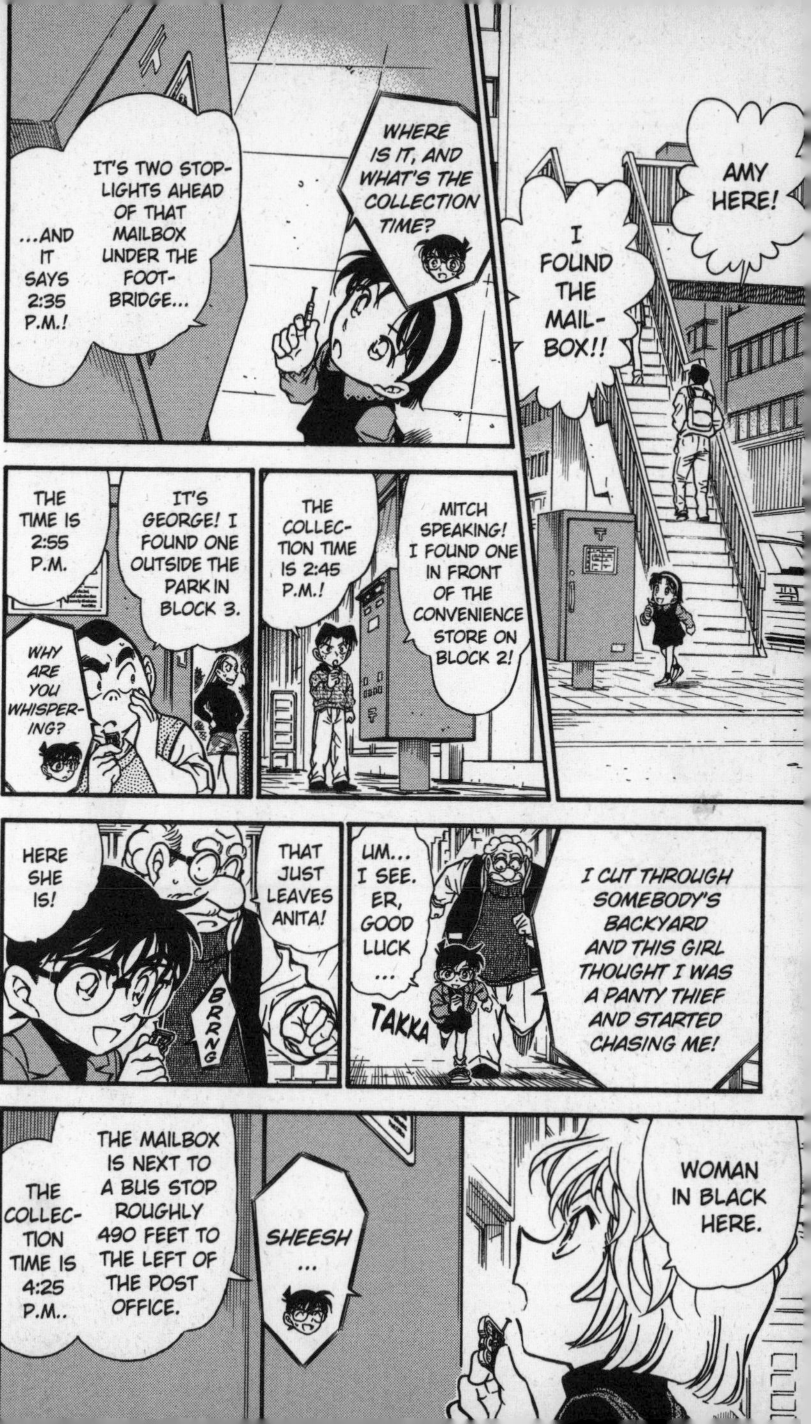
AMY HERE!
I FOUND THE MAILBOX!!
WHERE IS IT, AND WHAT'S THE COLLECTION TIME?
IT'S TWO STOPLIGHTS AHEAD OF THAT MAILBOX UNDER THE FOOTBRIDGE...
...AND IT SAYS 2:35 P.M.!
MITCH SPEAKING! I FOUND ONE IN FRONT OF THE CONVENIENCE STORE ON BLOCK 2!
THE COLLECTION TIME IS 2:45 P.M.!
IT'S GEORGE! I FOUND ONE OUTSIDE THE PARK IN BLOCK 3.
THE TIME IS 2:55 P.M.
WHY ARE YOU WHISPERING?
I CUT THROUGH SOMEBODY'S BACKYARD AND THIS GIRL THOUGHT I WAS A PANTY THIEF AND STARTED CHASING ME!
UM... I SEE. ER, GOOD LUCK ...
TAKKA
THAT JUST LEAVES ANITA!
HERE SHE IS!
BRRRNG
WOMAN IN BLACK HERE.
SHEESH ...
THE MAILBOX IS NEXT TO A BUS STOP ROUGHLY 490 FEET TO THE LEFT OF THE POST OFFICE.
THE COLLECTION TIME IS 4:25 P.M..

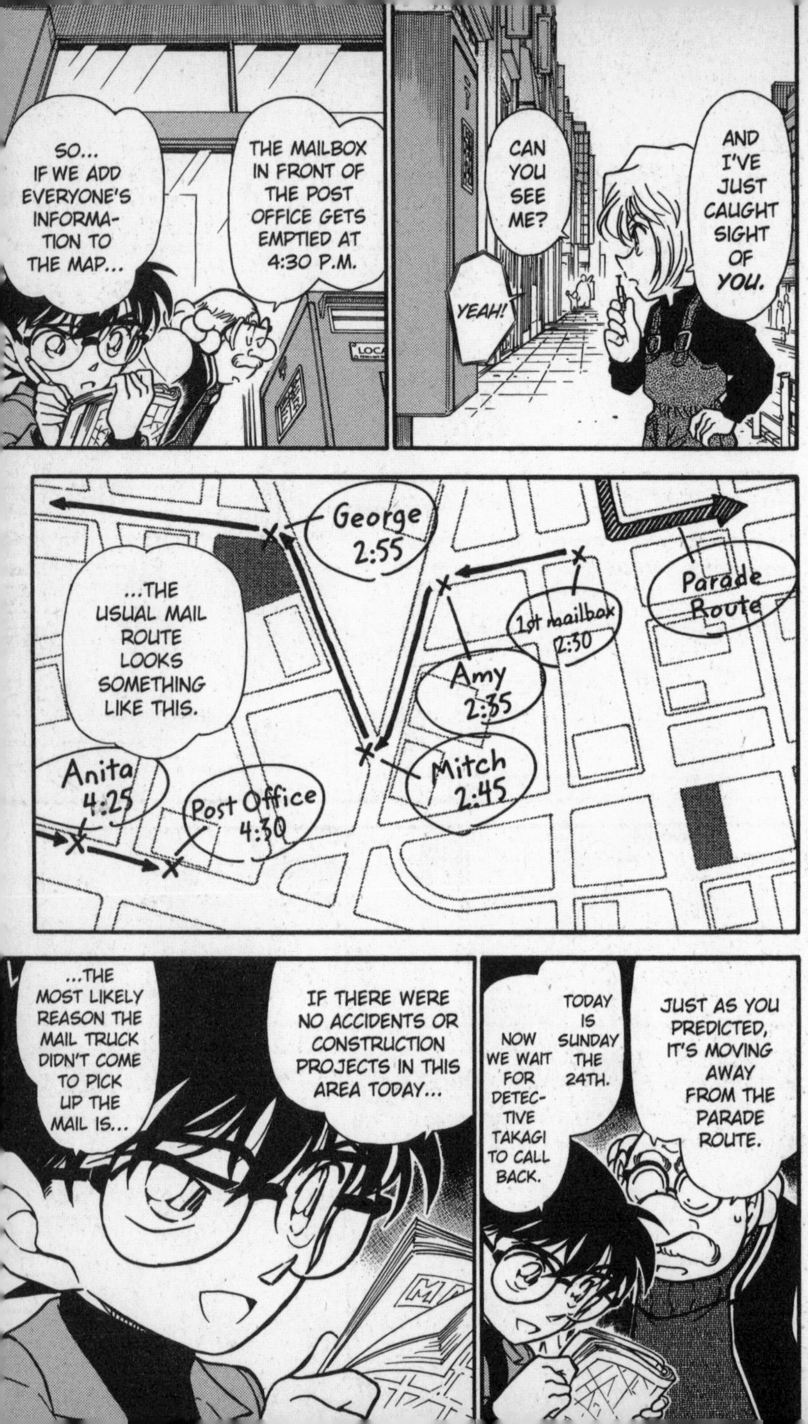
AND I'VE JUST CAUGHT SIGHT OF YOU.
CAN YOU SEE ME?
YEAH!
THE MAILBOX IN FRONT OF THE POST OFFICE GETS EMPTIED AT 4:30 P.M.
SO... IF WE ADD EVERYONE'S INFORMATION TO THE MAP...
LOCA
Parade Route
George 2:55
1st mailbox 2:30
...THE USUAL MAIL ROUTE LOOKS SOMETHING LIKE THIS.
Amy 2:35
Mitch 2:45
Post Office 4:30
Anita 4:25
JUST AS YOU PREDICTED, IT'S MOVING AWAY FROM THE PARADE ROUTE.
TODAY IS SUNDAY THE 24TH.
NOW WE WAIT FOR DETECTIVE TAKAGI TO CALL BACK.
IF THERE WERE NO ACCIDENTS OR CONSTRUCTION PROJECTS IN THIS AREA TODAY...
...THE MOST LIKELY REASON THE MAIL TRUCK DIDN'T COME TO PICK UP THE MAIL IS...

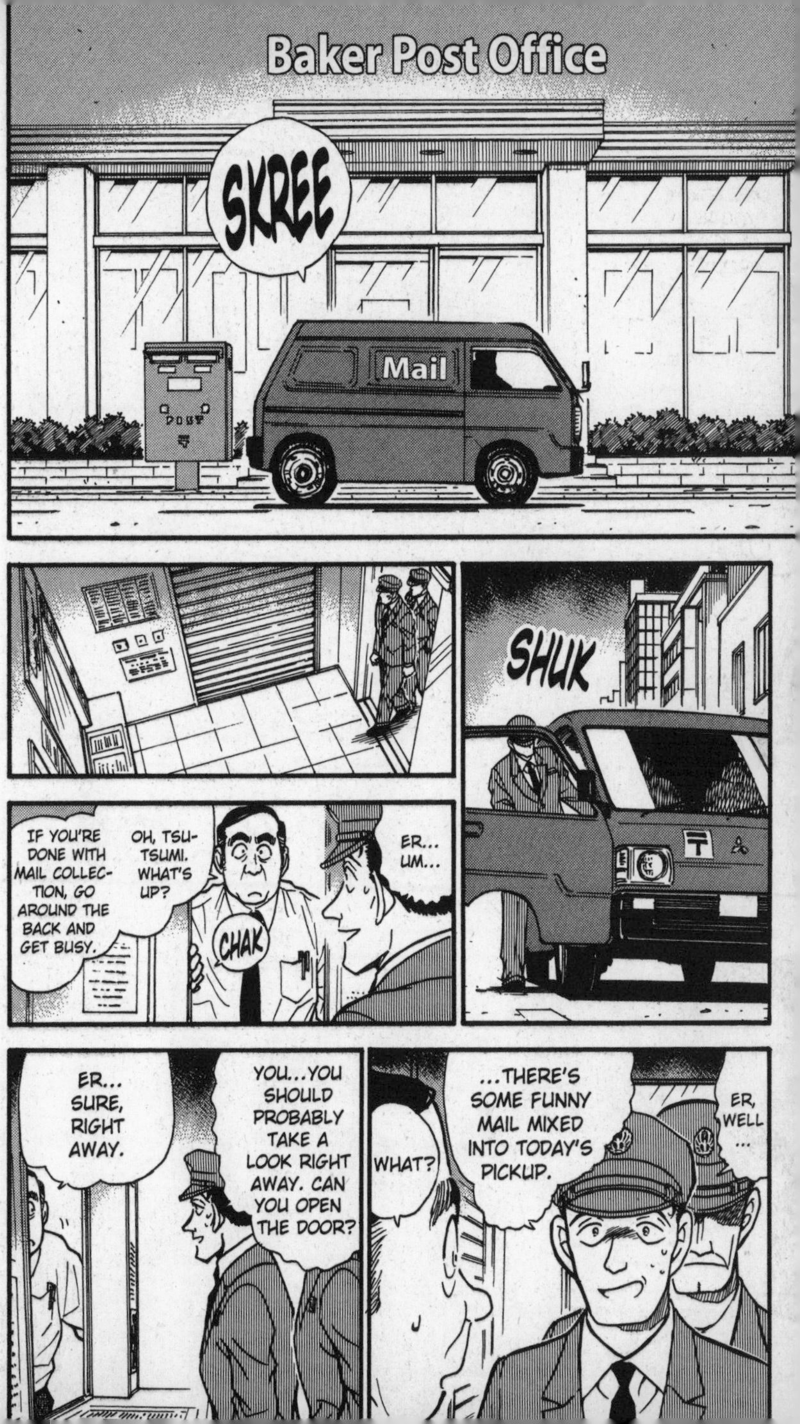
Baker Post Office
SKREE
Mail
SHUK
ER... UM...
OH, TSU-TSUMI. WHAT'S UP?
CHAK
IF YOU'RE DONE WITH MAIL COLLEC-TION, GO AROUND THE BACK AND GET BUSY.
ER, WELL ...
...THERE'S SOME FUNNY MAIL MIXED INTO TODAY'S PICKUP.
WHAT?
YOU...YOU SHOULD PROBABLY TAKE A LOOK RIGHT AWAY. CAN YOU OPEN THE DOOR?
ER... SURE, RIGHT AWAY.

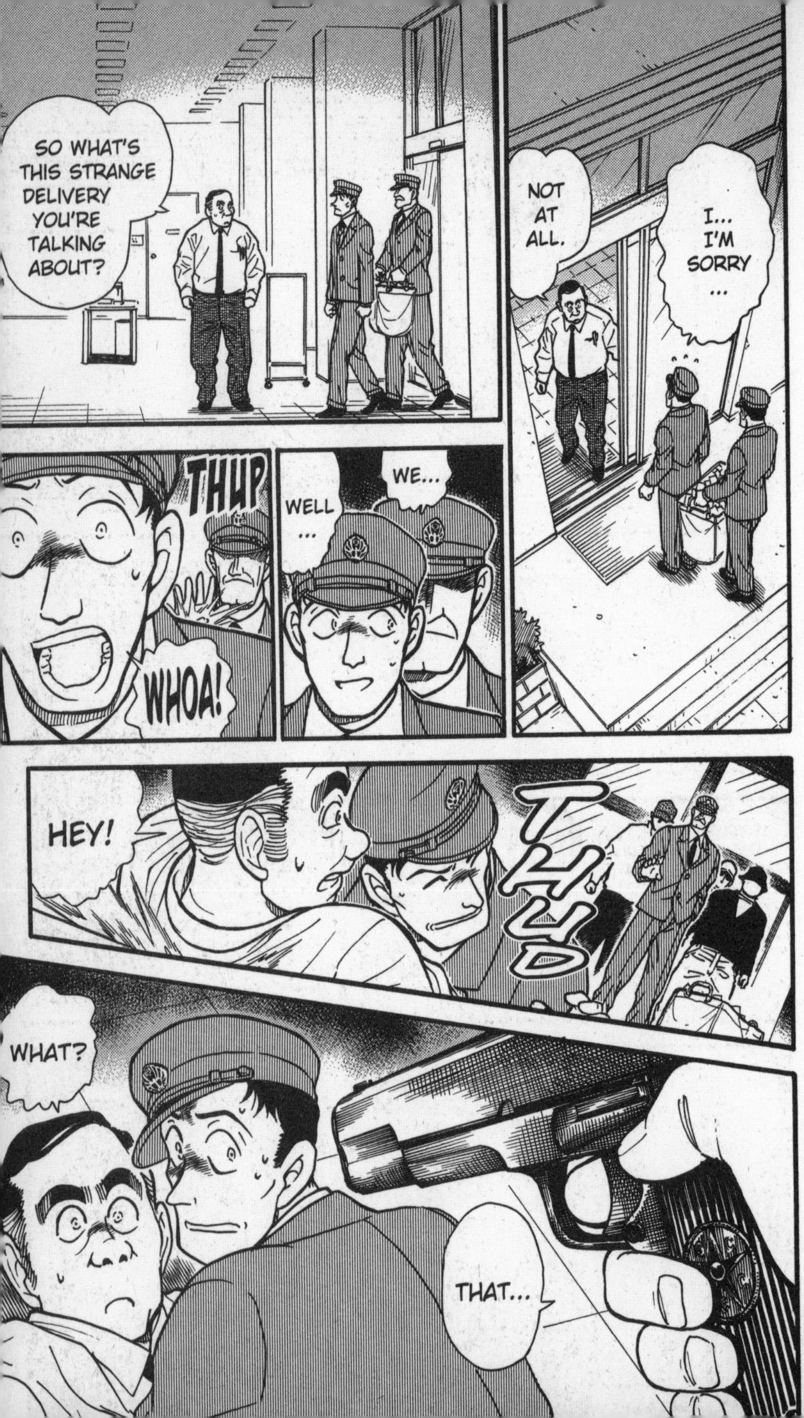
I... I'M SORRY...
NOT AT ALL.
SO WHAT'S THIS STRANGE DELIVERY YOU'RE TALKING ABOUT?
WE...
WELL...
THUP
WHOA!
THUD
HEY!
THAT...
WHAT?

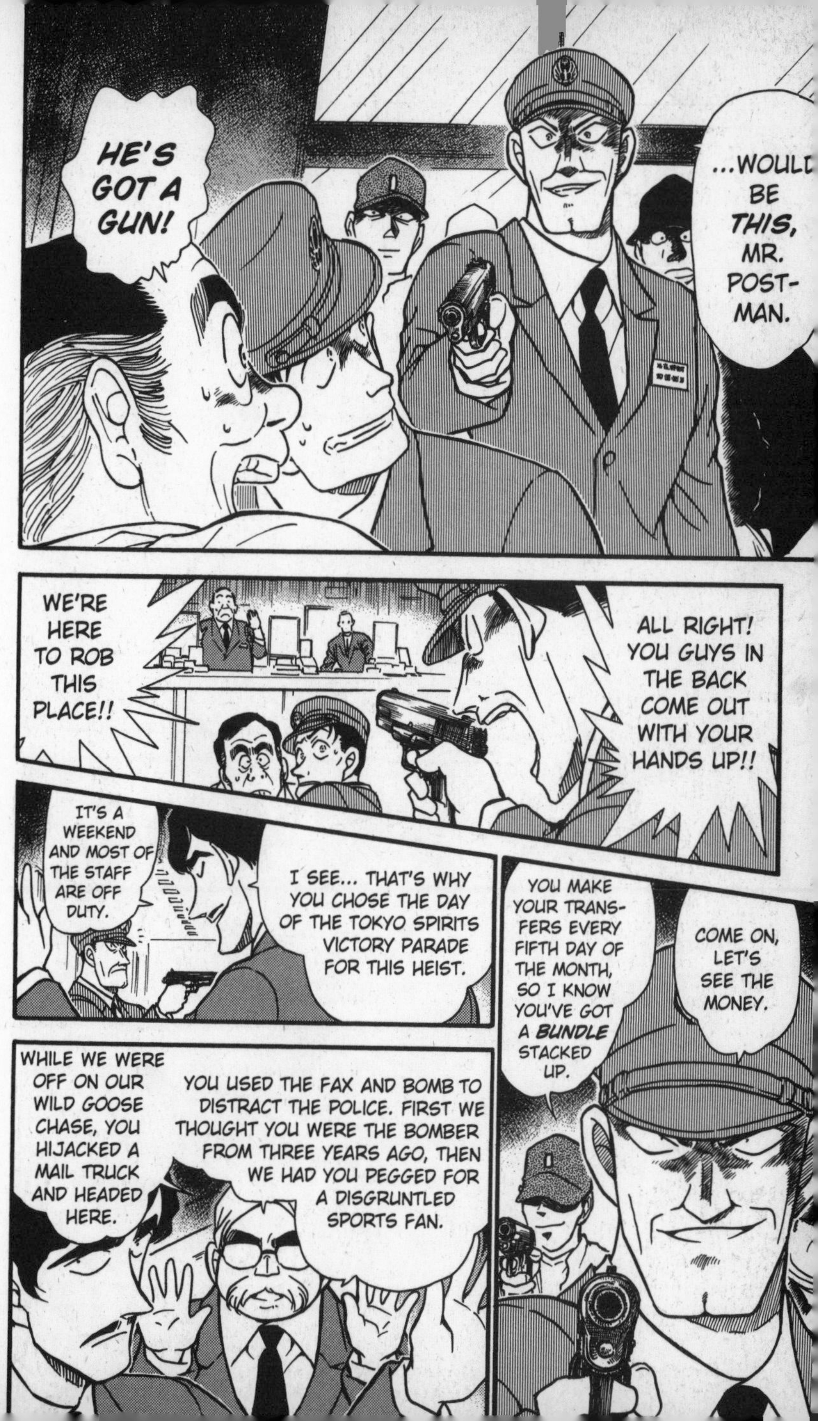
...WOULD BE THIS, MR. POSTMAN.
HE'S GOT A GUN!
ALL RIGHT! YOU GUYS IN THE BACK COME OUT WITH YOUR HANDS UP!!
WE'RE HERE TO ROB THIS PLACE!!
COME ON, LET'S SEE THE MONEY.
YOU MAKE YOUR TRANSFERS EVERY FIFTH DAY OF THE MONTH, SO I KNOW YOU'VE GOT A BUNDLE STACKED UP.
I SEE... THAT'S WHY YOU CHOSE THE DAY OF THE TOKYO SPIRITS VICTORY PARADE FOR THIS HEIST.
IT'S A WEEKEND AND MOST OF THE STAFF ARE OFF DUTY.
YOU USED THE FAX AND BOMB TO DISTRACT THE POLICE. FIRST WE THOUGHT YOU WERE THE BOMBER FROM THREE YEARS AGO, THEN WE HAD YOU PEGGED FOR A DISGRUNTLED SPORTS FAN.
WHILE WE WERE OFF ON OUR WILD GOOSE CHASE, YOU HIJACKED A MAIL TRUCK AND HEADED HERE.

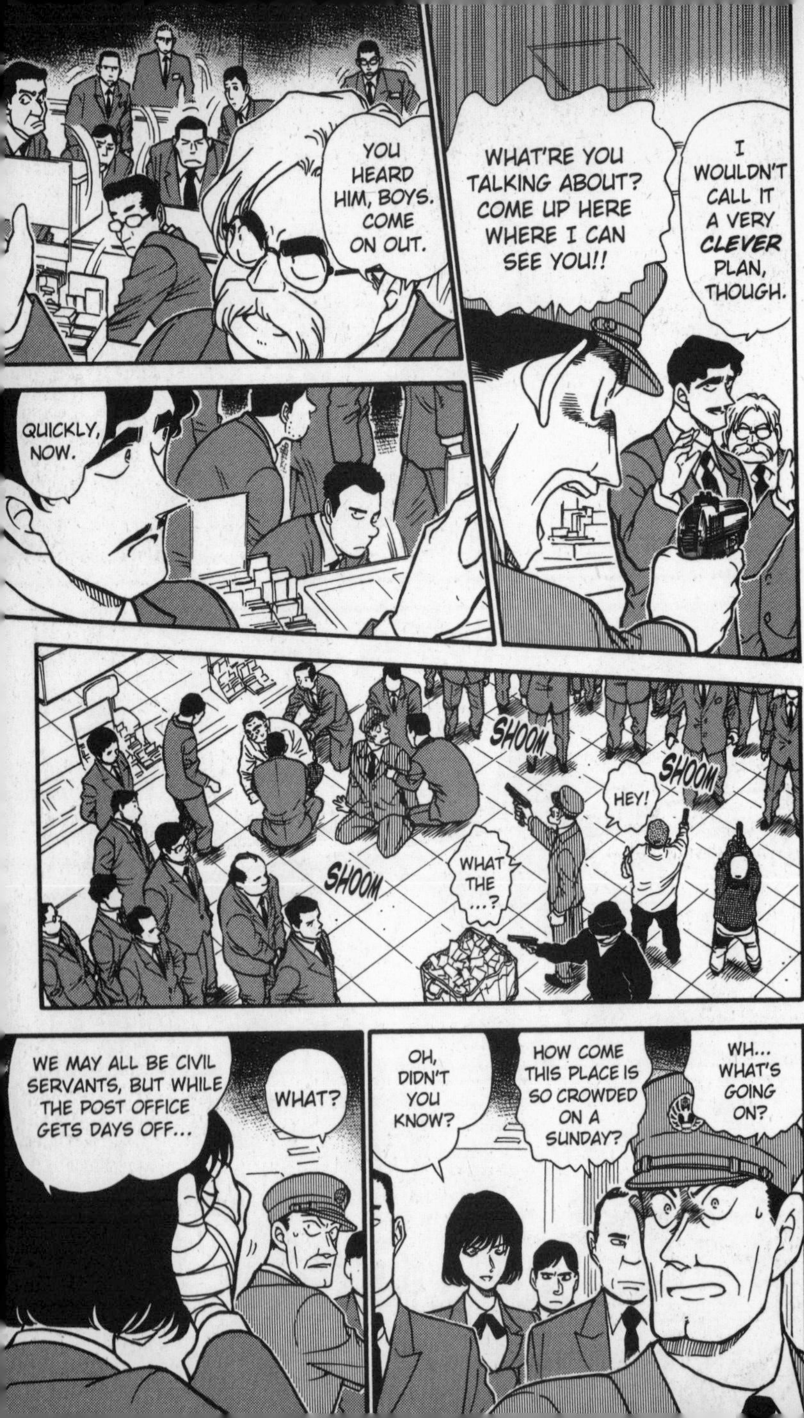
I WOULDN'T CALL IT A VERY *CLEVER* PLAN, THOUGH.
WHAT'RE YOU TALKING ABOUT? COME UP HERE WHERE I CAN SEE YOU!!
YOU HEARD HIM, BOYS. COME ON OUT.
QUICKLY, NOW.
SHOOM
SHOOM
HEY!
WHAT THE ...?
SHOOM
WH... WHAT'S GOING ON?
HOW COME THIS PLACE IS SO CROWDED ON A SUNDAY?
OH, DIDN'T YOU KNOW?
WHAT?
WE MAY ALL BE CIVIL SERVANTS, BUT WHILE THE POST OFFICE GETS DAYS OFF...

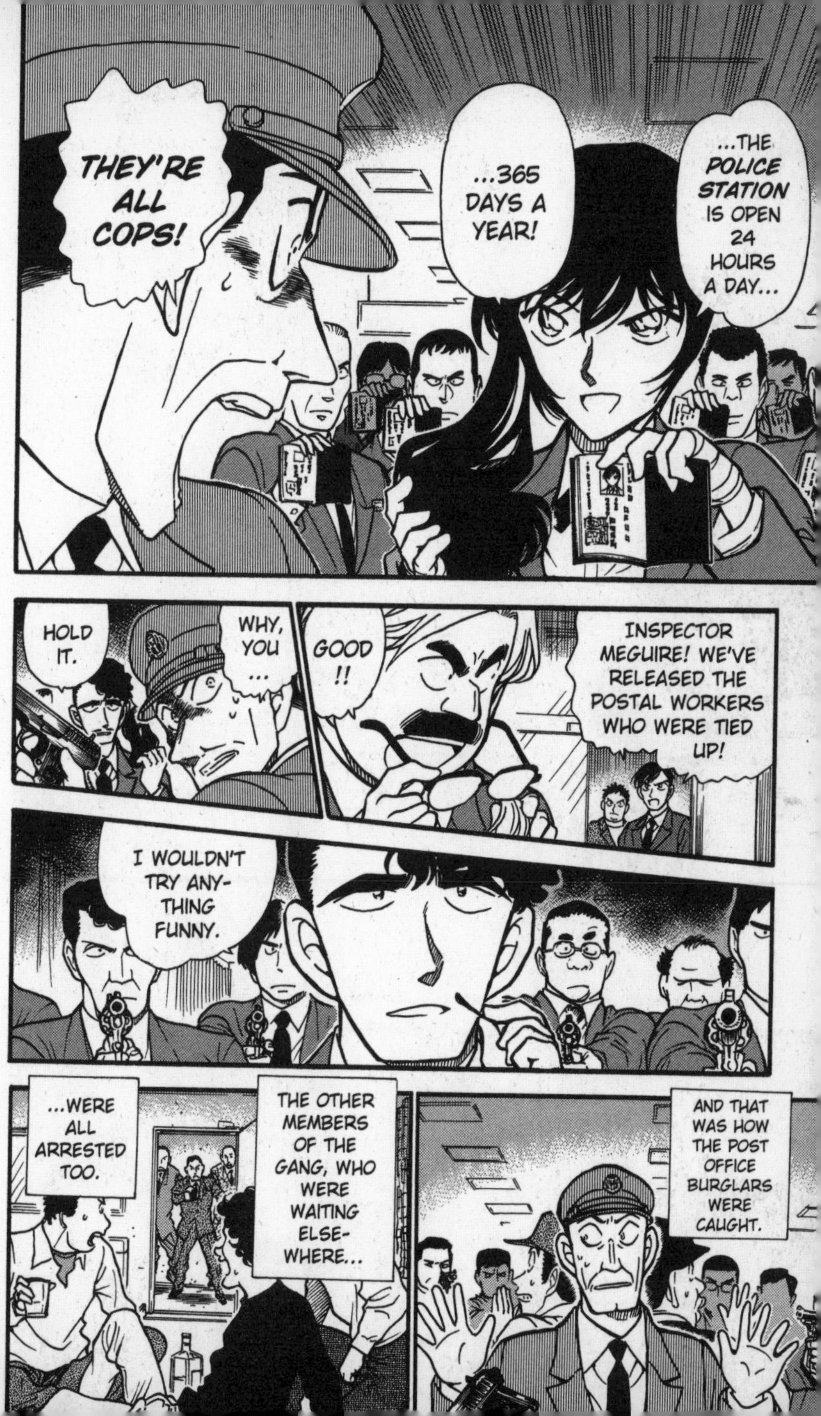
...THE POLICE STATION IS OPEN 24 HOURS A DAY...
...365 DAYS A YEAR!
THEY'RE ALL COPS!
INSPECTOR MEGUIRE! WE'VE RELEASED THE POSTAL WORKERS WHO WERE TIED UP!
GOOD!!
WHY, YOU ...
HOLD IT.
I WOULDN'T TRY ANY-THING FUNNY.
AND THAT WAS HOW THE POST OFFICE BURGLARS WERE CAUGHT.
THE OTHER MEMBERS OF THE GANG, WHO WERE WAITING ELSE-WHERE...
...WERE ALL ARRESTED TOO.

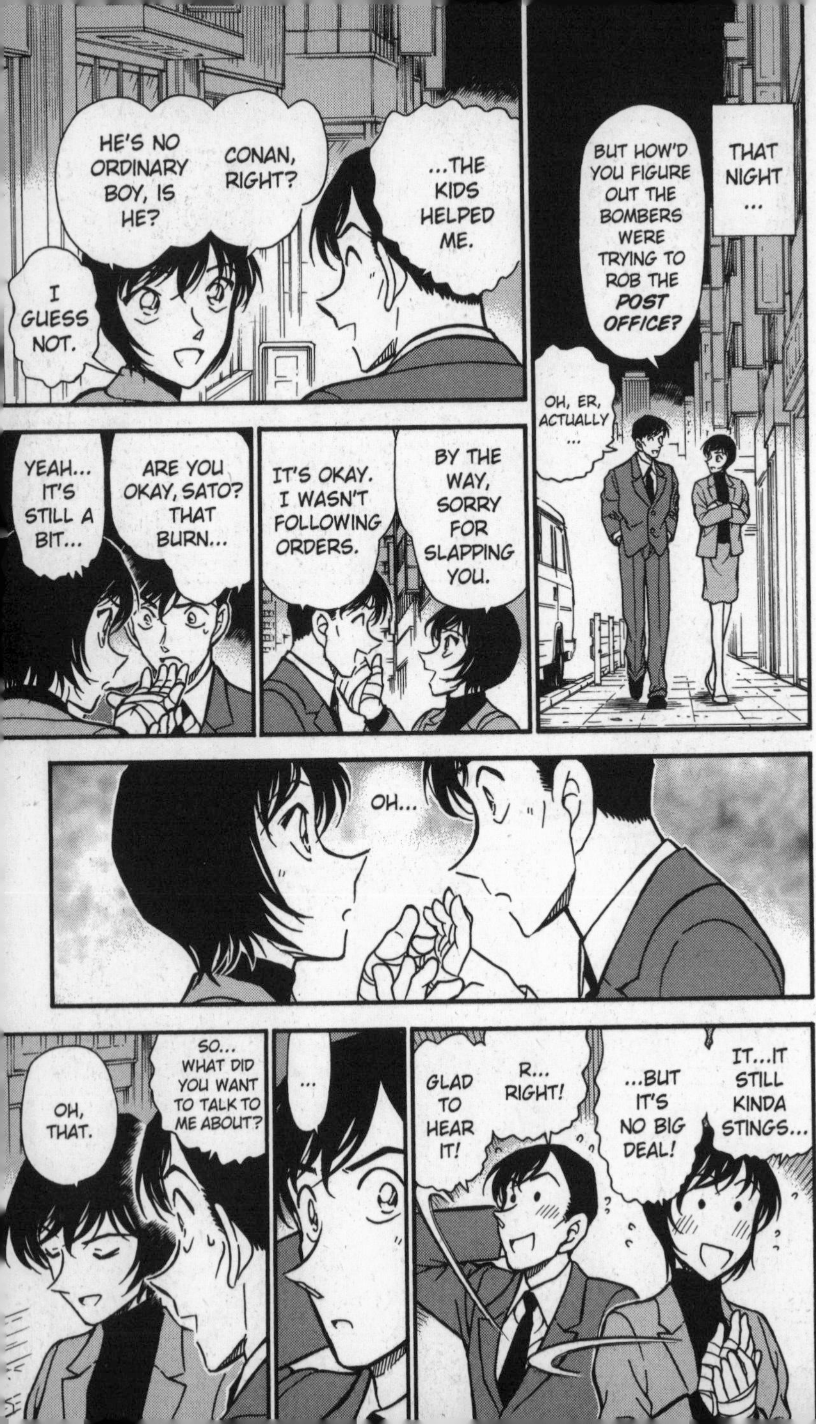
THAT NIGHT...
BUT HOW'D YOU FIGURE OUT THE BOMBERS WERE TRYING TO ROB THE ***POST OFFICE?***
OH, ER, ACTUALLY...
...THE KIDS HELPED ME.
CONAN, RIGHT?
HE'S NO ORDINARY BOY, IS HE?
I GUESS NOT.
BY THE WAY, SORRY FOR SLAPPING YOU.
IT'S OKAY. I WASN'T FOLLOWING ORDERS.
ARE YOU OKAY, SATO? THAT BURN...
YEAH... IT'S STILL A BIT...
OH...
IT...IT STILL KINDA STINGS...
...BUT IT'S NO BIG DEAL!
R... RIGHT!
GLAD TO HEAR IT!
...
SO... WHAT DID YOU WANT TO TALK TO ME ABOUT?
OH, THAT.

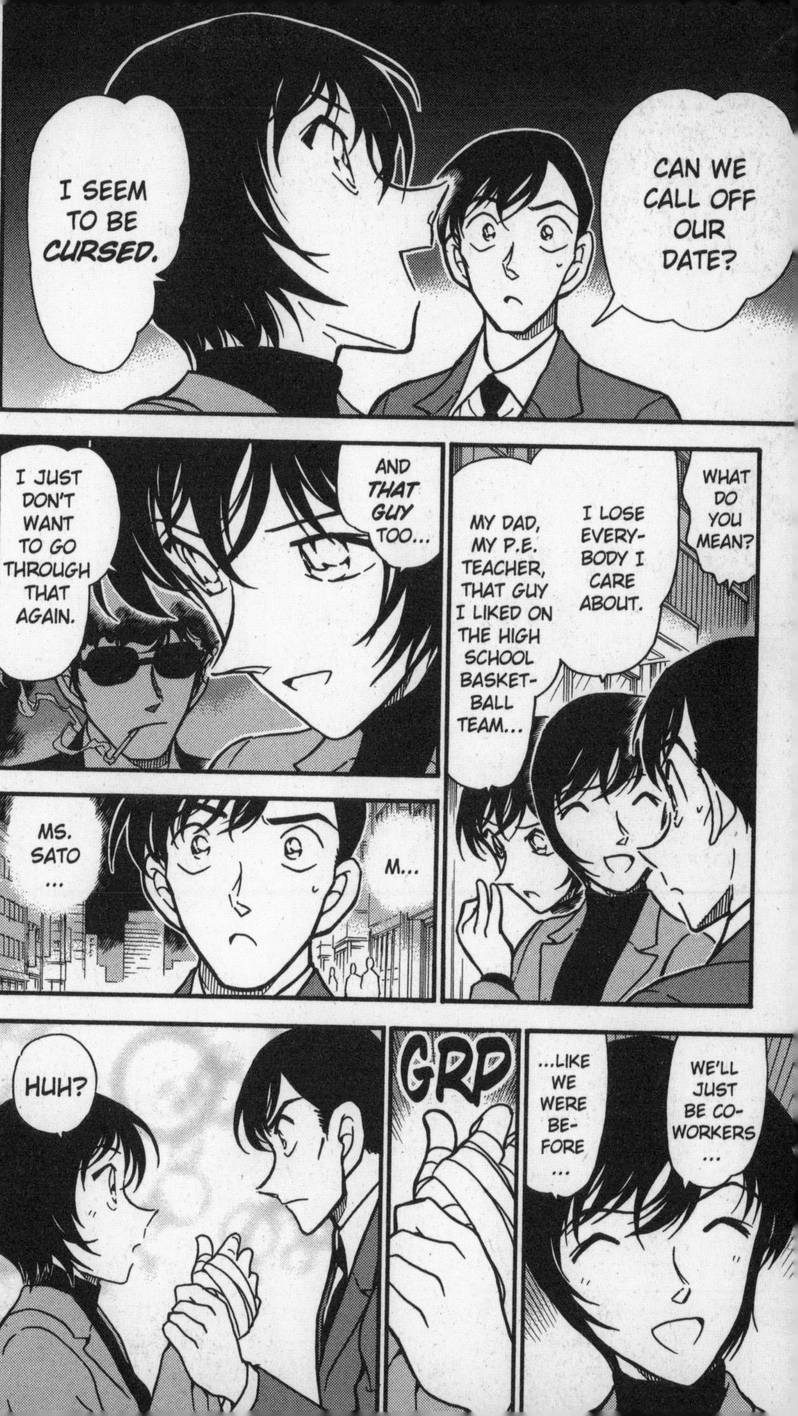
CAN WE CALL OFF OUR DATE?
I SEEM TO BE *CURSED.*
WHAT DO YOU MEAN?
I LOSE EVERY-BODY I CARE ABOUT.
MY DAD, MY P.E. TEACHER, THAT GUY I LIKED ON THE HIGH SCHOOL BASKET-BALL TEAM...
AND *THAT GUY* TOO...
I JUST DON'T WANT TO GO THROUGH THAT AGAIN.
M...
MS. SATO ...
WE'LL JUST BE CO-WORKERS ...
...LIKE WE WERE BE-FORE ...
GRP
HUH?

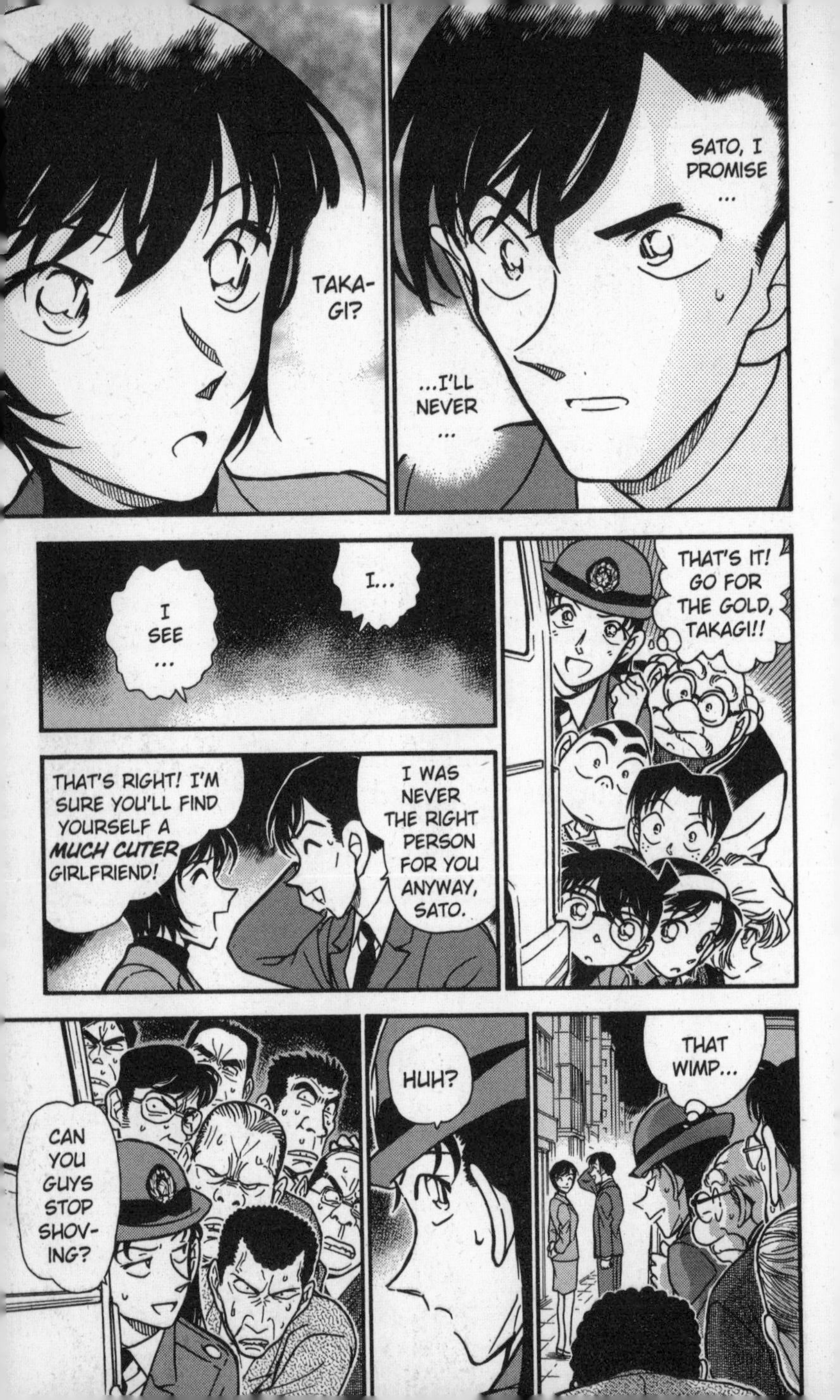
SATO, I PROMISE ...
...I'LL NEVER ...
TAKA-GI?
THAT'S IT! GO FOR THE GOLD, TAKAGI!!
I...
I SEE ...
I WAS NEVER THE RIGHT PERSON FOR YOU ANYWAY, SATO.
THAT'S RIGHT! I'M SURE YOU'LL FIND YOURSELF A *MUCH CUTER* GIRLFRIEND!
THAT WIMP...
HUH?
CAN YOU GUYS STOP SHOV-ING?

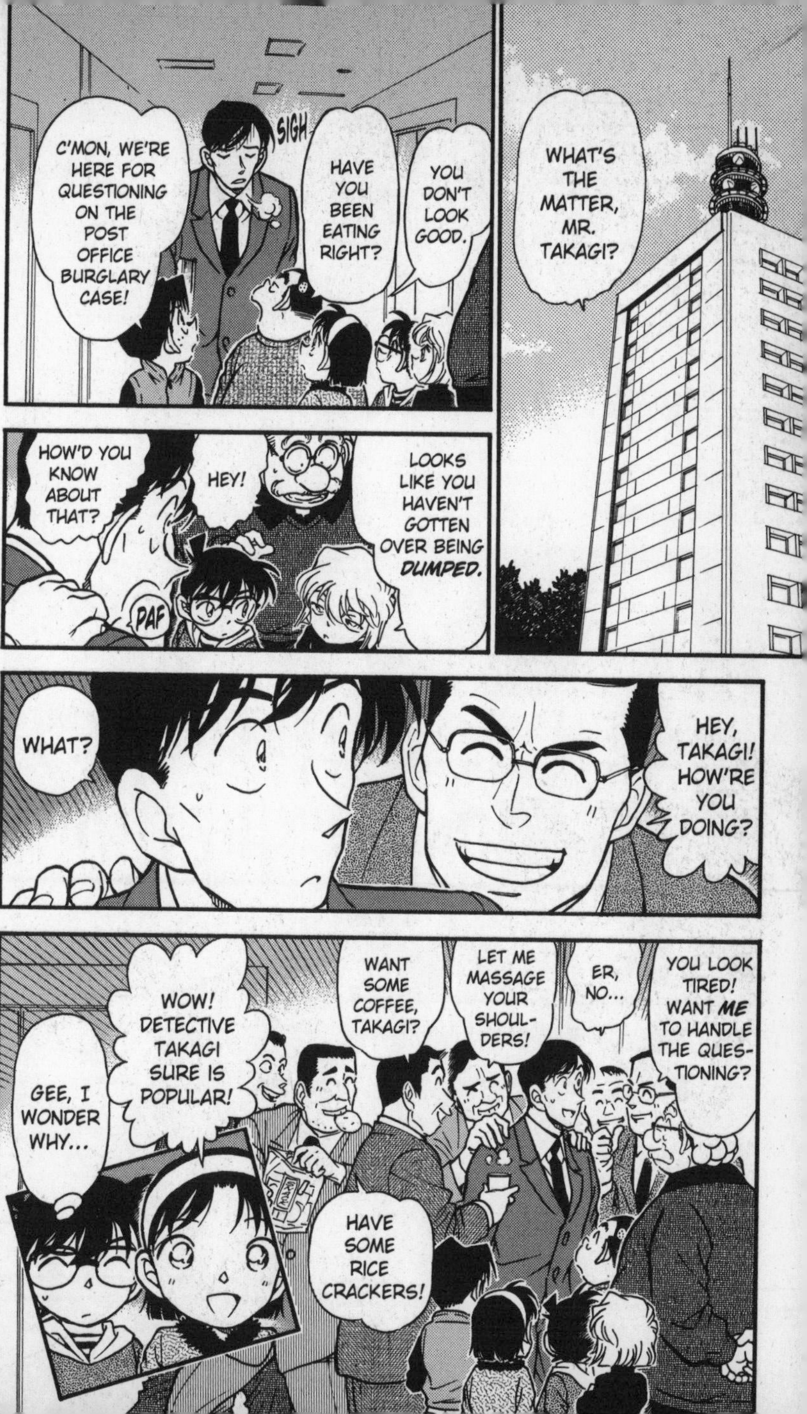
WHAT'S THE MATTER, MR. TAKAGI?
YOU DON'T LOOK GOOD.
HAVE YOU BEEN EATING RIGHT?
SIGH
C'MON, WE'RE HERE FOR QUESTIONING ON THE POST OFFICE BURGLARY CASE!
LOOKS LIKE YOU HAVEN'T GOTTEN OVER BEING *DUMPED*.
HEY!
HOW'D YOU KNOW ABOUT THAT?
PAF
HEY, TAKAGI! HOW'RE YOU DOING?
WHAT?
YOU LOOK TIRED! WANT *ME* TO HANDLE THE QUESTIONING?
ER, NO...
LET ME MASSAGE YOUR SHOULDERS!
WANT SOME COFFEE, TAKAGI?
WOW! DETECTIVE TAKAGI SURE IS POPULAR!
HAVE SOME RICE CRACKERS!
GEE, I WONDER WHY...

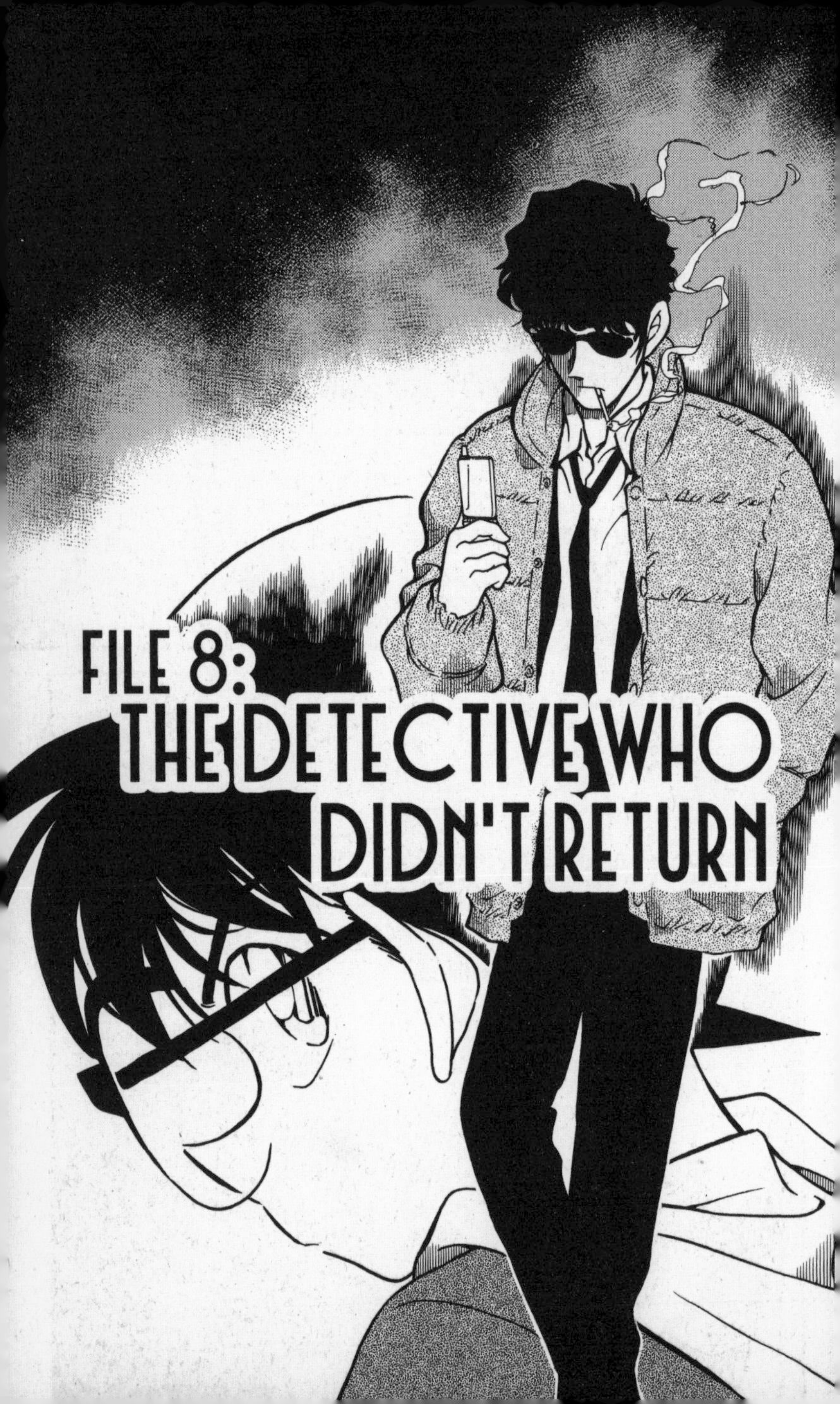
FILE 8:
THE DETECTIVE WHO
DIDN'T RETURN

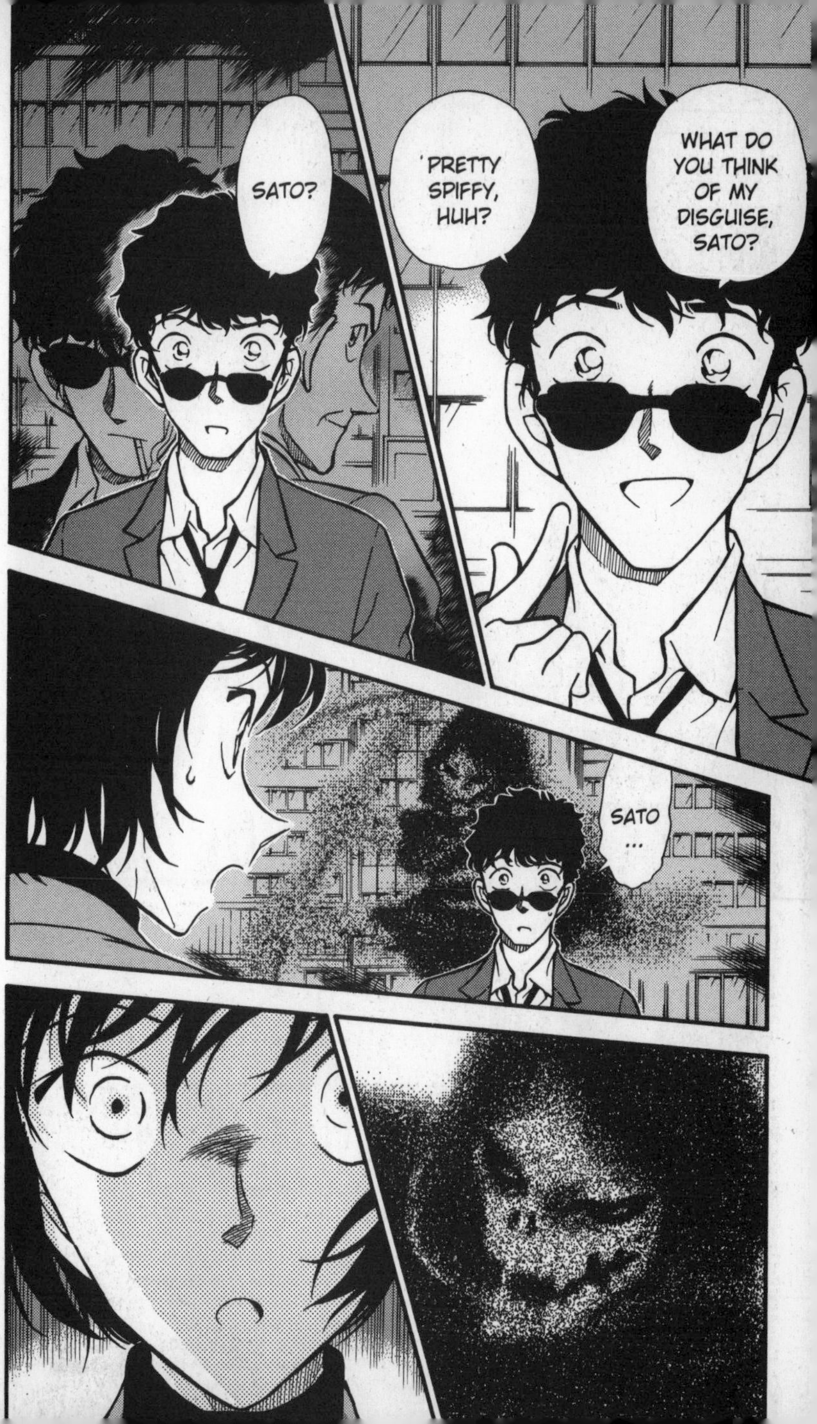
WHAT DO YOU THINK OF MY DISGUISE, SATO?
'PRETTY SPIFFY, HUH?
SATO?
SATO ...

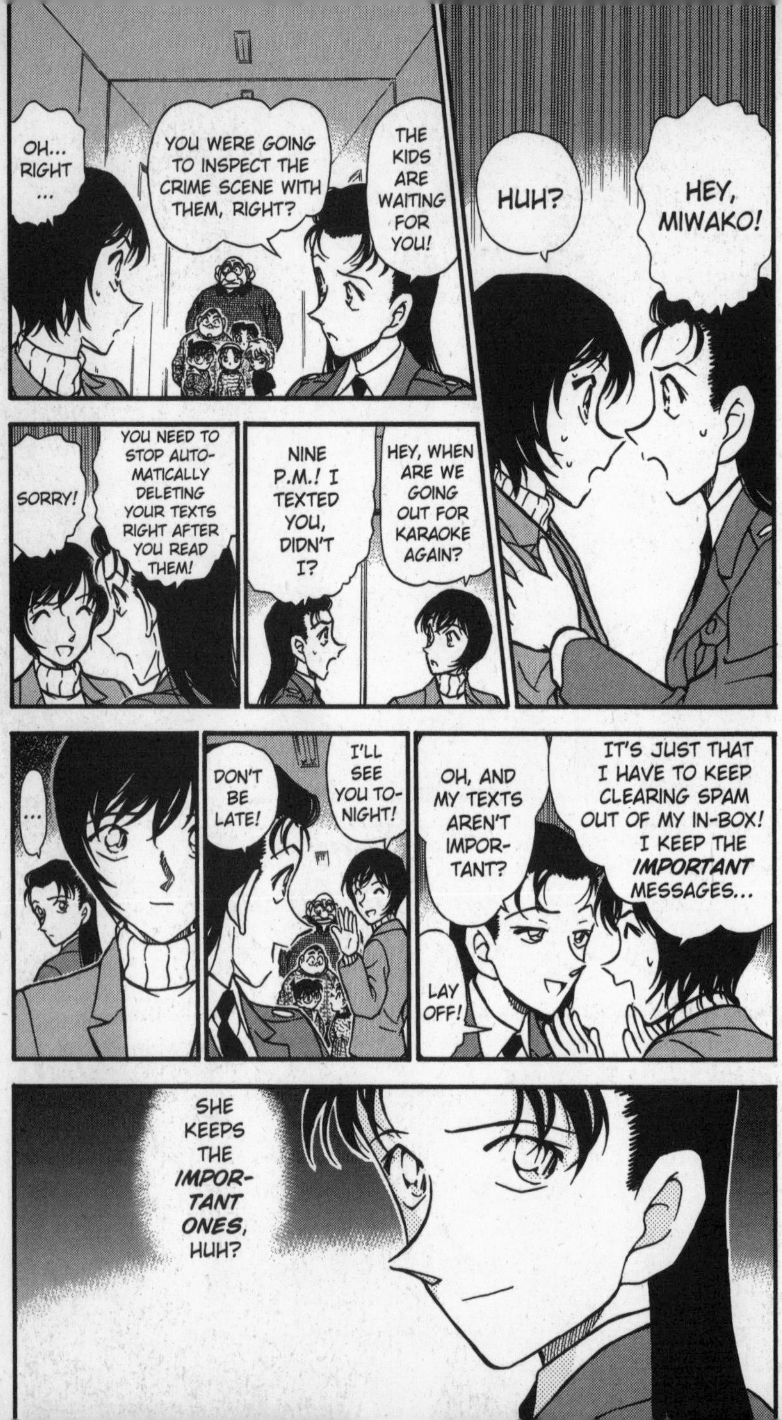
HEY, MIWAKO!
HUH?
THE KIDS ARE WAITING FOR YOU!
YOU WERE GOING TO INSPECT THE CRIME SCENE WITH THEM, RIGHT?
OH... RIGHT ...
HEY, WHEN ARE WE GOING OUT FOR KARAOKE AGAIN?
NINE P.M.! I TEXTED YOU, DIDN'T I?
YOU NEED TO STOP AUTO-MATICALLY DELETING YOUR TEXTS RIGHT AFTER YOU READ THEM!
SORRY!
IT'S JUST THAT I HAVE TO KEEP CLEARING SPAM OUT OF MY IN-BOX! I KEEP THE *IMPORTANT* MESSAGES...
OH, AND MY TEXTS AREN'T IMPOR-TANT?
LAY OFF!
I'LL SEE YOU TO-NIGHT!
DON'T BE LATE!
...
SHE KEEPS THE *IMPOR-TANT ONES*, HUH?

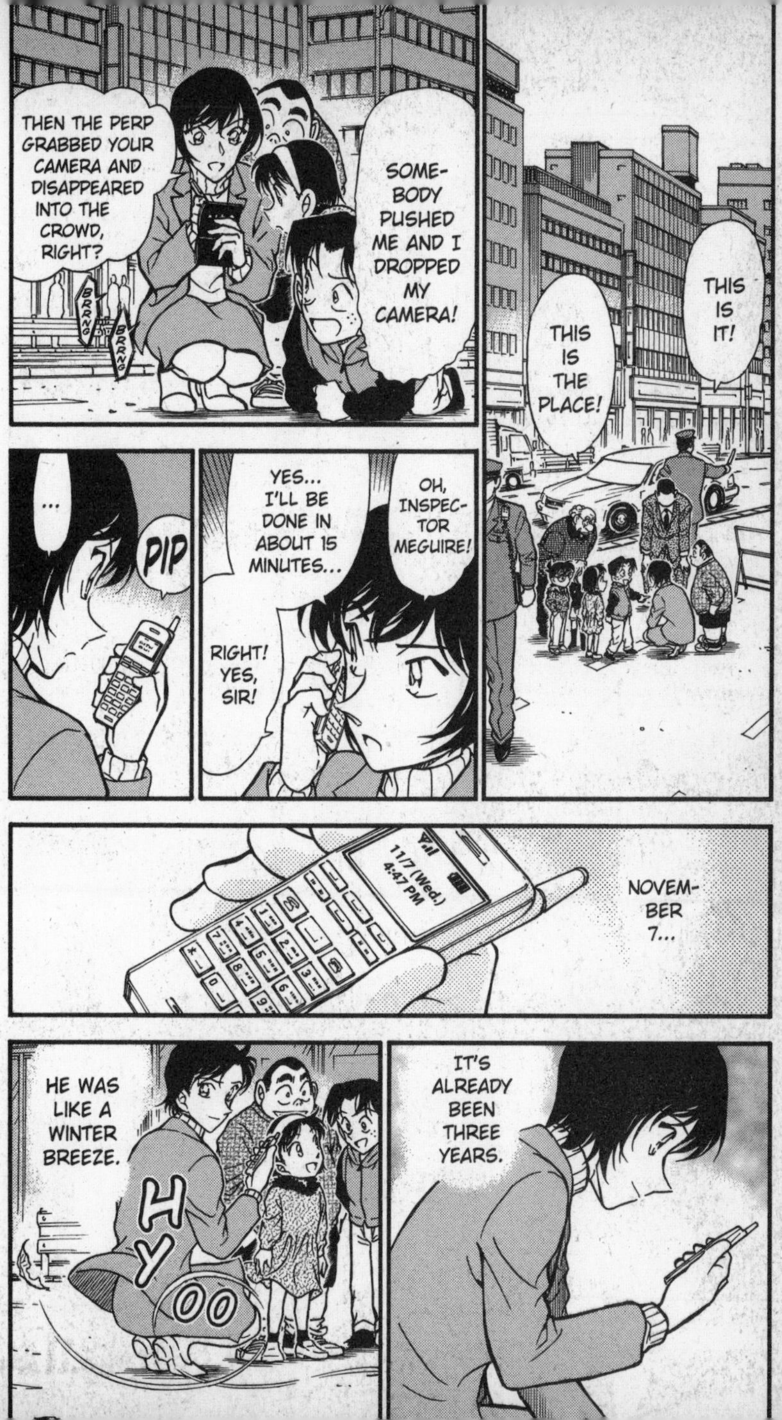
THIS IS IT!
THIS IS THE PLACE!
SOME-BODY PUSHED ME AND I DROPPED MY CAMERA!
THEN THE PERP GRABBED YOUR CAMERA AND DISAPPEARED INTO THE CROWD, RIGHT?
BRRNG
BRRNG
OH, INSPEC-TOR MEGUIRE!
YES... I'LL BE DONE IN ABOUT 15 MINUTES...
RIGHT! YES, SIR!
PIP
...
11/7 (Wed.)
4:47 PM
NOVEM-BER 7...
IT'S ALREADY BEEN THREE YEARS.
HE WAS LIKE A WINTER BREEZE.
HYOO

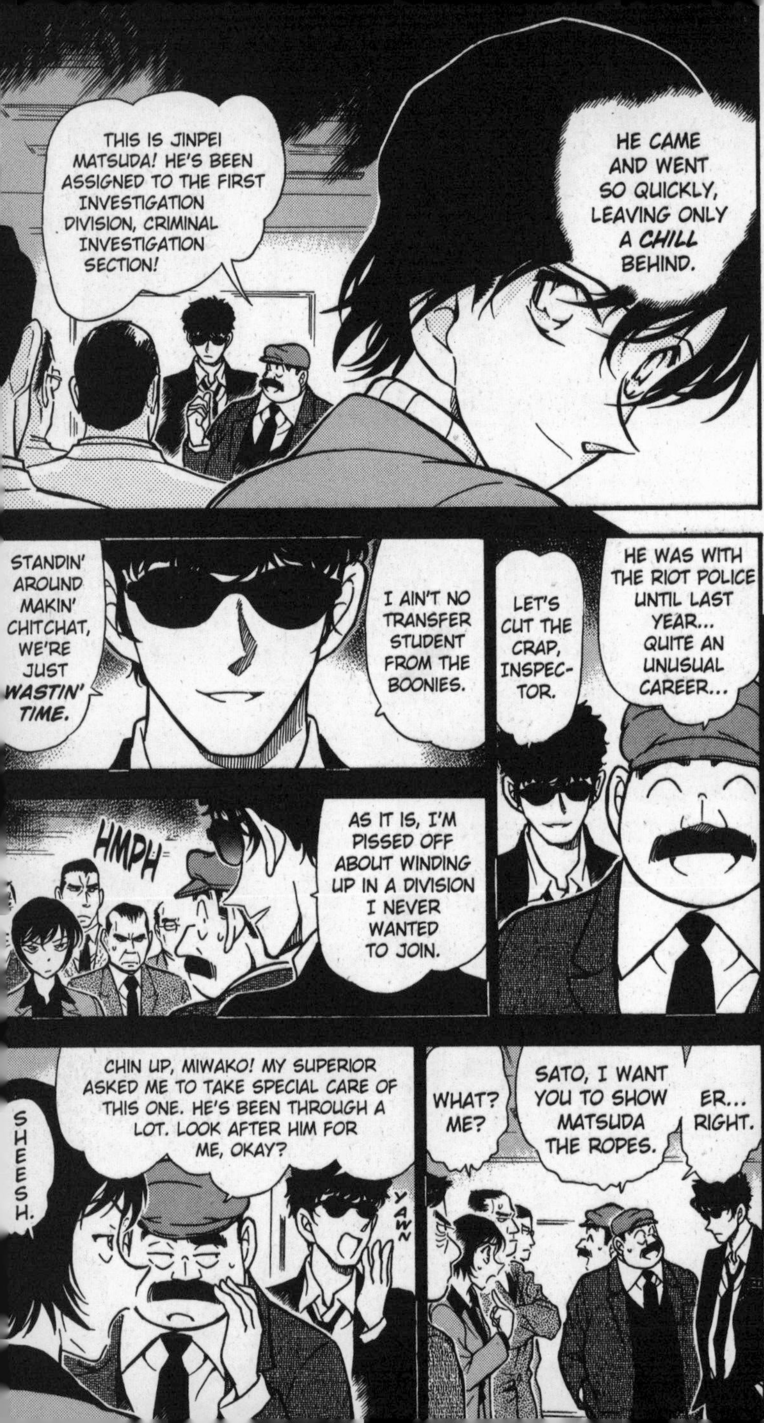
HE CAME AND WENT SO QUICKLY, LEAVING ONLY A CHILL BEHIND.
THIS IS JINPEI MATSUDA! HE'S BEEN ASSIGNED TO THE FIRST INVESTIGATION DIVISION, CRIMINAL INVESTIGATION SECTION!
HE WAS WITH THE RIOT POLICE UNTIL LAST YEAR... QUITE AN UNUSUAL CAREER...
LET'S CUT THE CRAP, INSPECTOR.
I AIN'T NO TRANSFER STUDENT FROM THE BOONIES.
STANDIN' AROUND MAKIN' CHITCHAT, WE'RE JUST WASTIN' TIME.
AS IT IS, I'M PISSED OFF ABOUT WINDING UP IN A DIVISION I NEVER WANTED TO JOIN.
HMPH
ER... RIGHT.
SATO, I WANT YOU TO SHOW MATSUDA THE ROPES.
WHAT? ME?
CHIN UP, MIWAKO! MY SUPERIOR ASKED ME TO TAKE SPECIAL CARE OF THIS ONE. HE'S BEEN THROUGH A LOT. LOOK AFTER HIM FOR ME, OKAY?
YAWN
SHEESH.

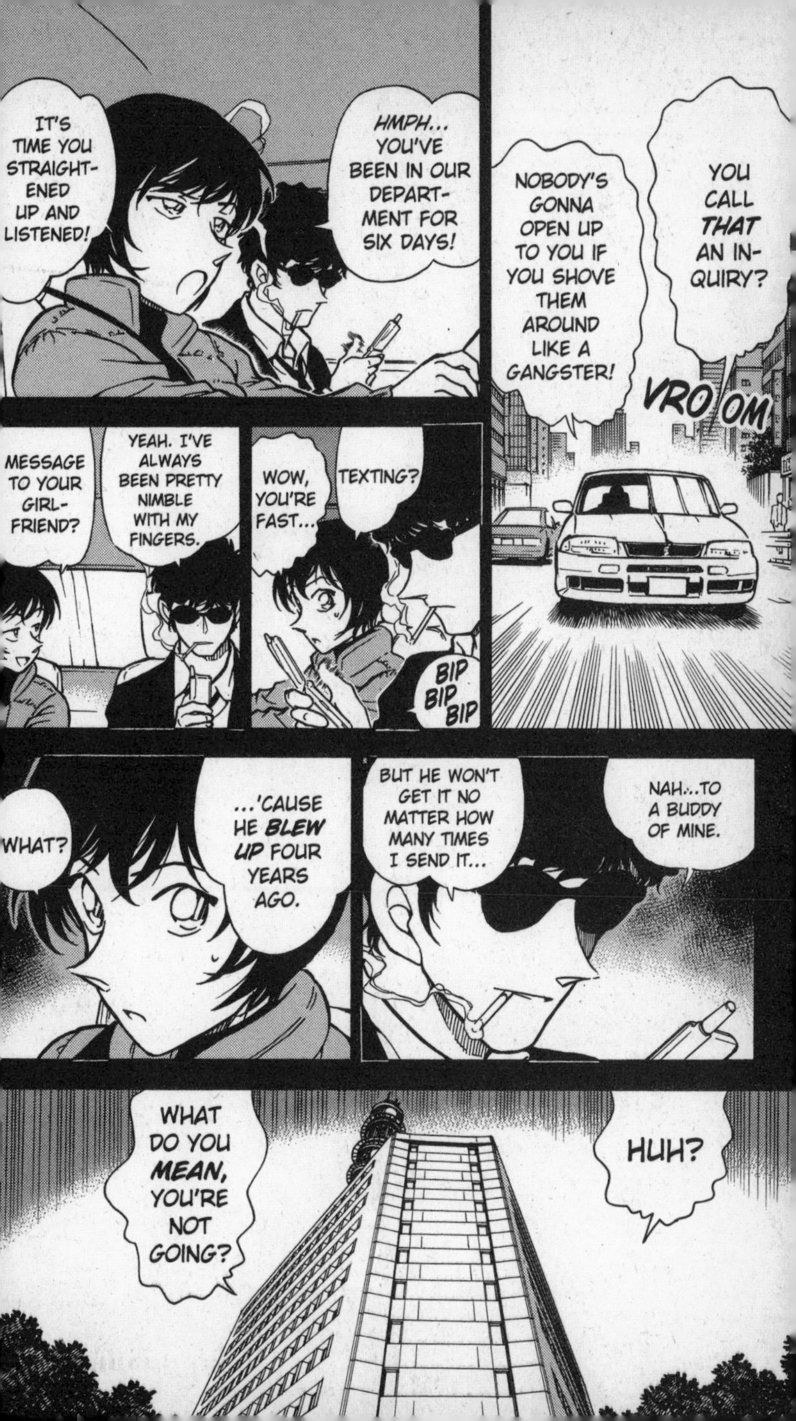
YOU CALL THAT AN INQUIRY?
NOBODY'S GONNA OPEN UP TO YOU IF YOU SHOVE THEM AROUND LIKE A GANGSTER!
VROOM
HMPH... YOU'VE BEEN IN OUR DEPARTMENT FOR SIX DAYS!
IT'S TIME YOU STRAIGHTENED UP AND LISTENED!
TEXTING?
WOW, YOU'RE FAST...
BIP BIP BIP
YEAH. I'VE ALWAYS BEEN PRETTY NIMBLE WITH MY FINGERS.
MESSAGE TO YOUR GIRLFRIEND?
NAH...TO A BUDDY OF MINE.
BUT HE WON'T GET IT NO MATTER HOW MANY TIMES I SEND IT...
...'CAUSE HE BLEW UP FOUR YEARS AGO.
WHAT?
HUH?
WHAT DO YOU MEAN, YOU'RE NOT GOING?

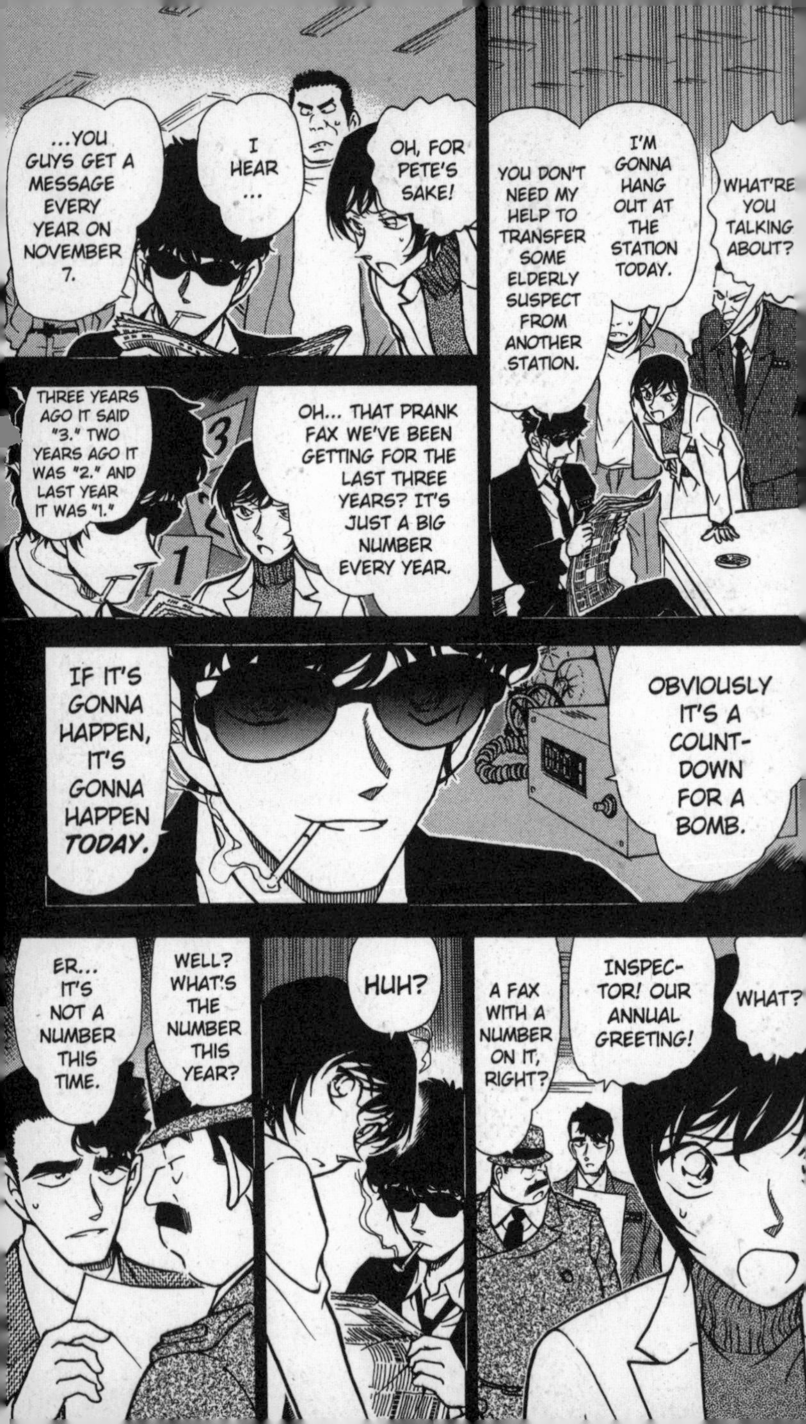
WHAT'RE YOU TALKING ABOUT?
I'M GONNA HANG OUT AT THE STATION TODAY.
YOU DON'T NEED MY HELP TO TRANSFER SOME ELDERLY SUSPECT FROM ANOTHER STATION.
OH, FOR PETE'S SAKE!
I HEAR...
...YOU GUYS GET A MESSAGE EVERY YEAR ON NOVEMBER 7.
OH... THAT PRANK FAX WE'VE BEEN GETTING FOR THE LAST THREE YEARS? IT'S JUST A BIG NUMBER EVERY YEAR.
THREE YEARS AGO IT SAID "3." TWO YEARS AGO IT WAS "2." AND LAST YEAR IT WAS "1."
OBVIOUSLY IT'S A COUNT-DOWN FOR A BOMB.
IF IT'S GONNA HAPPEN, IT'S GONNA HAPPEN *TODAY.*
WHAT?
INSPEC-TOR! OUR ANNUAL GREETING!
A FAX WITH A NUMBER ON IT, RIGHT?
HUH?
WELL? WHAT'S THE NUMBER THIS YEAR?
ER... IT'S NOT A NUMBER THIS TIME.

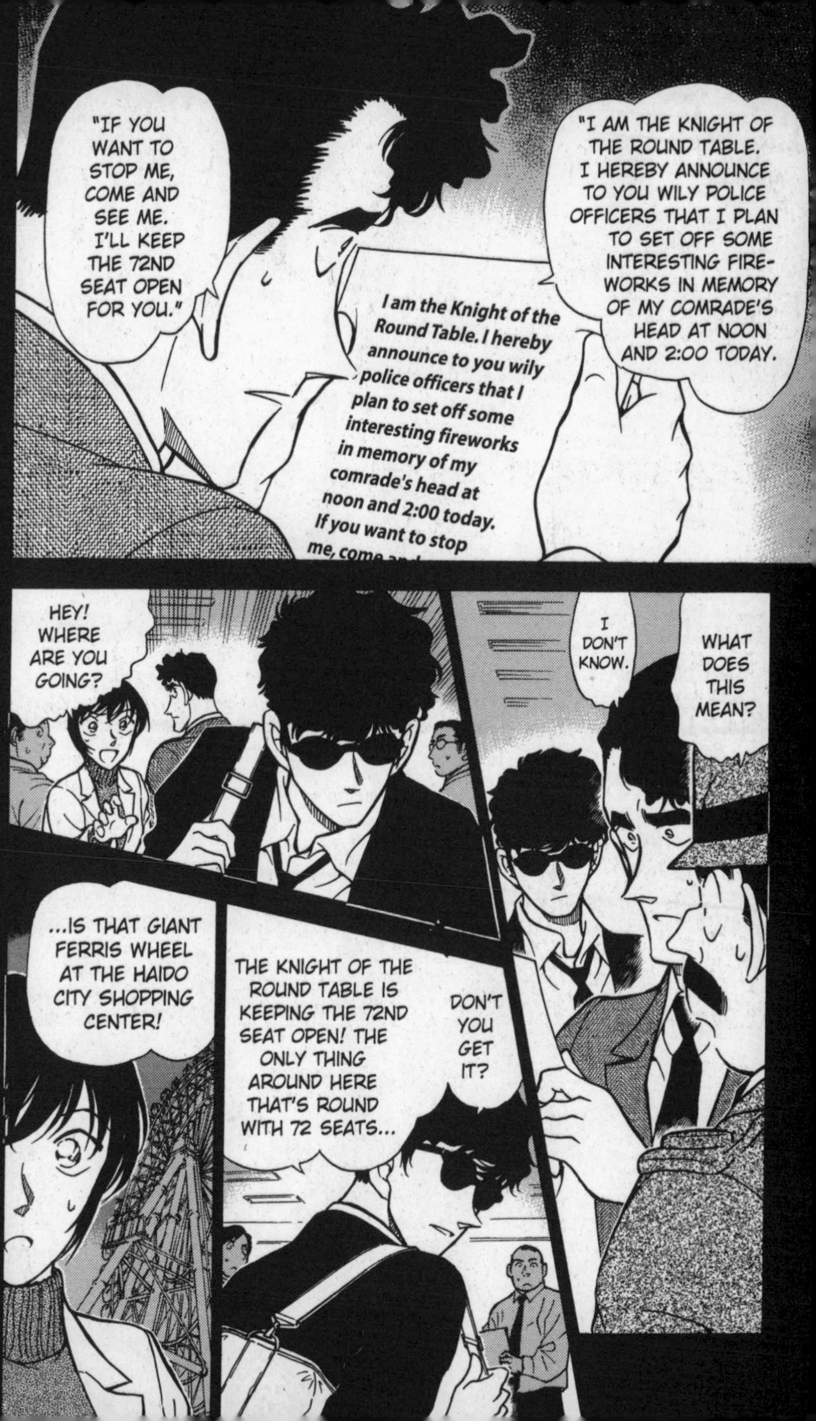
"I AM THE KNIGHT OF THE ROUND TABLE. I HEREBY ANNOUNCE TO YOU WILY POLICE OFFICERS THAT I PLAN TO SET OFF SOME INTERESTING FIRE-WORKS IN MEMORY OF MY COMRADE'S HEAD AT NOON AND 2:00 TODAY.
I am the Knight of the Round Table. I hereby announce to you wily police officers that I plan to set off some interesting fireworks in memory of my comrade's head at noon and 2:00 today. If you want to stop me, come
"IF YOU WANT TO STOP ME, COME AND SEE ME. I'LL KEEP THE 72ND SEAT OPEN FOR YOU."
WHAT DOES THIS MEAN?
I DON'T KNOW.
HEY! WHERE ARE YOU GOING?
DON'T YOU GET IT?
THE KNIGHT OF THE ROUND TABLE IS KEEPING THE 72ND SEAT OPEN! THE ONLY THING AROUND HERE THAT'S ROUND WITH 72 SEATS...
...IS THAT GIANT FERRIS WHEEL AT THE HAIDO CITY SHOPPING CENTER!

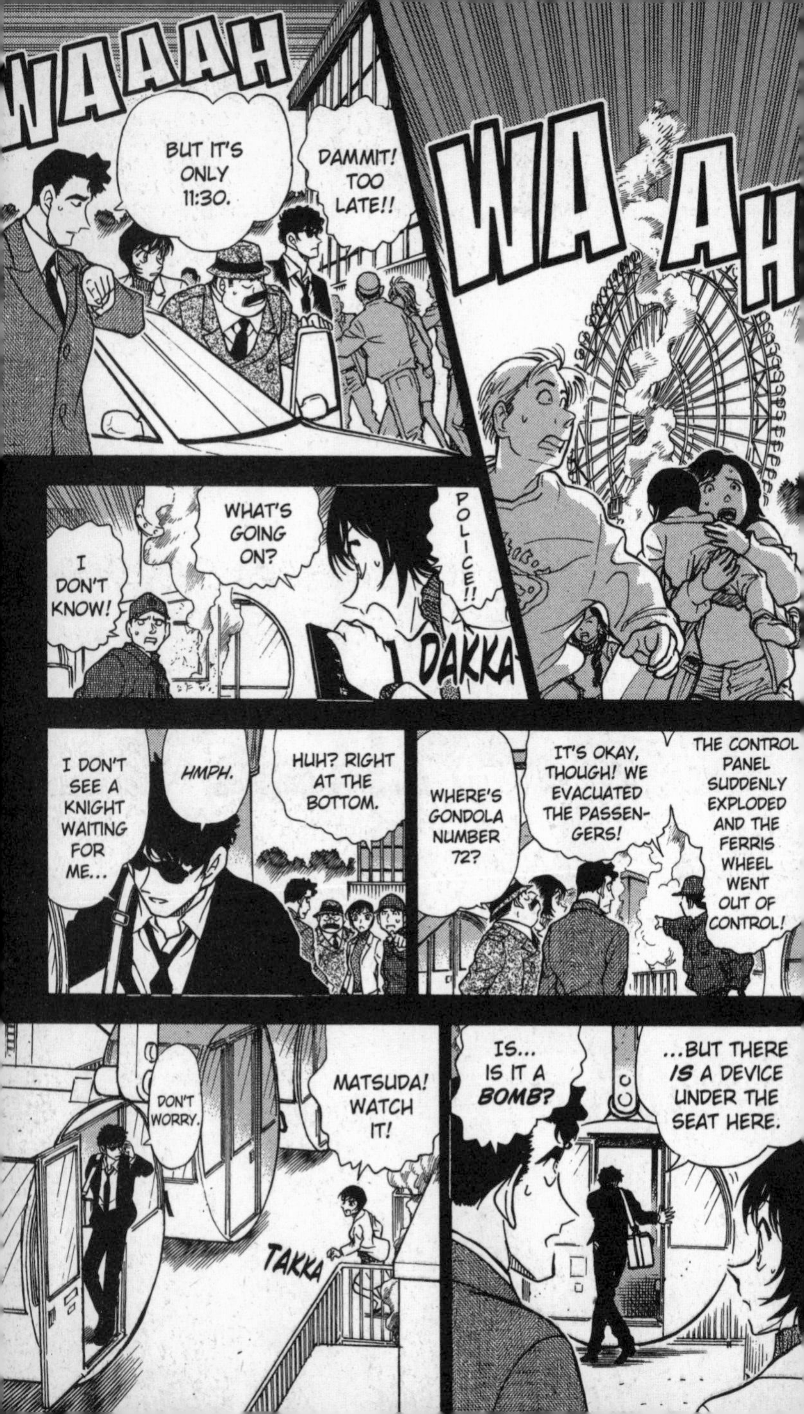
WA AH
DAMMIT! TOO LATE!!
BUT IT'S ONLY 11:30.
WAAAH
POLICE!!
DAKKA
WHAT'S GOING ON?
I DON'T KNOW!
THE CONTROL PANEL SUDDENLY EXPLODED AND THE FERRIS WHEEL WENT OUT OF CONTROL!
IT'S OKAY, THOUGH! WE EVACUATED THE PASSENGERS!
WHERE'S GONDOLA NUMBER 72?
HUH? RIGHT AT THE BOTTOM.
HMPH.
I DON'T SEE A KNIGHT WAITING FOR ME...
...BUT THERE IS A DEVICE UNDER THE SEAT HERE.
IS... IS IT A BOMB?
MATSUDA! WATCH IT!
TAKKA
DON'T WORRY.

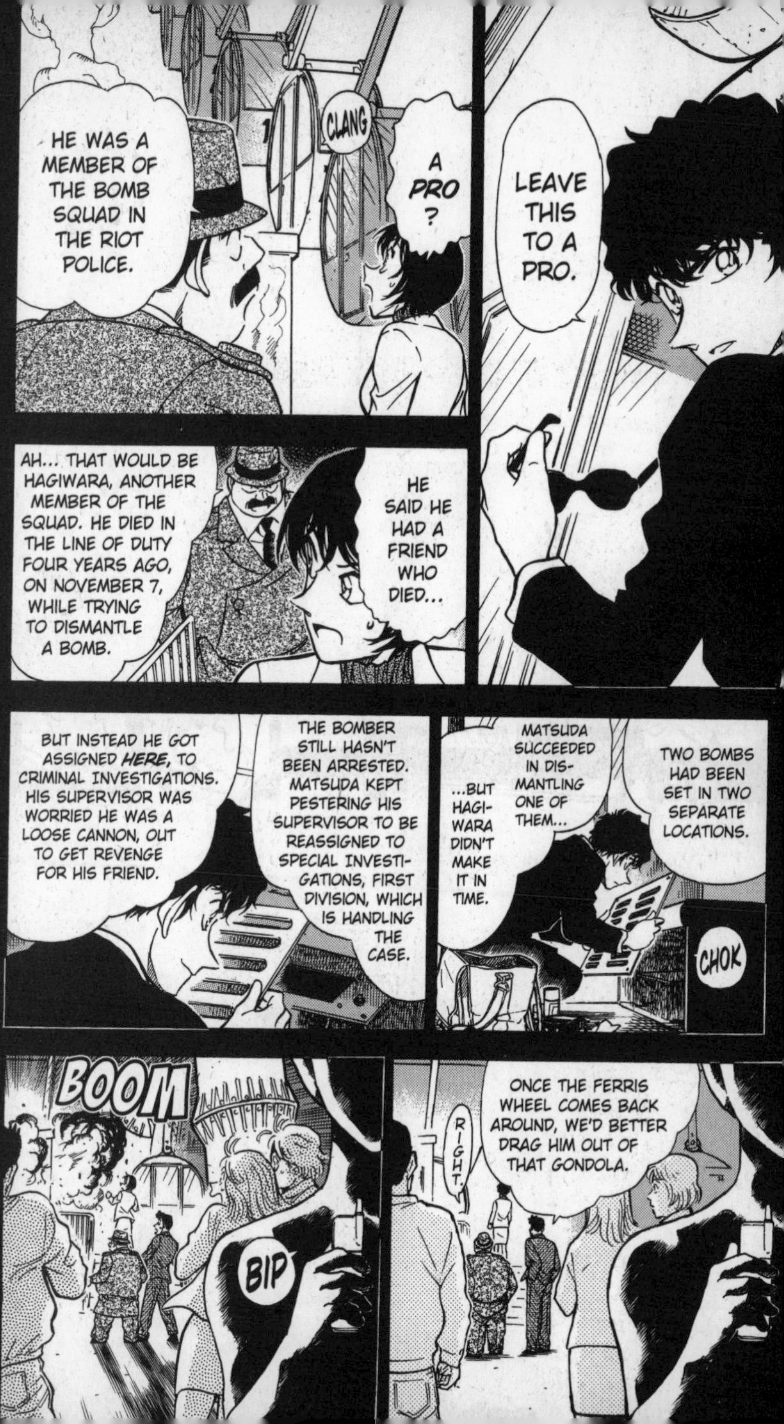
LEAVE THIS TO A PRO.
CLANG
A PRO?
HE WAS A MEMBER OF THE BOMB SQUAD IN THE RIOT POLICE.
HE SAID HE HAD A FRIEND WHO DIED...
AH... THAT WOULD BE HAGIWARA, ANOTHER MEMBER OF THE SQUAD. HE DIED IN THE LINE OF DUTY FOUR YEARS AGO, ON NOVEMBER 7, WHILE TRYING TO DISMANTLE A BOMB.
TWO BOMBS HAD BEEN SET IN TWO SEPARATE LOCATIONS.
MATSUDA SUCCEEDED IN DISMANTLING ONE OF THEM...
...BUT HAGIWARA DIDN'T MAKE IT IN TIME.
CHOK
THE BOMBER STILL HASN'T BEEN ARRESTED. MATSUDA KEPT PESTERING HIS SUPERVISOR TO BE REASSIGNED TO SPECIAL INVESTIGATIONS, FIRST DIVISION, WHICH IS HANDLING THE CASE.
BUT INSTEAD HE GOT ASSIGNED *HERE,* TO CRIMINAL INVESTIGATIONS. HIS SUPERVISOR WAS WORRIED HE WAS A LOOSE CANNON, OUT TO GET REVENGE FOR HIS FRIEND.
ONCE THE FERRIS WHEEL COMES BACK AROUND, WE'D BETTER DRAG HIM OUT OF THAT GONDOLA.
RIGHT.
BOOM
BIP

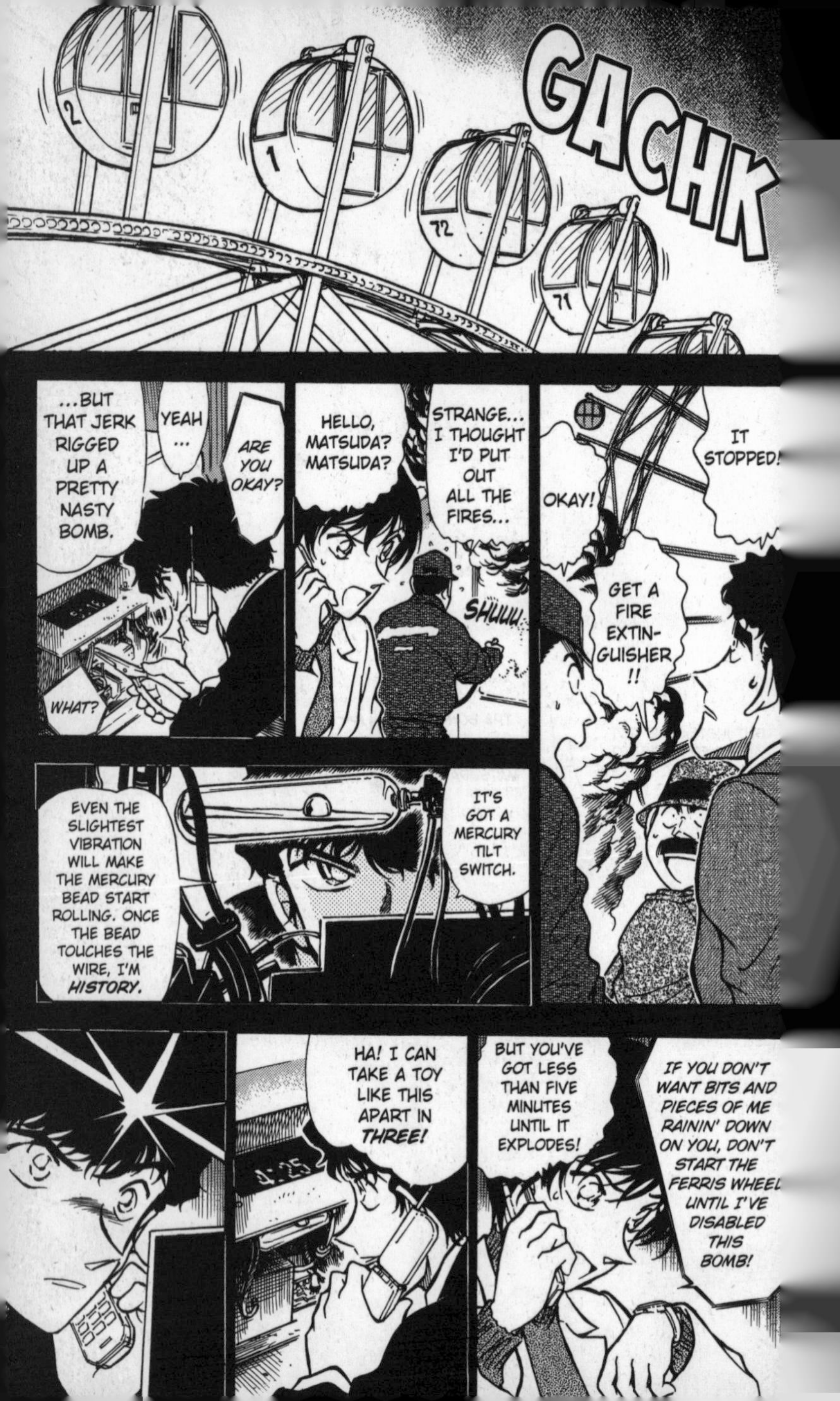
GACHK
IT STOPPED!
OKAY!
GET A FIRE EXTIN-GUISHER!!
STRANGE... I THOUGHT I'D PUT OUT ALL THE FIRES...
HELLO, MATSUDA? MATSUDA?
SHUUU
ARE YOU OKAY?
YEAH...
...BUT THAT JERK RIGGED UP A PRETTY NASTY BOMB.
WHAT?
IT'S GOT A MERCURY TILT SWITCH.
EVEN THE SLIGHTEST VIBRATION WILL MAKE THE MERCURY BEAD START ROLLING. ONCE THE BEAD TOUCHES THE WIRE, I'M *HISTORY*.
IF YOU DON'T WANT BITS AND PIECES OF ME RAININ' DOWN ON YOU, DON'T START THE FERRIS WHEEL UNTIL I'VE DISABLED THIS BOMB!
BUT YOU'VE GOT LESS THAN FIVE MINUTES UNTIL IT EXPLODES!
HA! I CAN TAKE A TOY LIKE THIS APART IN *THREE!*

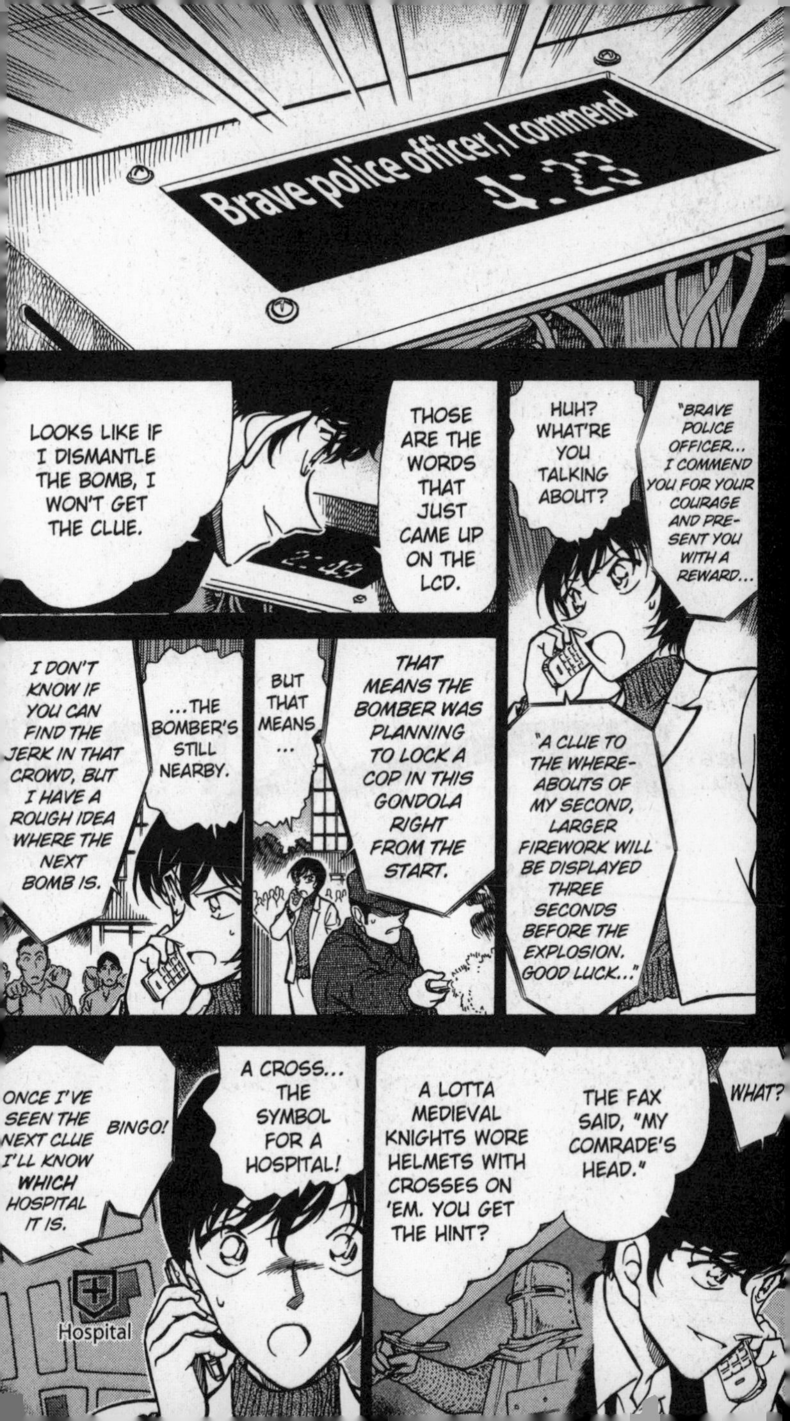
Brave police officer, I commend
4:23
"BRAVE POLICE OFFICER... I COMMEND YOU FOR YOUR COURAGE AND PRESENT YOU WITH A REWARD...
HUH? WHAT'RE YOU TALKING ABOUT?
"A CLUE TO THE WHEREABOUTS OF MY SECOND, LARGER FIREWORK WILL BE DISPLAYED THREE SECONDS BEFORE THE EXPLOSION. GOOD LUCK..."
THOSE ARE THE WORDS THAT JUST CAME UP ON THE LCD.
2:49
LOOKS LIKE IF I DISMANTLE THE BOMB, I WON'T GET THE CLUE.
THAT MEANS THE BOMBER WAS PLANNING TO LOCK A COP IN THIS GONDOLA RIGHT FROM THE START.
BUT THAT MEANS...
...THE BOMBER'S STILL NEARBY.
I DON'T KNOW IF YOU CAN FIND THE JERK IN THAT CROWD, BUT I HAVE A ROUGH IDEA WHERE THE NEXT BOMB IS.
WHAT?
THE FAX SAID, "MY COMRADE'S HEAD."
A LOTTA MEDIEVAL KNIGHTS WORE HELMETS WITH CROSSES ON 'EM. YOU GET THE HINT?
A CROSS... THE SYMBOL FOR A HOSPITAL!
BINGO!
ONCE I'VE SEEN THE NEXT CLUE I'LL KNOW WHICH HOSPITAL IT IS.
Hospital

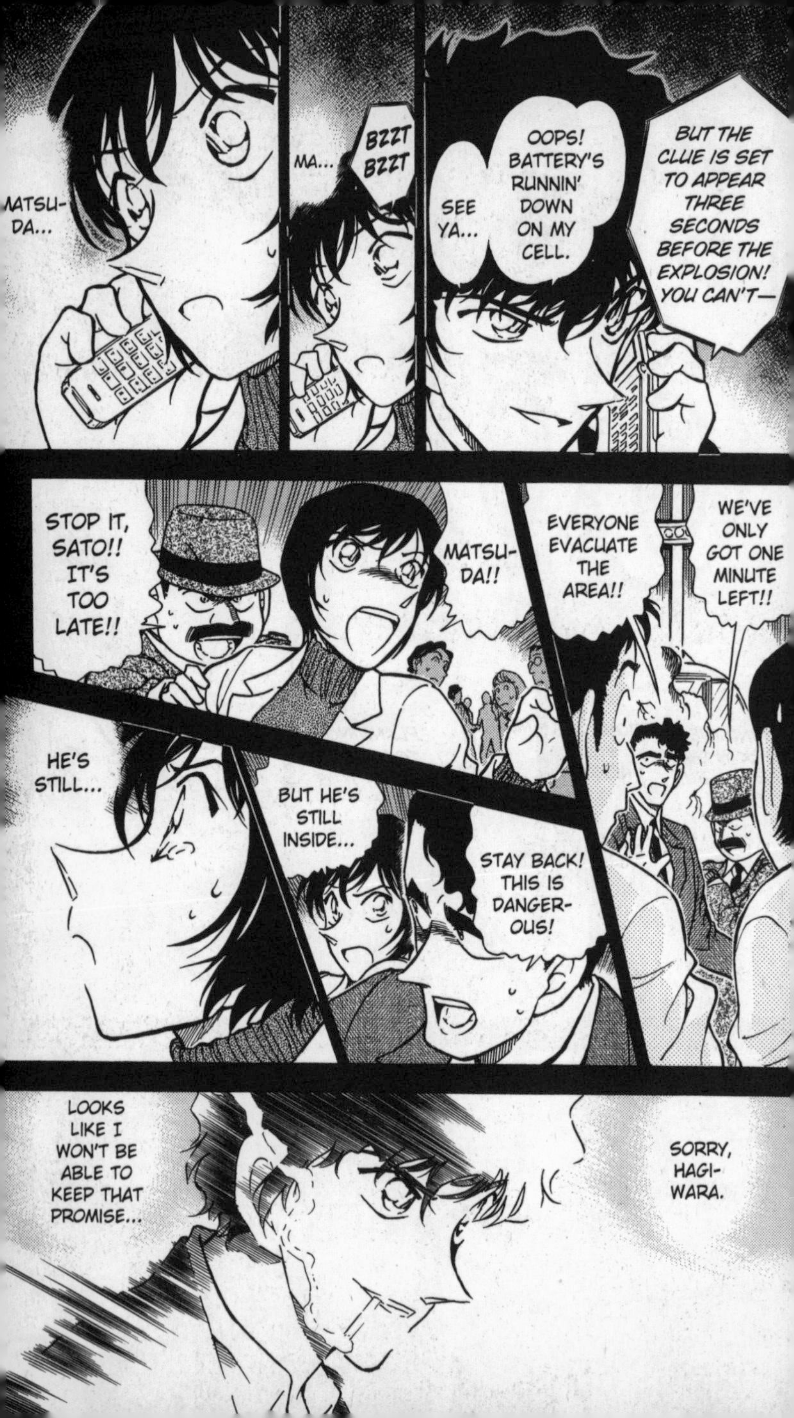
BUT THE CLUE IS SET TO APPEAR THREE SECONDS BEFORE THE EXPLOSION! YOU CAN'T—
OOPS! BATTERY'S RUNNIN' DOWN ON MY CELL.
SEE YA...
BZZT BZZT
MA...
MATSU-DA...
WE'VE ONLY GOT ONE MINUTE LEFT!!
EVERYONE EVACUATE THE AREA!!
MATSU-DA!!
STOP IT, SATO!! IT'S TOO LATE!!
STAY BACK! THIS IS DANGER-OUS!
BUT HE'S STILL INSIDE...
HE'S STILL...
SORRY, HAGI-WARA.
LOOKS LIKE I WON'T BE ABLE TO KEEP THAT PROMISE...

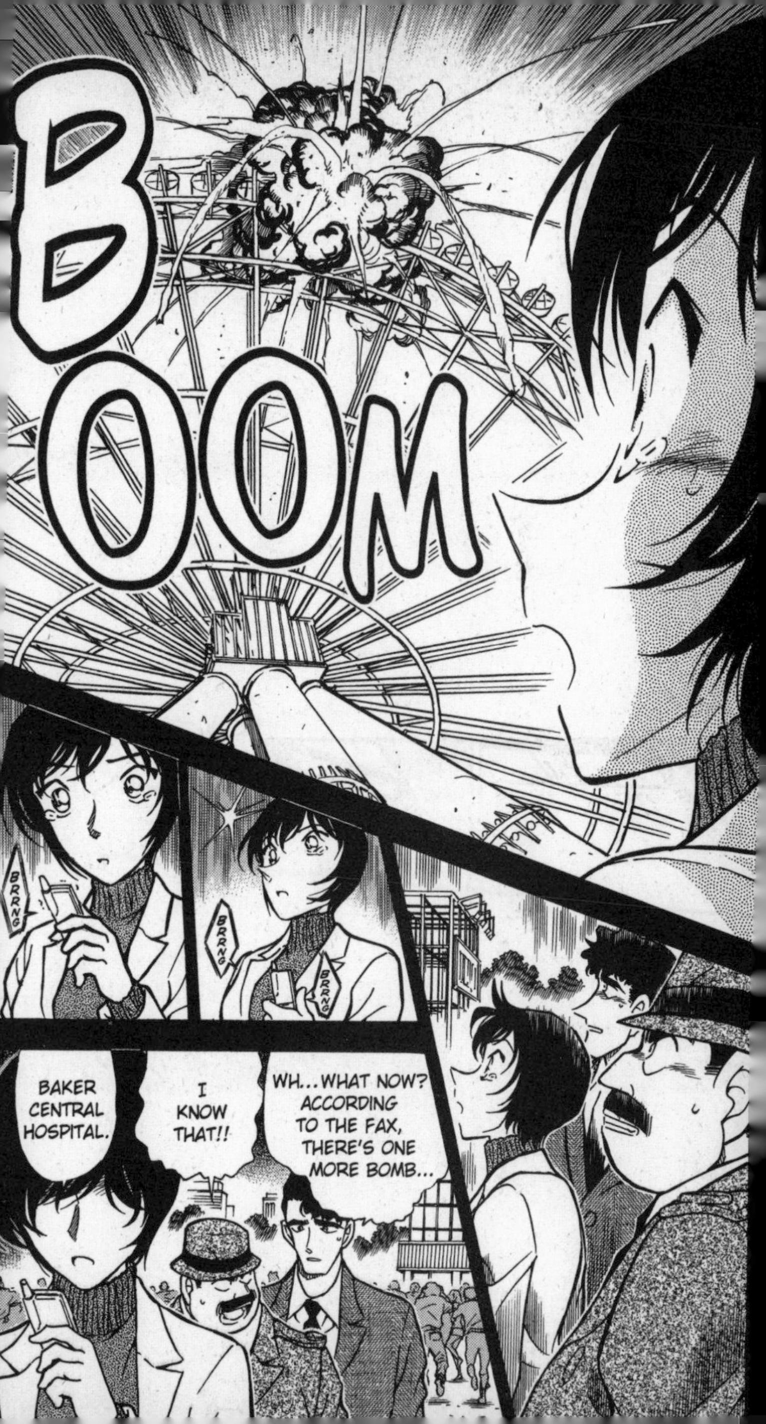
BOOOM
BRRNG
BRRNG
BRRNG
WH...WHAT NOW? ACCORDING TO THE FAX, THERE'S ONE MORE BOMB...
I KNOW THAT!!
BAKER CENTRAL HOSPITAL.

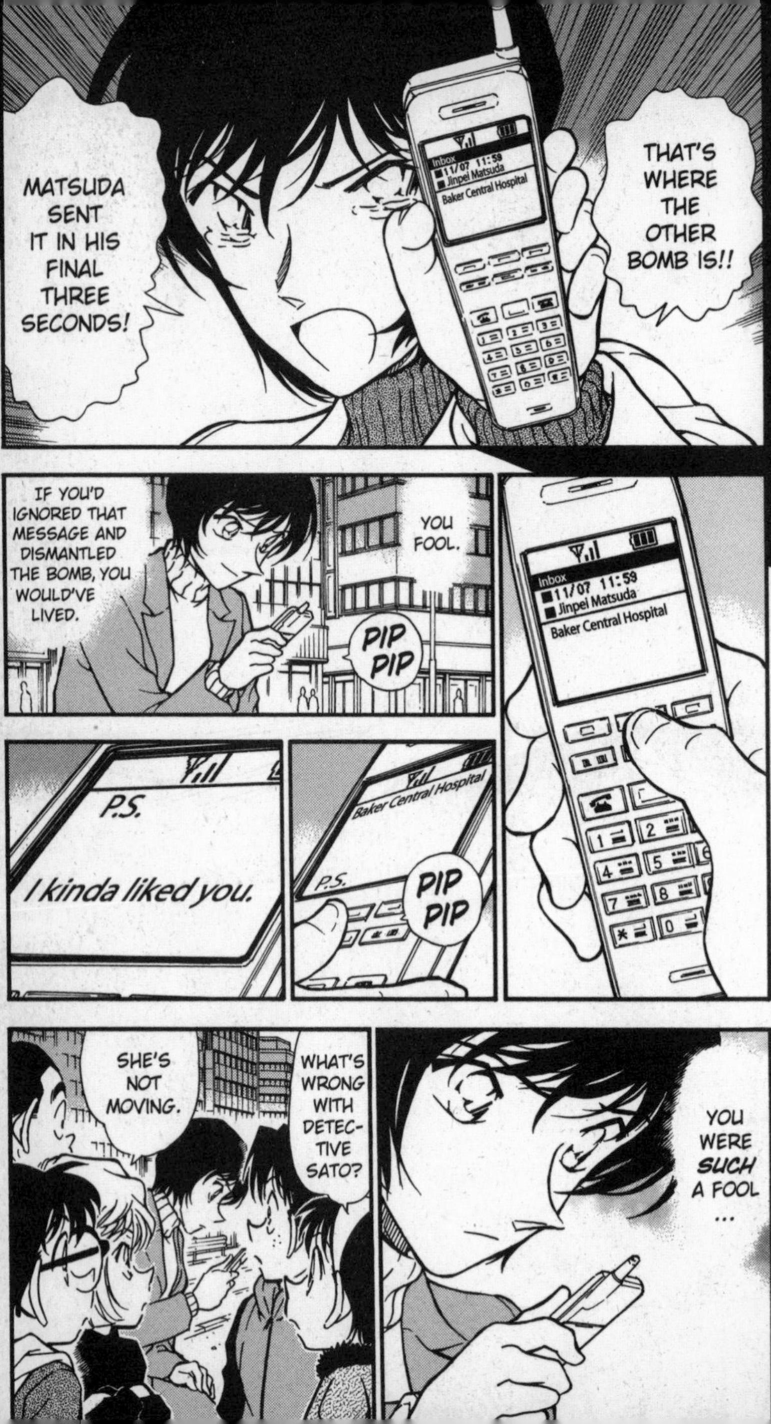
THAT'S WHERE THE OTHER BOMB IS!!
MATSUDA SENT IT IN HIS FINAL THREE SECONDS!
Inbox
11/07 11:59
Jinpei Matsuda
Baker Central Hospital
Inbox
11/07 11:59
Jinpei Matsuda
Baker Central Hospital
YOU FOOL.
IF YOU'D IGNORED THAT MESSAGE AND DISMANTLED THE BOMB, YOU WOULD'VE LIVED.
PIP PIP
Baker Central Hospital
P.S.
PIP PIP
P.S.
I kinda liked you.
YOU WERE *SUCH* A FOOL ...
WHAT'S WRONG WITH DETEC-TIVE SATO?
SHE'S NOT MOVING.

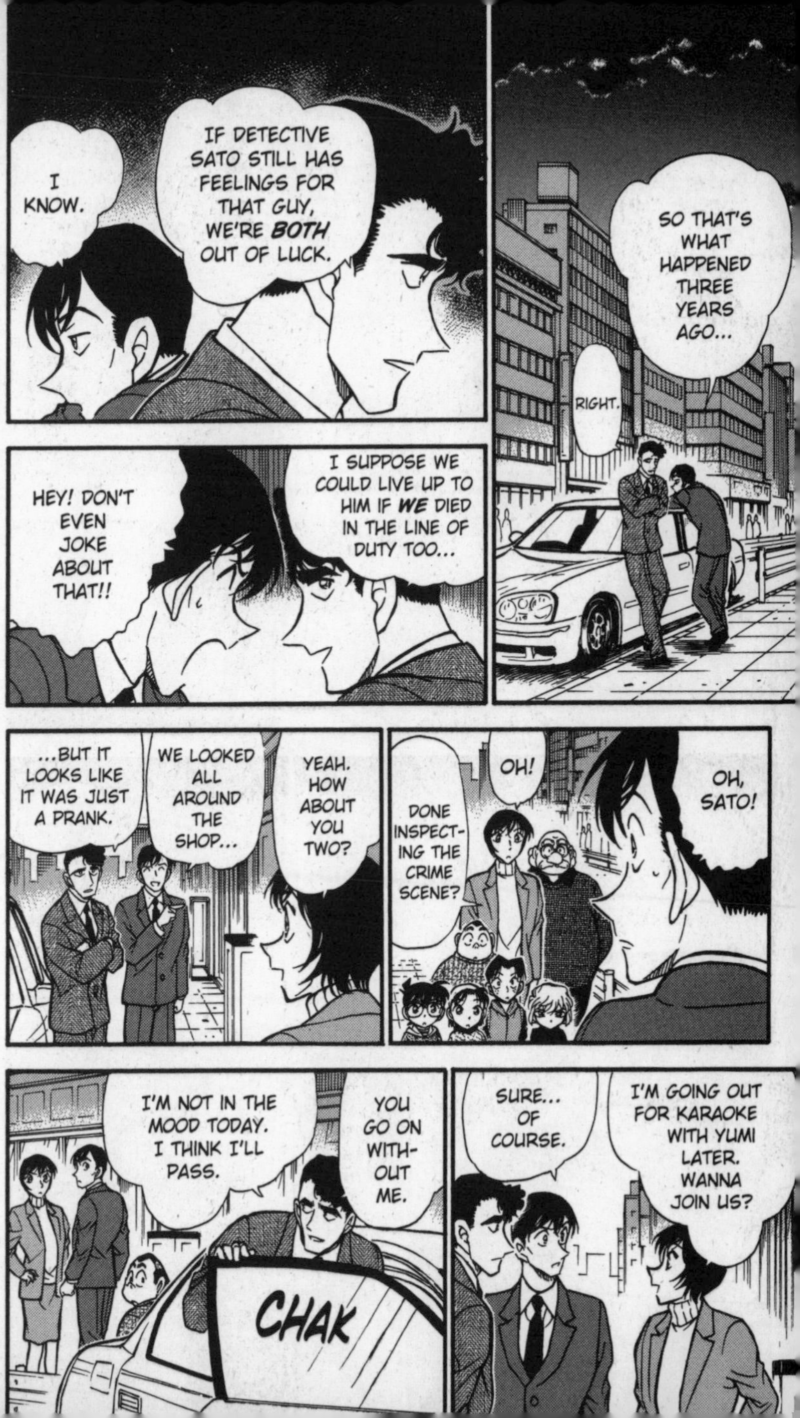
SO THAT'S WHAT HAPPENED THREE YEARS AGO...
RIGHT.
IF DETECTIVE SATO STILL HAS FEELINGS FOR THAT GUY, WE'RE *BOTH* OUT OF LUCK.
I KNOW.
I SUPPOSE WE COULD LIVE UP TO HIM IF *WE* DIED IN THE LINE OF DUTY TOO...
HEY! DON'T EVEN JOKE ABOUT THAT!!
OH, SATO!
OH!
DONE INSPECTING THE CRIME SCENE?
YEAH. HOW ABOUT YOU TWO?
WE LOOKED ALL AROUND THE SHOP...
...BUT IT LOOKS LIKE IT WAS JUST A PRANK.
I'M GOING OUT FOR KARAOKE WITH YUMI LATER. WANNA JOIN US?
SURE... OF COURSE.
YOU GO ON WITHOUT ME.
I'M NOT IN THE MOOD TODAY. I THINK I'LL PASS.
CHAK

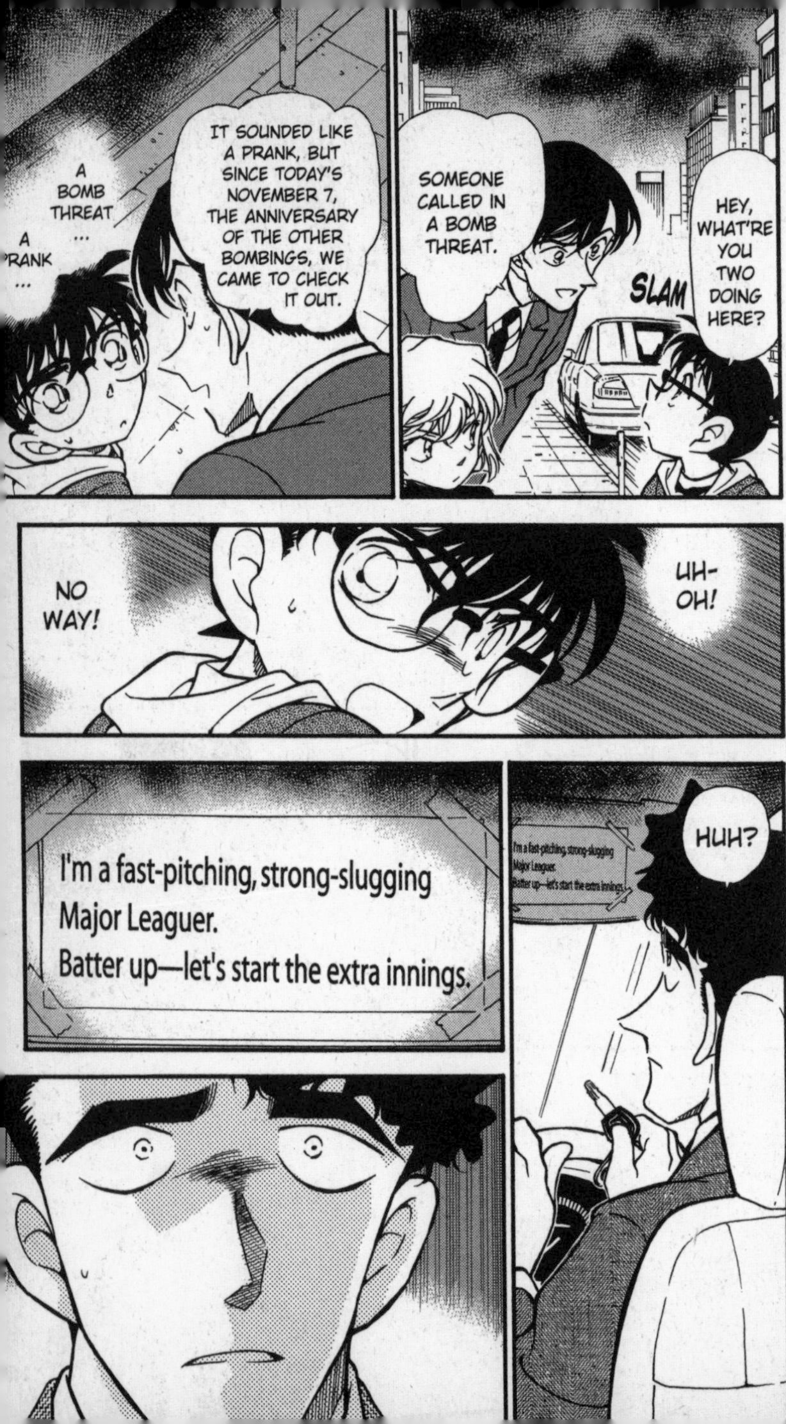
HEY, WHAT'RE YOU TWO DOING HERE?
SLAM
SOMEONE CALLED IN A BOMB THREAT.
IT SOUNDED LIKE A PRANK, BUT SINCE TODAY'S NOVEMBER 7, THE ANNIVERSARY OF THE OTHER BOMBINGS, WE CAME TO CHECK IT OUT.
A BOMB THREAT ...
A PRANK ...
UH-OH!
NO WAY!
HUH?
I'm a fast-pitching, strong-slugging Major Leaguer. Batter up—let's start the extra innings.
I'm a fast-pitching, strong-slugging
Major Leaguer.
Batter up—let's start the extra innings.

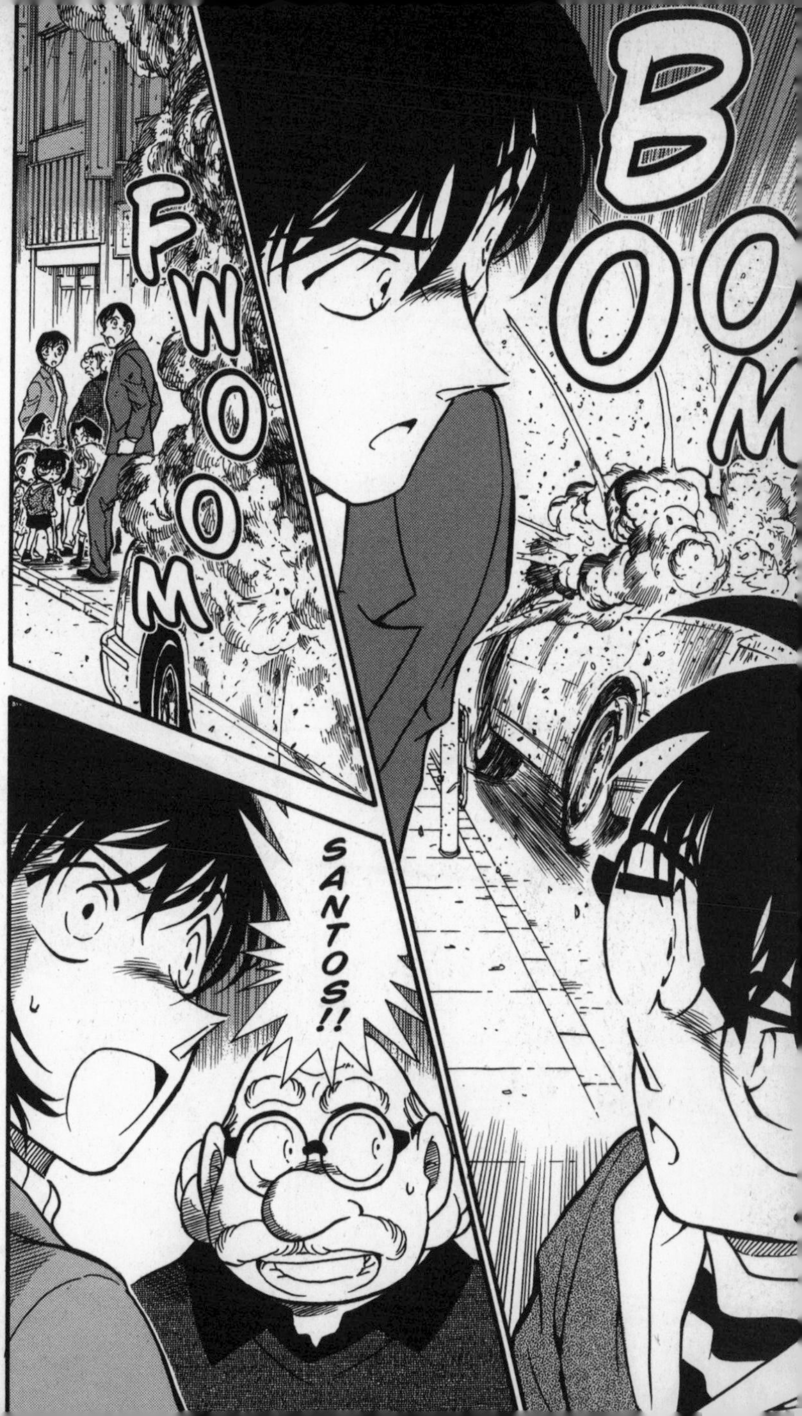
BOOOM
FWOOOM
SANTOS!!

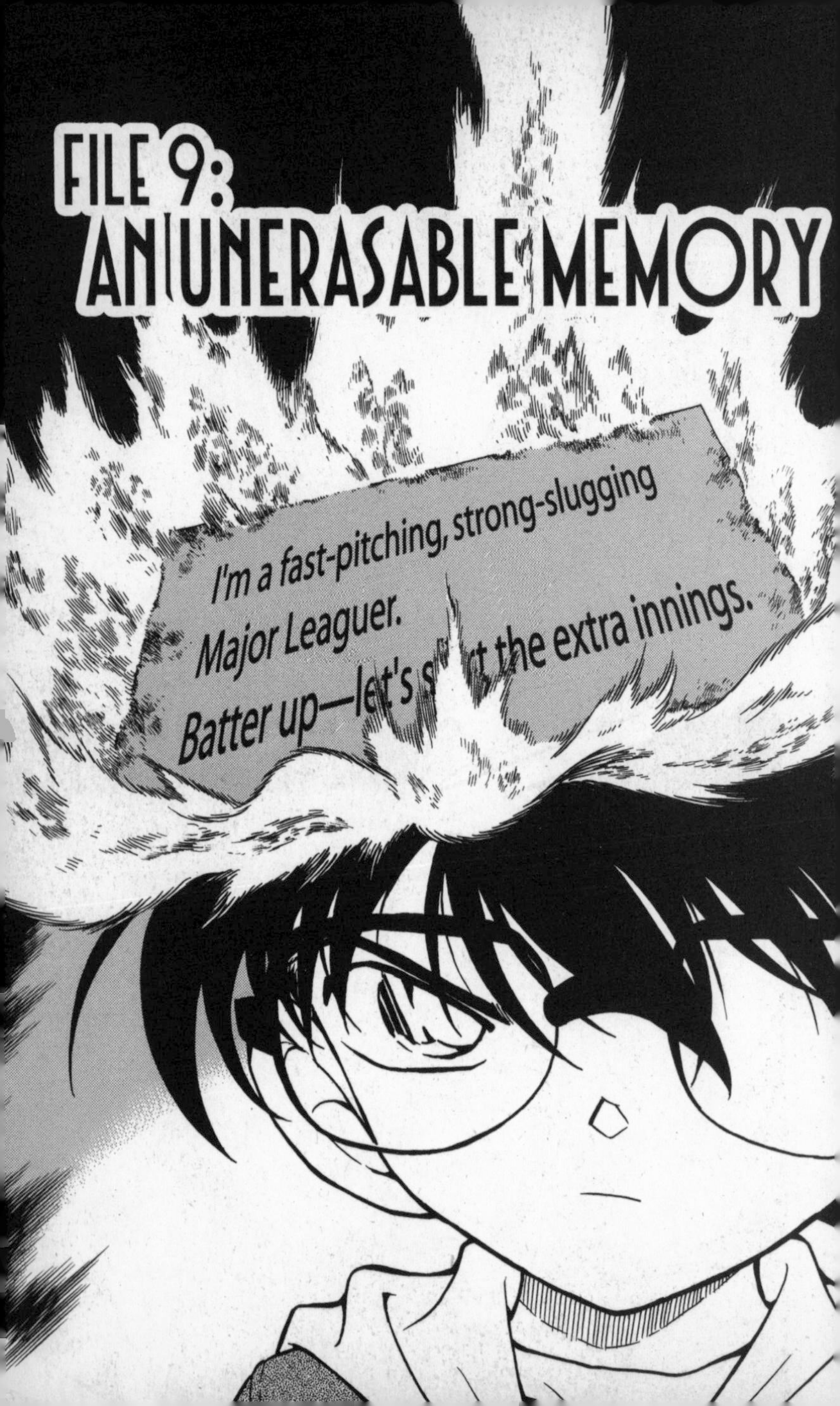
FILE 9:
AN UNERASABLE MEMORY
I'm a fast-pitching, strong-slugging
Major Leaguer.
Batter up—let's s rt the extra innings.

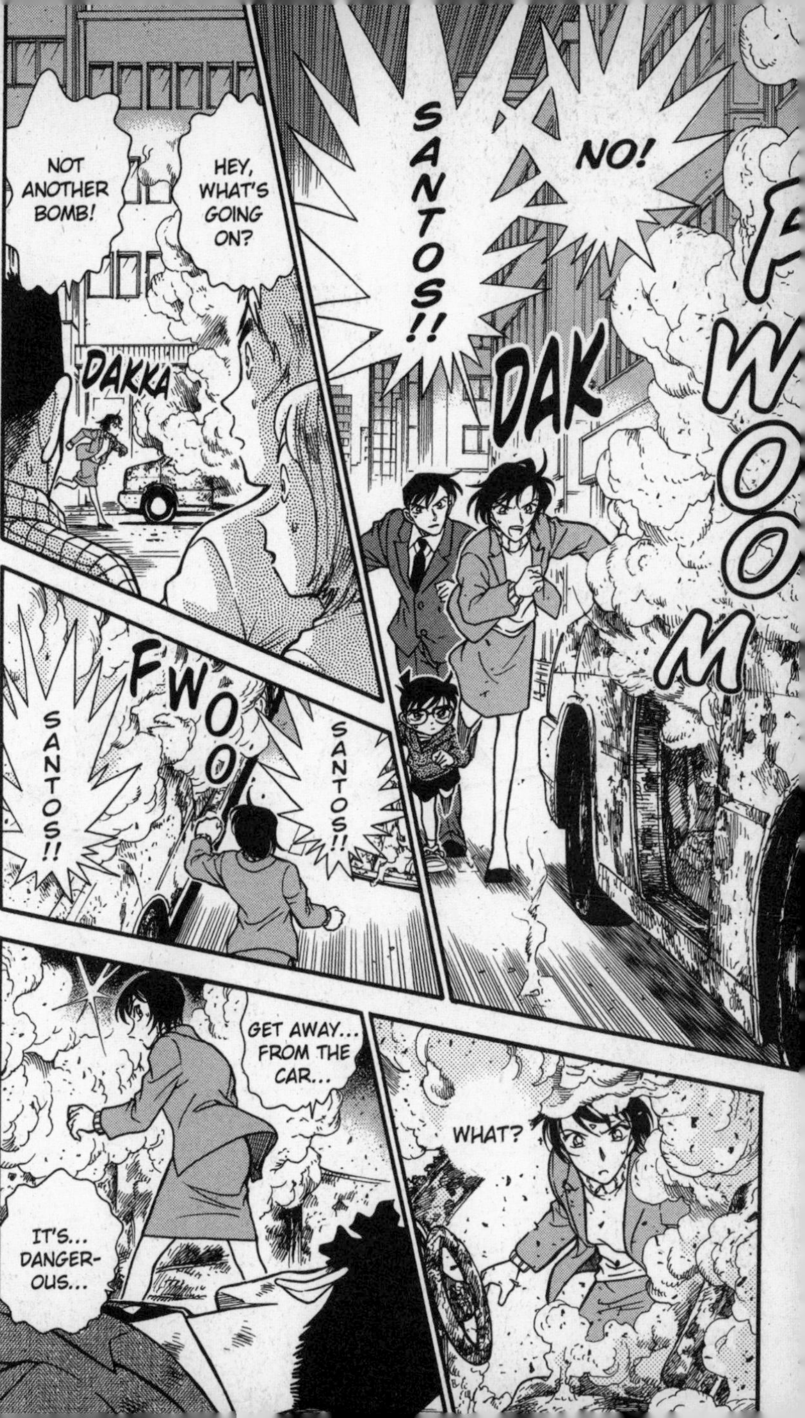
FWOOM
NO!
SANTOS!!
DAK
HEY, WHAT'S GOING ON?
NOT ANOTHER BOMB!
DAKKA
SANTOS!!
FWOO
SANTOS!!
WHAT?
GET AWAY... FROM THE CAR...
IT'S... DANGER-OUS...

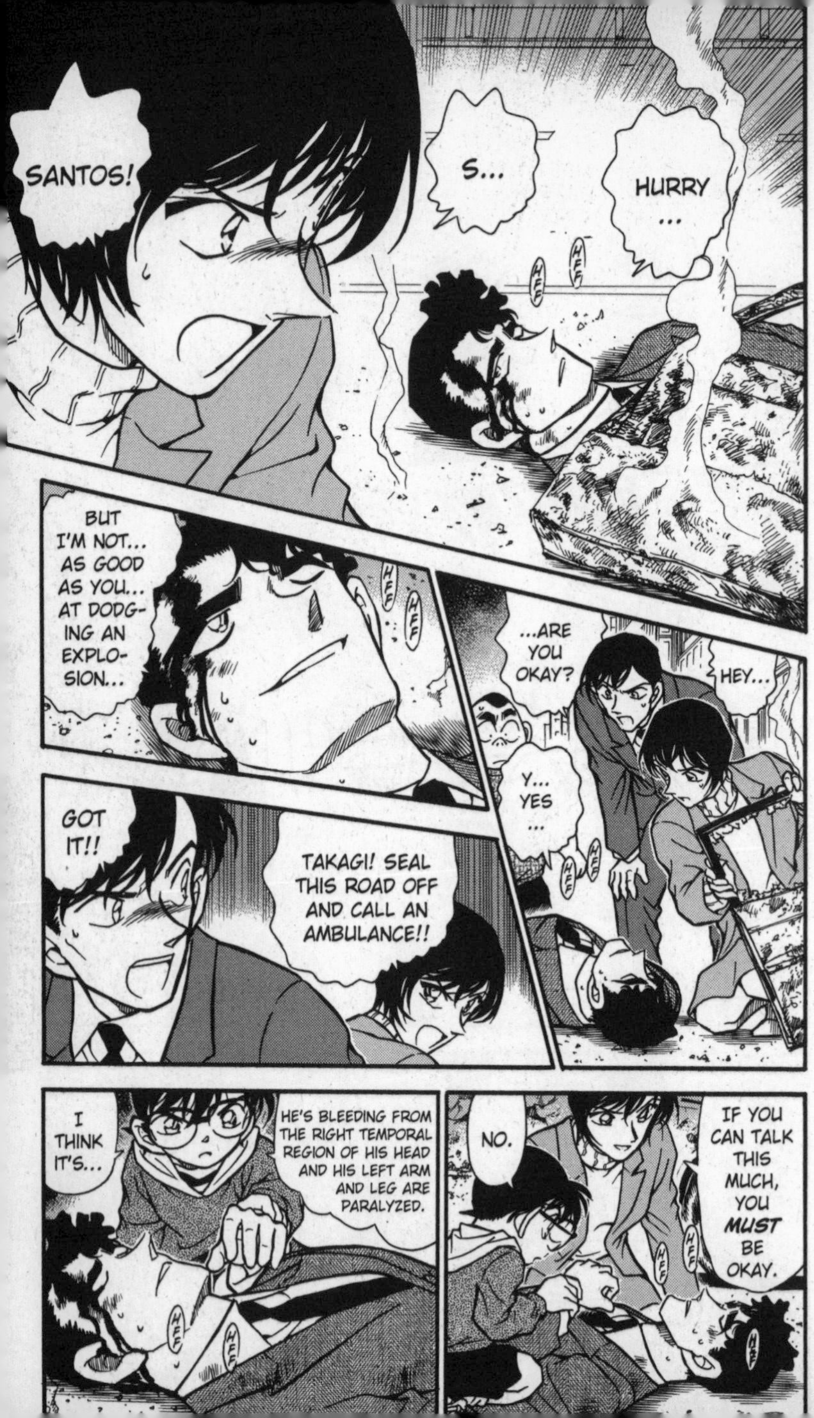
HURRY ...
S...
HEF HEF
SANTOS!
HEY...
...ARE YOU OKAY?
Y... YES ...
HEF HEF
BUT I'M NOT... AS GOOD AS YOU... AT DODGING AN EXPLOSION...
HEF HEF
TAKAGI! SEAL THIS ROAD OFF AND CALL AN AMBULANCE!!
GOT IT!!
IF YOU CAN TALK THIS MUCH, YOU *MUST* BE OKAY.
HEF
NO.
HEF
HE'S BLEEDING FROM THE RIGHT TEMPORAL REGION OF HIS HEAD AND HIS LEFT ARM AND LEG ARE PARALYZED.
I THINK IT'S...
HEF HEF

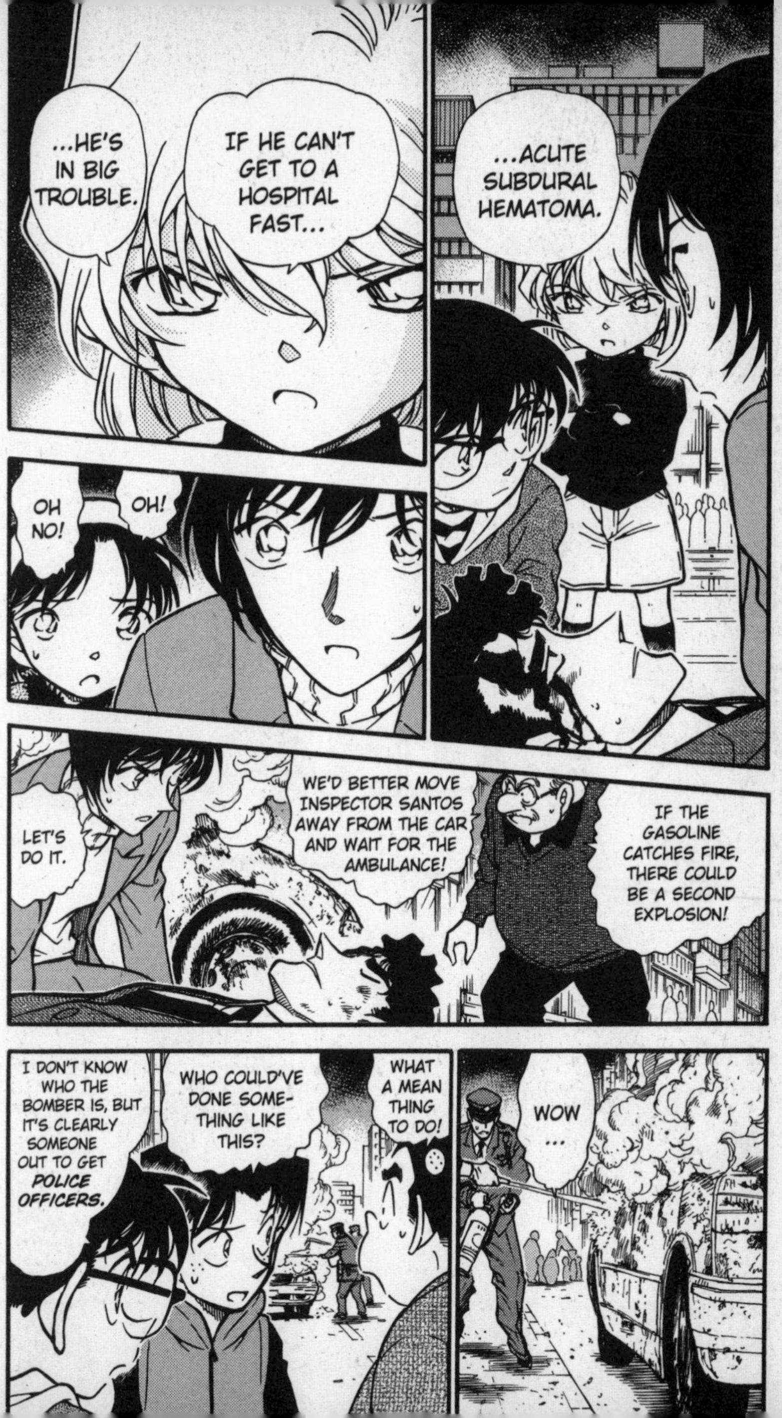
...ACUTE SUBDURAL HEMATOMA.
IF HE CAN'T GET TO A HOSPITAL FAST...
...HE'S IN BIG TROUBLE.
OH!
OH NO!
IF THE GASOLINE CATCHES FIRE, THERE COULD BE A SECOND EXPLOSION!
WE'D BETTER MOVE INSPECTOR SANTOS AWAY FROM THE CAR AND WAIT FOR THE AMBULANCE!
LET'S DO IT.
WOW ...
WHAT A MEAN THING TO DO!
WHO COULD'VE DONE SOME-THING LIKE THIS?
I DON'T KNOW WHO THE BOMBER IS, BUT IT'S CLEARLY SOMEONE OUT TO GET *POLICE OFFICERS.*

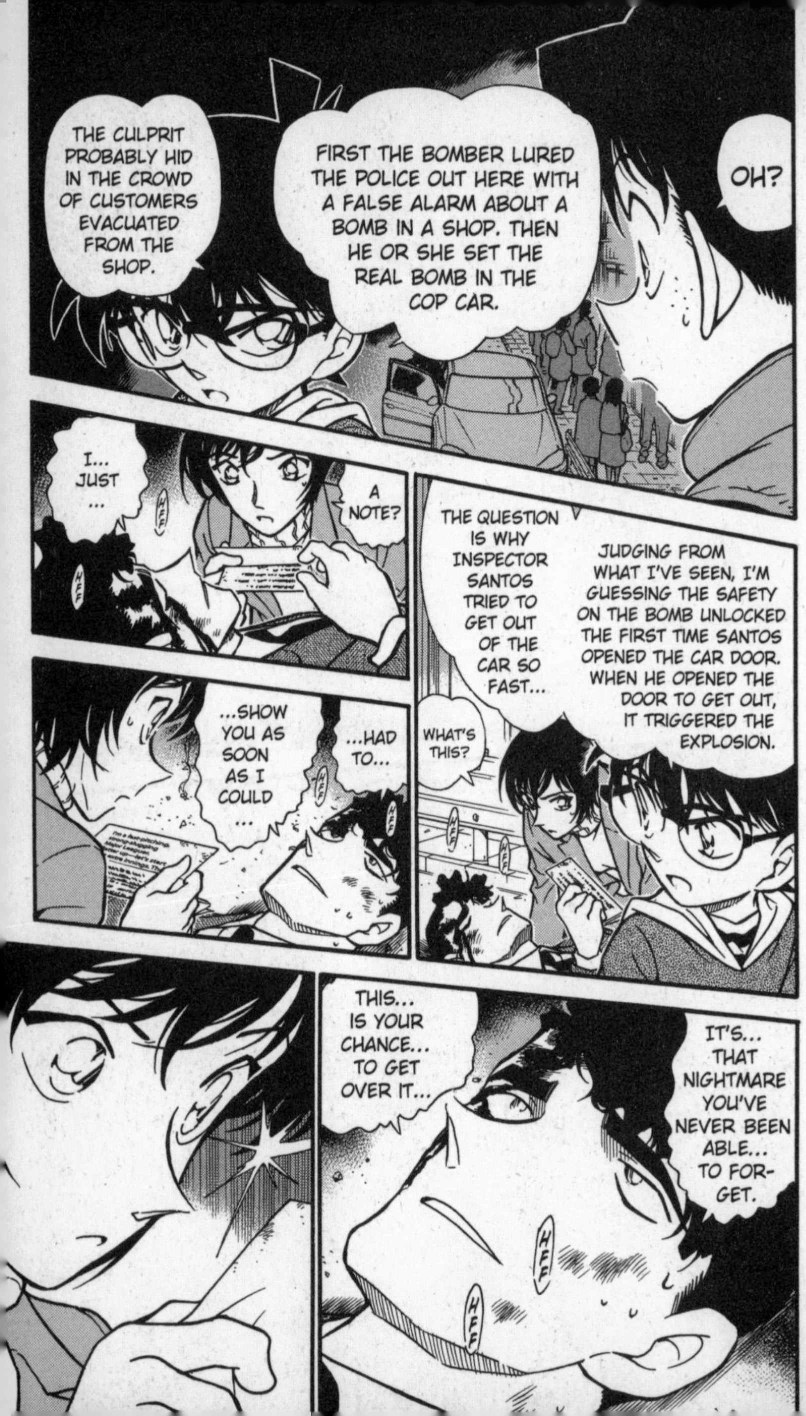
OH?
FIRST THE BOMBER LURED THE POLICE OUT HERE WITH A FALSE ALARM ABOUT A BOMB IN A SHOP. THEN HE OR SHE SET THE REAL BOMB IN THE COP CAR.
THE CULPRIT PROBABLY HID IN THE CROWD OF CUSTOMERS EVACUATED FROM THE SHOP.
THE QUESTION IS WHY INSPECTOR SANTOS TRIED TO GET OUT OF THE CAR SO FAST...
JUDGING FROM WHAT I'VE SEEN, I'M GUESSING THE SAFETY ON THE BOMB UNLOCKED THE FIRST TIME SANTOS OPENED THE CAR DOOR. WHEN HE OPENED THE DOOR TO GET OUT, IT TRIGGERED THE EXPLOSION.
WHAT'S THIS?
A NOTE?
I... JUST...
...HAD TO...
...SHOW YOU AS SOON AS I COULD...
IT'S... THAT NIGHTMARE YOU'VE NEVER BEEN ABLE... TO FOR-GET.
THIS... IS YOUR CHANCE... TO GET OVER IT...

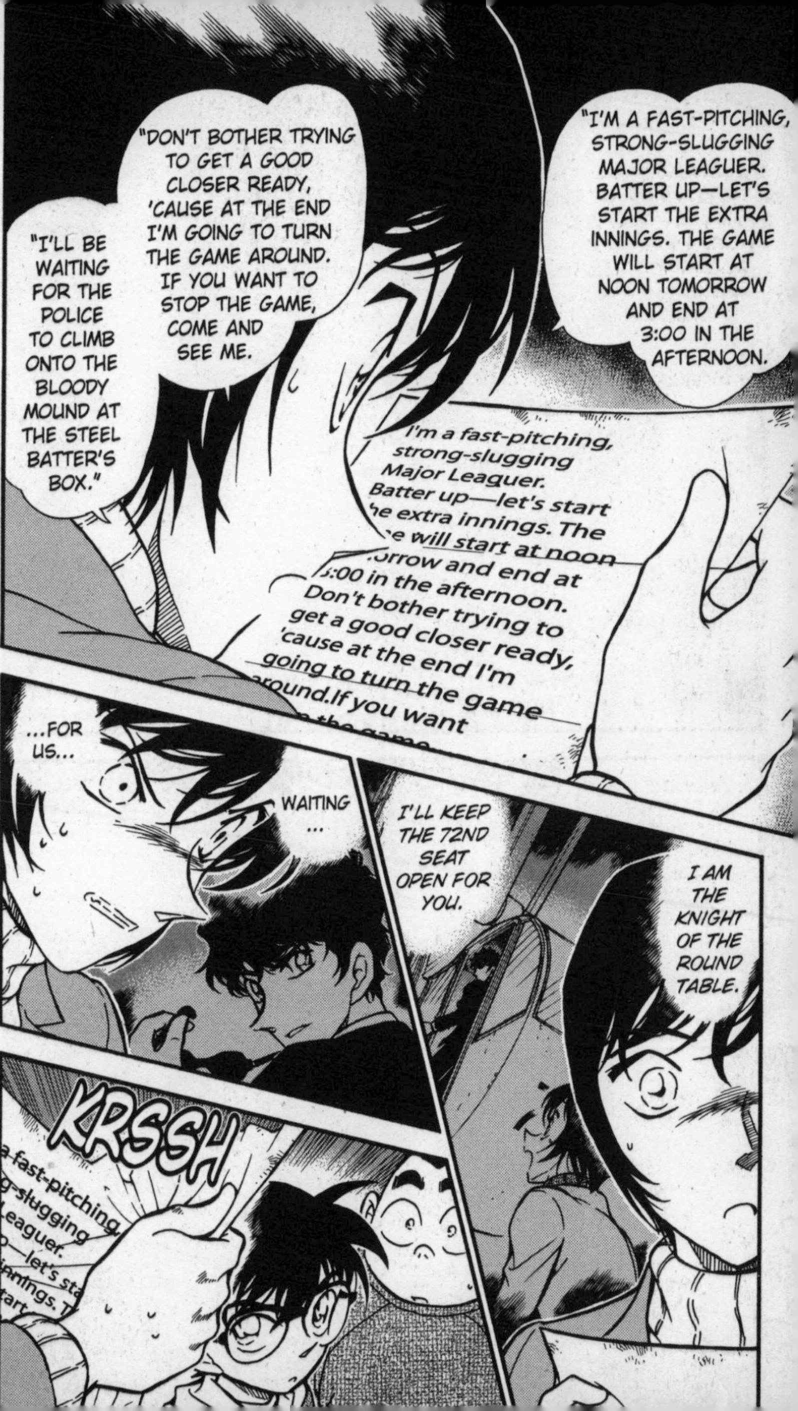
"I'M A FAST-PITCHING, STRONG-SLUGGING MAJOR LEAGUER. BATTER UP—LET'S START THE EXTRA INNINGS. THE GAME WILL START AT NOON TOMORROW AND END AT 3:00 IN THE AFTERNOON.
"DON'T BOTHER TRYING TO GET A GOOD CLOSER READY, 'CAUSE AT THE END I'M GOING TO TURN THE GAME AROUND. IF YOU WANT TO STOP THE GAME, COME AND SEE ME.
"I'LL BE WAITING FOR THE POLICE TO CLIMB ONTO THE BLOODY MOUND AT THE STEEL BATTER'S BOX."
I'm a fast-pitching,
strong-slugging
Major Leaguer.
Batter up—let's start
extra innings. The
will start at noon
orrow and end at
:00 in the afternoon.
Don't bother trying to
get a good closer ready,
'cause at the end I'm
going to turn the game
round.If you want
I AM THE KNIGHT OF THE ROUND TABLE.
I'LL KEEP THE 72ND SEAT OPEN FOR YOU.
WAITING...
...FOR US...
KRSSH
a fast-pitching,
g-slugging
Leaguer.
—let's sta
innings. T
tart.

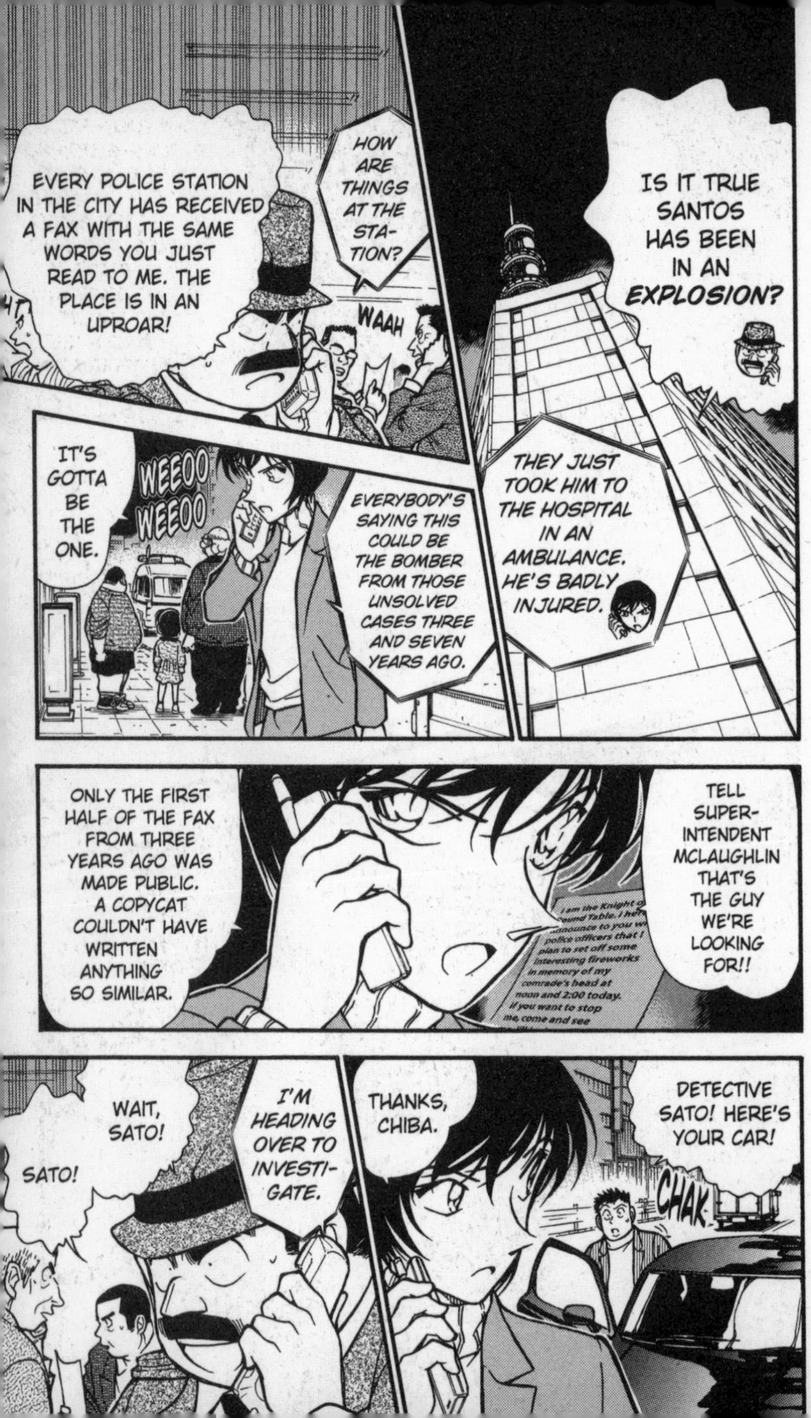
IS IT TRUE SANTOS HAS BEEN IN AN *EXPLOSION?*
THEY JUST TOOK HIM TO THE HOSPITAL IN AN AMBULANCE. HE'S BADLY INJURED.
HOW ARE THINGS AT THE STATION?
EVERY POLICE STATION IN THE CITY HAS RECEIVED A FAX WITH THE SAME WORDS YOU JUST READ TO ME. THE PLACE IS IN AN UPROAR!
WAAH
EVERYBODY'S SAYING THIS COULD BE THE BOMBER FROM THOSE UNSOLVED CASES THREE AND SEVEN YEARS AGO.
WEEOO WEEOO
IT'S GOTTA BE THE ONE.
TELL SUPER-INTENDENT MCLAUGHLIN THAT'S THE GUY WE'RE LOOKING FOR!!
ONLY THE FIRST HALF OF THE FAX FROM THREE YEARS AGO WAS MADE PUBLIC. A COPYCAT COULDN'T HAVE WRITTEN ANYTHING SO SIMILAR.
plan to set off some interesting fireworks in memory of my comrade's head at noon and 2:00 today. If you want to stop me, come and see
DETECTIVE SATO! HERE'S YOUR CAR!
CHAK
THANKS, CHIBA.
I'M HEADING OVER TO INVESTI-GATE.
WAIT, SATO!
SATO!

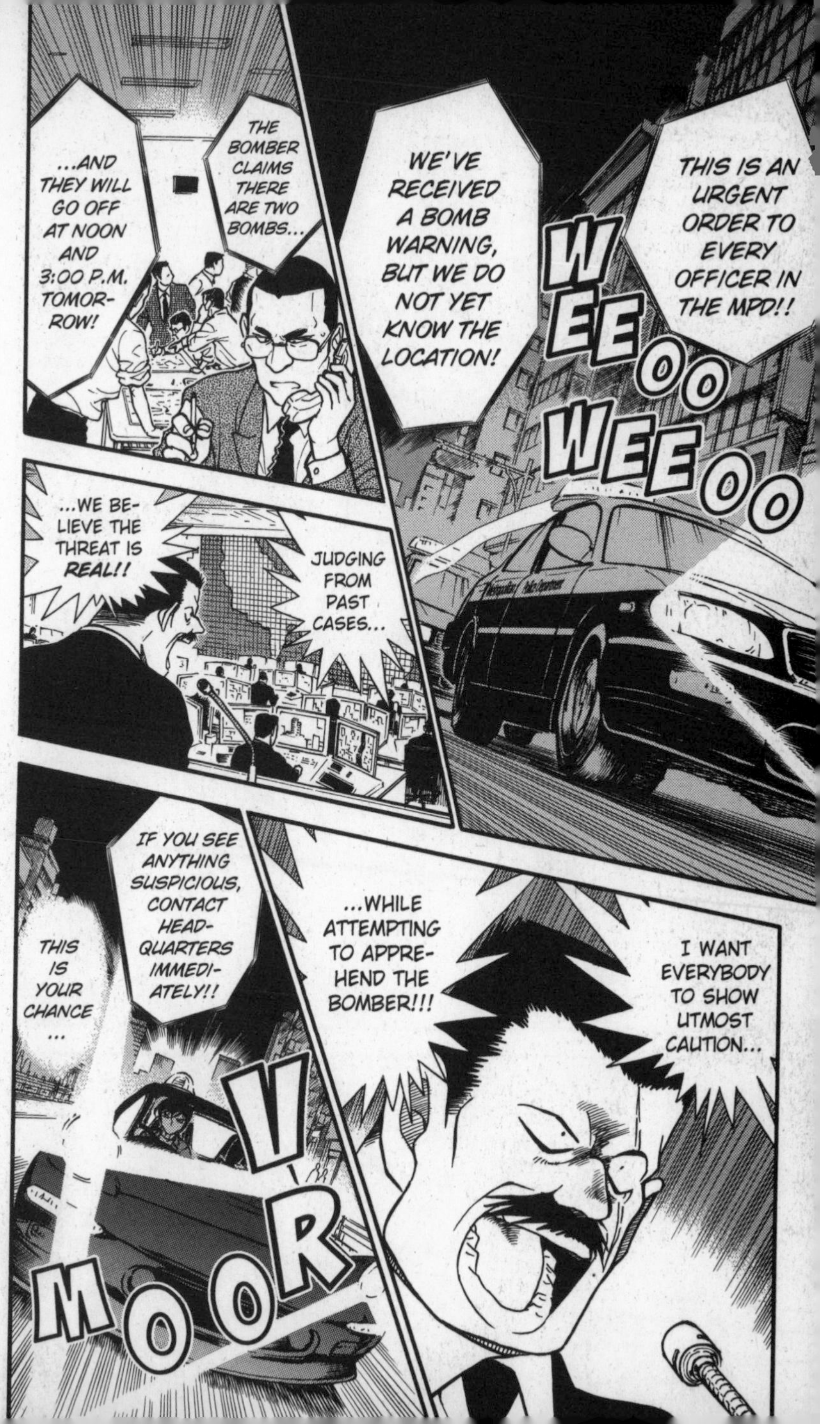
THIS IS AN URGENT ORDER TO EVERY OFFICER IN THE MPD!!
WEEOO WEEOO
WE'VE RECEIVED A BOMB WARNING, BUT WE DO NOT YET KNOW THE LOCATION!
THE BOMBER CLAIMS THERE ARE TWO BOMBS...
...AND THEY WILL GO OFF AT NOON AND 3:00 P.M. TOMORROW!
JUDGING FROM PAST CASES...
...WE BELIEVE THE THREAT IS REAL!!
I WANT EVERYBODY TO SHOW UTMOST CAUTION...
...WHILE ATTEMPTING TO APPREHEND THE BOMBER!!!
IF YOU SEE ANYTHING SUSPICIOUS, CONTACT HEADQUARTERS IMMEDIATELY!!
THIS IS YOUR CHANCE...
VROOM

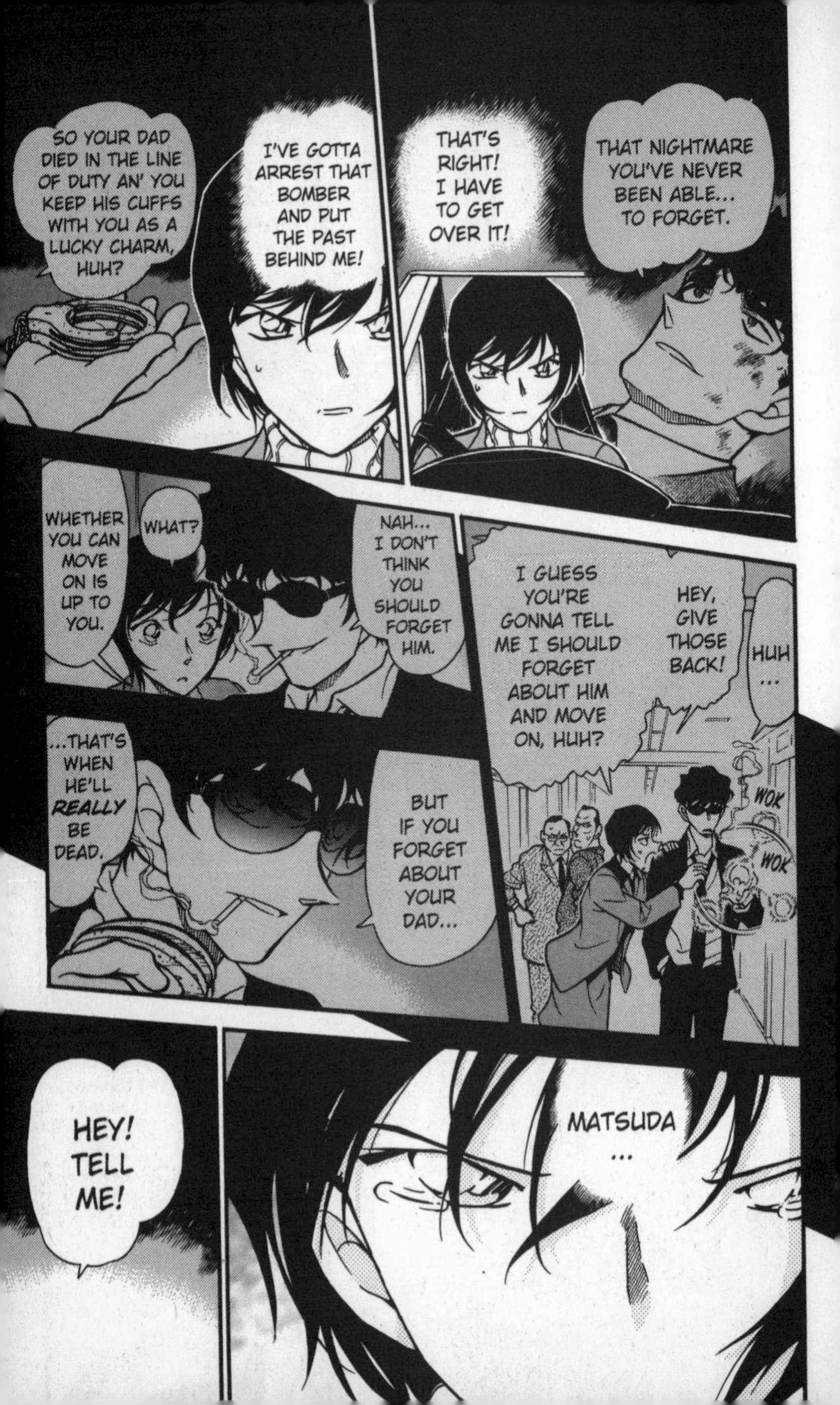
THAT NIGHTMARE YOU'VE NEVER BEEN ABLE... TO FORGET.
THAT'S RIGHT! I HAVE TO GET OVER IT!
I'VE GOTTA ARREST THAT BOMBER AND PUT THE PAST BEHIND ME!
SO YOUR DAD DIED IN THE LINE OF DUTY AN' YOU KEEP HIS CUFFS WITH YOU AS A LUCKY CHARM, HUH?
HUH...
HEY, GIVE THOSE BACK!
I GUESS YOU'RE GONNA TELL ME I SHOULD FORGET ABOUT HIM AND MOVE ON, HUH?
WOK
WOK
NAH... I DON'T THINK YOU SHOULD FORGET HIM.
WHAT?
WHETHER YOU CAN MOVE ON IS UP TO YOU.
BUT IF YOU FORGET ABOUT YOUR DAD...
...THAT'S WHEN HE'LL *REALLY* BE DEAD.
MATSUDA...
HEY! TELL ME!

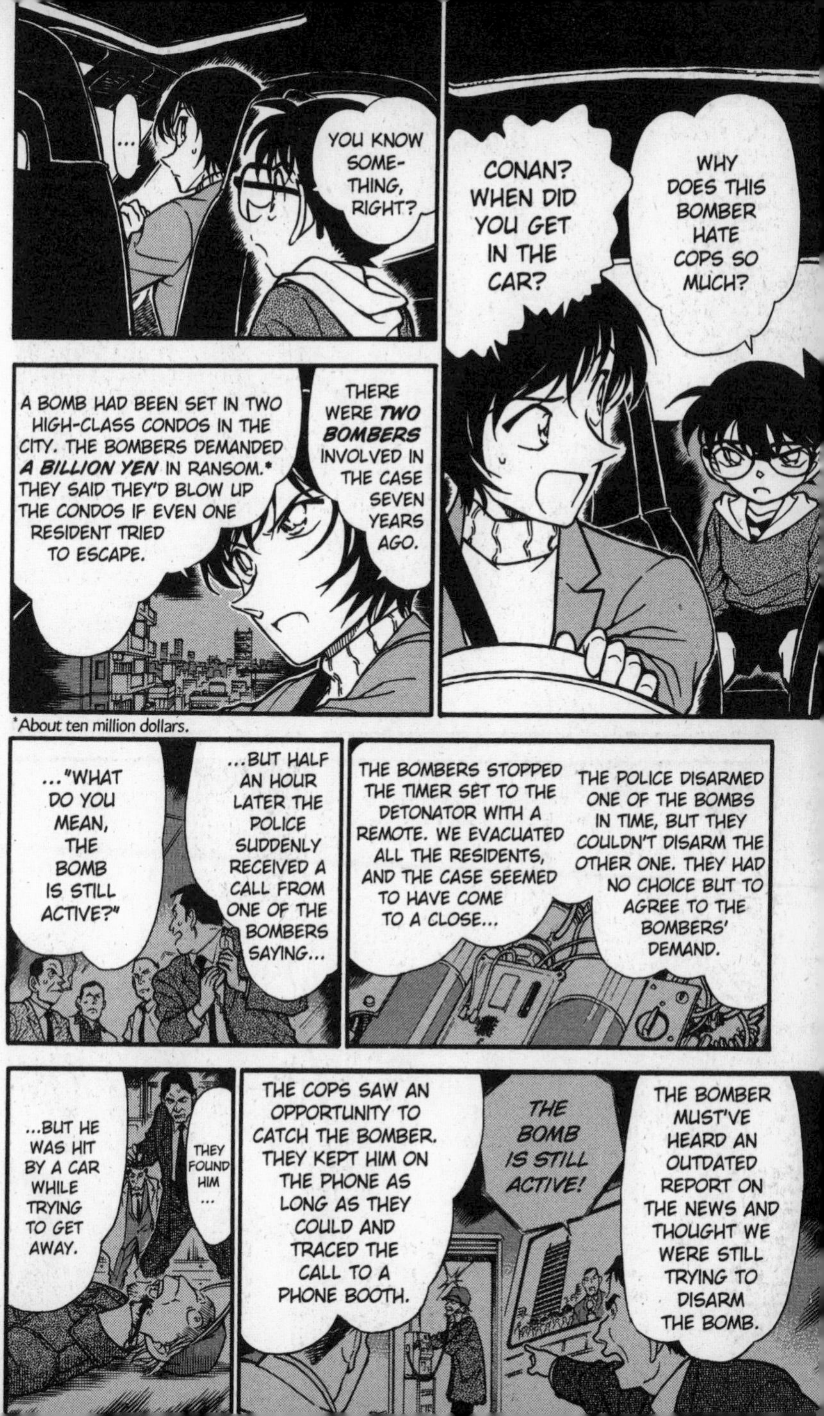
WHY DOES THIS BOMBER HATE COPS SO MUCH?
CONAN? WHEN DID YOU GET IN THE CAR?
YOU KNOW SOME-THING, RIGHT?
...
THERE WERE TWO BOMBERS INVOLVED IN THE CASE SEVEN YEARS AGO.
A BOMB HAD BEEN SET IN TWO HIGH-CLASS CONDOS IN THE CITY. THE BOMBERS DEMANDED A BILLION YEN IN RANSOM.* THEY SAID THEY'D BLOW UP THE CONDOS IF EVEN ONE RESIDENT TRIED TO ESCAPE.
THE POLICE DISARMED ONE OF THE BOMBS IN TIME, BUT THEY COULDN'T DISARM THE OTHER ONE. THEY HAD NO CHOICE BUT TO AGREE TO THE BOMBERS' DEMAND.
THE BOMBERS STOPPED THE TIMER SET TO THE DETONATOR WITH A REMOTE. WE EVACUATED ALL THE RESIDENTS, AND THE CASE SEEMED TO HAVE COME TO A CLOSE...
...BUT HALF AN HOUR LATER THE POLICE SUDDENLY RECEIVED A CALL FROM ONE OF THE BOMBERS SAYING...
..."WHAT DO YOU MEAN, THE BOMB IS STILL ACTIVE?"
THE BOMBER MUST'VE HEARD AN OUTDATED REPORT ON THE NEWS AND THOUGHT WE WERE STILL TRYING TO DISARM THE BOMB.
THE BOMB IS STILL ACTIVE!
THE COPS SAW AN OPPORTUNITY TO CATCH THE BOMBER. THEY KEPT HIM ON THE PHONE AS LONG AS THEY COULD AND TRACED THE CALL TO A PHONE BOOTH.
THEY FOUND HIM...
...BUT HE WAS HIT BY A CAR WHILE TRYING TO GET AWAY.
*About ten million dollars.

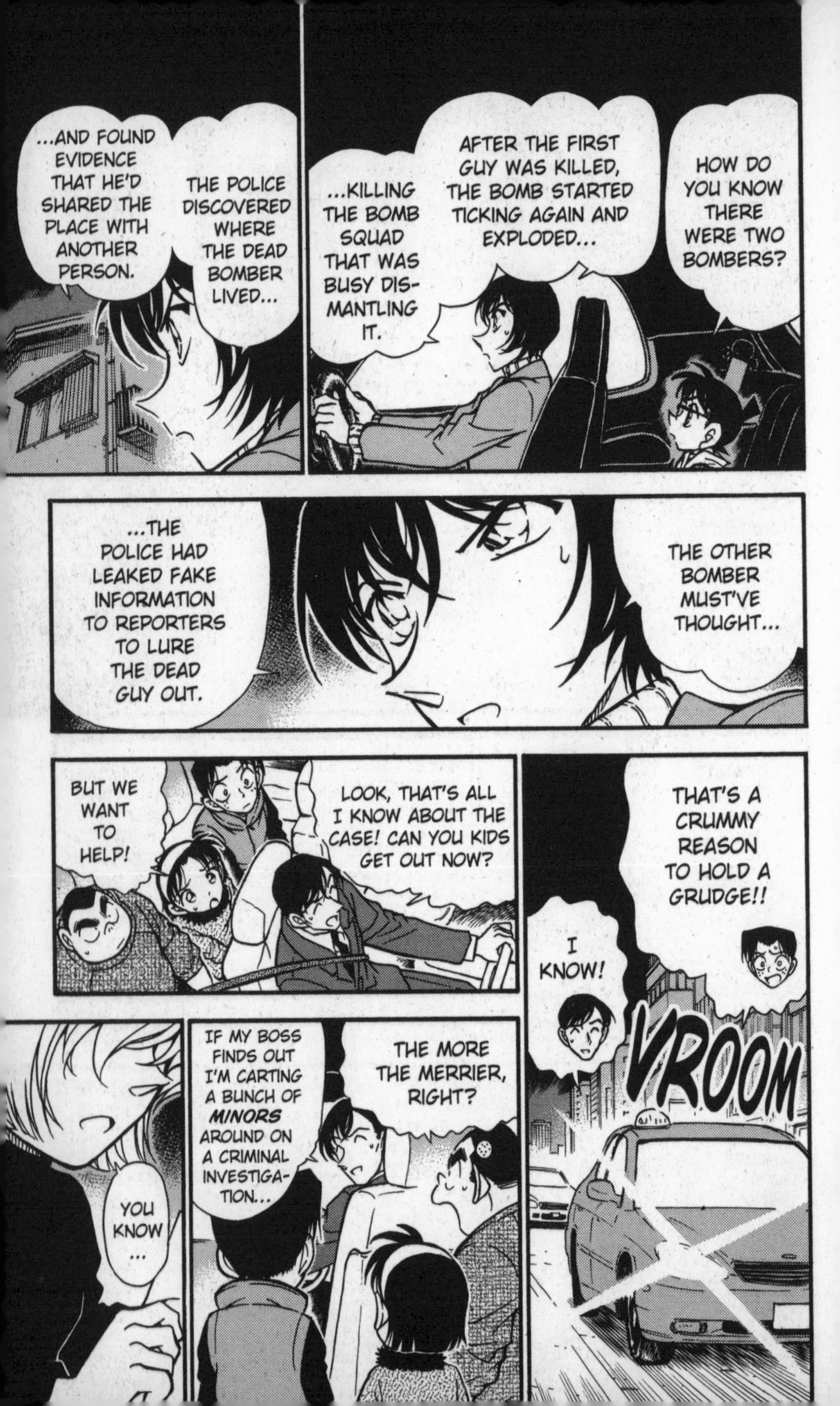

HOW DO YOU KNOW THERE WERE TWO BOMBERS?
AFTER THE FIRST GUY WAS KILLED, THE BOMB STARTED TICKING AGAIN AND EXPLODED...
...KILLING THE BOMB SQUAD THAT WAS BUSY DIS-MANTLING IT.
THE POLICE DISCOVERED WHERE THE DEAD BOMBER LIVED...
...AND FOUND EVIDENCE THAT HE'D SHARED THE PLACE WITH ANOTHER PERSON.
THE OTHER BOMBER MUST'VE THOUGHT...
...THE POLICE HAD LEAKED FAKE INFORMATION TO REPORTERS TO LURE THE DEAD GUY OUT.
THAT'S A CRUMMY REASON TO HOLD A GRUDGE!!
I KNOW!
VROOM
LOOK, THAT'S ALL I KNOW ABOUT THE CASE! CAN YOU KIDS GET OUT NOW?
BUT WE WANT TO HELP!
THE MORE THE MERRIER, RIGHT?
IF MY BOSS FINDS OUT I'M CARTING A BUNCH OF MINORS AROUND ON A CRIMINAL INVESTIGA-TION...
YOU KNOW ...

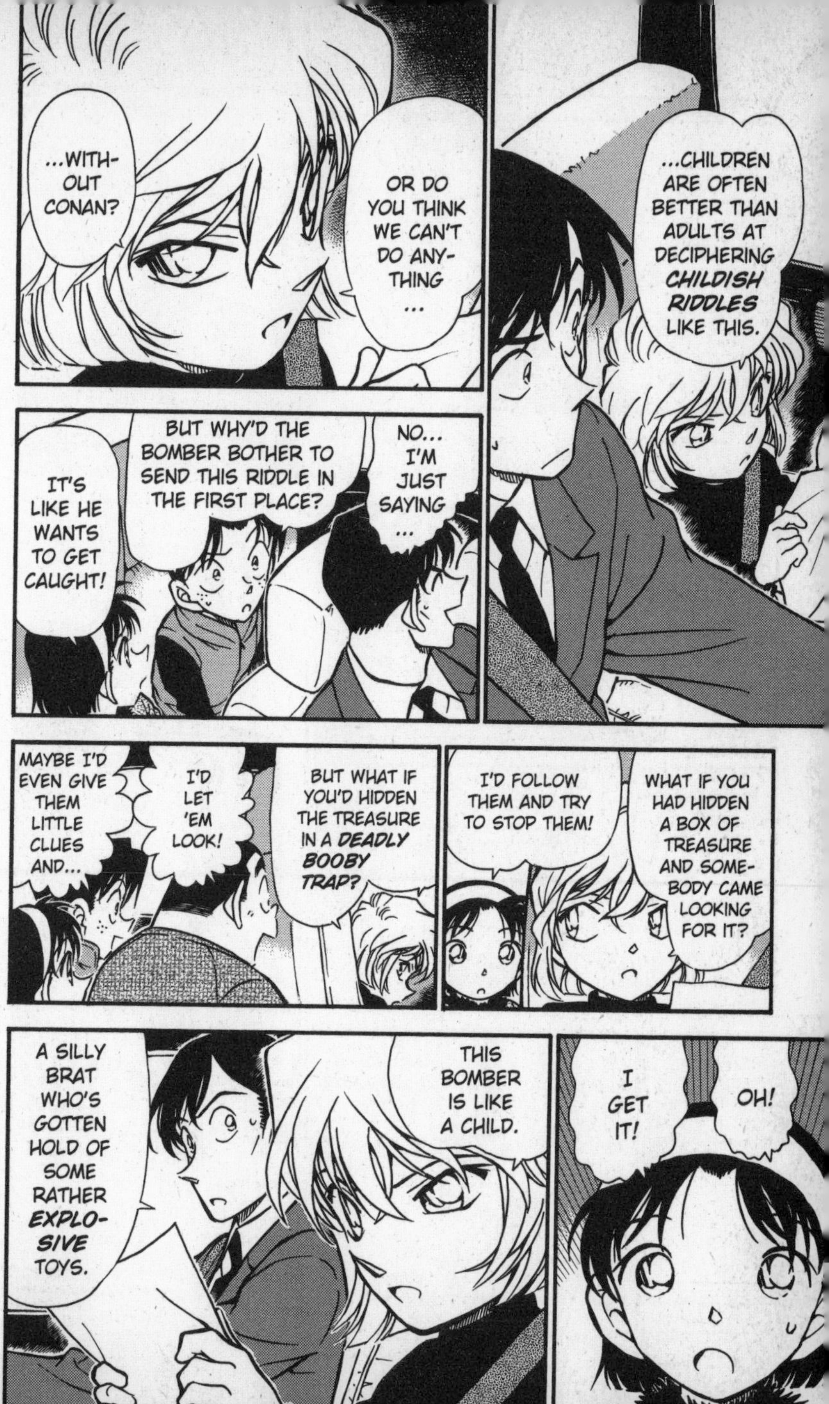

...CHILDREN ARE OFTEN BETTER THAN ADULTS AT DECIPHERING ***CHILDISH RIDDLES*** LIKE THIS.
OR DO YOU THINK WE CAN'T DO ANYTHING...
...WITHOUT CONAN?
NO... I'M JUST SAYING...
BUT WHY'D THE BOMBER BOTHER TO SEND THIS RIDDLE IN THE FIRST PLACE?
IT'S LIKE HE WANTS TO GET CAUGHT!
WHAT IF YOU HAD HIDDEN A BOX OF TREASURE AND SOMEBODY CAME LOOKING FOR IT?
I'D FOLLOW THEM AND TRY TO STOP THEM!
BUT WHAT IF YOU'D HIDDEN THE TREASURE IN A ***DEADLY BOOBY TRAP?***
I'D LET 'EM LOOK!
MAYBE I'D EVEN GIVE THEM LITTLE CLUES AND...
OH!
I GET IT!
THIS BOMBER IS LIKE A CHILD.
A SILLY BRAT WHO'S GOTTEN HOLD OF SOME RATHER ***EXPLOSIVE*** TOYS.

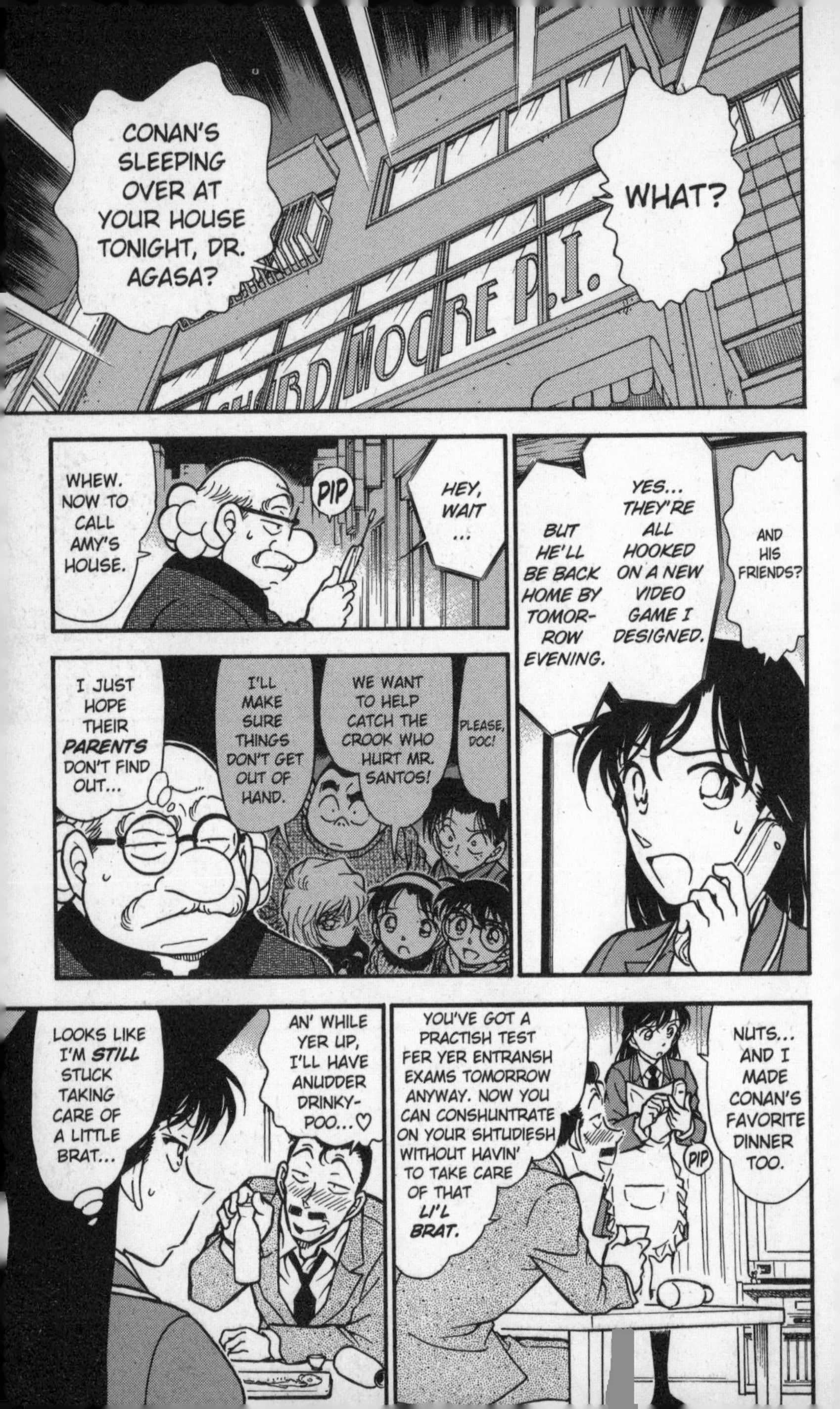
WHAT?
CONAN'S SLEEPING OVER AT YOUR HOUSE TONIGHT, DR. AGASA?
RICHARD MOORE P.I.
AND HIS FRIENDS?
YES... THEY'RE ALL HOOKED ON A NEW VIDEO GAME I DESIGNED.
BUT HE'LL BE BACK HOME BY TOMORROW EVENING.
HEY, WAIT...
PIP
WHEW. NOW TO CALL AMY'S HOUSE.
PLEASE, DOC!
WE WANT TO HELP CATCH THE CROOK WHO HURT MR. SANTOS!
I'LL MAKE SURE THINGS DON'T GET OUT OF HAND.
I JUST HOPE THEIR *PARENTS* DON'T FIND OUT...
NUTS... AND I MADE CONAN'S FAVORITE DINNER TOO.
PIP
YOU'VE GOT A PRACTISH TEST FER YER ENTRANSH EXAMS TOMORROW ANYWAY. NOW YOU CAN CONSHUNTRATE ON YOUR SHTUDIESH WITHOUT HAVIN' TO TAKE CARE OF THAT *LI'L BRAT.*
AN' WHILE YER UP, I'LL HAVE ANUDDER DRINKY-POO...♡
LOOKS LIKE I'M *STILL* STUCK TAKING CARE OF A LITTLE BRAT...

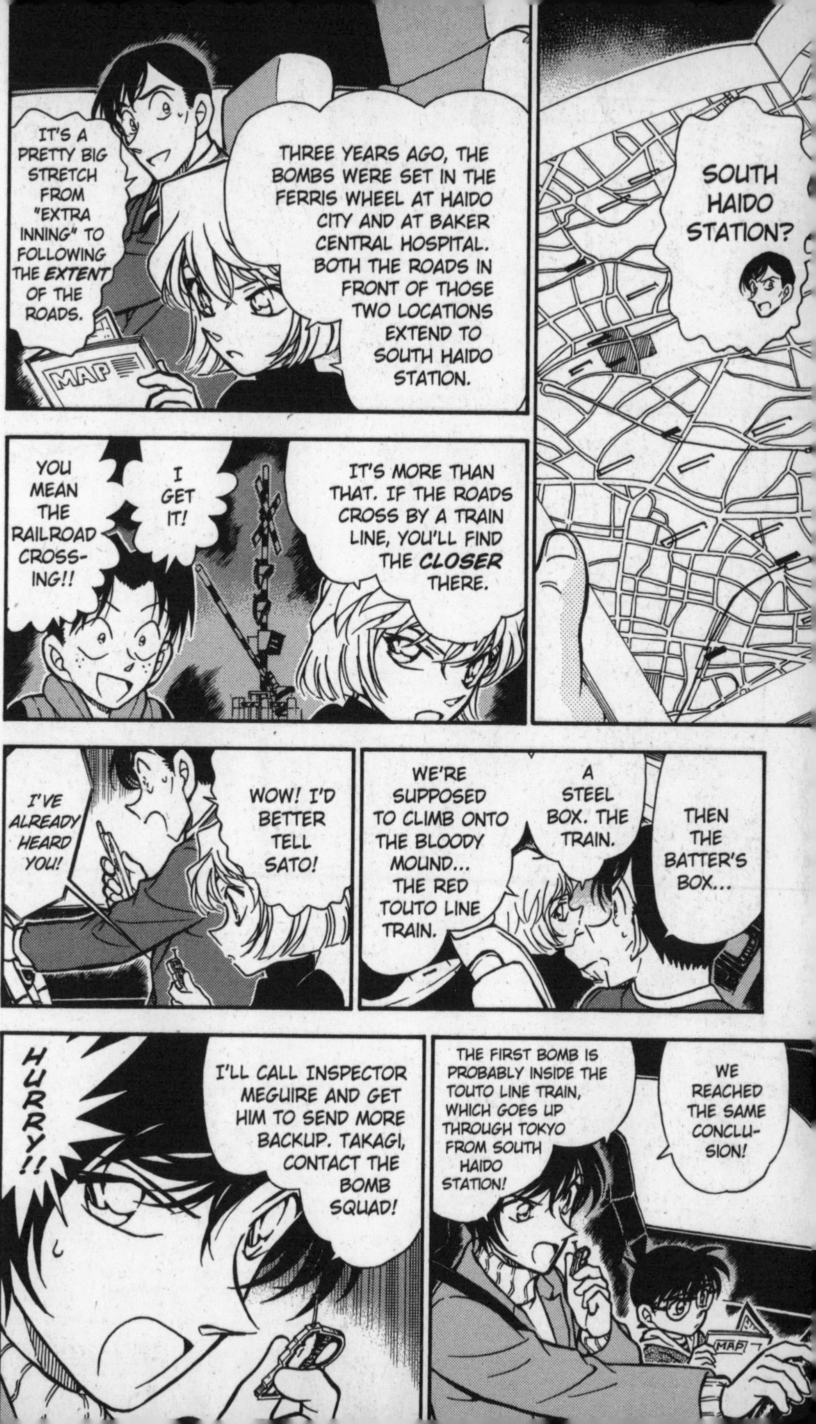
SOUTH HAIDO STATION?
THREE YEARS AGO, THE BOMBS WERE SET IN THE FERRIS WHEEL AT HAIDO CITY AND AT BAKER CENTRAL HOSPITAL. BOTH THE ROADS IN FRONT OF THOSE TWO LOCATIONS EXTEND TO SOUTH HAIDO STATION.
IT'S A PRETTY BIG STRETCH FROM "EXTRA INNING" TO FOLLOWING THE *EXTENT* OF THE ROADS.
MAP
IT'S MORE THAN THAT. IF THE ROADS CROSS BY A TRAIN LINE, YOU'LL FIND THE *CLOSER* THERE.
I GET IT!
YOU MEAN THE RAILROAD CROSSING!!
THEN THE BATTER'S BOX...
A STEEL BOX. THE TRAIN.
WE'RE SUPPOSED TO CLIMB ONTO THE BLOODY MOUND... THE RED TOUTO LINE TRAIN.
WOW! I'D BETTER TELL SATO!
I'VE ALREADY HEARD YOU!
WE REACHED THE SAME CONCLUSION!
THE FIRST BOMB IS PROBABLY INSIDE THE TOUTO LINE TRAIN, WHICH GOES UP THROUGH TOKYO FROM SOUTH HAIDO STATION!
MAP
I'LL CALL INSPECTOR MEGUIRE AND GET HIM TO SEND MORE BACKUP. TAKAGI, CONTACT THE BOMB SQUAD!
HURRY!!

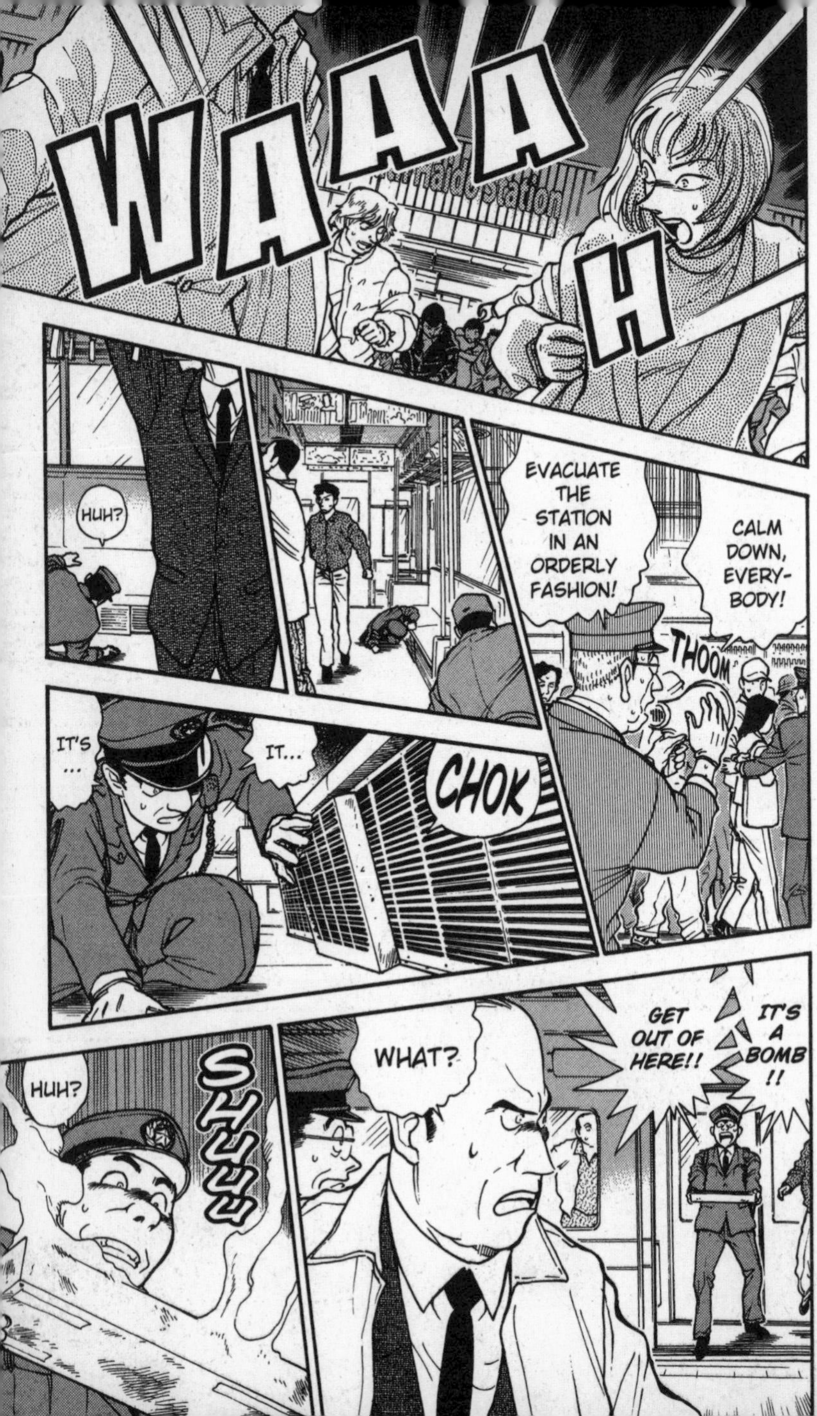
WAAAAH
CALM DOWN, EVERY-BODY!
EVACUATE THE STATION IN AN ORDERLY FASHION!
THOOM
HUH?
CHOK
IT...
IT'S ...
IT'S A BOMB !!
GET OUT OF HERE!!
WHAT?
SHUUU
HUH?

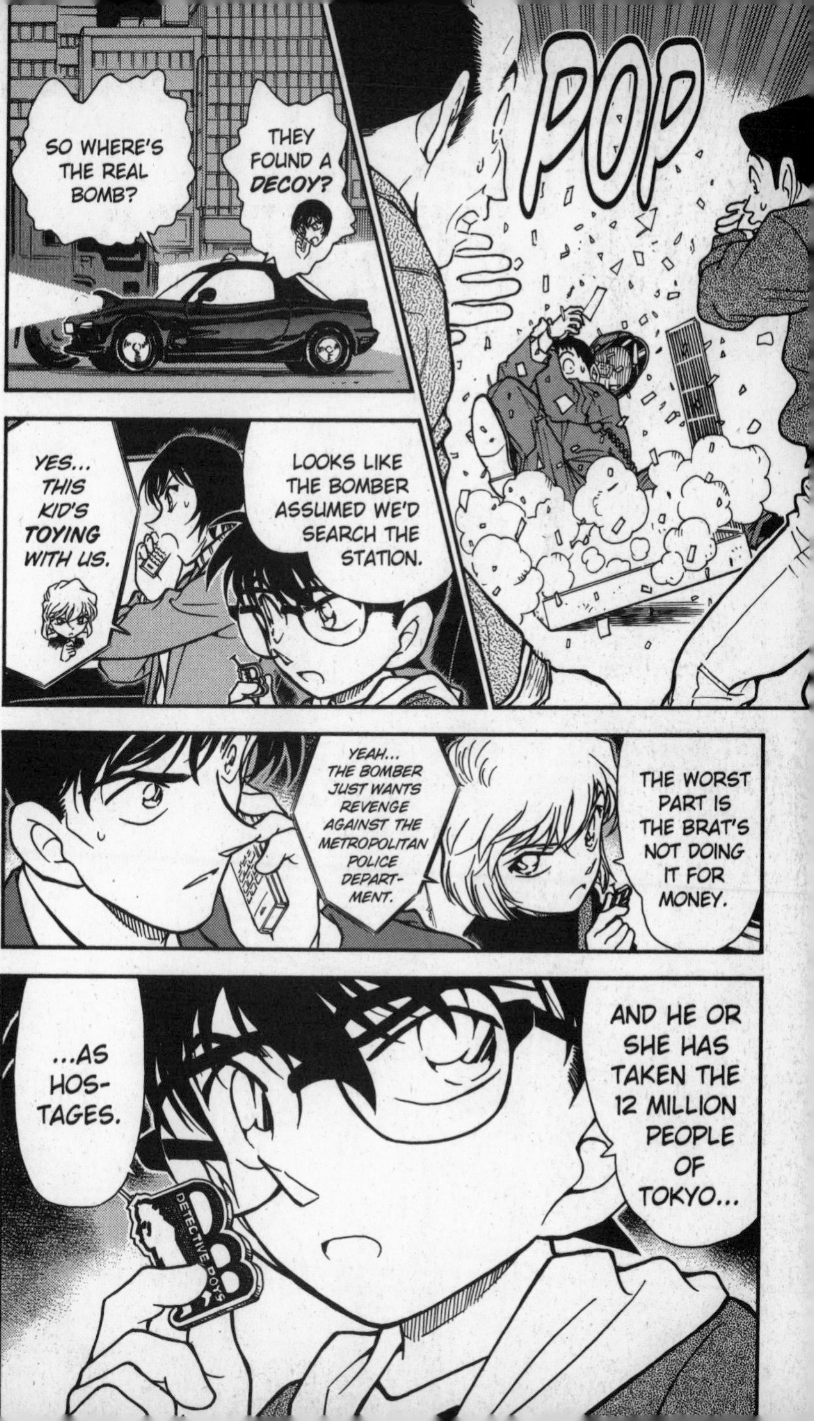
POP
THEY FOUND A DECOY?
SO WHERE'S THE REAL BOMB?
LOOKS LIKE THE BOMBER ASSUMED WE'D SEARCH THE STATION.
YES... THIS KID'S TOYING WITH US.
THE WORST PART IS THE BRAT'S NOT DOING IT FOR MONEY.
YEAH... THE BOMBER JUST WANTS REVENGE AGAINST THE METROPOLITAN POLICE DEPARTMENT.
AND HE OR SHE HAS TAKEN THE 12 MILLION PEOPLE OF TOKYO...
...AS HOSTAGES.
DETECTIVE BOYS

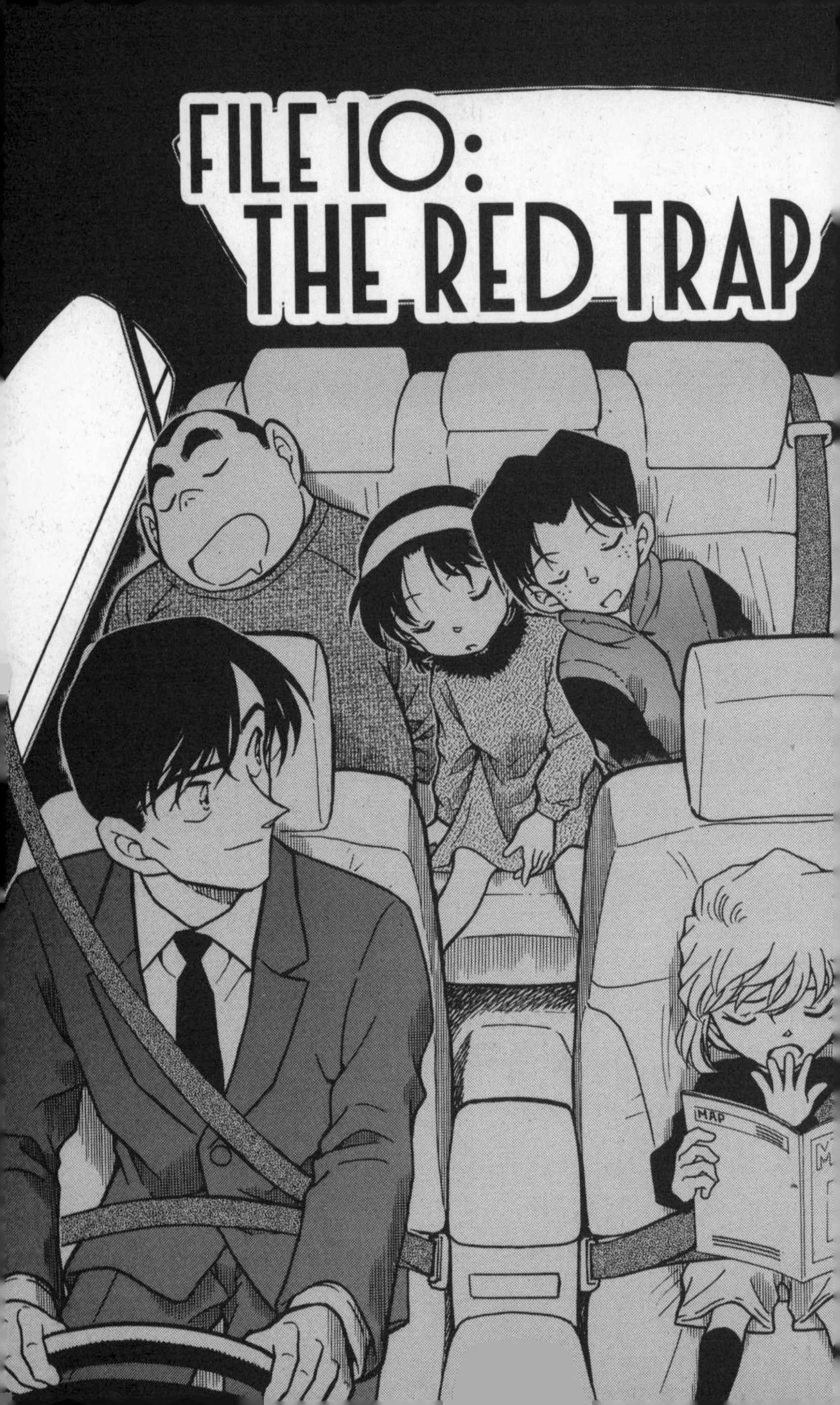
FILE 10:
THE RED TRAP
MAP

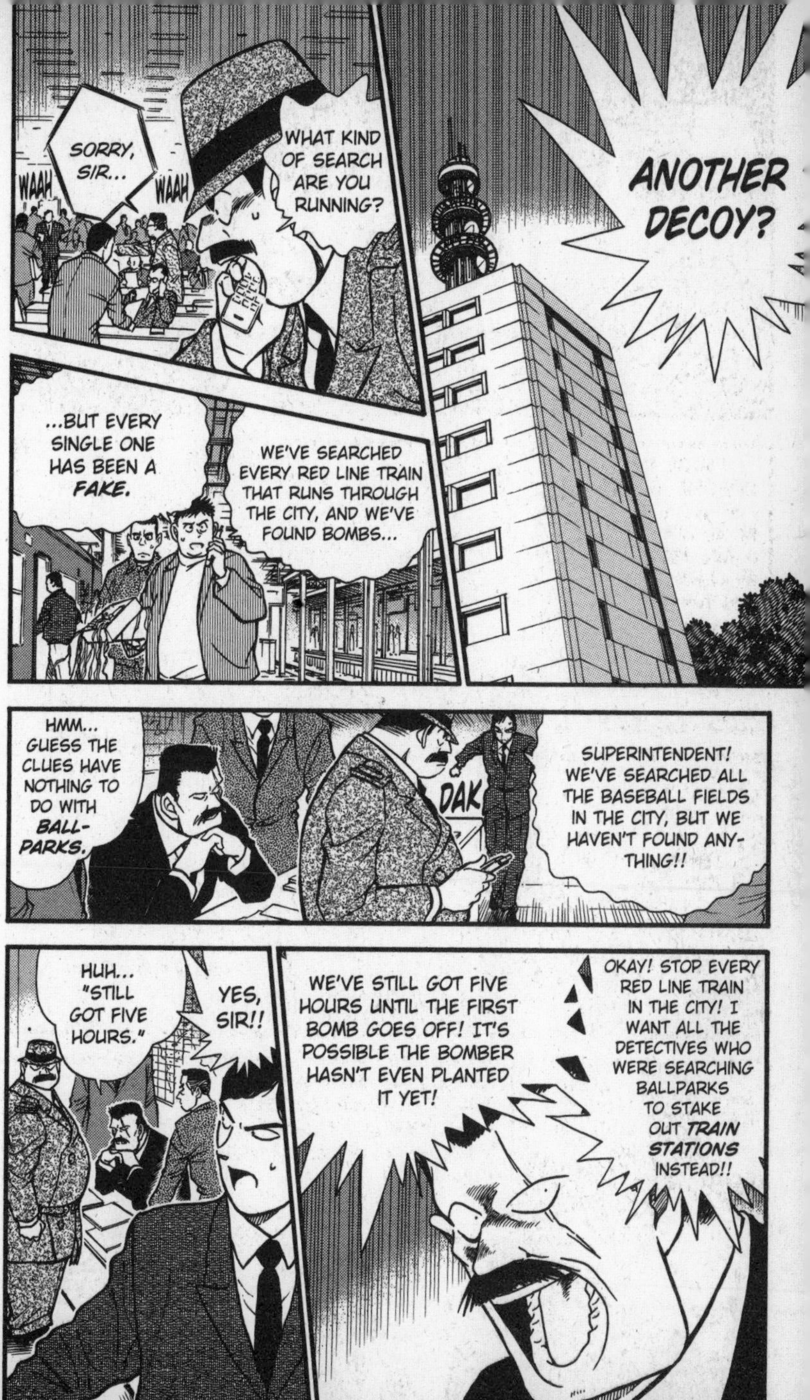
ANOTHER DECOY?
WHAT KIND OF SEARCH ARE YOU RUNNING?
WAAH
SORRY, SIR...
WAAH
WE'VE SEARCHED EVERY RED LINE TRAIN THAT RUNS THROUGH THE CITY, AND WE'VE FOUND BOMBS...
...BUT EVERY SINGLE ONE HAS BEEN A FAKE.
SUPERINTENDENT! WE'VE SEARCHED ALL THE BASEBALL FIELDS IN THE CITY, BUT WE HAVEN'T FOUND ANYTHING!!
DAK
HMM... GUESS THE CLUES HAVE NOTHING TO DO WITH BALLPARKS.
OKAY! STOP EVERY RED LINE TRAIN IN THE CITY! I WANT ALL THE DETECTIVES WHO WERE SEARCHING BALLPARKS TO STAKE OUT TRAIN STATIONS INSTEAD!!
WE'VE STILL GOT FIVE HOURS UNTIL THE FIRST BOMB GOES OFF! IT'S POSSIBLE THE BOMBER HASN'T EVEN PLANTED IT YET!
YES, SIR!!
HUH... "STILL GOT FIVE HOURS."

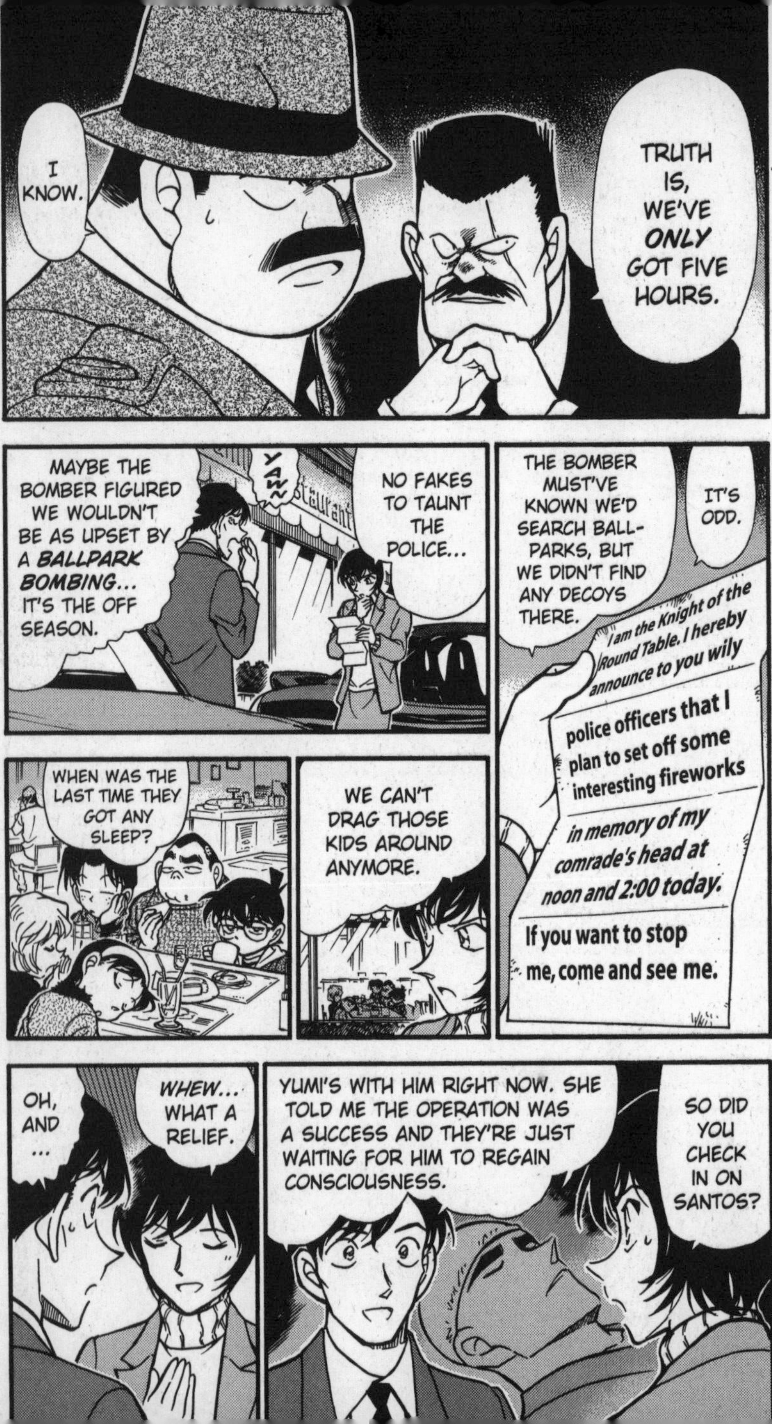
TRUTH IS, WE'VE ONLY GOT FIVE HOURS.
I KNOW.
IT'S ODD.
THE BOMBER MUST'VE KNOWN WE'D SEARCH BALL-PARKS, BUT WE DIDN'T FIND ANY DECOYS THERE.
I am the Knight of the Round Table. I hereby announce to you wily police officers that I plan to set off some interesting fireworks in memory of my comrade's head at noon and 2:00 today. If you want to stop me, come and see me.
NO FAKES TO TAUNT THE POLICE...
YAWN
Restaurant
MAYBE THE BOMBER FIGURED WE WOULDN'T BE AS UPSET BY A BALLPARK BOMBING... IT'S THE OFF SEASON.
WE CAN'T DRAG THOSE KIDS AROUND ANYMORE.
WHEN WAS THE LAST TIME THEY GOT ANY SLEEP?
SO DID YOU CHECK IN ON SANTOS?
YUMI'S WITH HIM RIGHT NOW. SHE TOLD ME THE OPERATION WAS A SUCCESS AND THEY'RE JUST WAITING FOR HIM TO REGAIN CONSCIOUSNESS.
WHEW... WHAT A RELIEF.
OH, AND ...

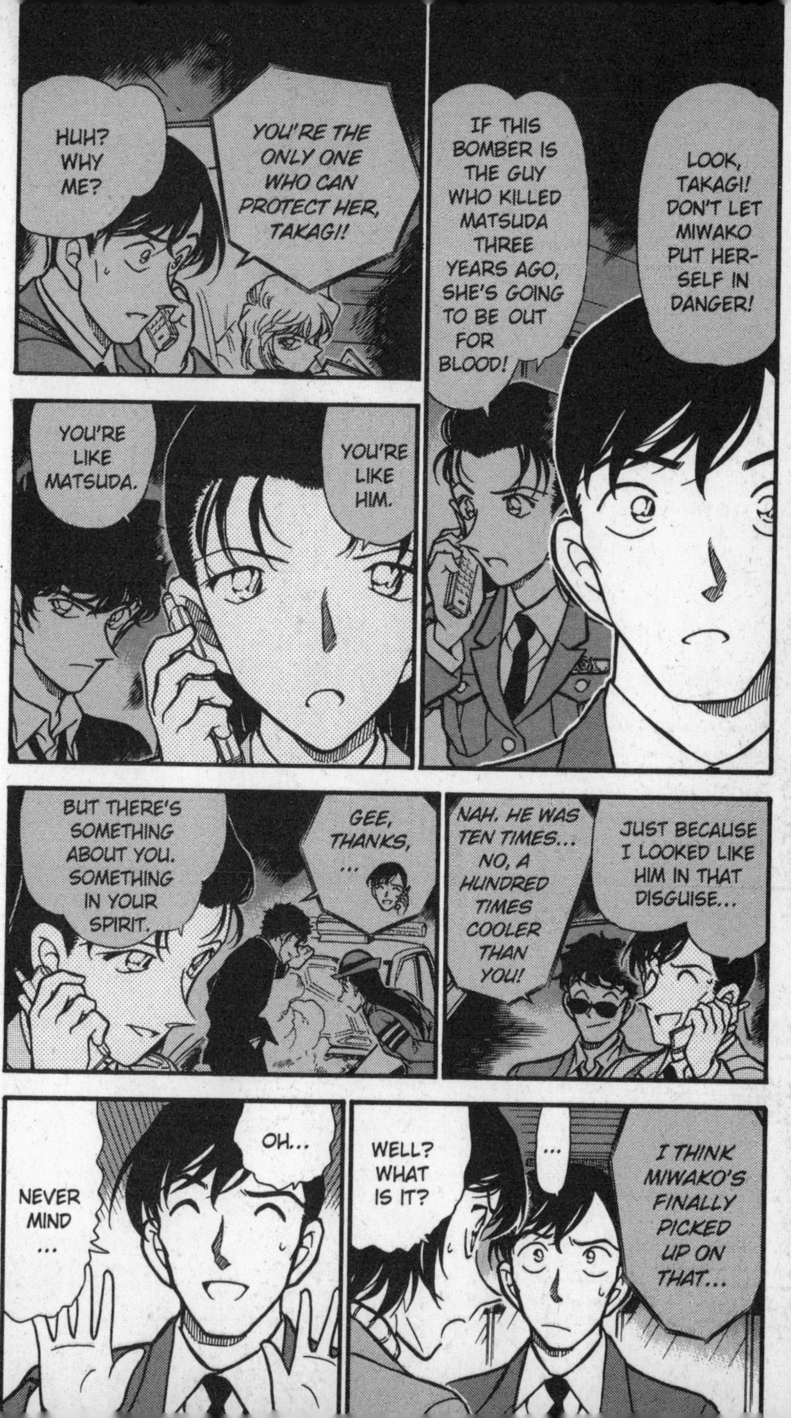

LOOK, TAKAGI! DON'T LET MIWAKO PUT HER-SELF IN DANGER!
IF THIS BOMBER IS THE GUY WHO KILLED MATSUDA THREE YEARS AGO, SHE'S GOING TO BE OUT FOR BLOOD!
YOU'RE THE ONLY ONE WHO CAN PROTECT HER, TAKAGI!
HUH? WHY ME?
YOU'RE LIKE HIM.
YOU'RE LIKE MATSUDA.
JUST BECAUSE I LOOKED LIKE HIM IN THAT DISGUISE...
NAH. HE WAS TEN TIMES... NO, A HUNDRED TIMES COOLER THAN YOU!
GEE, THANKS, ...
BUT THERE'S SOMETHING ABOUT YOU. SOMETHING IN YOUR SPIRIT.
I THINK MIWAKO'S FINALLY PICKED UP ON THAT...
...
WELL? WHAT IS IT?
OH...
NEVER MIND ...

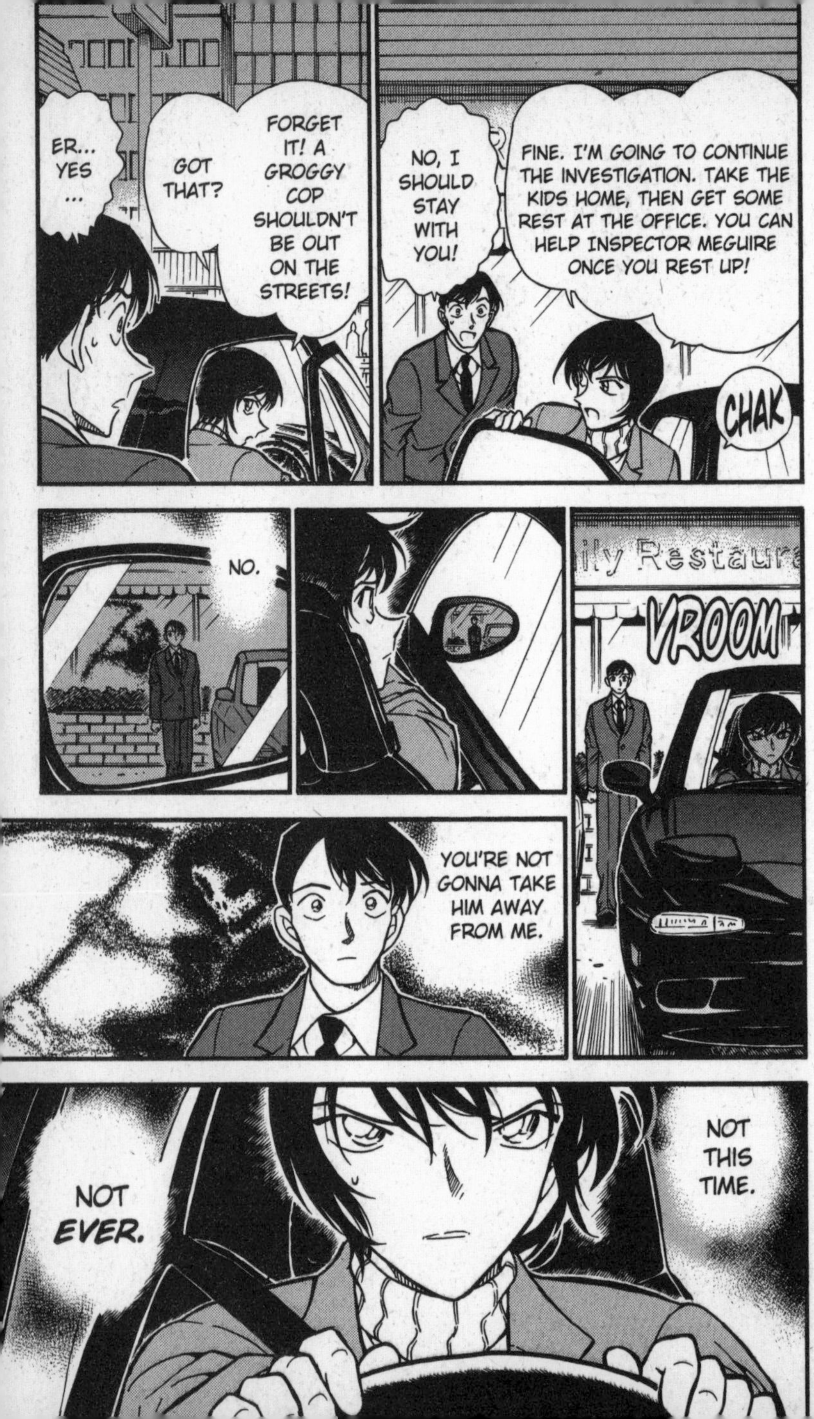
FINE. I'M GOING TO CONTINUE THE INVESTIGATION. TAKE THE KIDS HOME, THEN GET SOME REST AT THE OFFICE. YOU CAN HELP INSPECTOR MEGUIRE ONCE YOU REST UP!
NO, I SHOULD STAY WITH YOU!
CHAK
FORGET IT! A GROGGY COP SHOULDN'T BE OUT ON THE STREETS!
GOT THAT?
ER... YES ...
ily Restaura
VROOM
NO.
YOU'RE NOT GONNA TAKE HIM AWAY FROM ME.
NOT THIS TIME.
NOT *EVER.*

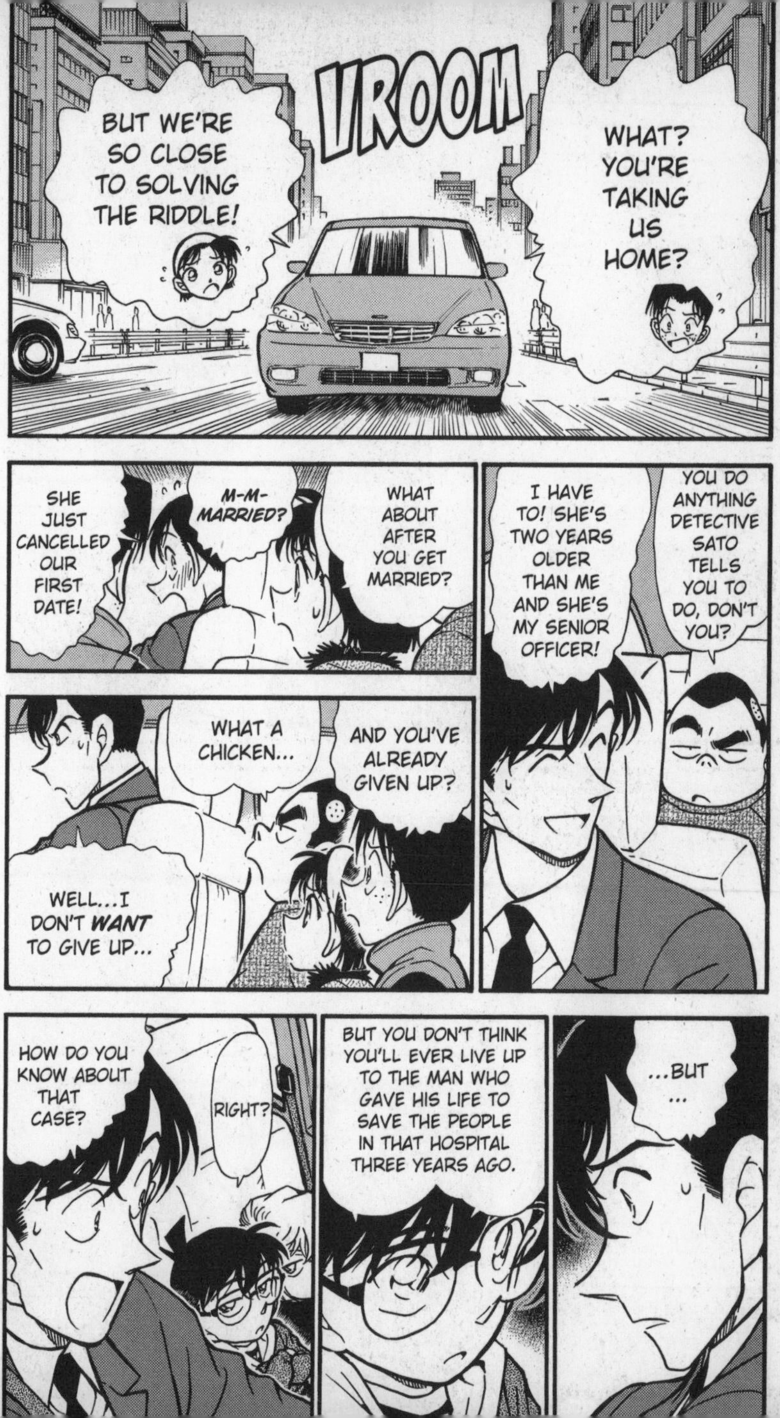
VROOM
WHAT? YOU'RE TAKING US HOME?
BUT WE'RE SO CLOSE TO SOLVING THE RIDDLE!
YOU DO ANYTHING DETECTIVE SATO TELLS YOU TO DO, DON'T YOU?
I HAVE TO! SHE'S TWO YEARS OLDER THAN ME AND SHE'S MY SENIOR OFFICER!
WHAT ABOUT AFTER YOU GET MARRIED?
M-M-MARRIED?
SHE JUST CANCELLED OUR FIRST DATE!
AND YOU'VE ALREADY GIVEN UP?
WHAT A CHICKEN...
WELL...I DON'T WANT TO GIVE UP...
...BUT ...
BUT YOU DON'T THINK YOU'LL EVER LIVE UP TO THE MAN WHO GAVE HIS LIFE TO SAVE THE PEOPLE IN THAT HOSPITAL THREE YEARS AGO.
RIGHT?
HOW DO YOU KNOW ABOUT THAT CASE?

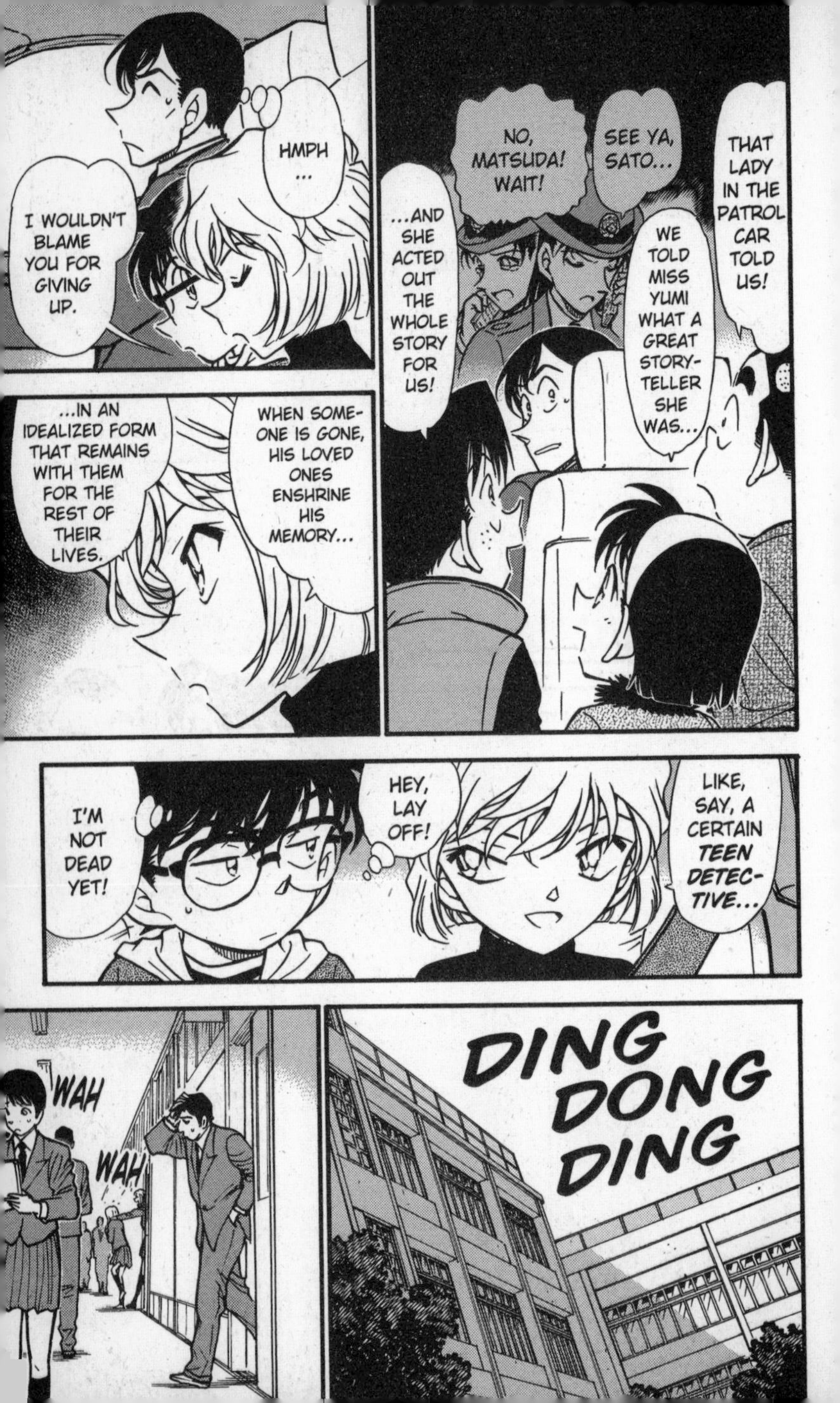
THAT LADY IN THE PATROL CAR TOLD US!
SEE YA, SATO...
NO, MATSUDA! WAIT!
WE TOLD MISS YUMI WHAT A GREAT STORY-TELLER SHE WAS...
...AND SHE ACTED OUT THE WHOLE STORY FOR US!
HMPH ...
I WOULDN'T BLAME YOU FOR GIVING UP.
WHEN SOME-ONE IS GONE, HIS LOVED ONES ENSHRINE HIS MEMORY...
...IN AN IDEALIZED FORM THAT REMAINS WITH THEM FOR THE REST OF THEIR LIVES.
LIKE, SAY, A CERTAIN *TEEN DETECTIVE*...
HEY, LAY OFF!
I'M NOT DEAD YET!
DING DONG DING
WAH
WAH

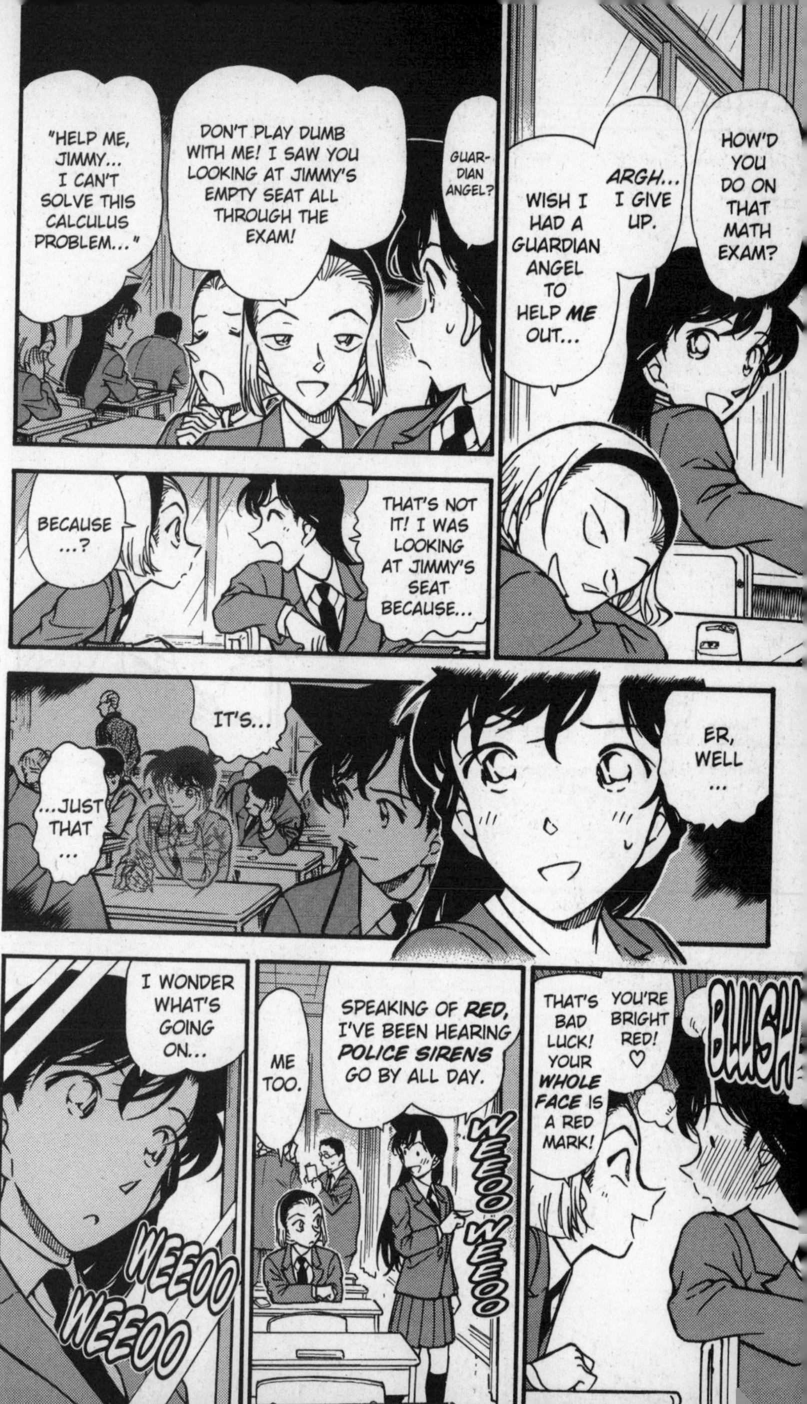
HOW'D YOU DO ON THAT MATH EXAM?
ARGH... I GIVE UP.
WISH I HAD A GUARDIAN ANGEL TO HELP ME OUT...
GUARDIAN ANGEL?
DON'T PLAY DUMB WITH ME! I SAW YOU LOOKING AT JIMMY'S EMPTY SEAT ALL THROUGH THE EXAM!
"HELP ME, JIMMY... I CAN'T SOLVE THIS CALCULUS PROBLEM..."
THAT'S NOT IT! I WAS LOOKING AT JIMMY'S SEAT BECAUSE...
BECAUSE ...?
ER, WELL ...
IT'S...
...JUST THAT ...
BLUSH
YOU'RE BRIGHT RED! ♡
THAT'S BAD LUCK! YOUR WHOLE FACE IS A RED MARK!
SPEAKING OF RED, I'VE BEEN HEARING POLICE SIRENS GO BY ALL DAY.
ME TOO.
WEEOO WEEOO
I WONDER WHAT'S GOING ON...
WEEOO WEEOO

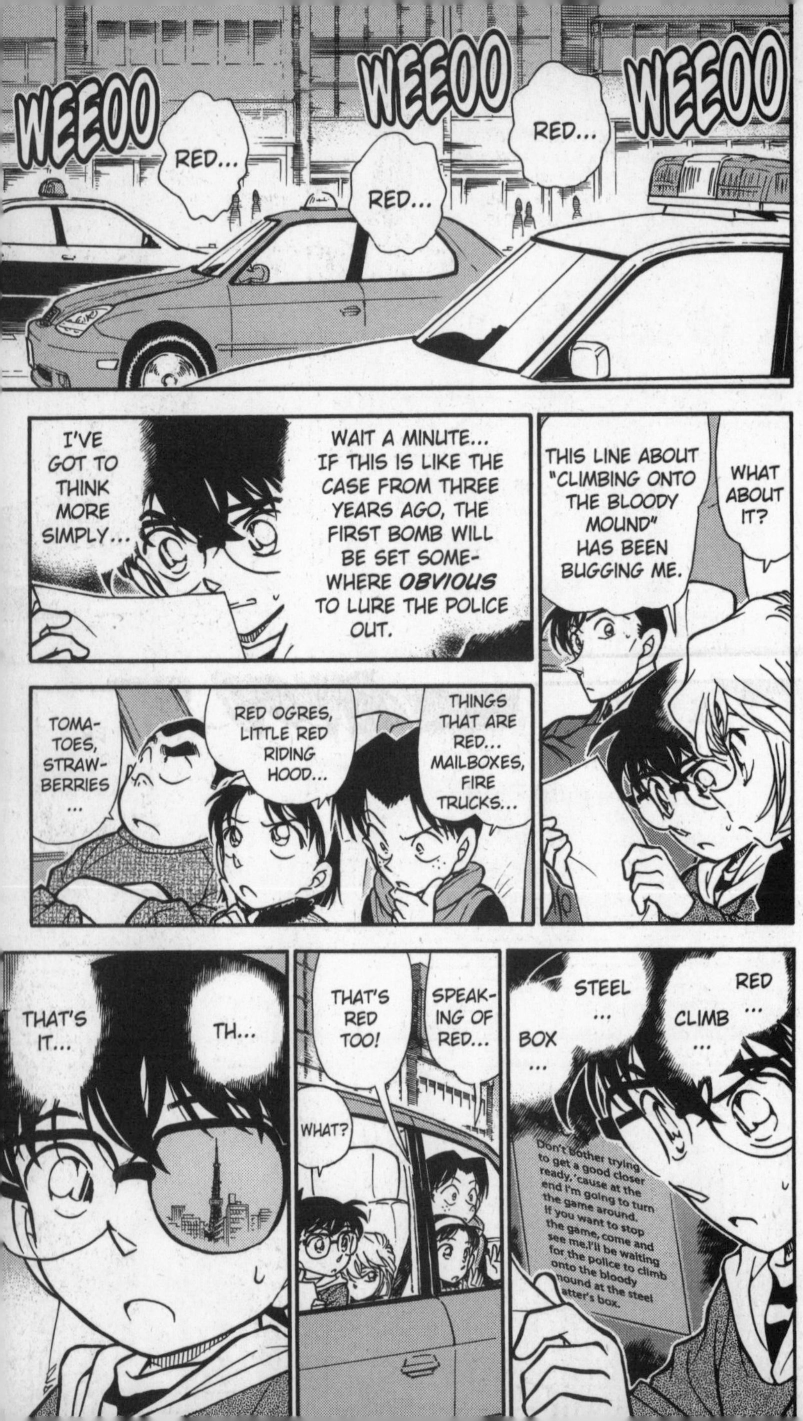
WEEOO
RED...
WEEOO
RED...
RED...
WEEOO
THIS LINE ABOUT "CLIMBING ONTO THE BLOODY MOUND" HAS BEEN BUGGING ME.
WHAT ABOUT IT?
WAIT A MINUTE... IF THIS IS LIKE THE CASE FROM THREE YEARS AGO, THE FIRST BOMB WILL BE SET SOME-WHERE OBVIOUS TO LURE THE POLICE OUT.
I'VE GOT TO THINK MORE SIMPLY...
THINGS THAT ARE RED... MAILBOXES, FIRE TRUCKS...
RED OGRES, LITTLE RED RIDING HOOD...
TOMA-TOES, STRAW-BERRIES ...
RED ...
CLIMB ...
STEEL ...
BOX ...
Don't bother trying to get a good closer ready, 'cause at the end I'm going to turn the game around. If you want to stop the game, come and see me. I'll be waiting for the police to climb onto the bloody mound at the steel atter's box.
SPEAK-ING OF RED...
THAT'S RED TOO!
WHAT?
TH...
THAT'S IT...

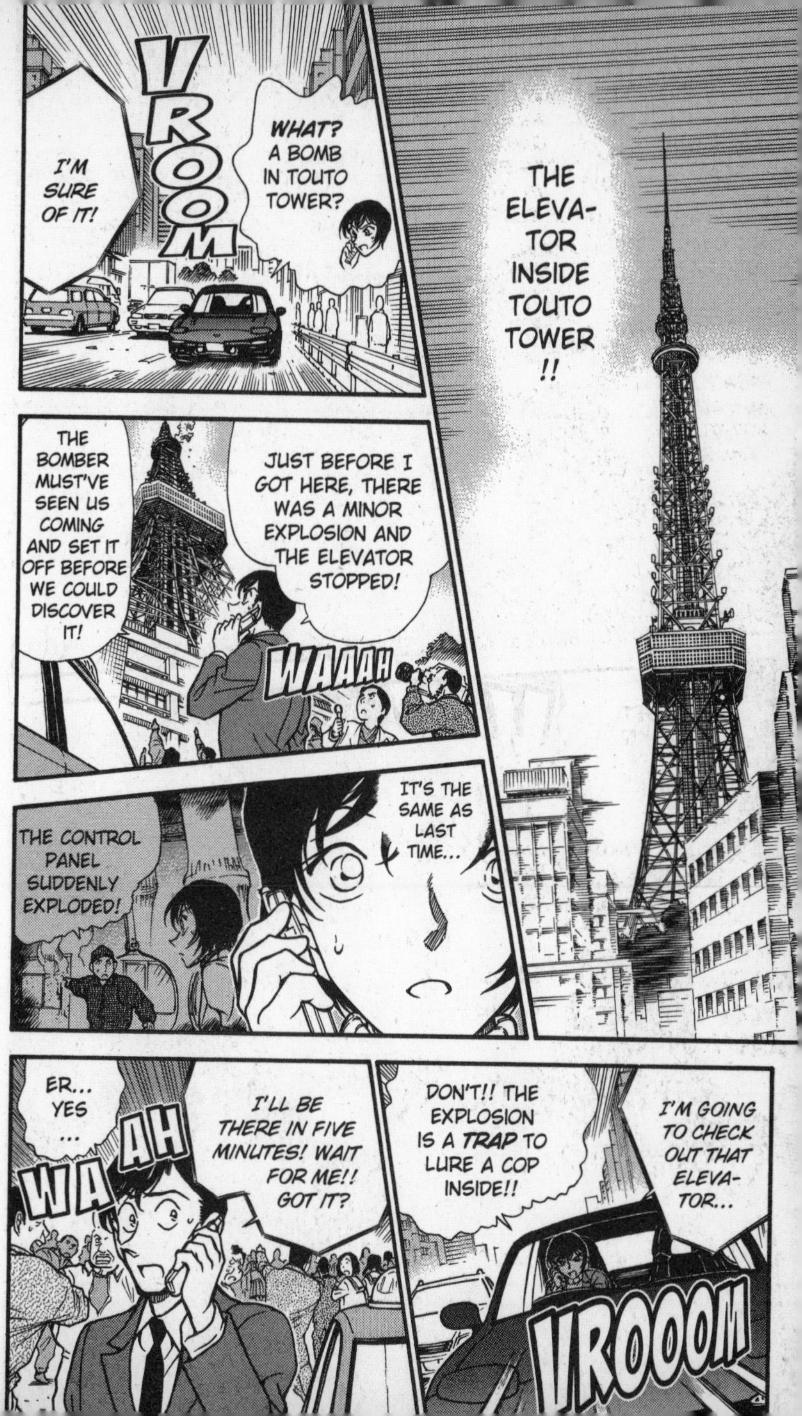
THE ELEVATOR INSIDE TOUTO TOWER!!
WHAT? A BOMB IN TOUTO TOWER?
VROOM
I'M SURE OF IT!
JUST BEFORE I GOT HERE, THERE WAS A MINOR EXPLOSION AND THE ELEVATOR STOPPED!
THE BOMBER MUST'VE SEEN US COMING AND SET IT OFF BEFORE WE COULD DISCOVER IT!
WAAAH
IT'S THE SAME AS LAST TIME...
THE CONTROL PANEL SUDDENLY EXPLODED!
I'M GOING TO CHECK OUT THAT ELEVATOR...
DON'T!! THE EXPLOSION IS A TRAP TO LURE A COP INSIDE!!
VROOOM
I'LL BE THERE IN FIVE MINUTES! WAIT FOR ME!! GOT IT?
WAAH
ER... YES ...

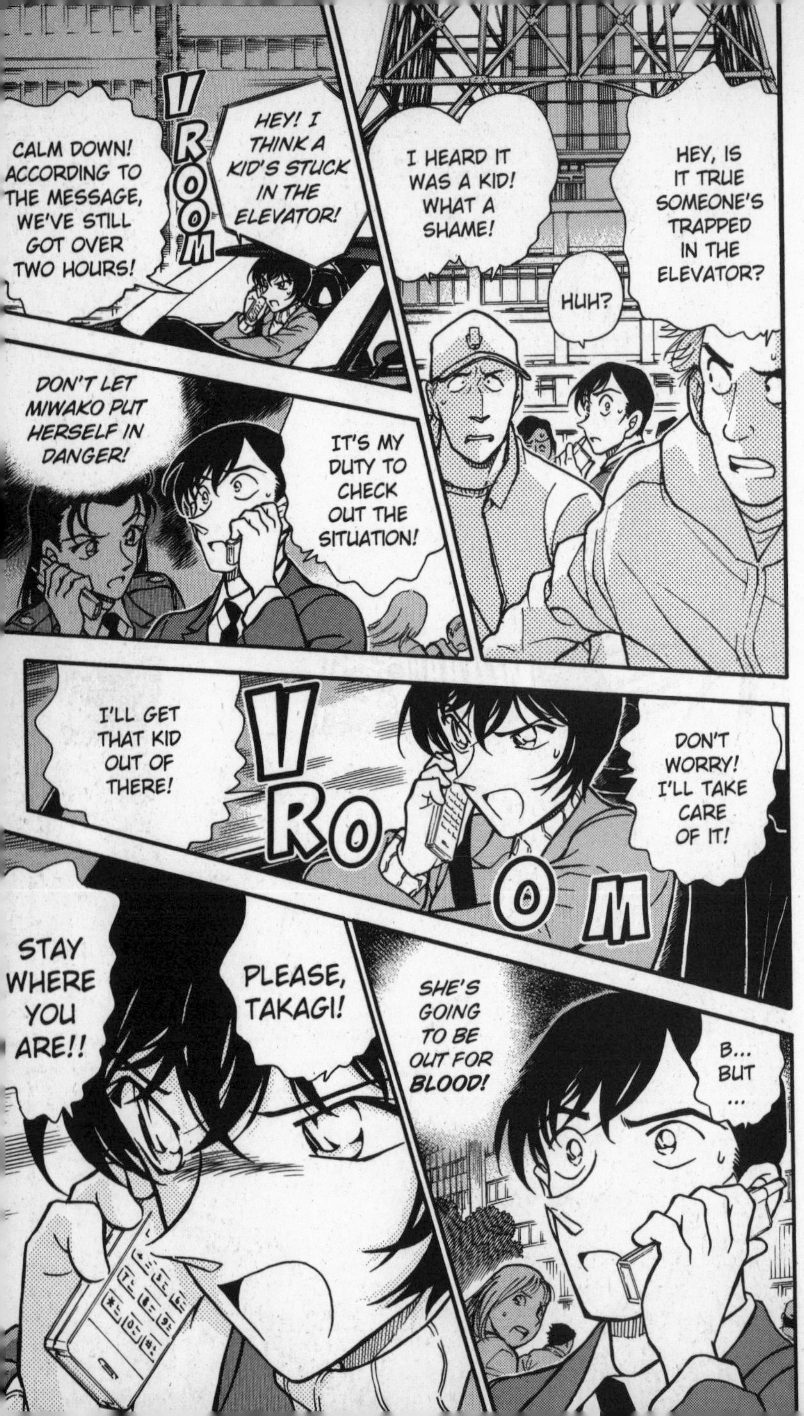
HEY, IS IT TRUE SOMEONE'S TRAPPED IN THE ELEVATOR?
HUH?
I HEARD IT WAS A KID! WHAT A SHAME!
HEY! I THINK A KID'S STUCK IN THE ELEVATOR!
VROOM
CALM DOWN! ACCORDING TO THE MESSAGE, WE'VE STILL GOT OVER TWO HOURS!
IT'S MY DUTY TO CHECK OUT THE SITUATION!
DON'T LET MIWAKO PUT HERSELF IN DANGER!
DON'T WORRY! I'LL TAKE CARE OF IT!
VROOM
I'LL GET THAT KID OUT OF THERE!
B... BUT ...
SHE'S GOING TO BE OUT FOR BLOOD!
PLEASE, TAKAGI!
STAY WHERE YOU ARE!!

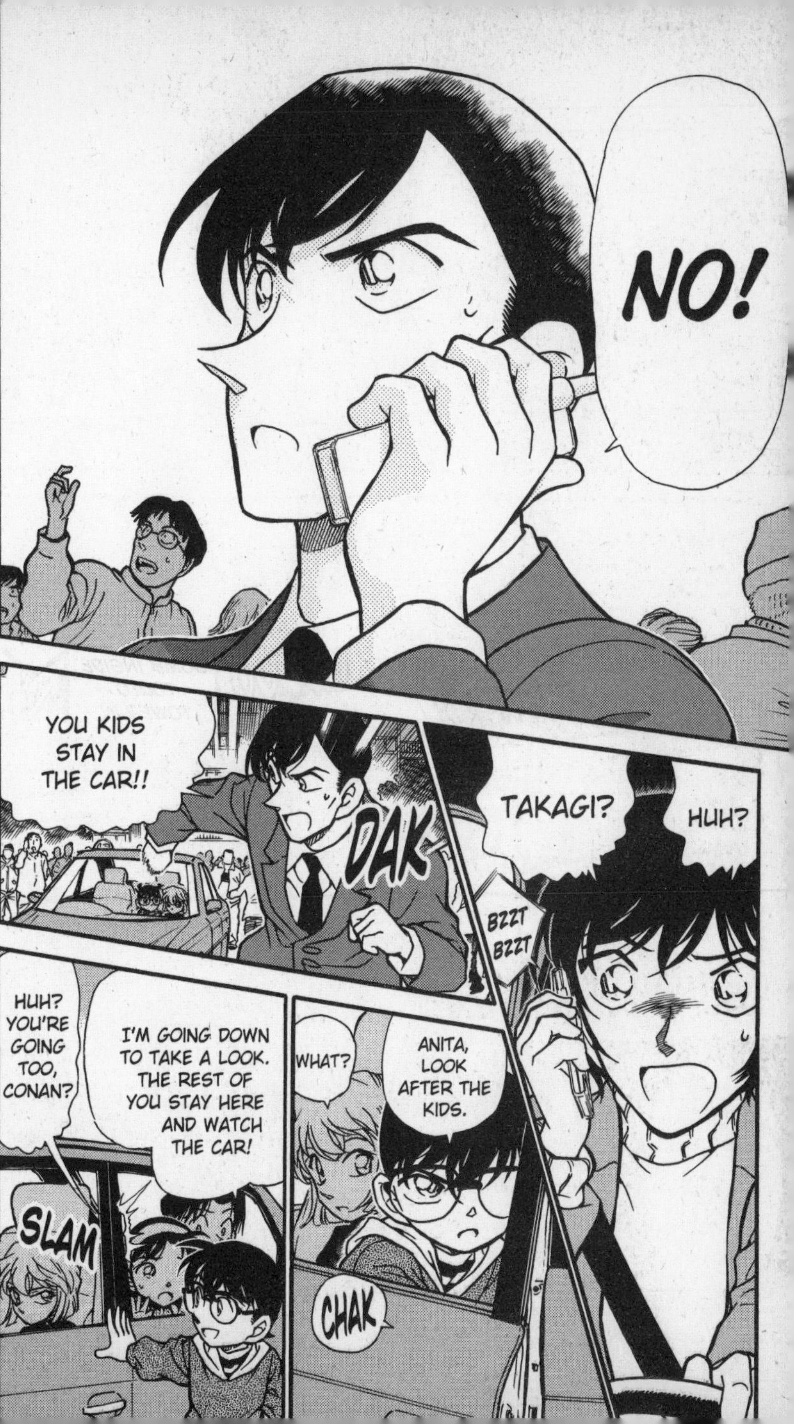
NO!
HUH?
TAKAGI?
BZZT BZZT
YOU KIDS STAY IN THE CAR!!
DAK
ANITA, LOOK AFTER THE KIDS.
WHAT?
CHAK
I'M GOING DOWN TO TAKE A LOOK. THE REST OF YOU STAY HERE AND WATCH THE CAR!
HUH? YOU'RE GOING TOO, CONAN?
SLAM

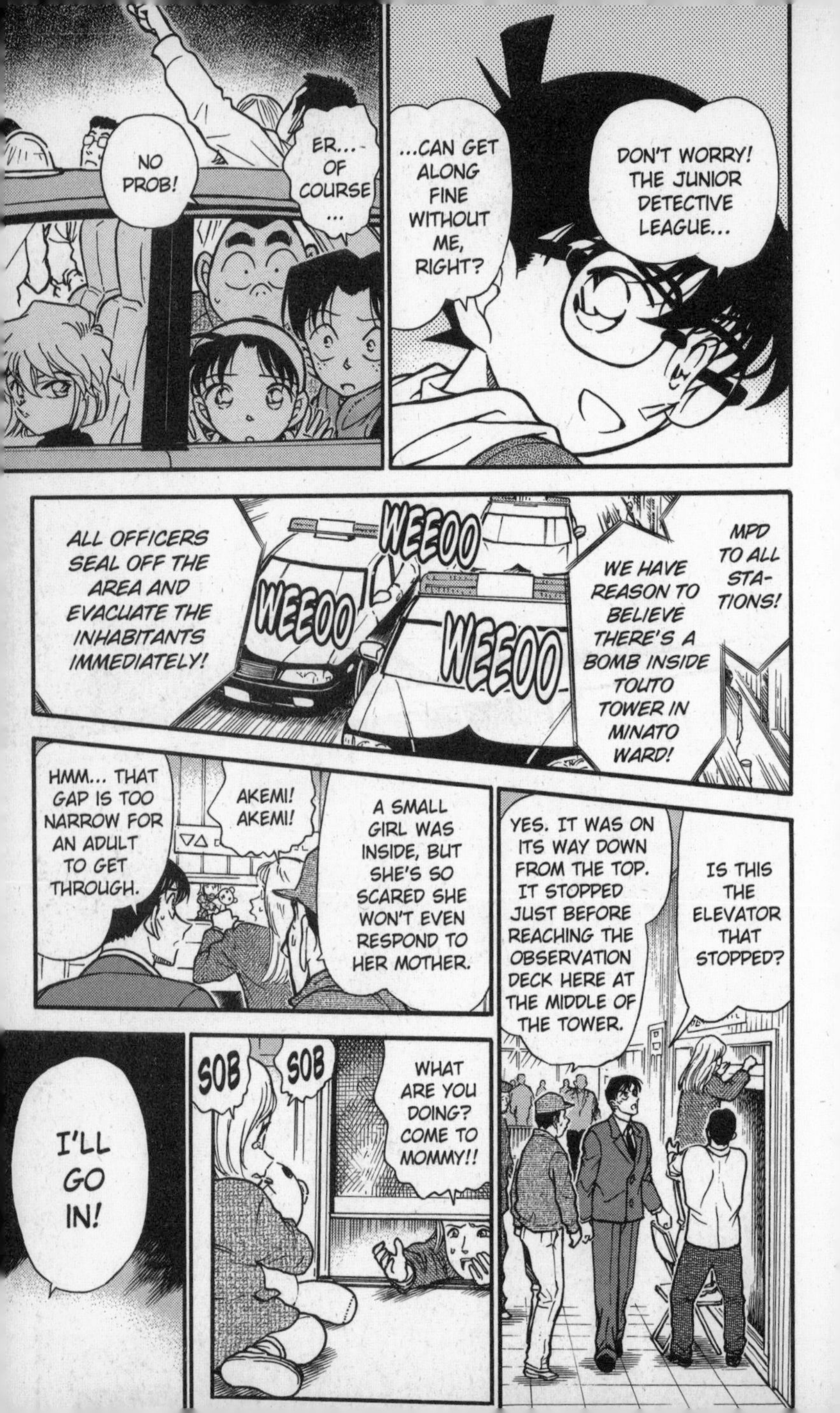
DON'T WORRY! THE JUNIOR DETECTIVE LEAGUE...
...CAN GET ALONG FINE WITHOUT ME, RIGHT?
ER... OF COURSE ...
NO PROB!
MPD TO ALL STATIONS!
WE HAVE REASON TO BELIEVE THERE'S A BOMB INSIDE TOUTO TOWER IN MINATO WARD!
WEEOO
WEEOO
WEEOO
ALL OFFICERS SEAL OFF THE AREA AND EVACUATE THE INHABITANTS IMMEDIATELY!
IS THIS THE ELEVATOR THAT STOPPED?
YES. IT WAS ON ITS WAY DOWN FROM THE TOP. IT STOPPED JUST BEFORE REACHING THE OBSERVATION DECK HERE AT THE MIDDLE OF THE TOWER.
A SMALL GIRL WAS INSIDE, BUT SHE'S SO SCARED SHE WON'T EVEN RESPOND TO HER MOTHER.
AKEMI! AKEMI!
HMM... THAT GAP IS TOO NARROW FOR AN ADULT TO GET THROUGH.
WHAT ARE YOU DOING? COME TO MOMMY!!
SOB
SOB
I'LL GO IN!

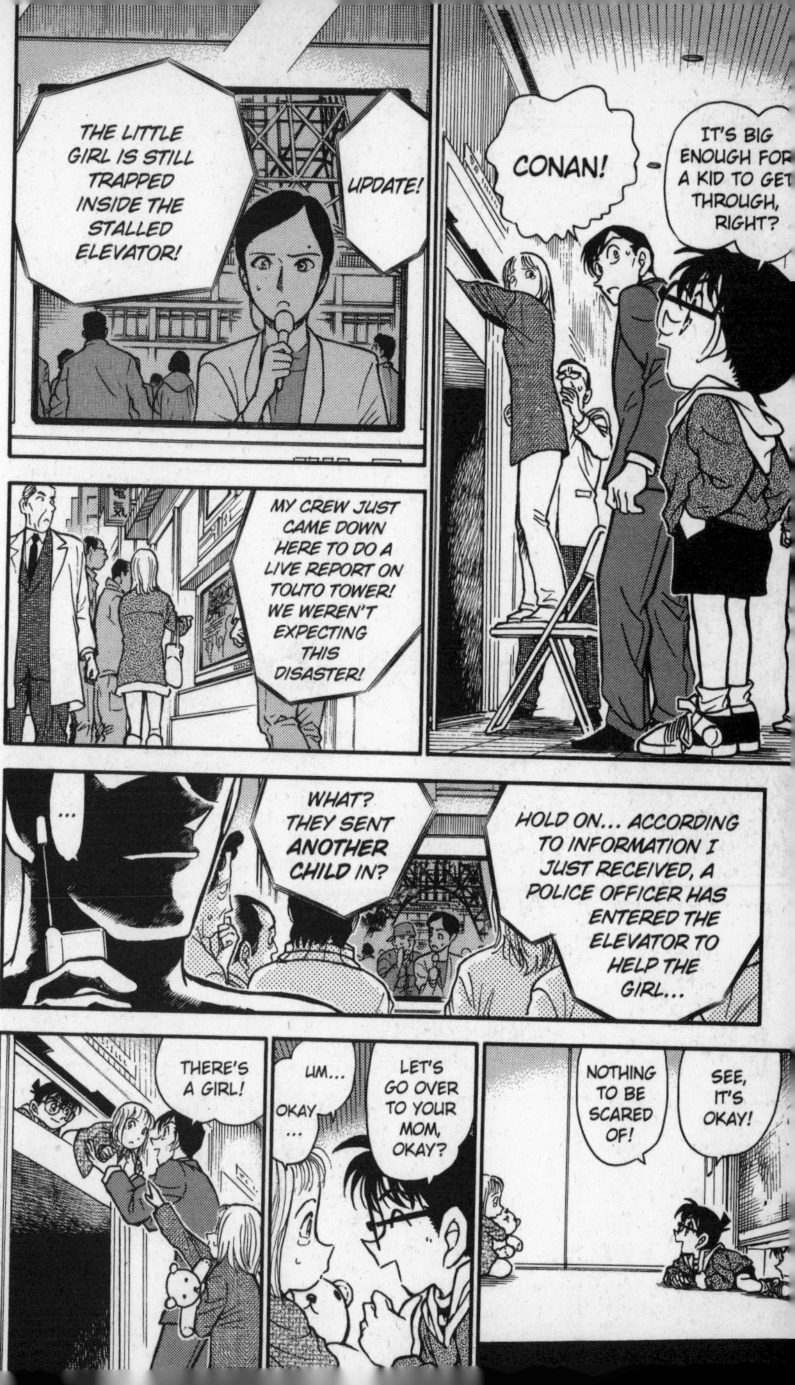
IT'S BIG ENOUGH FOR A KID TO GET THROUGH, RIGHT?
CONAN!
UPDATE!
THE LITTLE GIRL IS STILL TRAPPED INSIDE THE STALLED ELEVATOR!
MY CREW JUST CAME DOWN HERE TO DO A LIVE REPORT ON TOUTO TOWER! WE WEREN'T EXPECTING THIS DISASTER!
HOLD ON... ACCORDING TO INFORMATION I JUST RECEIVED, A POLICE OFFICER HAS ENTERED THE ELEVATOR TO HELP THE GIRL...
WHAT? THEY SENT ANOTHER CHILD IN?
...
SEE, IT'S OKAY!
NOTHING TO BE SCARED OF!
LET'S GO OVER TO YOUR MOM, OKAY?
UM... OKAY...
THERE'S A GIRL!

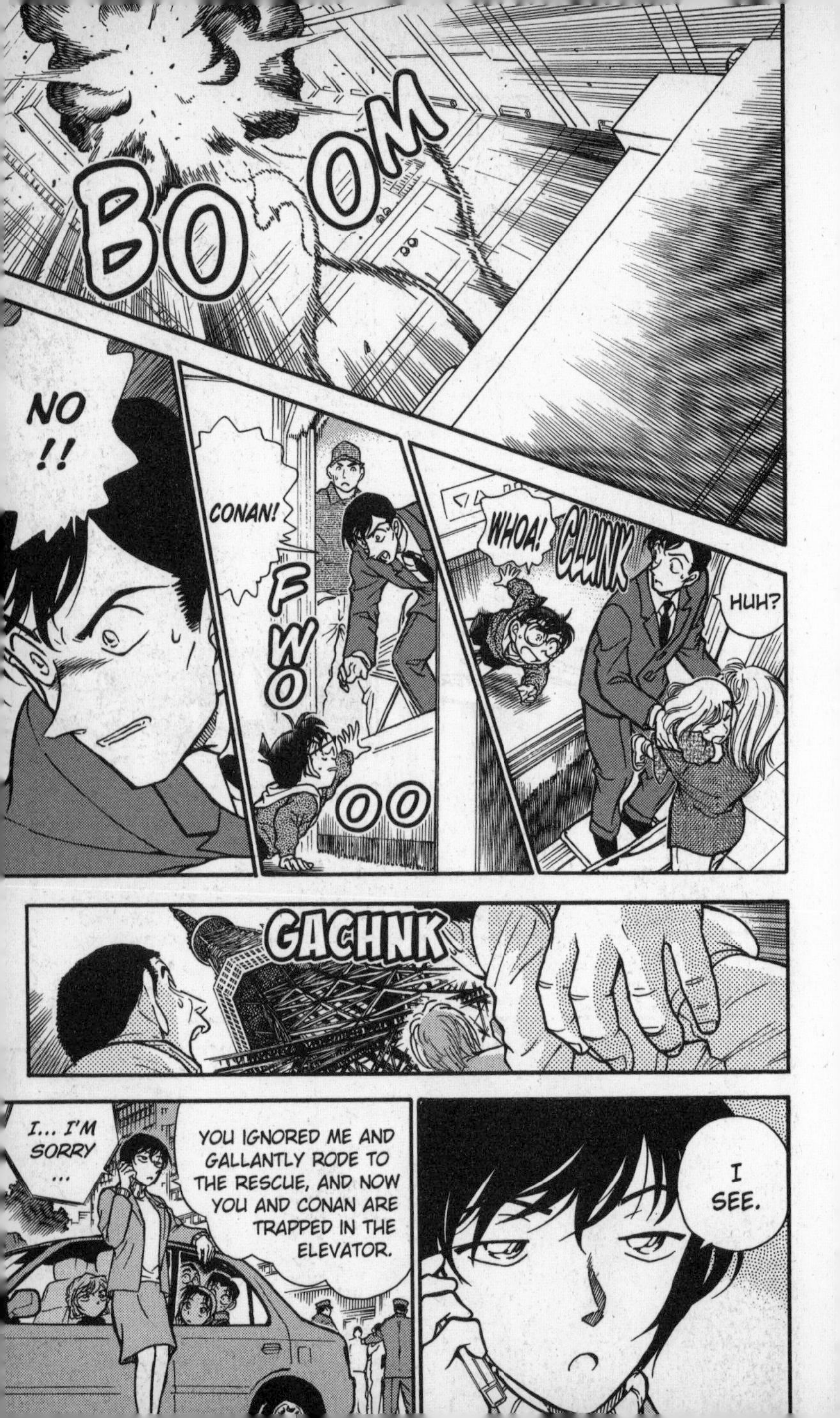
BOOM
WHOA!
CLUNK
HUH?
CONAN!
FWOOO
NO!!
GACHNK
I SEE.
YOU IGNORED ME AND GALLANTLY RODE TO THE RESCUE, AND NOW YOU AND CONAN ARE TRAPPED IN THE ELEVATOR.
I... I'M SORRY...

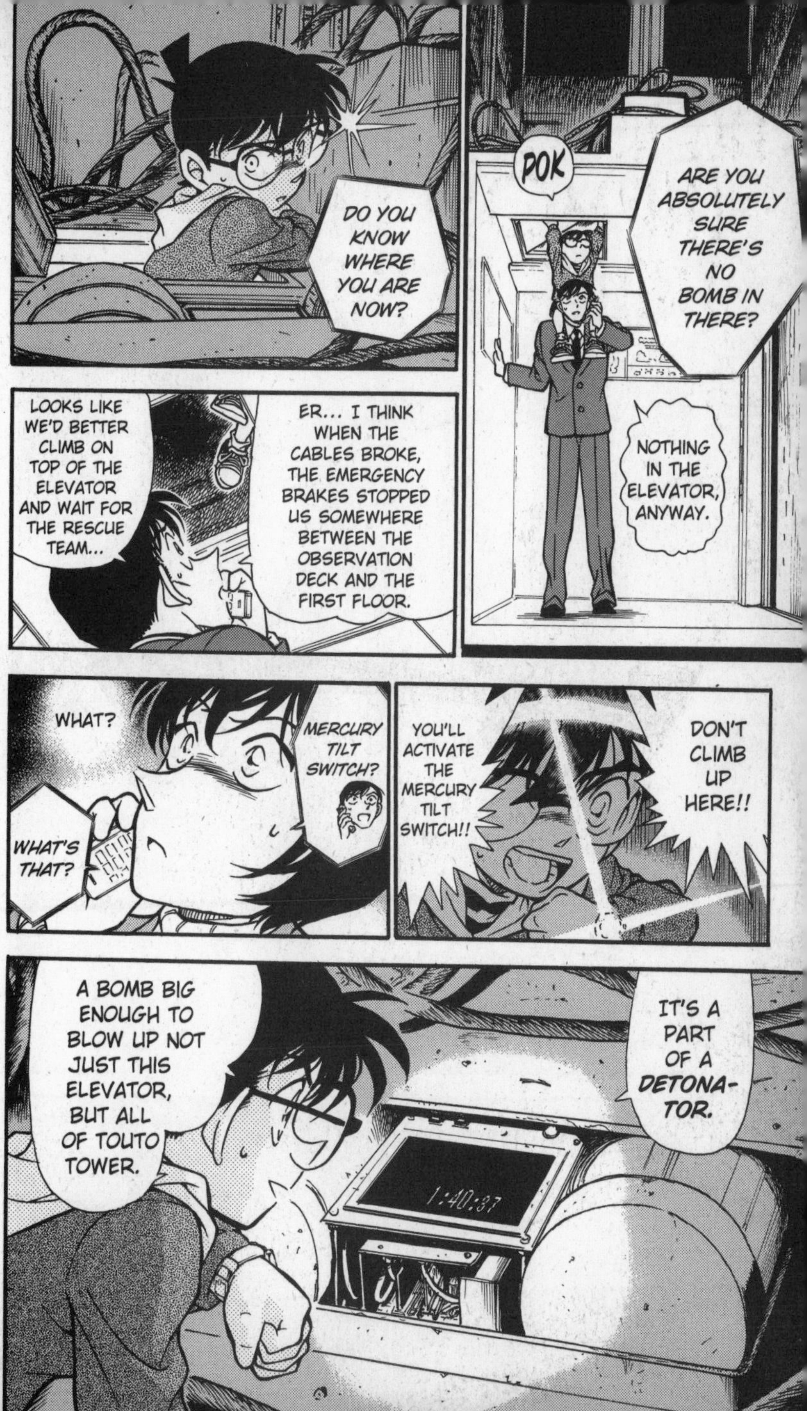
POK
ARE YOU ABSOLUTELY SURE THERE'S NO BOMB IN THERE?
NOTHING IN THE ELEVATOR, ANYWAY.
DO YOU KNOW WHERE YOU ARE NOW?
ER... I THINK WHEN THE CABLES BROKE, THE EMERGENCY BRAKES STOPPED US SOMEWHERE BETWEEN THE OBSERVATION DECK AND THE FIRST FLOOR.
LOOKS LIKE WE'D BETTER CLIMB ON TOP OF THE ELEVATOR AND WAIT FOR THE RESCUE TEAM...
DON'T CLIMB UP HERE!!
YOU'LL ACTIVATE THE MERCURY TILT SWITCH!!
MERCURY TILT SWITCH?
WHAT?
WHAT'S THAT?
IT'S A PART OF A DETONATOR.
A BOMB BIG ENOUGH TO BLOW UP NOT JUST THIS ELEVATOR, BUT ALL OF TOUTO TOWER.
1:40:37

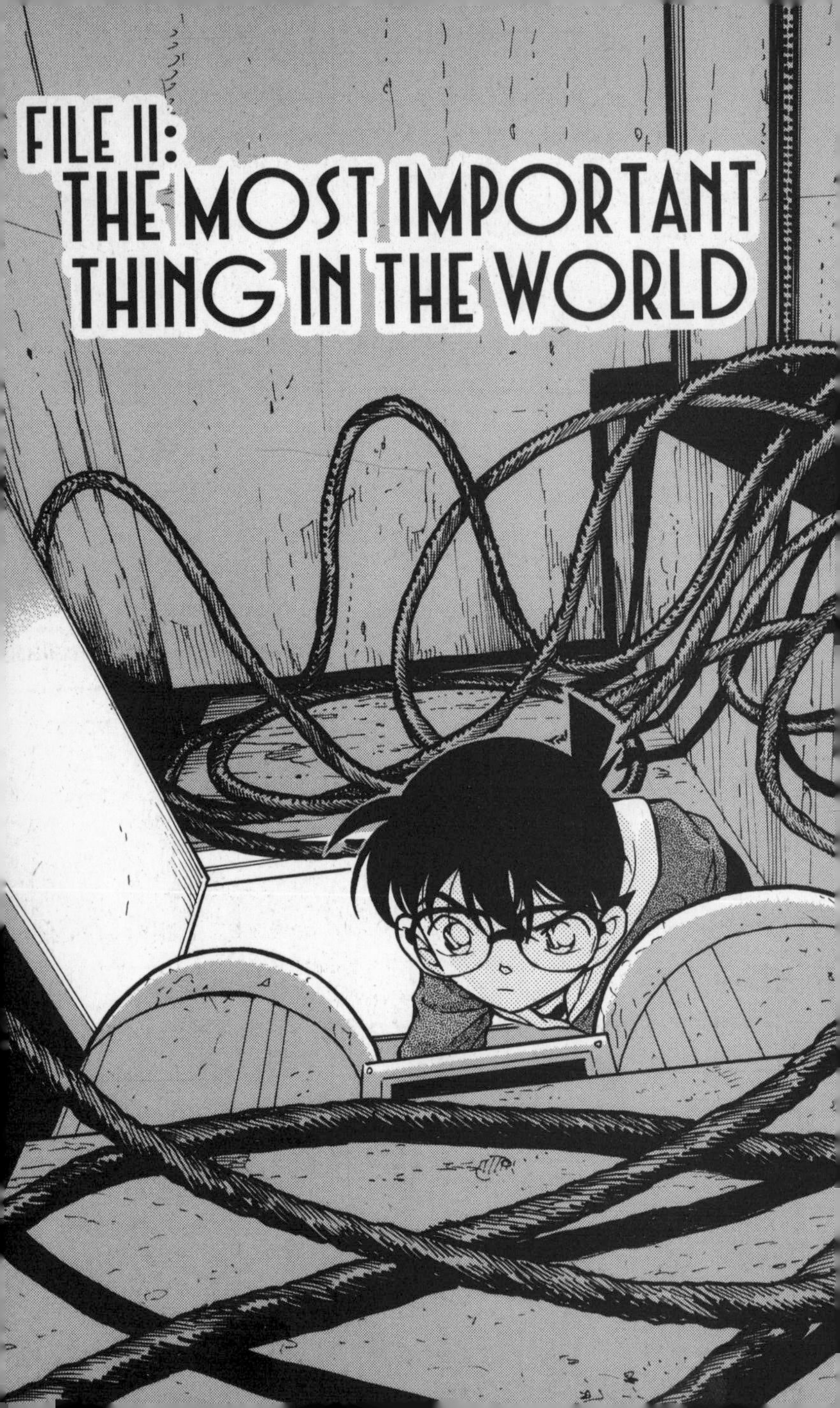
FILE 11:
THE MOST IMPORTANT
THING IN THE WORLD

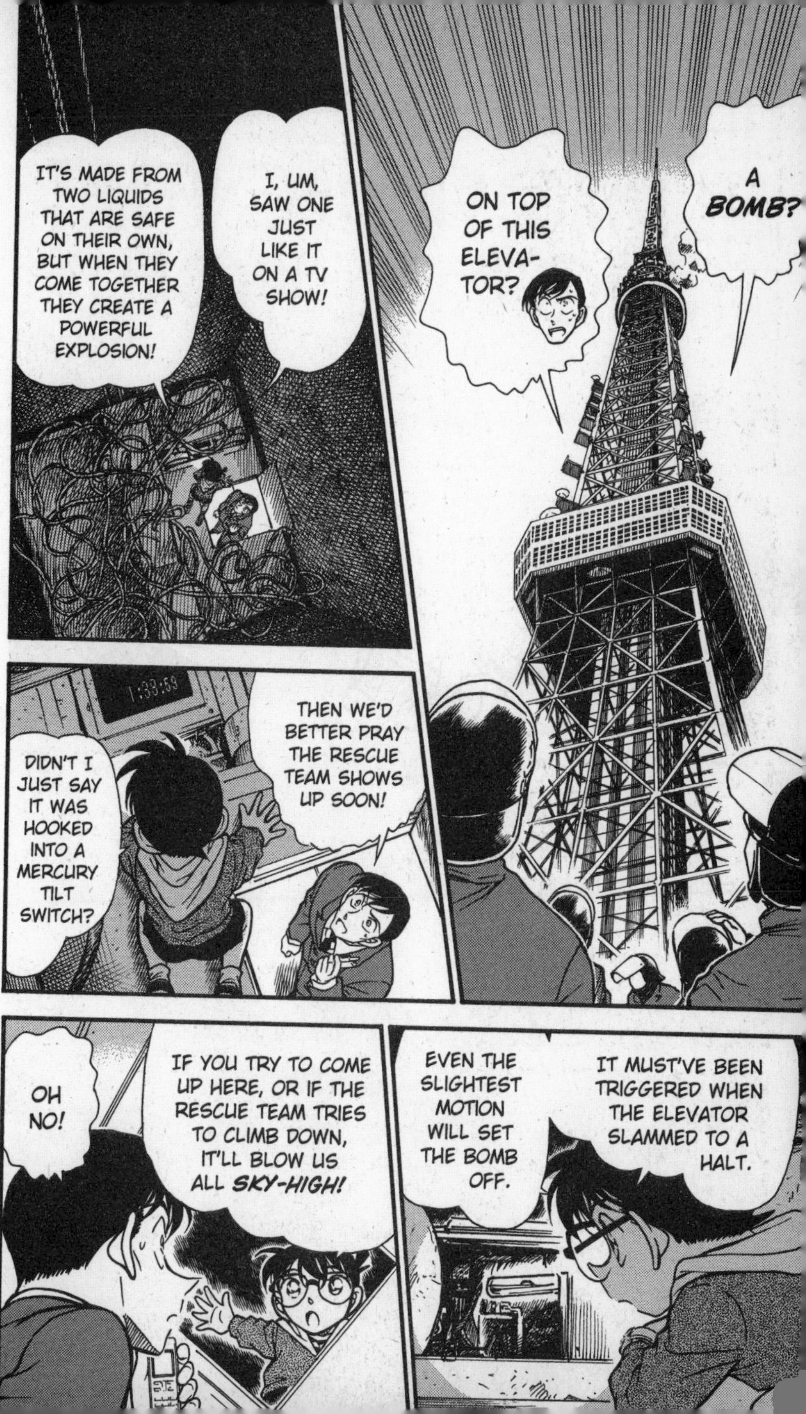

A BOMB?
ON TOP OF THIS ELEVATOR?
I, UM, SAW ONE JUST LIKE IT ON A TV SHOW!
IT'S MADE FROM TWO LIQUIDS THAT ARE SAFE ON THEIR OWN, BUT WHEN THEY COME TOGETHER THEY CREATE A POWERFUL EXPLOSION!
THEN WE'D BETTER PRAY THE RESCUE TEAM SHOWS UP SOON!
DIDN'T I JUST SAY IT WAS HOOKED INTO A MERCURY TILT SWITCH?
IT MUST'VE BEEN TRIGGERED WHEN THE ELEVATOR SLAMMED TO A HALT.
EVEN THE SLIGHTEST MOTION WILL SET THE BOMB OFF.
IF YOU TRY TO COME UP HERE, OR IF THE RESCUE TEAM TRIES TO CLIMB DOWN, IT'LL BLOW US ALL SKY-HIGH!
OH NO!

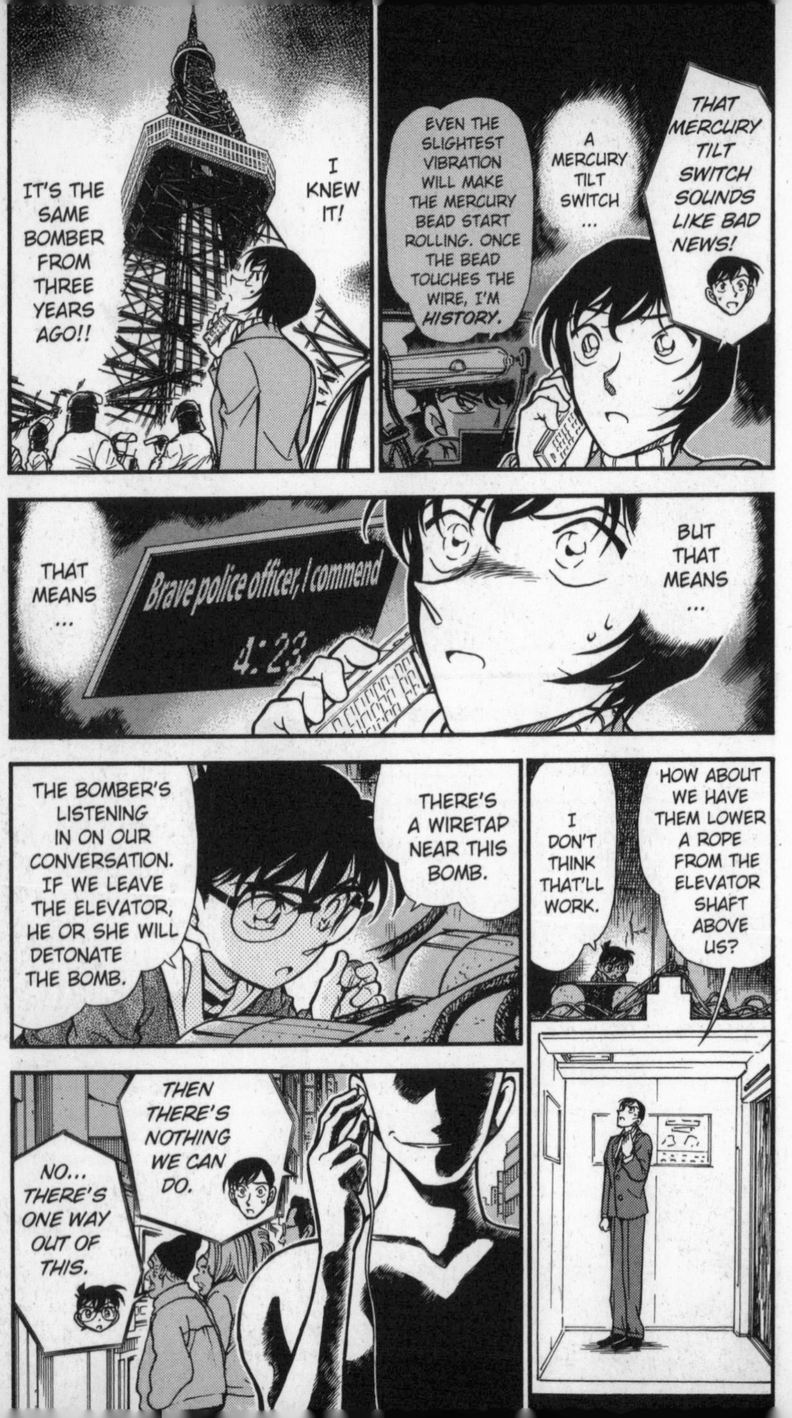
THAT MERCURY TILT SWITCH SOUNDS LIKE BAD NEWS!
A MERCURY TILT SWITCH ...
EVEN THE SLIGHTEST VIBRATION WILL MAKE THE MERCURY BEAD START ROLLING. ONCE THE BEAD TOUCHES THE WIRE, I'M HISTORY.
I KNEW IT!
IT'S THE SAME BOMBER FROM THREE YEARS AGO!!
BUT THAT MEANS ...
Brave police officer, I commend
4:23
THAT MEANS ...
HOW ABOUT WE HAVE THEM LOWER A ROPE FROM THE ELEVATOR SHAFT ABOVE US?
I DON'T THINK THAT'LL WORK.
THERE'S A WIRETAP NEAR THIS BOMB.
THE BOMBER'S LISTENING IN ON OUR CONVERSATION. IF WE LEAVE THE ELEVATOR, HE OR SHE WILL DETONATE THE BOMB.
THEN THERE'S NOTHING WE CAN DO.
NO... THERE'S ONE WAY OUT OF THIS.

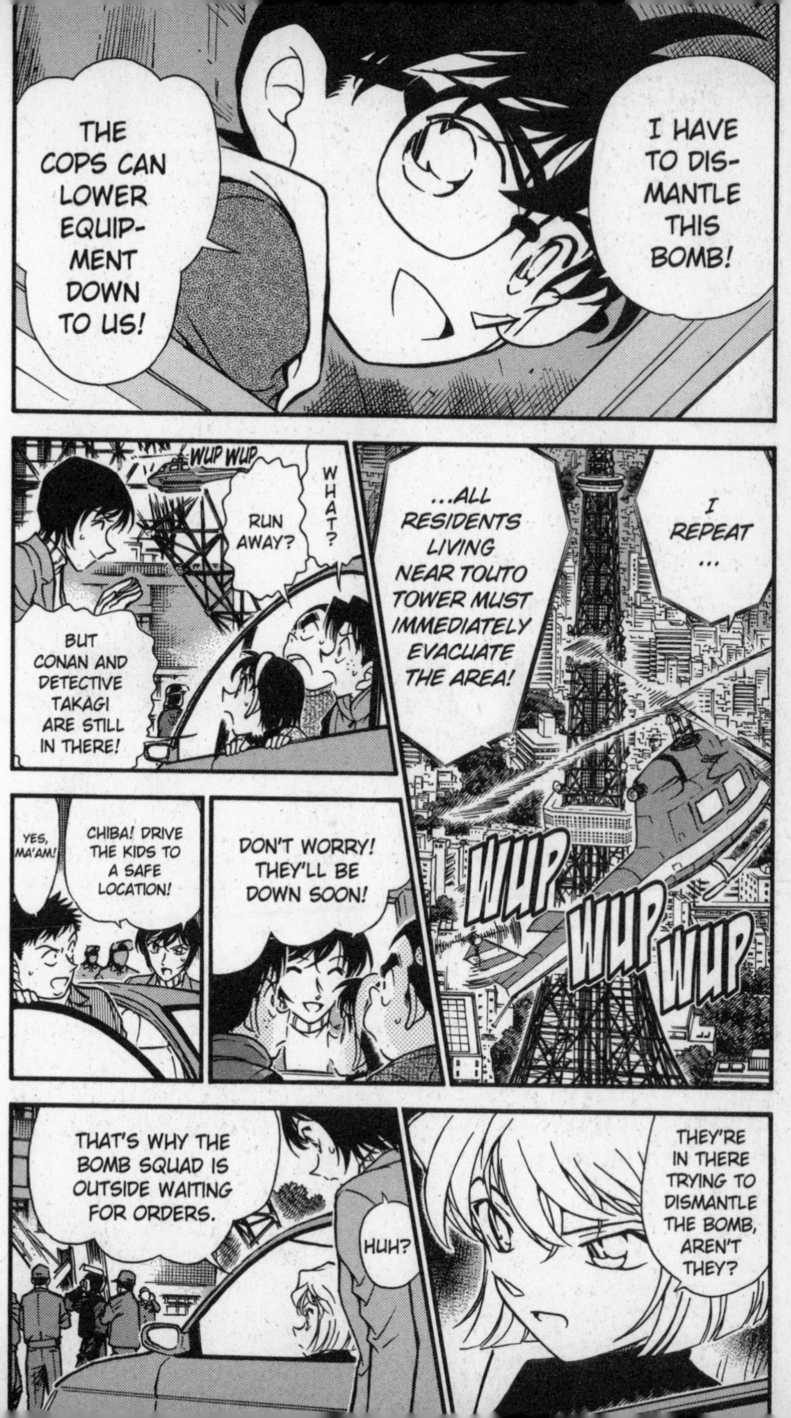
I HAVE TO DISMANTLE THIS BOMB!
THE COPS CAN LOWER EQUIPMENT DOWN TO US!
I REPEAT ...
...ALL RESIDENTS LIVING NEAR TOUTO TOWER MUST IMMEDIATELY EVACUATE THE AREA!
WUP
WUP
WUP
WUP WUP
WHAT?
RUN AWAY?
BUT CONAN AND DETECTIVE TAKAGI ARE STILL IN THERE!
DON'T WORRY! THEY'LL BE DOWN SOON!
CHIBA! DRIVE THE KIDS TO A SAFE LOCATION!
YES, MA'AM!
THEY'RE IN THERE TRYING TO DISMANTLE THE BOMB, AREN'T THEY?
HUH?
THAT'S WHY THE BOMB SQUAD IS OUTSIDE WAITING FOR ORDERS.

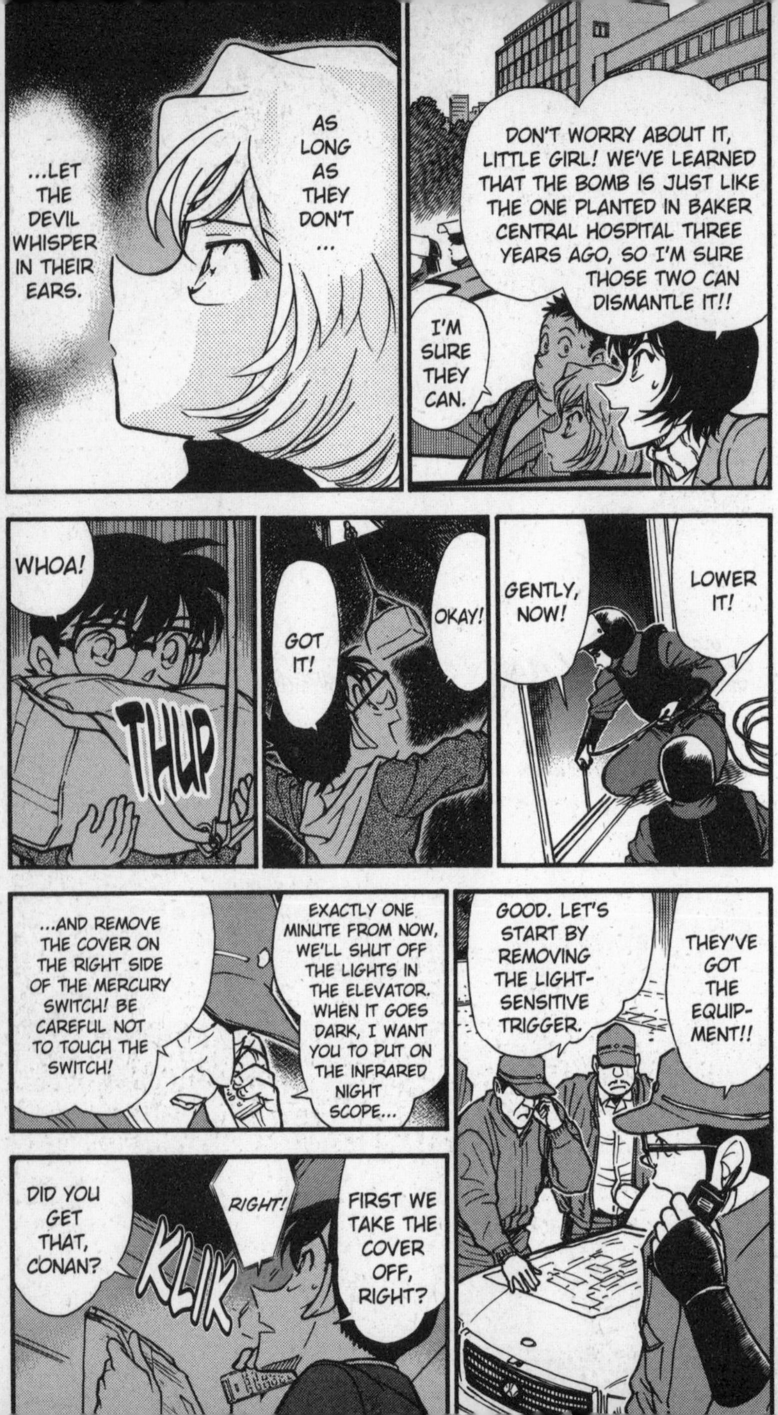
DON'T WORRY ABOUT IT, LITTLE GIRL! WE'VE LEARNED THAT THE BOMB IS JUST LIKE THE ONE PLANTED IN BAKER CENTRAL HOSPITAL THREE YEARS AGO, SO I'M SURE THOSE TWO CAN DISMANTLE IT!!
I'M SURE THEY CAN.
AS LONG AS THEY DON'T ...
...LET THE DEVIL WHISPER IN THEIR EARS.
LOWER IT!
GENTLY, NOW!
OKAY!
GOT IT!
WHOA!
THUP
THEY'VE GOT THE EQUIP-MENT!!
GOOD. LET'S START BY REMOVING THE LIGHT-SENSITIVE TRIGGER.
EXACTLY ONE MINUTE FROM NOW, WE'LL SHUT OFF THE LIGHTS IN THE ELEVATOR. WHEN IT GOES DARK, I WANT YOU TO PUT ON THE INFRARED NIGHT SCOPE...
...AND REMOVE THE COVER ON THE RIGHT SIDE OF THE MERCURY SWITCH! BE CAREFUL NOT TO TOUCH THE SWITCH!
FIRST WE TAKE THE COVER OFF, RIGHT?
RIGHT!
KLIK
DID YOU GET THAT, CONAN?

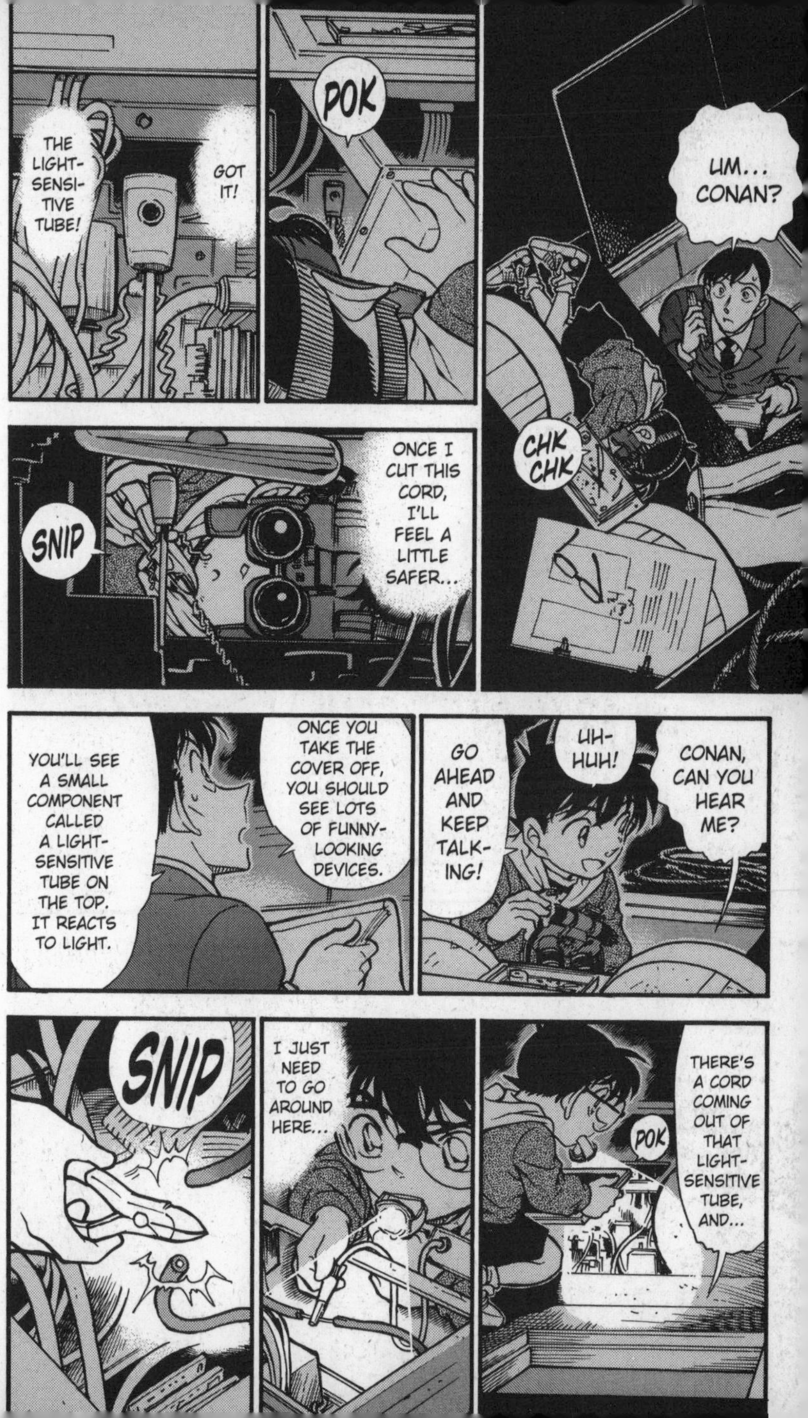
UM... CONAN?
CHK CHK
POK
GOT IT!
THE LIGHT-SENSITIVE TUBE!
ONCE I CUT THIS CORD, I'LL FEEL A LITTLE SAFER...
SNIP
CONAN, CAN YOU HEAR ME?
UH-HUH!
GO AHEAD AND KEEP TALKING!
ONCE YOU TAKE THE COVER OFF, YOU SHOULD SEE LOTS OF FUNNY-LOOKING DEVICES.
YOU'LL SEE A SMALL COMPONENT CALLED A LIGHT-SENSITIVE TUBE ON THE TOP. IT REACTS TO LIGHT.
THERE'S A CORD COMING OUT OF THAT LIGHT-SENSITIVE TUBE, AND...
POK
I JUST NEED TO GO AROUND HERE...
SNIP

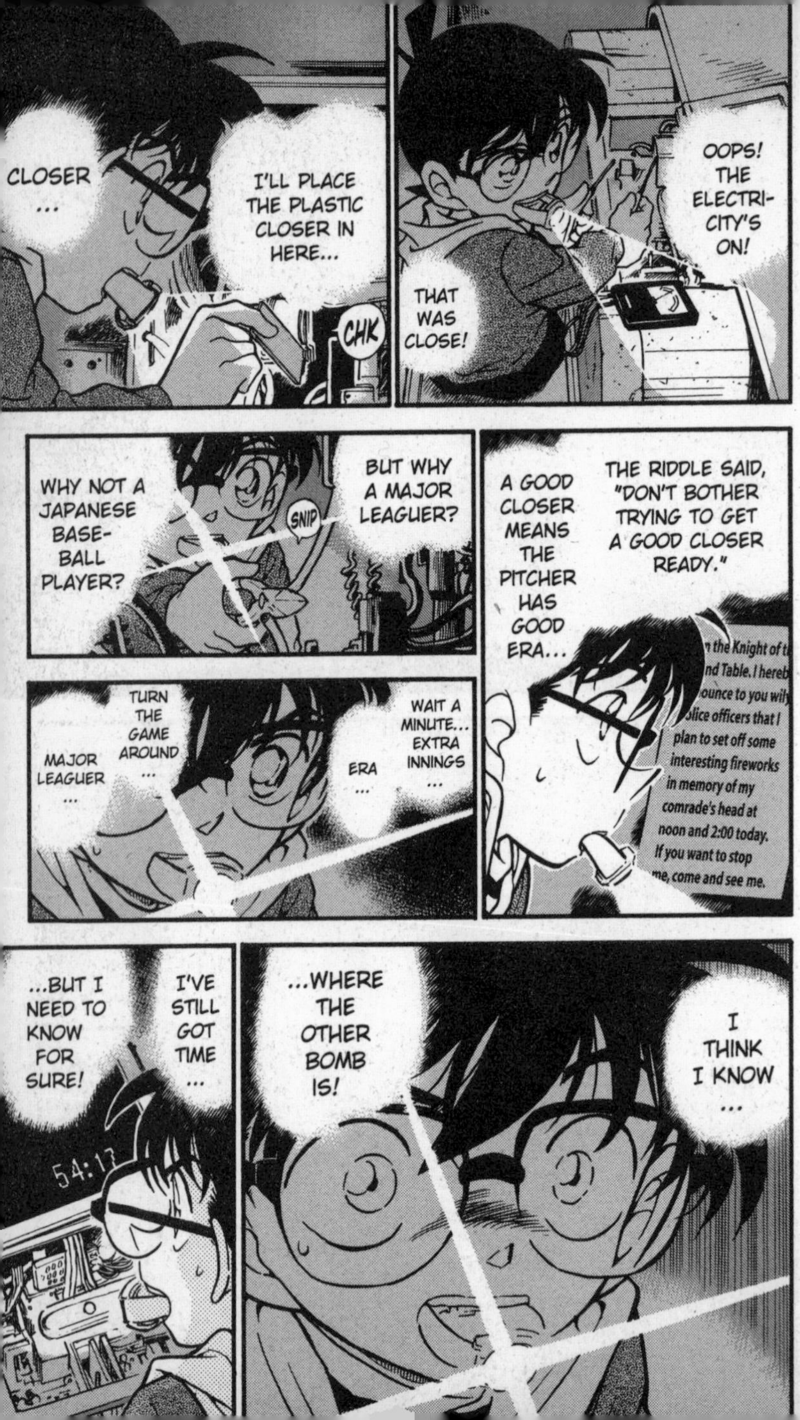

OOPS! THE ELECTRICITY'S ON!
THAT WAS CLOSE!
I'LL PLACE THE PLASTIC CLOSER IN HERE...
CHK
CLOSER...
THE RIDDLE SAID, "DON'T BOTHER TRYING TO GET A GOOD CLOSER READY."
A GOOD CLOSER MEANS THE PITCHER HAS GOOD ERA...
n the Knight of t
nd Table. I hereb
ounce to you wily
olice officers that I
plan to set off some
interesting fireworks
in memory of my
comrade's head at
noon and 2:00 today.
If you want to stop
me, come and see me.
BUT WHY A MAJOR LEAGUER?
SNIP
WHY NOT A JAPANESE BASE-BALL PLAYER?
WAIT A MINUTE... EXTRA INNINGS...
ERA...
TURN THE GAME AROUND...
MAJOR LEAGUER...
I THINK I KNOW...
...WHERE THE OTHER BOMB IS!
I'VE STILL GOT TIME...
...BUT I NEED TO KNOW FOR SURE!
54:17

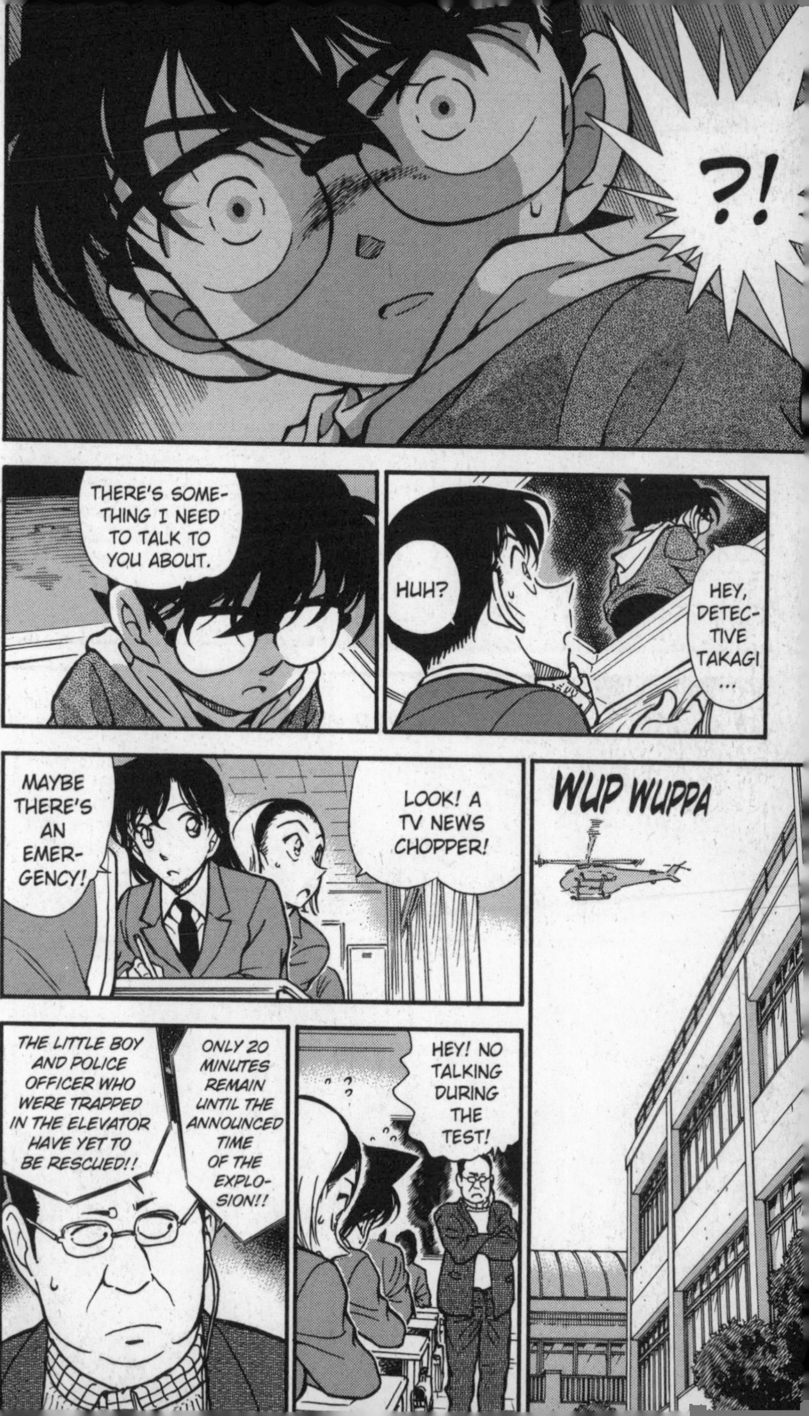

?!
HEY, DETECTIVE TAKAGI...
HUH?
THERE'S SOMETHING I NEED TO TALK TO YOU ABOUT.
WUP WUPPA
LOOK! A TV NEWS CHOPPER!
MAYBE THERE'S AN EMERGENCY!
HEY! NO TALKING DURING THE TEST!
ONLY 20 MINUTES REMAIN UNTIL THE ANNOUNCED TIME OF THE EXPLOSION!!
THE LITTLE BOY AND POLICE OFFICER WHO WERE TRAPPED IN THE ELEVATOR HAVE YET TO BE RESCUED!!

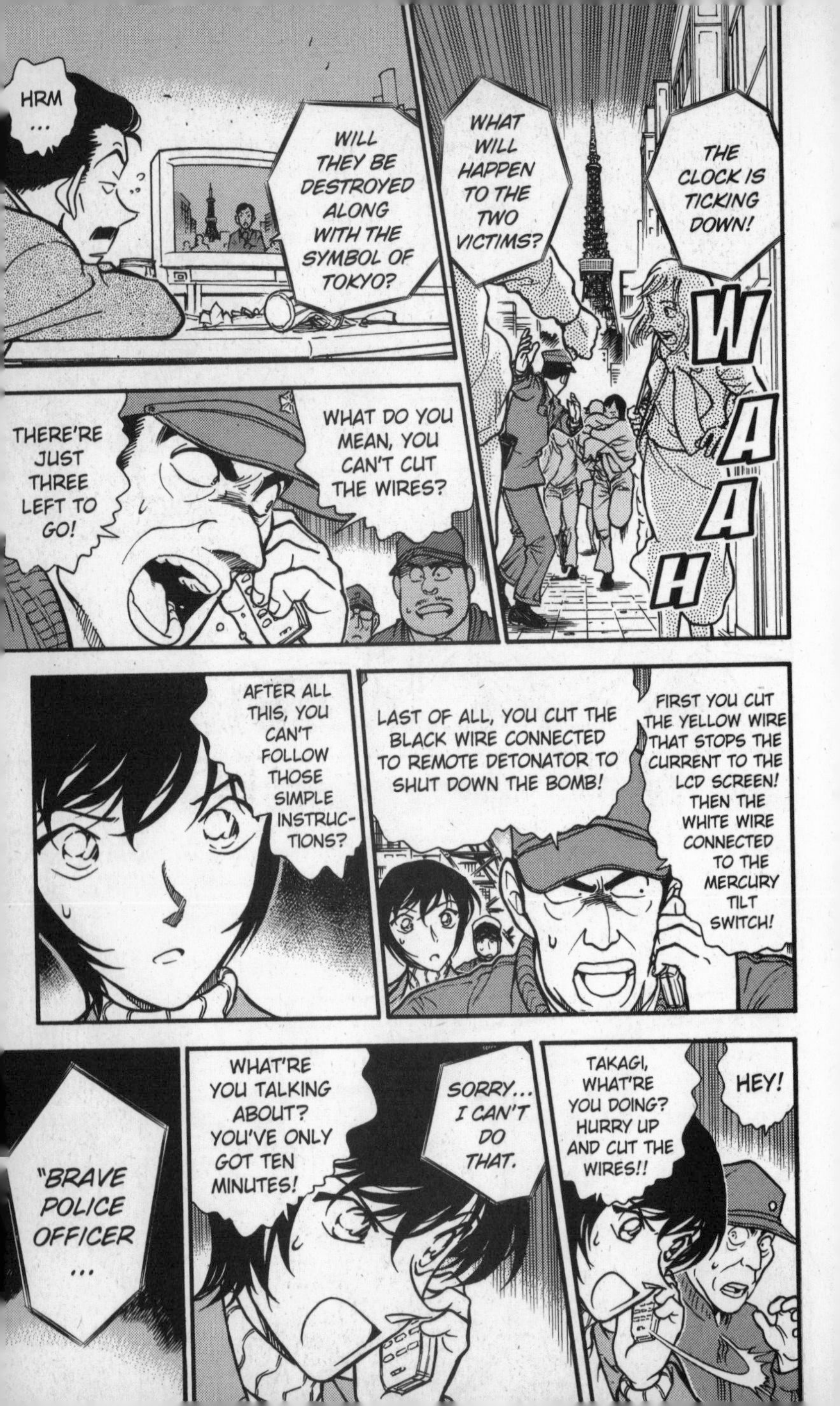
THE CLOCK IS TICKING DOWN!
WHAT WILL HAPPEN TO THE TWO VICTIMS?
WAAAH
WILL THEY BE DESTROYED ALONG WITH THE SYMBOL OF TOKYO?
HRM ...
WHAT DO YOU MEAN, YOU CAN'T CUT THE WIRES?
THERE'RE JUST THREE LEFT TO GO!
FIRST YOU CUT THE YELLOW WIRE THAT STOPS THE CURRENT TO THE LCD SCREEN! THEN THE WHITE WIRE CONNECTED TO THE MERCURY TILT SWITCH!
LAST OF ALL, YOU CUT THE BLACK WIRE CONNECTED TO REMOTE DETONATOR TO SHUT DOWN THE BOMB!
AFTER ALL THIS, YOU CAN'T FOLLOW THOSE SIMPLE INSTRUCTIONS?
HEY!
TAKAGI, WHAT'RE YOU DOING? HURRY UP AND CUT THE WIRES!!
SORRY... I CAN'T DO THAT.
WHAT'RE YOU TALKING ABOUT? YOU'VE ONLY GOT TEN MINUTES!
"BRAVE POLICE OFFICER ...

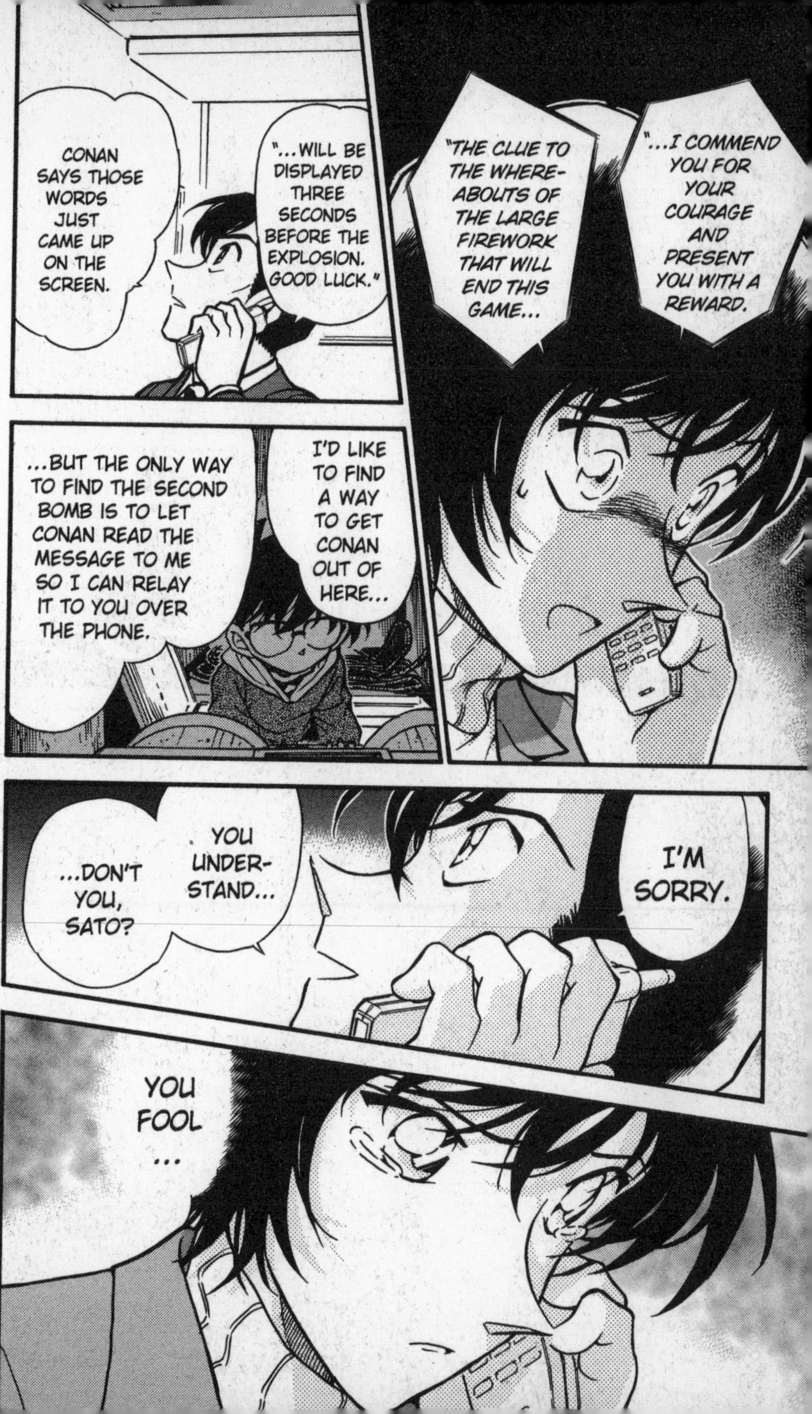
"...I COMMEND YOU FOR YOUR COURAGE AND PRESENT YOU WITH A REWARD.
"THE CLUE TO THE WHEREABOUTS OF THE LARGE FIREWORK THAT WILL END THIS GAME...
"...WILL BE DISPLAYED THREE SECONDS BEFORE THE EXPLOSION. GOOD LUCK."
CONAN SAYS THOSE WORDS JUST CAME UP ON THE SCREEN.
I'D LIKE TO FIND A WAY TO GET CONAN OUT OF HERE...
...BUT THE ONLY WAY TO FIND THE SECOND BOMB IS TO LET CONAN READ THE MESSAGE TO ME SO I CAN RELAY IT TO YOU OVER THE PHONE.
I'M SORRY.
YOU UNDERSTAND...
...DON'T YOU, SATO?
YOU FOOL ...

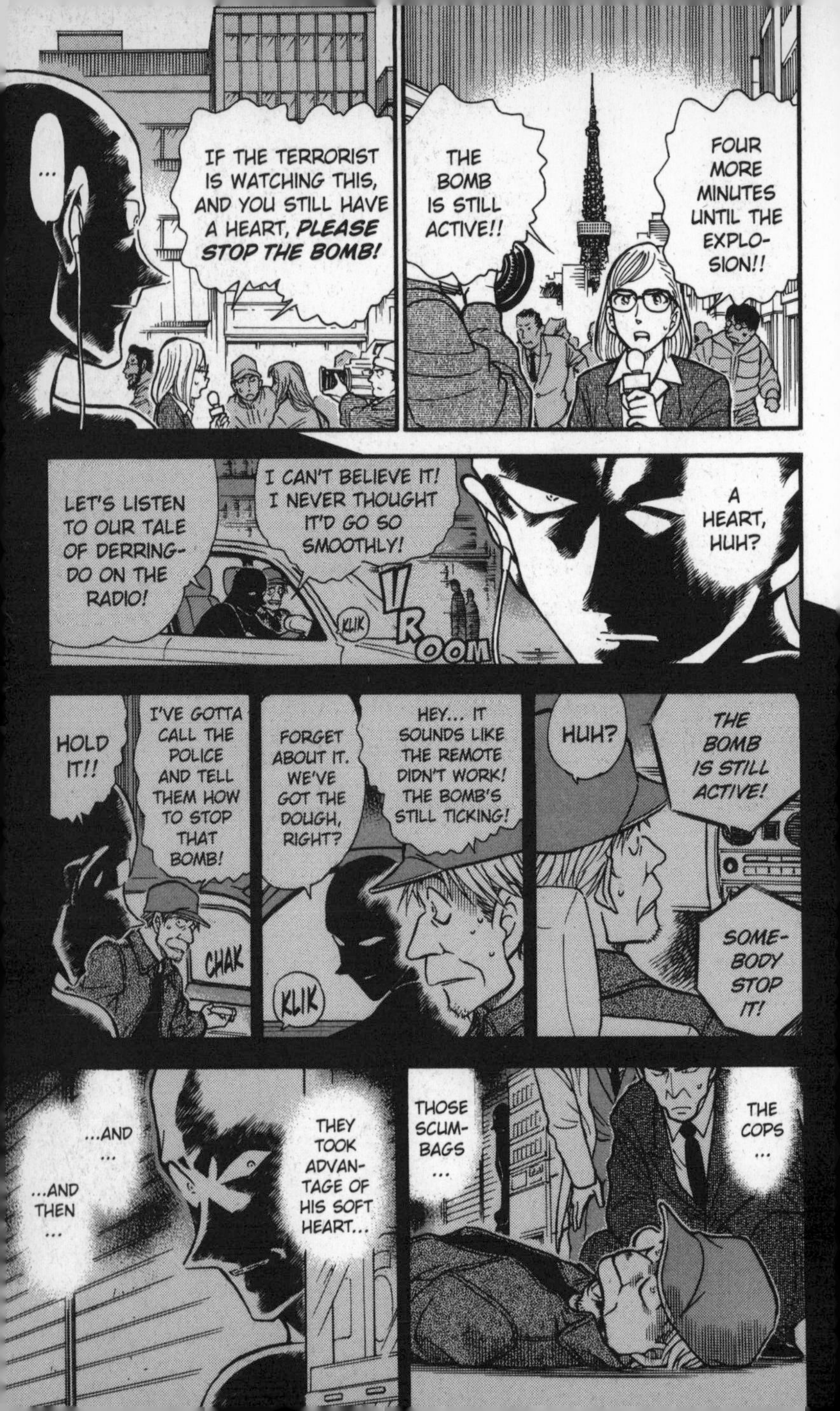
FOUR MORE MINUTES UNTIL THE EXPLOSION!!
THE BOMB IS STILL ACTIVE!!
IF THE TERRORIST IS WATCHING THIS, AND YOU STILL HAVE A HEART, *PLEASE STOP THE BOMB!*
...
A HEART, HUH?
I CAN'T BELIEVE IT! I NEVER THOUGHT IT'D GO SO SMOOTHLY!
LET'S LISTEN TO OUR TALE OF DERRING-DO ON THE RADIO!
KLIK
VROOM
THE BOMB IS STILL ACTIVE!
HUH?
SOMEBODY STOP IT!
HEY... IT SOUNDS LIKE THE REMOTE DIDN'T WORK! THE BOMB'S STILL TICKING!
FORGET ABOUT IT. WE'VE GOT THE DOUGH, RIGHT?
KLIK
I'VE GOTTA CALL THE POLICE AND TELL THEM HOW TO STOP THAT BOMB!
HOLD IT!!
CHAK
THE COPS ...
THOSE SCUMBAGS ...
THEY TOOK ADVANTAGE OF HIS SOFT HEART...
...AND ...
...AND THEN ...

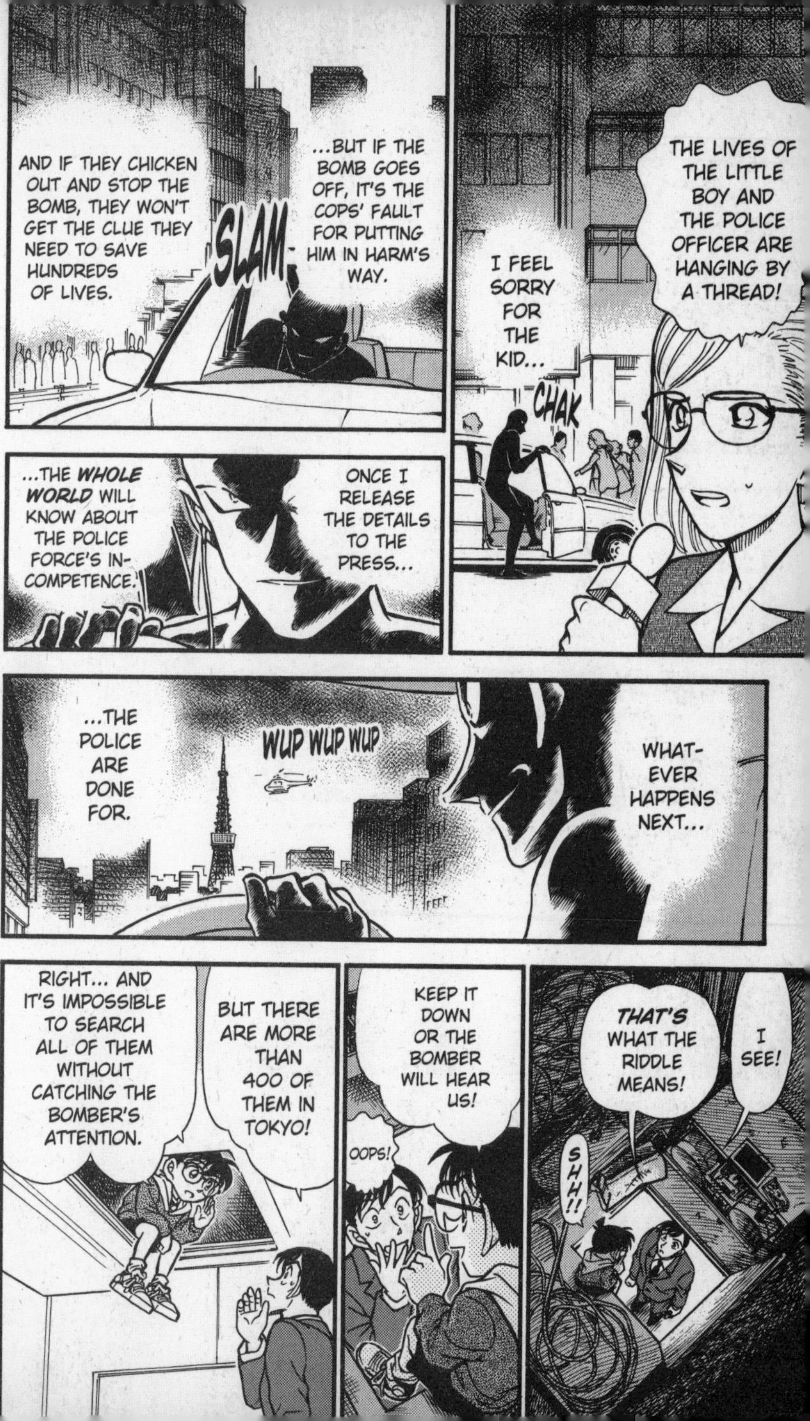
THE LIVES OF THE LITTLE BOY AND THE POLICE OFFICER ARE HANGING BY A THREAD!
I FEEL SORRY FOR THE KID...
CHAK
...BUT IF THE BOMB GOES OFF, IT'S THE COPS' FAULT FOR PUTTING HIM IN HARM'S WAY.
AND IF THEY CHICKEN OUT AND STOP THE BOMB, THEY WON'T GET THE CLUE THEY NEED TO SAVE HUNDREDS OF LIVES.
SLAM
ONCE I RELEASE THE DETAILS TO THE PRESS...
...THE *WHOLE WORLD* WILL KNOW ABOUT THE POLICE FORCE'S IN-COMPETENCE.
WHAT-EVER HAPPENS NEXT...
WUP WUP WUP
...THE POLICE ARE DONE FOR.
I SEE!
THAT'S WHAT THE RIDDLE MEANS!
SHH!!
KEEP IT DOWN OR THE BOMBER WILL HEAR US!
OOPS!
BUT THERE ARE MORE THAN 400 OF THEM IN TOKYO!
RIGHT... AND IT'S IMPOSSIBLE TO SEARCH ALL OF THEM WITHOUT CATCHING THE BOMBER'S ATTENTION.

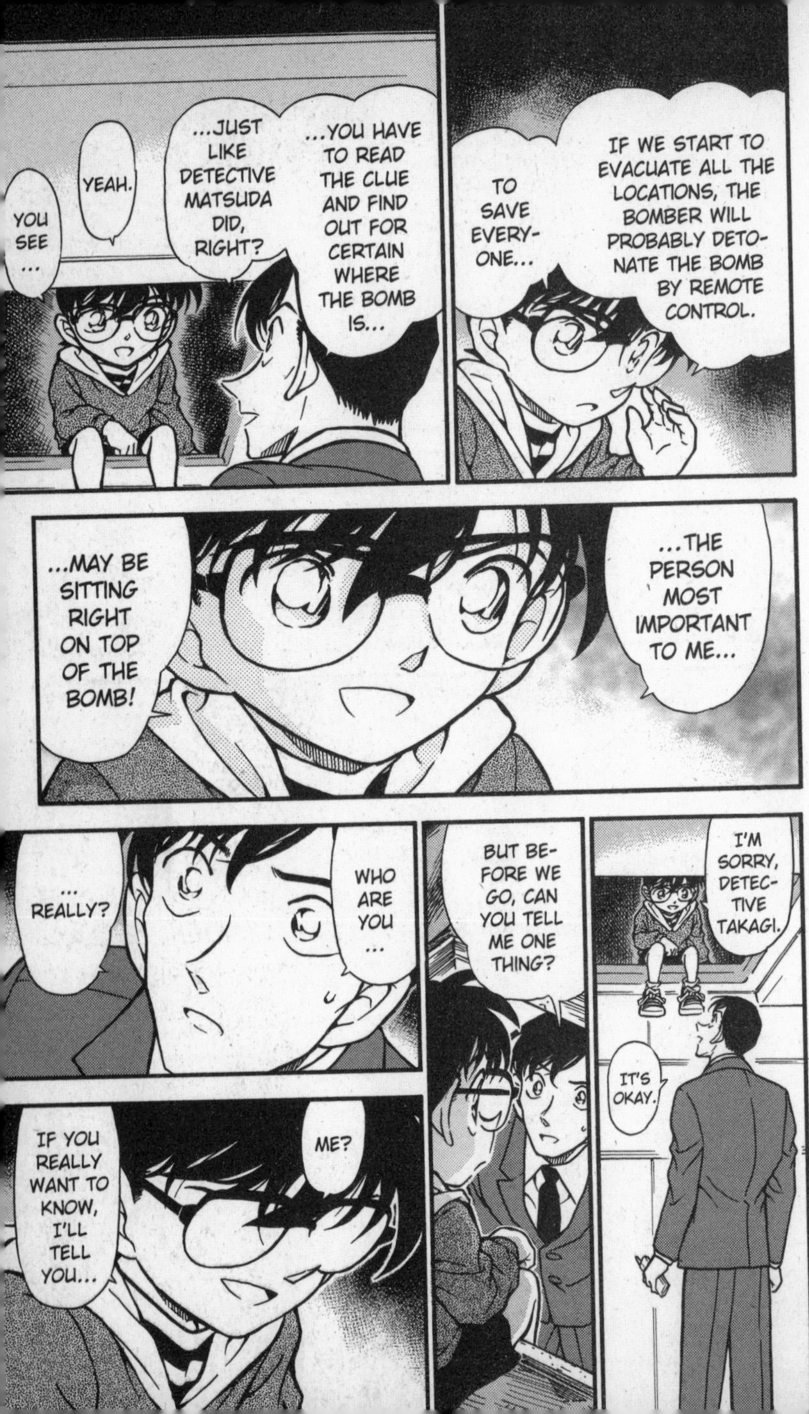
IF WE START TO EVACUATE ALL THE LOCATIONS, THE BOMBER WILL PROBABLY DETONATE THE BOMB BY REMOTE CONTROL.
TO SAVE EVERYONE...
...YOU HAVE TO READ THE CLUE AND FIND OUT FOR CERTAIN WHERE THE BOMB IS...
...JUST LIKE DETECTIVE MATSUDA DID, RIGHT?
YEAH.
YOU SEE...
...THE PERSON MOST IMPORTANT TO ME...
...MAY BE SITTING RIGHT ON TOP OF THE BOMB!
I'M SORRY, DETECTIVE TAKAGI.
IT'S OKAY.
BUT BEFORE WE GO, CAN YOU TELL ME ONE THING?
WHO ARE YOU...
...REALLY?
ME?
IF YOU REALLY WANT TO KNOW, I'LL TELL YOU...

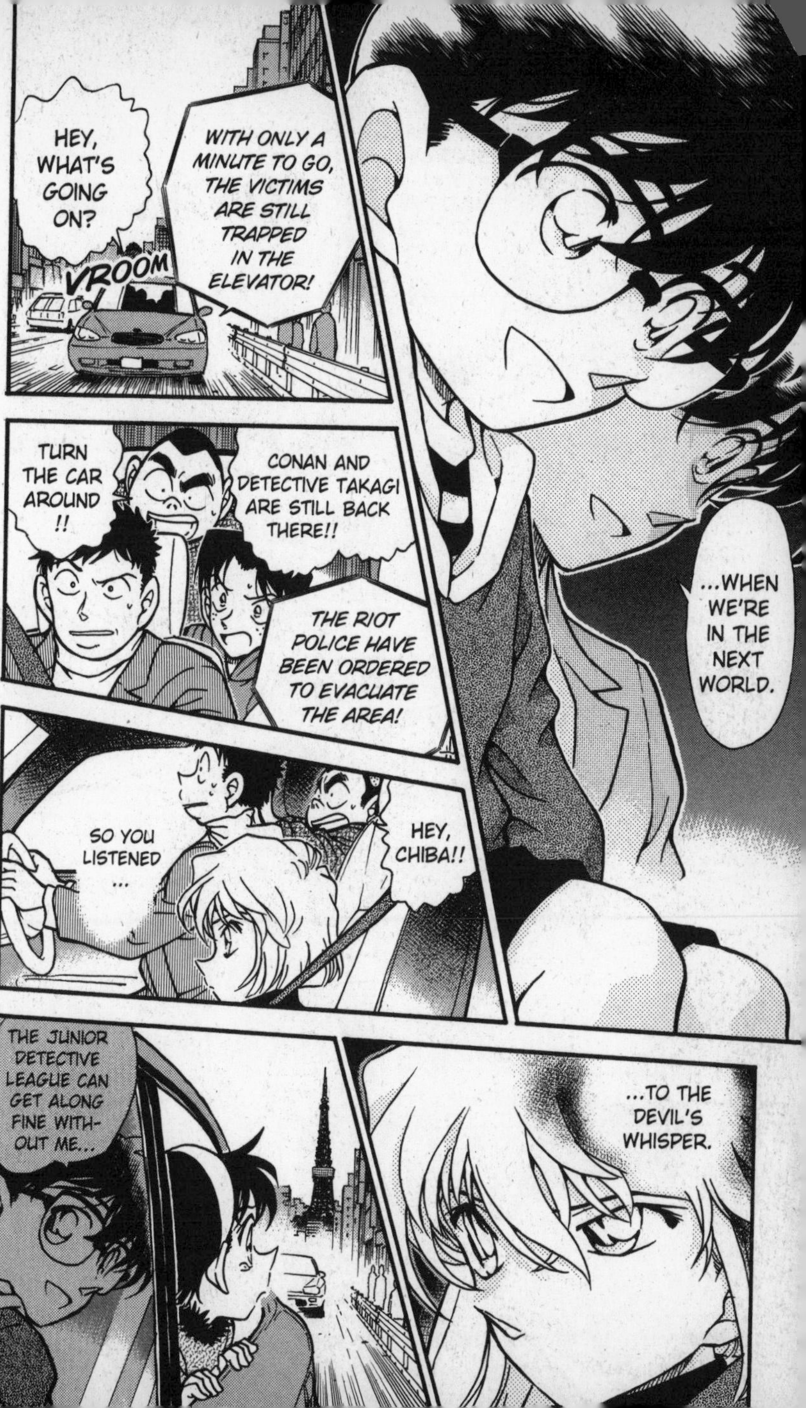
...WHEN WE'RE IN THE NEXT WORLD.
WITH ONLY A MINUTE TO GO, THE VICTIMS ARE STILL TRAPPED IN THE ELEVATOR!
HEY, WHAT'S GOING ON?
VROOM
CONAN AND DETECTIVE TAKAGI ARE STILL BACK THERE!!
TURN THE CAR AROUND!!
THE RIOT POLICE HAVE BEEN ORDERED TO EVACUATE THE AREA!
HEY, CHIBA!!
SO YOU LISTENED ...
...TO THE DEVIL'S WHISPER.
THE JUNIOR DETECTIVE LEAGUE CAN GET ALONG FINE WITH-OUT ME...

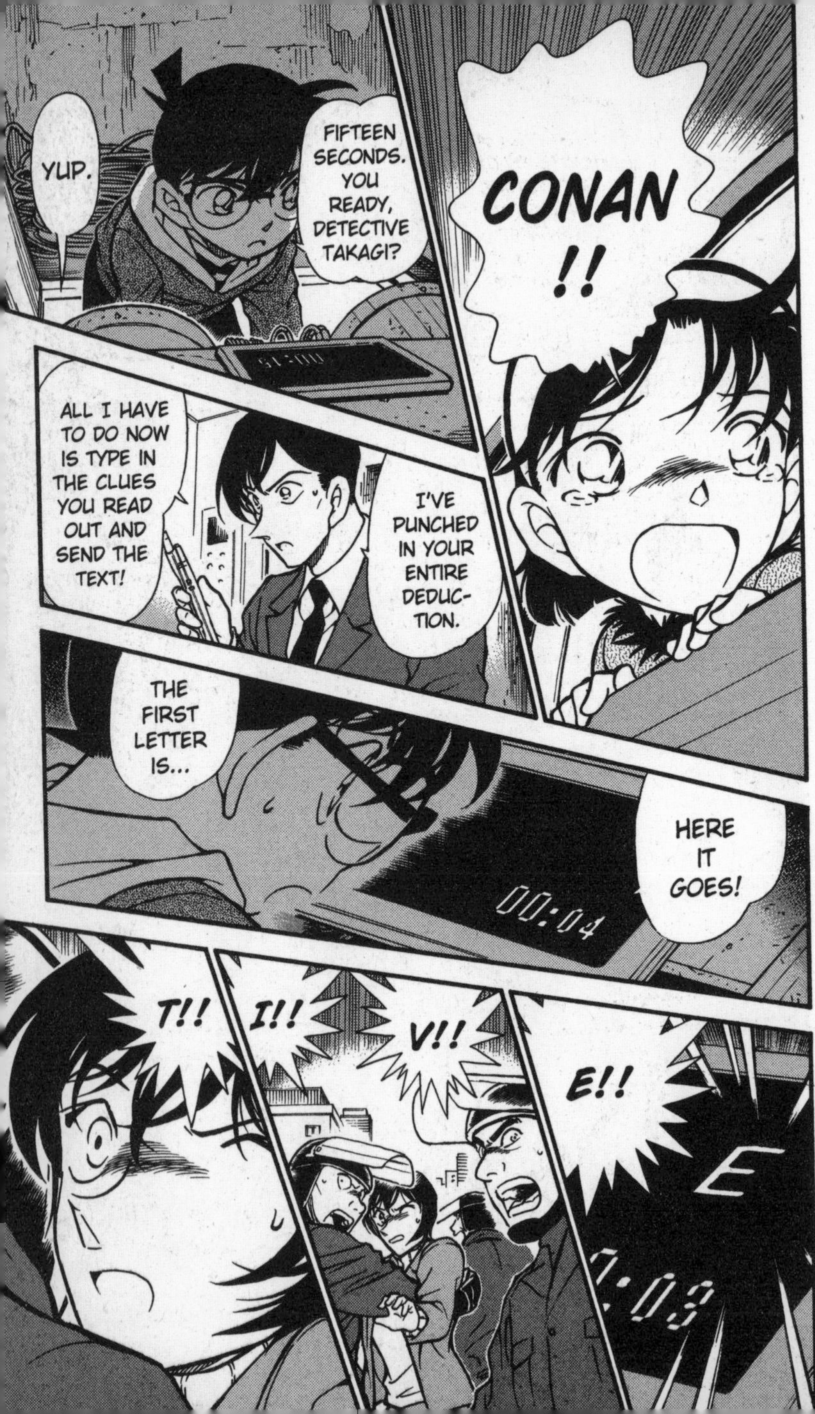
CONAN !!
FIFTEEN SECONDS. YOU READY, DETECTIVE TAKAGI?
YUP.
I'VE PUNCHED IN YOUR ENTIRE DEDUC-TION.
ALL I HAVE TO DO NOW IS TYPE IN THE CLUES YOU READ OUT AND SEND THE TEXT!
HERE IT GOES!
THE FIRST LETTER IS...
00:04
E!!
V!!
I!!
T!!

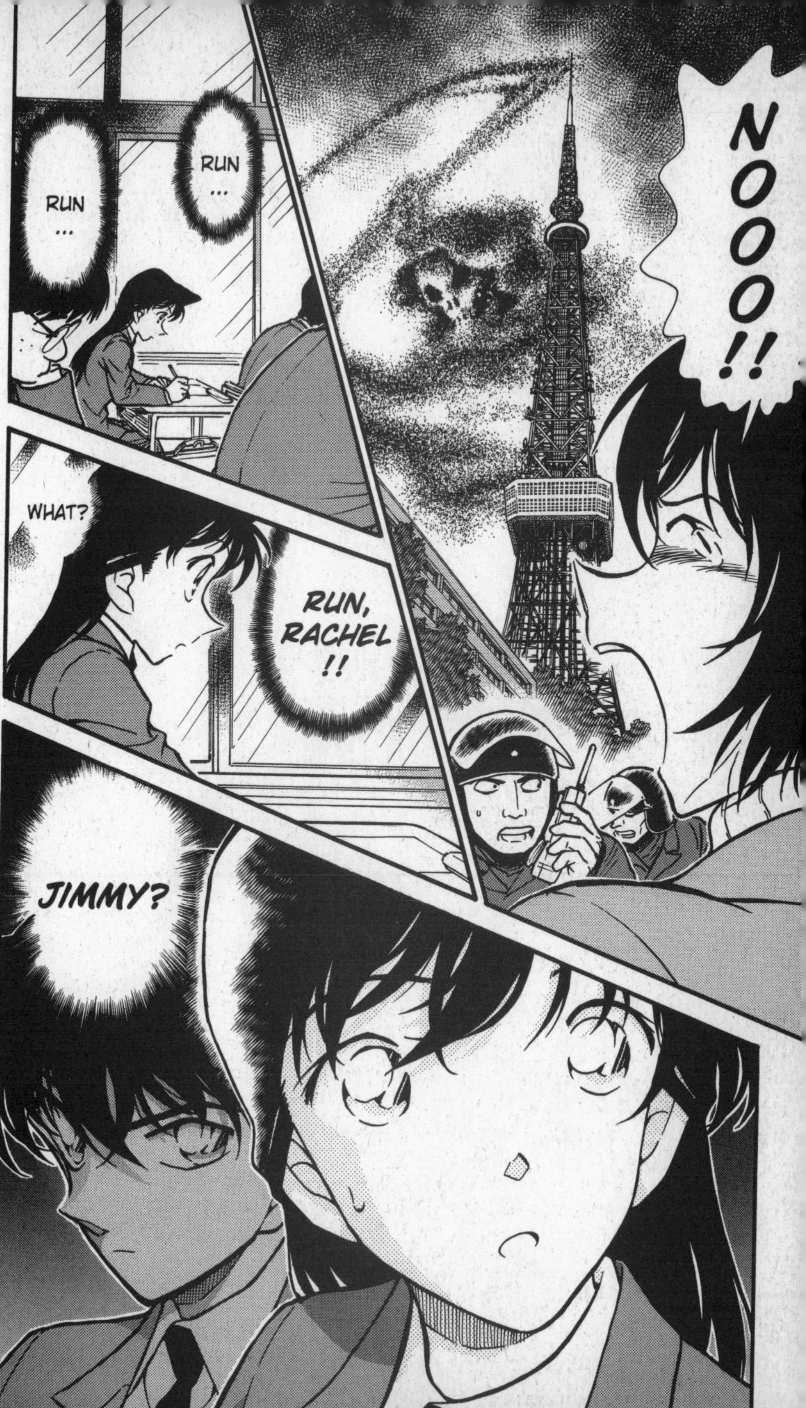
NOOOO!!
RUN ...
RUN ...
WHAT?
RUN, RACHEL !!
JIMMY?

Gosho Aoyama's
Mystery Library

36

CATHERINE TURNER

If there were ever a beauty pageant for detectives, Catherine Turner, created by Misa Yamamura, would definitely make it to the finals. The daughter of a millionaire and former vice president of the United States, Turner is a beautiful blue-eyed blond who was once crowned Miss University. Having moved to Kyoto to pursue her interest in traditional Japanese culture, she works as a journalist for a sophisticated fashion magazine. On the side, she often pokes her head into local cases as an amateur detective.

Turner's daring American attitude and free-spirited, outside-the-box thinking are her chief weapons against crime. Sometimes the cultural differences between the U.S. and Japan are crucial to cracking a case. Her partner in crime solving is Ichiro Hamaguchi, the son of a foreign minister, whom she's known since her first visit to Japan. They're in love, but she's so infatuated with "detectiving" that she has no interest in settling down yet...

I recommend *Hana no Hitsugi* (The Coffin of Flowers).

Hello, Aoyama here.

I had the honor of meeting the legendary Monkey Punch, creator of *Lupin III*, at a Tokyo Movie Co. party at the end of the year!

I shook his hand and was about to launch into a long conversation when my bridgework *fell off into my mouth*! I couldn't spit it out with him smiling and talking to me, so I just kept my mouth shut the whole time. Please, everyone, take good care of your teeth! Not another lecture... heh.

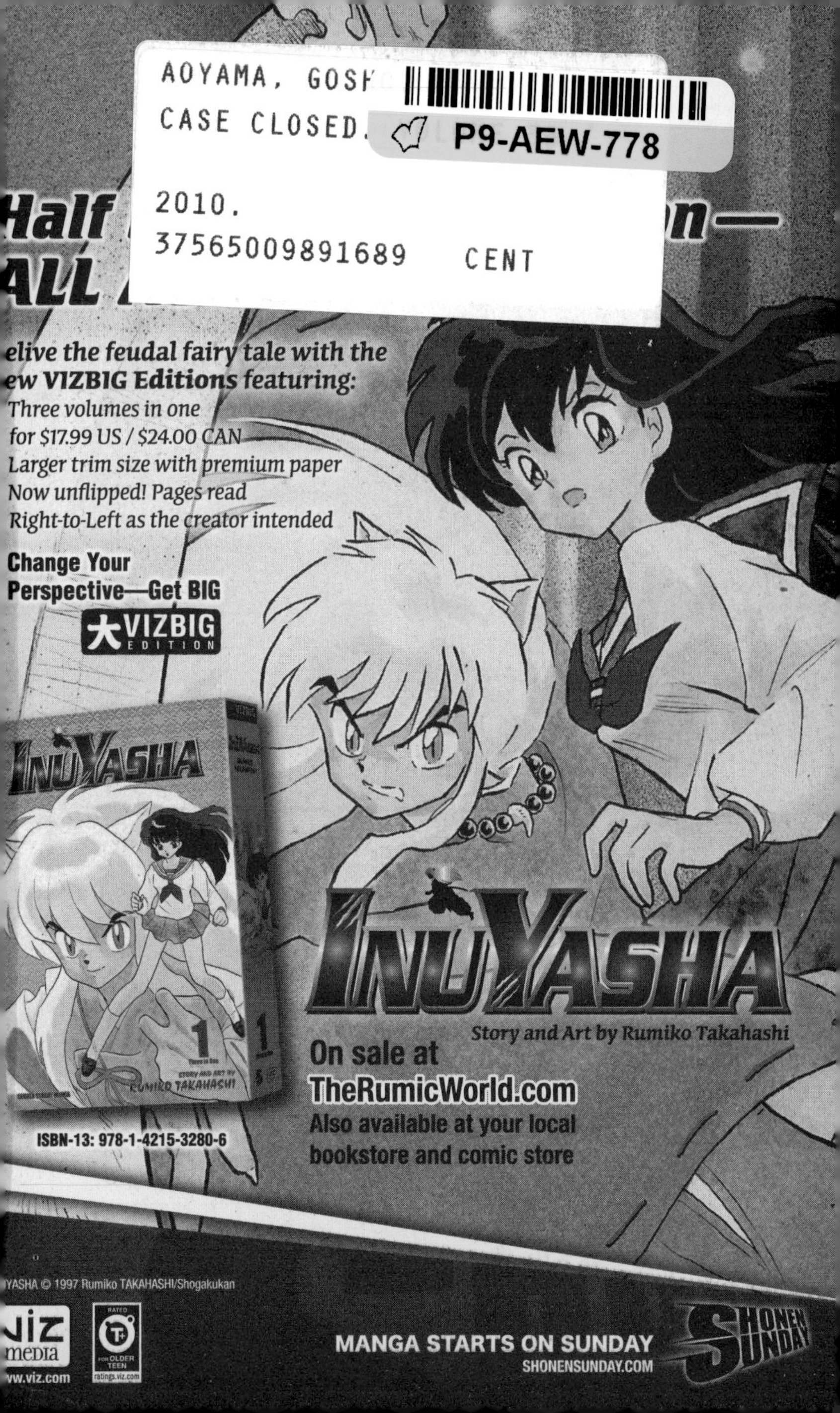
Half
n—
ALL
elive the feudal fairy tale with the
ew VIZBIG Editions featuring:
Three volumes in one
for $17.99 US / $24.00 CAN
Larger trim size with premium paper
Now unflipped! Pages read
Right-to-Left as the creator intended
Change Your
Perspective—Get BIG
大 VIZBIG EDITION
INUYASHA
1
STORY AND ART BY
RUMIKO TAKAHASHI
ISBN-13: 978-1-4215-3280-6
INUYASHA
Story and Art by Rumiko Takahashi
On sale at
TheRumicWorld.com
Also available at your local
bookstore and comic store
YASHA © 1997 Rumiko TAKAHASHI/Shogakukan
viz media
ww.viz.com
RATED T+ FOR OLDER TEEN
ratings.viz.com
MANGA STARTS ON SUNDAY
SHONENSUNDAY.COM
SHONEN SUNDAY